EARLY RESPONSES TO HUME

Volume 5

Edited and Introduced by
James Fieser
University of Tennessee at Martin

THOEMMES

Early Responses to Hume

Edited and Introduced by **James Fieser**
University of Tennessee at Martin, USA

Volumes 1 and 2
Early Responses to Hume's Moral, Literary and Political Writings

Volumes 3 and 4
Early Responses to Hume's Metaphysical and Epistemological Writings

Volumes 5 and 6
Early Responses to Hume's Writings on Religion

Volumes 7 and 8
Early Responses to Hume's *History of England* (2002)

Volumes 9 and 10
Early Hume Biographies and Bibliographies (2003)
Series Index

EARLY RESPONSES TO HUME'S WRITINGS ON RELIGION

I

Edited and Introduced by
James Fieser
University of Tennessee at Martin

THOEMMES PRESS

First published by Thoemmes Press, 2001

Thoemmes Press
11 Great George Street
Bristol BS1 5RR, England

http://www.thoemmes.com

Early Responses to Hume's Writings on Religion
2 Volumes : ISBN 1 85506 797 8

British Library Cataloguing-in-Publication Data
A CIP record of this title is available from the British Library

Printed on acid-free paper and bound in a durable library
buckram cloth by Antony Rowe Ltd, Chippenham, UK

CONTENTS

EARLY RESPONSES TO HUME'S WRITINGS ON RELIGION

VOLUME 1

INTRODUCTION

David Hume ranks among the most influential philosophers in the field of the philosophy of religion. He criticized the standard proofs for God's existence, traditional notions of God's nature and divine governance, the connection between morality and religion, and the rationality of belief in miracles. He also advanced theories on the origin of popular religious beliefs, grounding such notions in human psychology rather than in rational argument or divine revelation. The larger aim of his critique was to disentangle philosophy from religion and thus allow philosophy to pursue its ends without either rational over-extension or psychological corruption. This – the third part of the *Early Responses to Hume* series – collects reactions to Hume's writings on religion. Although we find religious themes throughout Hume's publications, the selections here are largely restricted to six items: (1) "Of Miracles", (2) "Of a Particular Providence and of a Future State", (3) "The Natural History of Religion", (4) *Dialogues Concerning Natural Religion*, (5) "Of Suicide", and, (6) "Of the Immortality of the Soul".

Hume's Place in Enlightenment Theories

During the Enlightenment, there were two pillars of traditional Christian belief: natural and revealed religion. One of the more routine charges brought against Hume by his early critics was that he sought to undermine both of these pillars.

Rooted in both ancient and medieval philosophy, *natural religion* involves knowledge of God drawn from nature through the use of logic and reason. Philosophers of the middle ages developed a variety of logical proofs regarding the existence and nature of God, three of which were especially influential in the centuries to come. First, the *design argument* (now called the teleological argument) infers the existence of a divine designer from the presence of natural order in the world. According to Aquinas's version of the argument, things in nature exhibit a purpose – or final cause – and this implies that there is an intelligence that guides things. Second, a collection of proofs now called *cosmological arguments* contends that the causes (or motion, or contingency) in the world around us must have an origin that is uncaused (or unmoved, or necessary). The most sophisticated of these is a causal argument that distinguishes between two kinds of causal sequences, namely, those that occur over a period of time and those that occur simultaneously. A classic example of a temporal causal sequence is Abraham begetting Isaac, who in turn begets Jacob. An example of a simultaneous causal sequence is a hand that moves a stick that in turn moves a stone, all at the same time. Proponents of the causal argument held that it is theoretically possible for a temporal causal sequence of events to trace back through time to infinity past. However, they argued, simultaneous causal sequences must terminate in a first cause. The point of the argument is that God is required at each moment to sustain the existence of the world. A third argument – now dubbed the *ontological argument* – maintains that the greatest possible being must exist since it is logically contradictory to assert otherwise.

All three of these arguments were modified and strengthened during the 17th and 18th centuries. The design argument was bolstered with the ever-growing body of scientific knowledge, particularly in the fields of biology and astronomy. Parallels were pointed out between intricate mechanisms of the cosmos and objects of human design, such as watches. Four especially influential works in this genre were John Ray's *The Wisdom of God Manifested in the Works of the Creation* (1691), Richard Bentley's *A Confutation of Atheism from the Origin and Frame of the World* (1692), William Derham's *Physico-Theology* (1713) and Derham's *Astro-Theology* (1715). Gottfried Wilhelm Leibniz and Samuel Clarke presented a more precise and somewhat different causal argument. Like their medieval predecessors, they agreed that it is theoretically possible for temporal causal sequences to trace back to infinity past. Nevertheless, they argued, an important fact still needs to be explained: the fact that this infinite temporal sequence of causal events exists at all. God, then, is the necessary cause of the whole series. Hume appears to have been unfamiliar with the medieval versions of the theistic proofs, and, like most of his British contemporaries, does not even discuss the ontological argument. His most direct source for the design and causal arguments were probably Cicero and the more contemporary discussions by Clarke and others.

Revealed religion, the second pillar of traditional Christian belief, involves knowledge of God contained in revelation, particularly the Bible. During the Enlightenment, religious writers continually defended the veracity of the Christian scriptures. Apologists argued that the biblical prophesies and miracles were true instances of God's intervention in earthly affairs, and this intervention confirmed the Bible's message of salvation. Challenged by voyagers' accounts of strange religions in the far corners of the world, some apologists argued further that Christianity was not just another religion. Instead, they believed, Christianity contains God's true revealed message, and other idolatrous religions are the result of human weakness or perhaps even demonic influence. Gerardus Joannes Vossius's

De Theologia Gentili (1641) is the most notable defence of this kind.

In spite of these valiant efforts to defend the Christian faith, several philosophers and theologians chiselled away at the notions of both natural and revealed religion. We know that Hume was acquainted with many of these criticisms, and Hume's respondents quickly associated his views with those of his forerunners.

Natural religion came under attack from two camps. First, within the Christian mainstream itself, religious fideists – particularly from the Augustinian tradition – argued that questions of God's existence and nature are matters of religious faith, and not matters of human reason. This is because of both the limits of human reason and the infinitely incomprehensible nature of God himself. French philosopher Blaise Pascal (1623–1662) boldly makes this point here:

> By faith we know God's existence. In the glorious state of heaven we will know his nature. ... If there is a God he is infinitely incomprehensible, since, having neither parts nor limits, he has no proportion to us. We are then incapable of knowing either what he is, or whether he is. This being true, who will dare to undertake to resolve this question? ...Who, then, will blame those Christians who are not able to give a reason for their belief insofar as they profess a religion for which they can give no reason? [*Thoughts*]

Scotland in Hume's time was influenced by Calvinistic fideism, which owed much of its theoretical position to Renaissance Augustinianism. The other attack on natural religion came from philosophical sceptics who – inspired by Sextus Empiricus and the Pyrrhonian sceptical tradition – pointed out the bankruptcy of human reason. No arguments, they contended, are immune from criticism, including theistic proofs. This sceptical conviction was especially strong among the French writers Michel Montaigne (1533–1592), Francois de la Mothe le Vayer (1588–1669), and Pierre Bayle (1647–1706). Like traditional fideists, many of these modern sceptics also held that questions of God's existence were matters of faith, not reason. Bayle, in fact, argues that scepticism is a wonderful preparation for religious faith:

> If a person is first convinced that he can expect no satisfaction from his philosophical studies, he will be more inclined to pray to God; he will ask God for the conviction of the truths which he ought to believe, rather than flattering himself with the success of his reasoning and disputing. It is therefore a welcom inclination to faith to know the defects of reason. ["Pyrrho", *Dictionary*]

Reassessments of revealed religion came in varying degrees from writers connected with non-traditional theological movements. *Latitudinarianism* – a movement within the Church of England – advocated religious toleration and attempted to hold a middle ground between religious dogmatism and scepticism. Although they were believers in biblical miracles, Latitudinarians such as John Tillotson (1730–1694) and Edward Stillingfleet (1635–1699) established criteria for distinguishing true miracles from false ones, particularly alleged miracles within the Catholic tradition. These criteria were influential in subsequent discussions of miracles. Perhaps the strongest attacks on revealed religion came from *Deism*, a heterogeneous movement which held that God created the universe, but thereafter left it alone without further interfering in the established course of nature. Deists had a notorious reputation for denying that God intervened through revealed texts such as the Bible or through miraculous suspensions of laws of nature. Whereas Latitudinarians tried to distinguish the Gospel miracles from Catholic ones, deists such as Thomas Chubb (1679–1747) often blurred the distinction. Charles Blount (1654–1693) argues similarly that pagan miracles have the same credibility as the Christian miracles. Their point was either to discredit biblical miracles by association, or to at least show that no religion has exclusive claim to miracles.

In addition to attacks on revealed religion from within these religious movements, some more independent philosophers also joined in the assault. Benedict de Spinoza (1632–1677) argues that the very facts attested in miracles count against them: "if anyone asserted that God acts in contravention to the laws of nature, he, *ipso facto*, would be compelled to assert that God acted against his own nature – an evident absurdity" (*Tractatus Theologico-Politicus*, Sect. 6). A similar attack appears in the posthumously published philosophical essays of Henry St. John, Viscount Bolingbroke (1678–1751) where he argues that miracles "are incredible, because [they are] contrary to all experience, and to the established course of Nature" (*Philosophical Works*, 1754, Vol. 5, pp. 99–102). Andrew Michael Ramsay (1686–1743), in his posthumously published *Philosophical Principles of Natural and Revealed Religion* (1748–1749), suggests that, to someone outside the Christian faith, the Biblical miracle accounts are inherently counter-intuitive.

Hume's Writings on Religion

To avoid being fined, imprisoned, or worse, critics of religion during Hume's time needed to express themselves cautiously. Sometimes this involved placing controversial views in the mouth of a character in a dialogue. Other times it involved adopting the persona of a deist or fideist as a means of concealing a more extreme religious scepticism. Hume used all of the rhetorical devices at his disposal, and left it to his readers to decode his most controversial conclusions.

His first sustained attack on natural and revealed religion appears in his *Enquiry Concerning Human Understanding* (1748), specifically in two essays, "Of Miracles", and "Of a Particular Providence and of a Future State". "Of Miracles" contains an assortment of attacks on the belief in miracles; the thrust of the essay is that it is unreasonable for anyone to believe in testimonies involving miraculous violations of laws of nature. The first of this two-part essay contains the argument for which Hume is most famous: uniform experience of natural law outweighs the testimony of any alleged miracle. We might imagine a scale with two balancing pans. In the first pan we place the strongest evidence in support of the occurrence of a miracle. In the second we place our life-long experience of consistent laws of nature. According to Hume, the second pan will always outweigh the first. Regardless of how strong the testimony is in favour of a given miracle, it can never come close to counterbalancing the overwhelming experience of unvaried laws of nature. Thus, proportioning one's belief to the evidence, the wise person must reject the weaker evidence concerning the alleged miracle. In a 1737 letter to Henry Home, Hume states that he intended to include a discussion of miracles in his *Treatise of Human Nature* (1739–1740), but ultimately left it out for fear of offending readers. It is probably this main argument to which Hume refers.

The second part of "Of Miracles" presents a potpourri of criticisms. Hume begins by offering four factors that count against the credibility of most miracle testimonies: (1) witnesses of miracles typically lack integrity; (2) we have a propensity to sensationalize, which prompts us to uncritically perpetuate miracle stories; (3) miracle testimonies abound in barbarous nations; and (4) miracles support rival religious systems and thus discredit each other. Like Chubb and Blount, Hume also discusses three non-biblical miracles that are supported by reliable testimony – one from ancient Rome and two recent Catholic miracles. Although they are backed by strong testimony, Hume argues that we nevertheless reject these alleged miracles since they are contrary to our consistent experience of laws of nature. He concludes noting that theologians invite problems when they attempt to ground their religion in miracles. Christianity, he concludes, certainly requires belief in miracles, but such belief should involve an act of faith and not reason.

As Hume's "Of Miracles" was an attack on *revealed* religion, he followed this with an attack on *natural* religion in the essay "Of a Particular Providence and of a Future State", which was originally titled "Of the Practical Consequences of Natural Religion". The essay presents a fictional conversation in which two characters examine the design argument. The characters give three key criticisms. First, our knowledge of God as creator is restricted to the effects that we see in his creation; since the world (the effect) is imperfect, we cannot conclude that God (the cause) is perfect. Second, justice in the universe is restricted to the imperfect justice that we see around us. Third, the singular and unparalleled nature of the universe prevents us from making analogical inferences about the creator.

In 1757 Hume published a work titled *Four Dissertations*, the first and longest essay of which was "The Natural History of Religion". The essay is one of the first attempts to explain the causes of religious belief solely in terms of psychological and sociological factors.[1] We might see the "Natural History" as an answer to a challenge, such as the sort that William Adams poses here in his attack on Hume's "Of Miracles":

> Whence could the religion and laws of this people [i.e., the Jews] so far exceed those of the wisest Heathens, and come out at once, in their first infancy, thus perfect and entire; when all human systems are found to grow up by degrees, and to ripen, after many improvements; into perfection? [*An Essay*, Part 2]

According to Adams, only divine intervention can account for the sophistication of the ancient Jewish religion. In the "Natural History", though, Hume offers an alternative explanation, and one that is grounded solely in human nature. His critics saw this work as an attack on revealed religion, since it brushes aside the contention that religious belief hinges on God's direct involvement within human history. The work may be divided into three parts. In the first part (Sections 1 and 4), Hume argues that polytheism, and not monotheism, was the original religion of primitive humans. Monotheism, he believes, was only a later development that emerged with the progress of various societies. The standard theory in Judeo-Christian theology was that early humans first believed in a single God, but as religious corruption crept in, people lapsed into polytheism. Hume was the first writer to systematically defend the position of original polytheism. In the second part (Sections 2–3, 5–8), Hume establishes the psychological principles that give rise to popular religious belief. His thesis is that natural instincts – such as fear and the propensity to adulate – are the true causes of popular religious belief, and not divine intervention or rational argument. The third part of this work (Sections 9–15) compares various aspects of polytheism with monotheism, showing that one is no more superior than the other. Both contain points of absurdity. From this he concludes that we should suspend belief on the entire subject of religious truth.

---

[1]   See James Fieser, "Introduction" to Hume's *The Natural History of Religion*, Prentice Hall, 1992.

Around the same time that Hume was composing his "Natural History of Religion" he was also working on his *Dialogues Concerning Natural Religion*, which appeared in print two decades later, after his death. The work is perhaps Hume's greatest philosophical writing, both in terms of content and composition. There are three principal characters in the *Dialogues*. A character named Cleanthes defends an *a posteriori* design argument for God's existence. Next, a character named Demea defends an *a priori* casual argument for God's existence, particularly Leibniz's and Clarke's version. Finally, a character named Philo is a sceptic who argues against both *a posteriori* and *a priori* proofs. Philo offers a stream of criticisms against the design argument, many of which are now standard in discussions of the issue. For Philo, the design argument is based on a faulty analogy: we do not know whether the order in nature was the result of design, since, unlike our experience with the creation of machines, we did not witness the formation of the world. The vastness of the universe also weakens any comparison with human artefacts. Although the universe is orderly here, it may be chaotic elsewhere. Similarly, if intelligent design is exhibited only in a small fraction of the universe, then we cannot say that it is the productive force of the *whole* universe. Philo also contends that natural design may be accounted for by nature alone, insofar as matter may contain within itself a principle of order. And even if the design of the universe is of divine origin, we are not justified in concluding that this divine cause is a single, all powerful, or all good being. As to the causal argument, Philo argues that once we have a sufficient explanation for each particular fact in the infinite sequence of facts, it makes no sense to inquire about the origin of the *collection* of these facts. That is, once we adequately account for each individual fact, this constitutes a sufficient explanation of the whole collection.

In 1755 Hume's essays "Of Suicide" and "Of the Immortality of the Soul" were printed along with the "Natural History of Religion" in a book titled *Five Dissertations*. When pre-release copies of *Five Dissertations* provoked controversy among influential readers, Hume and his publisher Andrew Millar agreed to have the two essays physically removed from the printed copies. They were replaced with a more innocent essay titled "Of the Standard of Taste", and the book of essays appeared in 1757 under the title *Four Dissertations*. Rumours about the two withdrawn essays circulated for years, and clandestine copies appeared anonymously in French (1770) and later in English (1777). In 1783 a reprint of the 1777 version was published more openly, and this time with Hume's name attached. Along with Hume's two essays, the anonymous editor of the 1783 edition included his own critical notes to Hume's two pieces, and excerpts from Rousseau's *La Nouvelle Heloise* on the subject of suicide. "Of Suicide" defends the moral permissibility of suicide by arguing that it does not violate our duties to God, oneself, or others. "Of the Immortality of the Soul" disputes a series of metaphysical, moral, and physical arguments for the soul's immortality. Pages of the original two essays as they were printed in *Five Dissertations* are in the possession of the National Library of Scotland. These contain nineteen corrections in Hume's hand and are his final surviving revisions of the essays. He sent the revised pages to his printer William Strahan, who then suppressed them. It is only since the twentieth century that these revisions appear in editions of the two essays.

Overview of Early Responses to Hume's Writings on Religion

Only a few of Hume's early respondents were active philosophers; most, instead, were theologians who believed that Hume posed a real threat to religion and they accordingly responded as defenders of their faith. These theologians fall into several groups. First, an initial group were Anglican clergy or members of that theological camp. Anthony Ellys, Thomas Rutherforth, Owen Manning, William Adams, and William Samuel Powell were clergy of the Church of England; John Douglas was a Scottish Episcopalian cleric, and Philip Skelton was a cleric of the Church of Ireland. William Warburton was a polemicist for this group. Second, there were dissenters who were members of non-Anglican church bodies in England and Ireland. Most of these were non-Calvinistic and classified as *rational dissenters*. William Rose was a layman in this group. John Leland, Richard Price, Joseph Priestley, and Thomas Cogan were ministers at different positions along the theological spectrum. Third, there were ministers of the Church of Scotland – a Presbyterian rather than an Episcopalian body. Henry Home was a layman in this group. George Anderson, George Campbell, and James Oswald were ministers.

The early responses to Hume's writings on religion differ from early responses to his metaphysical and moral writings in three key ways. First, there are many more responses to his religious writings, undoubtedly because of the perceived threat that they posed. Second, critics of Hume's other writings frequently misunderstood his views; however, as professionally trained theologians, the respondents to Hume's religious writings typically had a good grasp of his arguments, even if they did not offer convincing refutations. Third, although all early responses to Hume are intrinsically interesting, the responses to his religious writings are invaluable for helping decipher Hume's frequently concealed attacks on religion. Having the advantage of living during Hume's time, early critics understood Hume's implications better than we might today. And, in their responses, they routinely interpret Hume's hidden meaning.[2]

---

[2] See James Fieser, "Hume's Concealed Attack on Religion and his Early Critics", *Journal of Philosophical Research*, 1995, Vol. 20, pp. 83–101.

The first early response to "Of Miracles" appeared in 1749 by Philip Skelton, and a steady stream of responses has continued to the present time. The longest of these were by William Adams (1752), John Leland (1755), and George Campbell (1762). Although Hume avoided responding to his critics as a matter of principle, he nevertheless kept track of printed criticisms as they appeared. In the last decade of his life he wrote "I cou'd cover the Floor of a large Room with Books and Pamphlets wrote against me". His interest in critical responses to "Of Miracles" in particular started early. Writing to his friend Robert Wallace in 1753, Hume stated that he saw three pamphlets that attacked "Of Miracles", two of which he owned. Some time later, Hume told Richard Kirwan that "twenty-two answers had been made [to "Of Miracles"], hinting, that if any of them had been satisfactory any other would have been judged superfluous" ("Remarks", included below). In addition to works devoted exclusively to "Of Miracles", critics of Hume's other writings on religion routinely included brief attacks on that essay. Some critics attacked a single point in his essay, whereas others carefully dissected the work sentence by sentence. The respondents were typically acquainted with the critiques of Hume that appeared prior to their own, and they often stated their intention to offer a new angle in their attack.

The principal objections raised by respondents regarding "Of Miracles" Part 1 are these. (1) Hume's use of the word "experience" is ambiguous, sometimes meaning an individual's private experience, other times meaning human collective experience. (2) Our limited experience of natural laws does not make it unreasonable to believe that God altered natural laws. (3) Miraculous intervention is reasonable to believe when we recognize God's existence, God's nature, and God's interest in redeeming humanity. (4) Contrary to Hume, it is perfectly reasonable for the Indian prince to believe that water freezes, even though his limited experience suggests otherwise. (5) Experience of natural laws is not as weighty as Hume maintains since some commonly believed laws are overturned by a single experiment. (6) Strong testimony of miracles can in fact outweigh our experience of consistent natural laws. (7) Hume misconstrues the notion of probability when stating that we "subtract" contrary evidences from each other. (8) Hume's argument tells us only that miracles are highly unusual, which believers in miracles already acknowledge.

Concerning Part 2, these are the main objections. (1) The New Testament miracles were not in fact reported by ignorant people in a barbarous nation. (2) Miracle testimonies from rival religions do not nullify each other; upon examination, the New Testament miracles are the only ones that are credible. (3) Contrary to Hume, Muhammad never claimed to have performed miracles. (4) The alleged miracle done by Vespasian is not credible since it was done in front of gullible people with a clear political aim. (5) The alleged miracle at Saragossa was not thoroughly investigated by Cardinal de Retz, and it is likely that the man in question had a wooden leg. (6) Hume exaggerates the number and nature of the alleged miracles at the tomb of the Abbé De Pâris; the most notable ones were either frauds or the result of natural healings, as exposed by De Voeux in his *Lettres sur les Miracles* (1735) and *Critique Generale du livre de Mr. de Montgeron* (1741).

Early responses to "Of a Particular Providence" were more modest in number, and written by some of Hume's most notable critics: Henry Home (1751), George Anderson (1753), George Psalmanazar (1753), John Leland (1755), James Beattie (1770), James Oswald (1772), Joseph Priestley (1780), and Archibald Arthur (1803). Their main objection was with Hume's claim that our knowledge of God as creator is limited to the effects that we see in the creation. When Hume's "Natural History of Religion" appeared in 1757, four reviews of that work shortly followed, most of which found the work to be less original than Hume's other writings. The most sustained critiques of the "Natural History of Religion" were written by Caleb Fleming (1757), William Warburton (1757), Thomas Stona (1758), Voltaire (1764–1769), and Duncan Shaw (1776). Most of these writers focused on Hume's claim that polytheism was the original religion of humanity.

When Hume's *Dialogues* was published in 1777, at least six reviews of that work appeared, the majority of which were very critical. Throughout the eighteenth and nineteenth centuries, books, pamphlets and journal articles appeared that analysed different parts of the *Dialogues*, but the most systematic studies of that work only appeared later in the twentieth century. The early responses to the *Dialogues* presented in this volume are by Thomas Hayter (1780), Joseph Priestley (1780), Joseph Milner (1781), John Ogilvie (1783), Hugh Hamilton (1784), George Horne (1784), Archibald Arthur (1803), and Alexander Crombie (1829). "Of Suicide" and "Of the Immortality of the Soul" were openly published in 1783 with Hume's name attached, and most respondents were shocked by these essays. In fact, we find here some of the most negative comments about Hume that have appeared in print. Four review articles attacked the work, and parts of the essays were analysed by the anonymous *An Essay on the Immortality of the Soul* (1784), and Charles Moore's *A Full Inquiry into the Subject of Suicide* (1790). The most systematic study of "Of Suicide" was presented by George Horne (1784).

Editorial Conventions

During the eighteenth and nineteenth centuries, there were enough responses to Hume's writings on religion to fill perhaps four volumes this size. Discretion being necessary, the selections made for these volumes were based on two key factors. First, in deference to the greater interest that Hume scholars have towards eighteenth-century responses, I have minimized the inclusion of nineteenth-century ones. Second, in 1996 Thoemmes Press published two shorter collections of early responses to Hume's writings on religion, edited by Stanley Tweyman: *Hume on Miracles* and *Hume on Natural Religion*. I have minimized redundancy here. Specifically, I have not included any of the nineteenth-century responses that appear in the 1996 volumes. Also, whereas some of the items in the 1996 volumes are short excerpts, I have included the more complete selections here. All totalled, only about 20 per cent of the present contents are covered in the 1996 volumes, and I have newly prepared that material here.

In preparing these selections, spelling and punctuation have not been modernised. Some original printers' conventions have been altered; for example, capitalisation of words at the beginning of sections and paragraphs have been eliminated. Also, when relevant, footnote references follow punctuation marks, rather than precede them. Unless noted otherwise, comments contained in square brackets are mine. For input and assistance on various phases of this volume, I express thanks to M.A. Stewart. I also express thanks to the editorial and production staff at Thoemmes Press, specifically Rudi Thoemmes, Chris Albury, Dan Broughton, Alan Rutherford and Jane Williamson.

1

PHILIP SKELTON

Philip Skelton, *Ophiomaches: or, Deism revealed*. London: printed for A. Millar, 1749, 2 vol.
Dialogue 5, selections; from *The Complete Works of the Late Rev. Philip Skelton*, ed. Robert Lynam (1824), vol. 4.

Irish cleric Philip Skelton (1707–1787) is best known among historians of philosophy for his attack on deism in *Ophiomaches, or Deism Revealed* (1749). The work is a dialogue on philosophical theology mainly between Shepherd, a conservative parson, and Dechaine, a deistic tutor. Dialogue 5 includes a discussion of miracles, which briefly addresses Hume's essay. Skelton presents two main criticisms of Hume, which appear in the mouth of Shepherd. (1) Experience has not ruled out some miracles, such as Jesus' resurrection, since a miracle assertion implies no contradiction. (2) God has compassion for humanity and, so, it is reasonable to assume that he would send a messenger who would perform miracles as proof of his authority. In his "Life of the Rev. Philip Skelton" (in volume 1 of Skelton's *Works*, 1824) Samuel Burdy notes that Hume looked over Skelton's manuscript prior to publication: "He came it seems to Andrew Millar's, took the manuscript to a room adjoining the shop, examined it here and there for about an hour, and then said to Andrew, print." In their review of Skelton's *Ophiomaches*, the *Literary Journal* stated that,

"Mr. Skelton is a Man of very great Parts, and his performance well deserves the serious Attention, and in some respects, the Thanks of every true Lover of Christianity; – and tho' I may doubt whether mine will be acceptable, as I differ from him on several Articles; Yet I venture to offer them here, in the full Sincerity of my Heart. [*Literary Journal*, 1749, Vol. 5, pp. 92–127]

The reviewer objects in particular to Skelton's contention that those who stray from orthodoxy on the slightest points are deists. Skelton's *Ophiomaches* was published again in 1751, under the title *Deism Revealed*, and is also included in the three editions of his works.

DIALOGUE V.

Dech. It seems not a little strange to me, that the abettors of Christianity should make the ignorance of those who first established that religion an argument in its favour, since all the world must own, that such simple folks might have been much more easily imposed on, than persons of greater knowledge and sagacity.

Shep. The ignorance of our Saviour's witnesses is with an ill grace turned into an objection against their veracity, by men, who cannot but be conscious to themselves, that in case persons of distinguished sense and ability had been employed for that purpose, the doubters and libertines of later ages would have ascribed all they said to artifice, policy, and combination. Ignorance and knowledge, it seems, although so opposite in themselves, are alike fit to disqualify those, in whom they are found, to bear witness to a religion we do not like.

Dech. Say what you will, those witnesses you speak of, were by either temporal, or spiritual considerations at least, strongly interested to vouch for your religion; and therefore their evidence must be of little weight.

Shep. This may account for their adhering privately to the religion of their Master, but could never of itself have induced them to labour in prose-lyting others; for that, as I have already observed, was directly against their temporal interest, and could never have been reconciled to their hopes in futurity, but by an express command from God.

Dech. When testimonies are alleged for facts, we are to weigh the improbability of the facts, against the credibility of the witnesses, before we give up our assent to either the one, or the other. If the improbability on the one side is equally balanced by the credibility on the other, there is a destruction of both, and the assent must be suspended. But, in case the arguments for the improbability appear to preponderate, then our assent must lean to the improbability in a ratio of the surplus; must be, as the superiority of the arguments to the testimonies. Now experience, and the evidence of our senses, prove to us, for instance, that the dead never revive; and that the stated laws of nature are never violated by God, nor can be by man. No testimony of men for the resurrection of one who was dead, can be so strong as this evidence of experience; and therefore the quantity of assent must be proportionable to the excess of experience over the credibility of those, who bear witness to the fact.[3]

Temp. I believe it will be no easy matter to answer this argument.

Shep. It was answered already, towards the close of our first conference. But, as it now comes forth in a new mathematical armour of ratios and equations, we must treat it as a new argument. However, it amounts to no

---

[3]   See the philosophical essays concerning human understanding, Essay 10.

more in English than this, that when reasons, or causes of assent, are brought for both sides of a question, we ought to close with the strongest, in proportion as it appears to be the strongest; and that experience, in the present question, appearing stronger than testimony, the assent ought to go along with experience.

Temp. That is all the argument contains; but it is a great deal.

Shep. Your experience, gentlemen, never furnished you with an instance of a resurrection, it is true; but neither does your experience tell you, that Christ did not rise again, after he was dead; nor that this was impossible. You have no evidence of sense against the fact; nor of reason, against the possibility of it. Judging by your experience, and past observation, you are confident 'the sun will rise to-morrow.' But no experience can make you sure of this, till it shall actually arise; 'for it implies no contradiction to say it will not arise.'[4] Neither does it imply a contradiction to say, Christ arose from the dead. If experience tells you, that dead men seldom, or never, revive; yet you cannot conclude, that no man ever did; 'for the contrary is possible.' Nay, no one thing in the world is more possible or easy, provided we ascribe the effect to a sufficient cause. That which is impossible to one agent, may be easy to another. That which a man, or nature, cannot effect, God can perform by a single act of his will. Now it is to the power of God we ascribe the resurrection of Christ; and therefore the power of the agent is sufficient. If, however, the fact, on account of its unusualness, appears improbable, it will, on account of its expediency appear, in a higher degree, probable, if duly considered. Such is the goodness and tender compassion of God, that we can hardly help concluding, he would some time or other use means to retrieve mankind from ignorance, wickedness, and misery. If philosophy, and other ordinary means, were insufficient, recourse must be had to extraordinary and super-natural means, that is, to revelation; for we cannot possibly conceive any other effectual expedient for such a purpose; nor can we conceive, how the person, by whom the revelation should be made, could prove himself to be a messenger, sent from God, without working miracles. Were he vested with no higher signs of power than other men, his plainer dictates would appear to be no more, than the obvious suggestions of common sense, or, at most, of philosophy; and if he delivered any doctrines, undiscoverable by the force of reason, they would appear to be less; in either respect he could only teach in his own name, not in that of God, and consequently without authority or effect. That it is highly probable God would send us an instructor, thus qualified and empowered, and that this is not a proba-bility, only invented by divines to serve the purposes of Christianity, appears evidently from hence, that Plato fell into the same way of thinking,

---

[4] See the philosophical essays concerning human understanding, Essay 4. part 1.

long before our Saviour came into the world. He was strongly of opinion, that God would send some person, or being, into the world, who should teach mankind how they ought to serve the Supreme Being. But, had such a person appeared in Plato's time, that philosopher would, no doubt, have expected from him the signs and credentials of a divine commission, which could have been nothing else, but miracles; for without miracles the pretended messenger could have had no right to dictate to Plato, nor to assume any higher character, than that of a philosopher. If he could have done no more than an ordinary man could do, how could he have answered the expectations of our philosopher, or have appeared to come from God? Now, gentlemen, if the fact of our Saviour's resurrection appears improbable, when nothing else is considered, but the common course and nature of things, it must appear in a quite contrary light, when what I have just now alleged is candidly taken into the account; if it is, it will at least balance the arguments for the improbability of that fact, and give the vouchers for it their full force, without any deductions or subtractions on account of the argument advanced from experience. Give me leave to illustrate what I have urged by an instance, wherein the assent is rationally given, against the current of experience, upon far less testimony, than that which supports the fact in question. A Negro hath a constant uninterrupted experience, that water is fluid, soft, and easily penetrated; yet from the repeated, disinterested testimony of northern people, who trade in Guinea, and of whose veracity he makes no question, he may have such reasons given him, as he cannot rationally resist, to believe that the water in northern countries is sometimes so hard, as to bear loaded waggons, &c. This testimony a Negro often receives, and often believes, without any farther proof than the concurrence of the reporters, who are known by him to be men of truth, and known also to have no temptation to combine, in order to impose on him in a thing of this nature. But if many or all of these reporters should, instead of gaining, lose a great deal by their report, this would help to raise his conviction still higher; or if they should suffer death, rather than give the lie to their own testimony, his dependence on their testimony would then be cleared of all doubts, and wholly overpower the arguments, drawn from experience, concerning the perpetual fluidity of water. Here is a rational conviction on testimony, against experience, without ascribing the extraordinary fact to the agency of a superior being, or rendering it at all probable by any previous proof of its expediency. Now this is so natural, and so common an instance, that I cannot but wonder at their assurance, who know it, as well as I do, and yet argue, as if the like could not or ought not, to take place, in other matters, wherein the reasons for it are much stronger.

Dech. After all you have said, it is hard to believe against experience, and a great inlet to imposture and superstition. I therefore cannot help thinking, that, if God intended we should give credit to facts so extraordinary, he would now and then exhibit, a little nearer to our view, somewhat of the like nature, that we might have an opportunity of examining into them by our own reason, and satisfying ourselves.

Shep. We are not to prescribe to God, nor to expect more evidence from him in religious matters, than we are ready to yield our assent to in things of another nature. Yet, if to grant even this your farther demand will satisfy you, a few words will shew, that some provision may have been made for that also. If the person, who is said to have wrought miracles, is likewise said to have uttered prophecies concerning events, which nothing but the wisdom of God could have foreseen; if we are satisfied of the antiquity ascribed to these prophecies, and of the exact conformity between them and some recent events; we cannot but look on them as equivalent to miracles, nor help believing, that he, who uttered them, might have performed other things, as demonstrative of the divine power, as these are of the divine wisdom, notwithstanding that his experience furnishes him with no instances of facts against the established laws, or the common course of nature. None but God could have enabled any man to foretell the destruction of Jerusalem, the persecutions set on foot against the Christians, the rise or progress of antichrist, or the pope, nor so exactly to characterize the principles and practices of our infidel apostles. If God hath bestowed such a supernatural gift on men, he may also have communicated with it the power of working miracles. Here experience and observation shift sides a little, and fall in with the testimony in favour of miracles.

Dech. For my part, I cannot see, that these prophecies were either intelligible in themselves, or cleared up by answerable events; but, be that as it will, contrary arguments and evidences destroy each other, in proportion to their respective degrees of strength: and therefore, although a rational person should believe in your religion, as a consequence of having first believed, that miracles were wrought in proof of its divinity; yet his experience must be a considerable clog on his assent, a weighty counterbalance to the grounds of his faith, which must therefore be, in a great measure, precarious and sceptical.

Shep. This way of balancing evidences, and subtracting the less from the greater, in order to proportion the assent to the overplus, ought not to be passed over without examination. As propositions, in themselves, are either true or false; so they must appear to be either true or false to the mind, before it fixes its assent. As soon as the judgment hath weighed the evidences for and against any proposition, and fully rests in the belief of that proposition, although the evidences against it were allowed all their weight in the scrutiny; yet they are now regarded as false, and thrown entirely out of the scales. Were not this the case, how could a jury, on oath, find their neighbour guilty of murder, after a trial, in which he had produced considerable evidence for his innocence against superior evidence for his guilt? Although all good jurors make it a rule, in doubtful cases, to err on the merciful side, rather than on the contrary; it is, however, plain, in this case, that they have no doubts, arising from the evidence in favour of the prisoner, notwithstanding the strength of that evidence. It is true, indeed, that when the evidences, on both sides of any point, appear equal, there can be no assent given, with the approbation of reason. It is likewise certain, that opposite arguments, not equal, but nearly equivalent, leave a faint and feeble assent on the side where the superiority seems to lie; but if the superiority appears to be very great on one side, the assent of a rational mind closes entirely with it, believes without reserve, and, having regarded the arguments against its assent, as nothing, ceases to attend to them, or entirely forgets them; acting, in this respect, as the mathematician does, who, after he hath drawn his conclusion, rests therein, and attends no longer either to the several steps in his demonstration, or to the difficulties that had impeded those steps.

Dech. Still the testimonies produced for miracles, are but the testimonies of interested persons, and therefore are not to be set in the balance against experience.

Shep. It seems, to me impossible, that those, who saw the miracles wrought, and yet were not converted, and interested on the side of Christianity, should become vouchers for those miracles, and advocates for that religion they were wrought in proof of: but how, in the name of common sense, were the first converts interested, on the side of Christianity? Were not all their hopes in another world? And was not the strength of these hopes, and the interest founded on them, a full proof of their own conviction? Could any reasonable man, to whom they bore testimony of the miracles, have desired from them a clearer proof, that they actually saw the miracles, than their becoming sincere converts to Christianity, and, in consequence of their conversion, renouncing all their temporal interests, in order to secure an eternal? But if the testimony of men, thus interested from the beginning on the side of Christianity, will not please you; What think you of those, who, from its bitterest enemies, were brought over, by miracles, to be its most zealous advocates? Their testimony is that of adversaries. Now of this sort Christianity is supported with not a few; among whom St. Paul appears as the most distinguished: his zeal against it required a peculiar miracle, wrought on himself, to overcome it; after which, being fully convinced of its truth and divinity, he interested himself as warmly in its defence, as he had done before in its suppression.

Dech. You will not, surely, maintain, that the speeches and epistles of St. Paul are to be reckoned among the testimonies of your adversaries, since they were all made and wrote after his conversion; unless you can prove to us, that his conversion was not sincere.

Shep. Is it to be expected, that a person, who is still an adversary to any particular cause, should speak, and write, and die, for that cause? *Dech.* No; but, when he actually labours in its defence, he cannot, I think, be called its adversary.

Shep. It is true; yet if, while he was busied in a bitter opposition to that cause, he received a full conviction in its favour, whatsoever he does, or says, afterward, towards its support, upon the strength of that conviction, is certainly the testimony of a person who, in the midst of his prejudices and virulence against it, saw sufficient reasons for going over to it; at least, if this kind of testimony is not, in strictness, the testimony of an adversary, it is of the same, or superior, nature or force. It is a full evidence of conviction against the most inveterate prejudices, and the strongest aversion. I forbear to expatiate on the irresistible proof, drawn, in favour of our religion, from the conversion of St. Paul: because you, and every one, must have seen Mr. Lyttleton's letter on that subject; in which there is such ample justice done to the argument I have been urging, as cannot but equally prevent all that otherwise might have been said, on either side of the question. The candid reader of that incomparable paper, whose author can be no more suspected of a previous bias to Christianity than St. Paul himself, stands in need of nothing else, to make him a sincere Christian.

Temp. I see, to my great satisfaction, that the evidences for the second step of tradition may be very strong: when multitudes of eye-witnesses die, to convince one of a fact, though it may be very strange, one can hardly help believing it. But still I am somewhat at a loss to foresee how you will bring down this evidence to me, who live at such a distance from the facts, and make it even clearer than the assassination of Cæsar, as you undertook to do.

Shep. This I am ready to do, if you, or Mr. Dechaine, will be pleased to state the difficulties, that seem to break the chain of evidence, by which you know the certainty of the gospel-history is usually deduced by Christians.

Dech. Although, in favour of the gospel-history, it may be said, that those who wrote it were not interested so to do, or to defend it; yet when the church, from being persecuted, came to be loaded with rich endowments, idly conferred by our bigoted ancestors on a set of men who pretended to divine assistance, and to a contempt for such support as mere worldly wealth and power could give them; then, I am sure, it will be owned, the sticklers for Christianity had worldly reasons enough for their attachment to it. Their testimony, therefore, must be of little weight with us, who know what they gained by it.

Shep. Howsoever interested they may have been, yet, as the original evidence for Christianity was fixed in the writings of the evangelists and the immediate disciples of our Saviour; their successors, in later ages, could have added little to that evidence: and the question is not now concerning any testimony we pretend to derive from them, in favour of facts said to have been done so long before; but how far the original evidence, reduced to writing, may be reasonably suspected to have suffered by the hands through which it hath passed.

Temp. That is our present question.

Dech. But might not the interested clergy, of the fourth or fifth century, for instance, have forged those evidences, which now pass for original, and brought them into credit, by degrees, among those bigots, the then laity, over whose understandings and consciences they had gained an entire ascendant? You know the very first ages produced abundance of gospels, epistles, Sibylline oracles, &c. which were received, for a time, in many churches, and afterward proved to be spurious. This being the case, those writings, which are now esteemed authentic, may have been forgeries too, for aught we, at this distance of time, can tell. Christians are not yet agreed about the canon of the Old Testament, nor were those of the first ages more unanimous about that of the New, several parts of which were not admitted into it till after a considerable tract of time, and many doubts concerning their genuineness.

Shep. All those doubts serve only to furnish us, in these ages, with the stronger assurances, that supposititious writings could not easily find admittance into the canon of the Scripture. ...

2
WILLIAM WARBURTON

William Warburton, paper on "Of Miracles" (1749?).
Complete paper; from Francis Kilvert, *A selection from unpublished papers of
... William Warburton*, London, J.B. Nichols and Son, 1841, xx, 449 p., pp.
311–315.

William Warburton (1698–1779) was an Anglican churchman and after 1760 bishop of Gloucester. He was known for his editions of Shakespeare and Pope, his attack on deism in the *Divine Legation of Moses Demonstrated* (1737–1741), and his involvement in numerous religious and literary controversies. Warburton's primary attack on Hume is in his *Remarks on... the Natural History of Religion* (1757), which is included later in this volume. According to his friend and biographer Richard Hurd, Warburton first became acquainted with Hume's *Enquiry* in 1749, just as Warburton was preparing his *Julian*[5] for publication. In Hurd's words, Warburton "had thoughts of closing that work with some strictures upon them [i.e., the *Philosophical Essays*]".[6] Writing to Hurd in 1749, Warburton asks Hurd whether Hume might be a worthwhile target of attack:

I have got but six sheets of Julian yet from under the press.... I am strongly tempted too to have a stroke at Hume in parting. He is the author of a little book called "Philosophical Essays", in one part of which he argues against the being of a God, and in another, (very needlessly you will say,) against the possibility of miracles. He has crowned the liberty of the press. And yet he has a considerable post under the Government. I have a great mind to do justice on his arguments against miracles, which I think might be done in a few words. But does he deserve notice? Is he known amongst you? Pray answer me these questions. For if his own weight keeps him down, I should be sorry to contribute to his

---

[5] *Julian. Or a discourse concerning the earthquake and fiery eruption, which defeated that Emperor's attempt to rebuild the temple at Jerusalem. ... By the Rev. Mr. Warburton*. London: printed for J. and P. Knapton, 1750, [2], xlii, 23, 22–286 p.

[6] Richard Hurd (1720–1808), *A discourse, by way of general preface to the quarto edition of Bishop Warburton's works, containing some account of the life, ... of the author*. London: printed by John Nichols, 1794, vii, [1], 150 p.

advancement to any place but the pillory. [Warburton to Hurd, in *Letters from a Late Eminent Prelate to One of his Friends*, Boston: 1806, p. 10].

Although the "strictures" did not appear in his *Julian*, Warburton did include the following comment against Hume:

> For the next objection to the fact arises from what, one would have hoped, should have been the chief support of it, THE TESTIMONY OF THE FATHERS. But their credit in the fashionable world is now so low, that if they do not dishonour the cause they appear in, it is all we are to expect from them. For as a late writer graciously allows us to believe every strange thing except a Miracle that is to say, any the most extraordinary phenomenon in Nature, but where Religion lends it support; so, to say the truth, we are enough disposed to credit the wonders of antiquity, all but the *Fathers* have officiously vouched for. [*Julian*, p. 94][7]

A little further in the text Warburton writes,

> Now, as Religion and religious purposes have nothing to do in this wonder, that extraordinary Philosopher, once before quoted, will permit us to give it credit. [*Julian*, p. 123]

Among Warburton's manuscripts there was a brief attack on Hume's "Of Miracles" that remained unpublished for almost 100 years, finally appearing in Francis Kilvert's *A Selection from Unpublished Papers of the Right Reverend William Warburton* (1841). Although Kilvert does not date this manuscript, it is likely that Warburton wrote it in 1749 within the context of the publication of his *Julian*. The following is as appears in Kilvert's *Selection*.

A late writer, who entitles his book Philosophical Essays concerning Human Understanding, printed for A. Millar, 1748, has a Discourse on Miracles, in which he endeavours to show that there is no probable evidence of the truth of such facts. His reasoning is summed up in what he calls "a general *maxim* worthy our attention, that no testimony is sufficient to establish a miracle, unless the testimony be of such a kind that its

---

[7]   In a footnote to this passage Warburton writes, "In a book, intituled, *Philosophical essays concerning human understanding*, printed 1748. p. 199". Warburton slightly revised his comment in the 1751 second edition of *Julian*. I thank John Gill for bringing these passages from *Julian* to my attention.

falsehood would be *more miraculous* than the fact which it endeavours to establish; and even in that case there is a mutual destruction of arguments, and the superior only gives us an assurance suitable to that degree of force which remains after deducting the inferior." (p. 182.)

Now, to pass at present the jargon of his *more miraculous*, and to suppose he may mean a testimony whose falsehood implies a miracle, I answer, that in order to render the miraculous fact related the object of our belief, it is not necessary that the falsehood of the relator should imply a miracle; and for this plain reason, because that testimony whose falsehood implies a miracle makes the fact attested not *credible*, but *certain*; for the falsehood of no testimony but the *testimony of sense* implies a miracle. Now, what the senses inform us of we call certain. If they deceive us, it must be by God's altering the established order of things, which this author agrees to be a true definition of a miracle; so that we see he mistakes the very nature of the evidence in question. But would you know why he uses his nonsense of *more miraculous*, instead of *miraculous*, it is to insinuate that *even the evidence of sense* is no sufficient proof of a miracle; for he confesses that the degree of evidence, in the case here put, is only the *remains* of his *more miraculous*, when the quantity in his *less miraculous* has been *deducted*; so that if the falsehood of the testimony and the fact testified were equally miraculous, from thence, we see, no proof would arise; i.e. we ought not to own the truth of a miraculous fact when it makes its appeal to the senses. But if this man's reasoning cannot verify his own maxim, his passions will at least verify that of our Heavenly Master, who long ago pronounced that "He who will not believe Moses and the Prophets will not believe though one arose from the dead."

But the unhappy man would exclude all miracles, because at all hazards he will exclude Christianity, as appears from another of his maxims, for he is not a dealer in small truths: "We may establish it as a maxim (says he), that no human testimony can have such force as to prove a miracle, and make it a just foundation for any *such* system of religion," (p. 199;) i.e. no possible proof can be given of miracles to establish any revelation or popular religion, as he just before expresses it; for he himself, forsooth, is of the religion of the philosophers. Yet, when he has said this, with an impartiality becoming the most *moral* of his tribe, he adds the following corrective; that in miracles, where religion has nothing to do, we may safely believe a miracle: If (says he) all authors agree that from 1st Jan. 1600 there was a total darkness over the whole earth for eight days, it is evident our present philosophers ought to receive it for a certain fact; but, should all the historians who treat of England agree that 1st Jan. 1600 Queen Elizabeth died, (who here, you are to observe, stands for Christ,) that she afterwards rose again, took possession of the throne, and governed publicly for three years, this you are to reject as an arrant fable. (pp. 199, 200.) His spite, we see, is not against miracles, but only against the workers of them; for why, I pray you, are we to make this distinction? Are not the two facts equally attested by the concurrent evidence of all concerned? Are they not equally miraculous? for the absence of the sun eight days together from the globe of the earth is surely as *contrary* to the common course of nature as the resurrection of one from the dead. If he believes that, from the beginning, none ever rose from the dead, he believes, too, that there never was a total darkness for eight days together. Here, then, the *uniform experience*, as he calls it, is, in both cases, the same; yet we must believe the one, and not the other. Here spoke the true sense, as well as spirit, of modern infidelity; – we must reject *that* miracle, for whose working, by the interposition of God, we *can* give a reasonable account, and embrace that for which there is *no account to be given at all.* But this circumstance of the *cause* of working the miracles recorded in Scripture, so worthy the exertion of the Divine power, is always, either for want of sense or honesty, omitted by this author, when he comes to balance what he calls his opposed proofs, on which all his jargon turns. And well would it be for our *moral philosopher* if this was the only one omitted; but every collateral circumstance that affords internal evidence of the truth of the Evangelic testimony, such as the state of the world that follows, and which must have been that very state consequent on miracles, had miracles been really performed; such again as the accomplishment of predictions recorded in books, as well known to be written after the facts, as that Julius Cæsar's Commentaries was written before the time of Henry VIII.; – none of these, I say, are ever brought into the balance of this fair accountant. Very suitably, therefore, is his reasoning supported on each hand, and of a piece with the modesty of his *introduction* and the decency of his *conclusion.*

Thus he begins: – "I flatter myself that I have *discovered* an argument, which, if just, will with the wise and learned be an *everlasting check* to all kinds of superstitious delusion, and, consequently, will be *useful as long as the world endures.*" (p. 174.) Thus he ends: – "Mere reason is insufficient to convince us of the veracity of the Christian religion; and whoever is moved by *faith* to assent to it, is conscious of a continued *miracle* in his own person, which *subverts all the principles of his understanding,* and gives him a demonstration to believe what is most contrary to custom and experience." (p. 203.)

Who, after this, will scruple to own that *freedom of thinking* is the source of our greatest blessings, and that the liberty of the press is the only means of conveying and preserving them pure and unpolluted to our posterity!!!

3

GILBERT ELLIOT OF MINTO

Gilbert Elliot of Minto, letter to Hume (c. March 1751), in Dugald Stewart's *Dissertation on the Progress of Philosophy* Part 2, supplemental volumes to the *Encyclopædia Britannica*, 1821.
Complete letter fragment; from Vol. 1 of Stewart's *Works* (1854–1858), pp. 606–609.

By early 1751, Hume had composed part of his *Dialogues Concerning Natural Religion* and sent a sample to his friend Gilbert Elliot of Minto (1722–1777). In March of that year, Hume penned a note to Elliot describing the purpose of the *Dialogues* and, in a postscript to this letter, he asks Elliot's help in strengthening Cleanthes' defence of the design argument:

> If you'll be persuaded to assist me in supporting Cleanthes, I fancy you need not take Matters any higher than Part 3. He allows, indeed, in Part 2, that all our Inference is founded on the Similitude of the Works of Nature to the usual Effects of Mind. Otherwise they must appear a mere Chaos. The only Difficulty is, why the other Dissimilitudes do not weaken the Argument. And indeed it woud seem from Experience & Feeling, that they do not weaken it so much as we might naturally expect. A Theory to solve this woud be very acceptable. [Hume to Gilbert Elliot, March 10, 1751]

Trained as a lawyer, Elliot was a politician and at this time was a member of the British Parliament. He indeed wrote a lengthy letter in response to Hume's request, an unfinished draft of which survives among his papers. He notes interesting limitations with Cleanthes' argument and suggests some ways of strengthening it. We do not know whether Elliot's letter – or some version of it – ever reached Hume. In the second part of his *Dissertation on the Progress of Philosophy* (1821) Dugald Stewart printed the letter in an endnote. Stewart's transcription cannot be entirely trusted, since it was his practice to truncate and edit quoted documents; nevertheless, it is all that we have. Stewart himself refers to this letter as a specimen of "sound philosophy". By contrast, in his *Letters of David Hume*, Greig makes the rather puzzling comment that the letter is "philosophically worthless".

DEAR SIR,

Inclosed I return your papers, which, since my coming to town, I have again read over with the greatest care. The thoughts which this last perusal of them has suggested I shall set down, merely in compliance with your desire, for I pretend not to say anything new upon a question which has already been examined so often and so accurately. I must freely own to you, that to me it appears extremely doubtful if the position which Cleanthes undertakes to maintain can be supported, at least in any satisfactory manner, upon the principles he establishes and the concessions he makes. If it be only from effects exactly similar that experience warrants us to infer a similar cause, then I am afraid it must be granted, that the works of Nature resemble not so nearly the productions of man as to support the conclusion which Cleanthes admits can be built only on that resemblance. The two instances he brings to illustrate his argument are indeed ingenious and elegant – the first, especially, which seemingly carries great weight along with it; the other, I mean that of the Vegetating Library, as it is of more difficult apprehension, so I think it is not easy for the mind either to retain or to apply it. But, if I mistake not, this strong objection strikes equally against them both. Cleanthes does no more than substitute two artificial instances in the place of natural ones; but if these bear no nearer a resemblance than natural ones to the effects which we have experienced to proceed from men, then nothing *can* justly be inferred from them; and if this resemblance be greater, then nothing farther *ought* to be inferred from them. In one respect, however, Cleanthes seems to limit his reasonings more than is necessary even upon his own principles. Admitting, for once, that experience is the only source of our knowledge, I cannot see how it follows, that, to enable us to infer a similar cause, the effects must not only be similar, but exactly and precisely so. Will not experience authorize me to conclude, that a machine or piece of mechanism was produced by human art, unless I have happened previously to see a machine or piece of mechanism exactly of the same sort? Point out, for instance, the contrivance and end of a watch to a peasant who had never before seen anything more curious than the coarsest instruments of husbandry, will he not immediately conclude, that this watch is an effect produced by human art and design? And I would still farther ask, does a spade or a plough much more resemble a watch than a watch does an organized animal? The result of our whole experience, if experience indeed be the only principle, seems rather to amount to this: There are but two ways in which we have ever observed the different parcels of matter to be thrown together; either at random, or with design and purpose. By the first we have never seen produced a regular complicated effect, corresponding to a certain end; by the second, we uniformly have. If, then, the works of nature, and the productions of man, resemble each other in this one general characteristic, will not even experience sufficiently warrant us to ascribe to both a similar though proportionable cause? If you answer, that abstracting from the experience we acquire in this world, order and adjustment of parts is no proof of design, my reply is, that no conclusions, drawn from the nature of so chimerical a being as man, considered abstracted from experience, can at all be listened to. The principles of the human mind are clearly so contrived as not to unfold themselves till the proper objects and proper opportunity and occasion be presented. There is no arguing upon the nature of man but by considering him as grown to maturity, placed in society, and become acquainted with surrounding objects. But if you should still farther urge, that, with regard to instances of which we have no experience, for aught we know, matter may contain the principles of order, arrangement, and the adjustment of final causes, I should only answer, that whoever can conceive this proposition to be true, has exactly the same idea of matter that I have of mind. I know not if I have reasoned justly upon Cleanthes's principles, nor is it indeed very material. The purpose of my letter is barely to point out what to me appears the fair and philosophical method of proceeding in this inquiry. That this universe is the effect of an intelligent designing cause, is a principle which has been most universally received in all ages and in all nations; the proof uniformly appealed to is, the admirable order and adjustment of the works of nature. To proceed, then, experimentally and philosophically, the first question in point of order seems to be, what is the effect which the contemplation of the universe, and the several parts of it, produces upon a considering mind? This is a question of fact; a popular question, the discussion of which depends not upon refinements and subtlety, but merely upon impartiality and attention. I ask, then, what is the sentiment which prevails in one's mind, after having considered not only the more familiar objects that surround him, but also all the discoveries of Natural Philosophy and Natural History; after having considered not only the general economy of the universe, but also the most minute parts of it, and the amazing adjustment of means to ends with a precision unknown to human art, and in instances innumerable? Tell me, (to use the words of Cleanthes,) does not the idea of a contriver flow in upon you with a force like that of sensation? Expressions how just! (yet in the mouth of Cleanthes you must allow me to doubt of their propriety.) Nor does this conviction only arise from the consideration of the inanimate parts of the creation, but still more strongly from the contemplation of the faculties of the understanding, the affections of the heart, and the various instincts discoverable both in men and brutes: all so properly adapted to the circumstances and situation both of the species and the individual. Yet this last observation, whatever may be in it, derives no force from experience. For whoever saw a mind produced? If we are desirous to push our experiments still farther, and inquire, whether the survey of the universe has regularly and uniformly led to the belief of an intelligent cause? Shall we not find, that, from the author of the book of Job to the preachers at Boyle's Lecture, the same language has been universally held? No writer, who has ever treated this subject, but has either applied himself to describe, in the most emphatical language, the beauty and order of the universe, or else to collect together and place in the most striking light, the many instances of contrivance and design which have been discovered by observation and experiment. And when they have done this, they seem to have imagined that their task was finished, and their demonstration complete; and indeed no wonder, – for it seems to me, that we are scarce more assured of our own existence, than that this well-ordered universe is the effect of an intelligent cause.

This first question, then, which is indeed a question of fact, being thus settled upon observations which are obvious and unrefined, but not on that account the less satisfactory, it becomes the business of the philosopher to inquire, whether the conviction arising from these observations be founded on the conclusions of reason, the reports of experience, or the dictates of feeling, or possibly upon all these together; but if his principles shall not be laid so wide as to account for the fact already established upon prior evidence, we may, I think, safely conclude, that his principles are erroneous. Should a philosopher pretend to demonstrate to me, by a system of optics, that I can only discern an object when placed directly opposite to my eye, I should certainly answer, your system must be defective, for it is contradicted by matter of fact.

4

HENRY HOME, LORD KAMES

[Henry Home, Lord Kames], *Essays on the principles of morality and natural religion in two parts*. Edinburgh: Printed by R. Fleming, for A. Kincaid and A. Donaldson, 1751, 394 p.
Selections from Essay 8; from 1751 edition.

Henry Home (1696–1782) – later Lord Kames after 1752 when he was appointed to the Scottish Court of Session and Justiciary – was a close friend to Hume. He was a professional lawyer and legal writer, but also authored works on a variety of topics, including natural philosophy, agricultural reform, criticism, and historical anthropology. The first of his philosophical works was *Essays on the Principles of Morality and Natural Religion* (1751), selections from which are contained in *Early Responses to Hume's Metaphysical and Epistemological Writings*. In Essay 8 of that work, Kames considers Hume's argument in "Of a Particular Providence" – formerly titled "Of the Practical Consequences of Natural Religion". Hume presents the argument there that we must ascribe only those qualities to a cause that are required to bring about an effect; since the world (the effect) is imperfect, we cannot conclude that God (the cause) is perfect. In response, Kames holds that we have a natural feeling that both *impels* us to infer and *justifies* us in inferring the greatness of a cause based only on a small effect. William Rose favourably reviewed Kames's *Essays* in the *Monthly Review*, stating that readers "will be pleased with his ingenuity, and the genteel and candid manner in which he writes" (*Monthly Review*, 1751, Vol. 5, pp. 129–155). In his *Estimate of the Profit and Loss of Religion* (1753) George Anderson critically comments on the selection from Kames below (Anderson's discussion is contained later in this volume). The following is from the 1751 first edition. In the face of criticism, Kames revised his *Essays* in the 1758 second edition and 1759 third edition. The later revisions to the selection below were largely stylistic.

ESSAY VIII.
Our KNOWLEDGE *of the* DEITY

Of the BENEVOLENCE *of the* DEITY.

The mixed nature of the events, which fall under our observation, seems, at first sight, to point out a mixed cause, partly good and partly evil. The author of "philosophical essays concerning human understanding," in his eleventh essay, "of the practical consequences of natural religion," puts in the mouth of an Epicurean philosopher, a very shrewd argument against the benevolence of the Deity. The sum of it is what follows.

"If the cause be known only by the effect, we never ought to assign to it any qualities, beyond what are precisely requisite to produce the effect. Allowing therefore God to be the Author of the existence and order of the universe; it follows, that he possesses that precise degree of power, intelligence and benevolence, which appears in his workmanship."

And hence, from the present scene of things, apparently so full of ill and disorder, it is concluded, "That we have no foundation for ascribing any attribute to the Deity, but what is precisely commensurate with the imperfection of this world." With regard to mankind, and exception is made.

"In works of human art and contrivance, it is admitted, that we can advance from the effect to the cause, and returning back from the cause, that we conclude new effects, which have not yet existed. Thus, for instance, from the sight of a half-finished building, surrounded with heaps of stones and mortar, and all the instruments of masonry, we naturally conclude, that the building will be finished, and receive all the farther improvements, which art can bestow upon it. But the foundation of this reasoning is, plainly, that man is a being whom we know by experience, and whose motives and designs we are acquainted with, which enables us to draw many inferences, concerning what may be expected from him. But did we know man only from a single work or production, which we examine, we could not argue in this manner; because our knowledge of all the qualities which we ascribe to him, being, upon that supposition, derived from the work or production, it is impossible they could point any thing farther, or be the foundation of any new inference."

Supposing reason to be our only guide in these matters, which is supposed by this philosopher in his argument, I cannot help seeing his reasoning to be just. It appears to be true, that by no inference of reason, can I conclude any power or benevolence in the cause, beyond what is displayed in the effect. But this is no wonderful discovery. The philosopher might have carried his argument a greater length. He might have observed, even with regard to a man I am perfectly acquainted with, that I cannot conclude, by any chain of reasoning, he will finish the house he has begun. 'Tis to no purpose to urge his temper and disposition. For, from what principle of reason can I infer, that these will continue the same as formerly? He might further have observed, that the difficulty is greater, with regard to a man I know nothing of, supposing him to have begun the building. For what foundation have I, to transfer the qualities of the persons I am acquainted with, to strangers? This surely is not performed by any process of reasoning. There is still a wider step, which is, that reason will not help me out in attributing to the Deity, even that precise degree of power, intelligence and benevolence, which appears in his workmanship. I find no inconsistency in supposing, that a blind and undesigning cause may be productive of excellent effects. It will, I presume, be difficult to produce a demonstration to the contrary. And supposing, at the instant of operation, the Deity to have been endued with these properties, can we make out, by any argument *a priori*, that they are still subsisting in him? Nay, this same philosopher might have gone a great way further, by observing, when any thing comes into existence, that, by no process of reasoning, can we so much as infer any cause of its existence.

But happily for man, where reason fails him, perception and feeling come to his assistance. By means of principles implanted in our nature, we are enabled to make the above conclusions and inferences, as, at full length is made out, in some of the foregoing essays. More particularly, power, discovered in any object, is perceived as a permanent quality, like figure or extension.[8] Upon this account, power discovered by a single effect, is considered, as sufficient, to produce the like effects without end. Further, great power may be discovered from a small effect; which holds even in bodily strength; as where an action is performed readily, and without effort. This is equally remarkable in wisdom and intelligence. A very short argument may unfold correctness of judgment and deep reach. The same holds in art and skill. Examining a slight piece of workmanship done with taste, we readily observe, that the artist was equal to a greater task. But it is most of all remarkable in the quality of benevolence. For even, from a single effect produced by an unknown cause, which appears to be accurately adapted to some good purpose, we necessarily attribute to this cause, benevolence, as well as power and wisdom.[9] It is indeed but a weak perception, which arises from a single effect: but still, it is a clear and

---

[8] Essay upon our knowledge of future events.

[9] Essay of our idea of power, at the close.

distinct perception of pure benevolence, without any mixture of malice; for such contradictory qualities, are not readily to be ascribed to the same cause. There may be a difficulty indeed, where the effect is of a mixt nature, partly evil, partly good; or where a variety of effects, having these opposite characters, proceed from the same cause. Such intricate cases cannot fail to embarass us. But, as we must form some sentiment, the resolution of the difficulty plainly is, that we must ascribe benevolence or malevolence to the cause, from the prevalence of the one or other quality in the effects. If evil makes the greatest figure, we perceive the cause to be malevolent, notwithstanding of opposite instances of goodness. If, upon the whole, goodness is supereminent, we perceive the cause to be benevolent; and are not moved by the cross instances of evil, which we endeavour to reconcile, as we can, to pure benevolence. It is, indeed, true, that where the opposite effects nearly balance each other, our perception cannot be entire upon the side of benevolence or malevolence. But, if good or evil greatly preponderate, the weight in the opposite scale goes for nothing: the perception is entire upon the one side or other. Because it is the tendency of our perceptions, to reject a mixt character made up of benevolence and malevolence, unless, where it is necessarily prest home upon us, by an equality of opposite effects.

Such are the conclusions, that we can with certainty draw, not indeed from reason, but from sense and feeling. So little are we acquainted with the essence and nature of things, that we cannot establish these conclusions upon any argument *a priori*. Nor would it be of great benefit to mankind, to have these conclusions demonstrated to them; few having either leisure or genius to deal in such profound speculations. It is more wisely ordered, that they appear to us intuitively certain. We feel that they are true, and our feelings have full authority over us. This is a solid foundation for our conviction of the benevolence of the Deity. If, from a single effect, pure benevolence in the cause can be perceived or felt; what doubt can there be, of the pure benevolence of the Deity, when we survey his works, pregnant with good-will to mankind? Innumerable instances, of things wisely adapted to good purposes, gives us the strongest feeling, of the goodness, as well as wisdom, of the Deity; which is joined with the firmest persuasion of constancy and uniformity in his operations. A few cross instances, which to us, weak-sighted mortals, may appear of evil tendency, ought not, and cannot make us waver. When we know so little of nature, it would be surprising, indeed, if we should be able to account for every event, and its final tendency. Unless we were let into the counsels of the Almighty, we can never hope to unravel all the mysteries of the creation.

...

5

THOMAS RUTHERFORTH

Thomas Rutherforth, *The credibility of miracles defended against the author of Philosophical essays in a discourse delivered at the primary visitation of the Right Reverend ... Thomas Lord Bishop of Ely in St. Michaels Church Cambridge Avg. XXIX. MDCCLI. By T. Rutherforth*. Cambridge: printed by J. Bentham; for W. Thurlbourn; and sold by W. Innys and J. Beecroft, London, 1751, [viii], 22 p.

Complete pamphlet; from 1751 edition.[10]

Thomas Rutherforth (1712–1771) held various positions in the Anglican Church throughout his life and was the author of several works in moral philosophy. In *The Credibility of Miracles Defended*, he contends that Hume changed the nature of miracle discussions, from problems with specific miracles to a problem with miracles in general. The crux of Rutherforth's defence is that experience (as Hume explains it) is only one possible source of rational conviction; but a claim may also be deemed credible according to the degree that it conforms with other kinds of knowledge – particularly demonstrable knowledge. And this, he believes, is the case with miracles. Rutherforth focuses on what he believes are the two key premises of Hume's argument. First, Hume argues that a firm and invariable experience amounts to a full proof. However, Rutherforth counters, "in respect of a power superior to nature, which is not the immediate object of experiences, but of demonstrative knowledge", proof is not limited to our invariable experiences. Second, Hume argues that no event is a miracle unless there is firm and invariable experience against it. Rutherforth concedes that a miracle must be inconsistent with our experience of nature; however, it is not inconsistent "with our knowledge of the power of God". In view of the limits of these two premises,

---

[10] Title Page: The Credibility of Miracles defended | Against the Author of | *Philosophical Essays* | IN A | DISCOURSE | DELIVERED AT THE | PRIMARY VISITATION | OF | THE RIGHT REVEREND | FATHER IN GOD | THOMAS | LORD BISHOP OF ELY | IN | St. MICHAELS CHURCH | CAMBRIDGE | AVG. XXIX | MDCCLI. | BY | T. RUTHERFORTH D.D. CHAPLAIN TO HER ROYAL | HIGHNESS THE PRINCESS DOWAGER OF WALES. | *CAMBRIDGE*, | PRINTED BY J. BENTHAM PRINTER TO THE UNIVERSITY; | FOR W. THURLBOURN BOOKSELLER IN CAMBRIDGE; AND SOLD BY | W. INNYS IN PATER-NOSTER ROW AND J. BEECROFT IN LOMBARD-STREET, LONDON. | MDCCLI.

Rutherforth shows that Hume cannot validly draw his conclusion that it is always unreasonable to believe testimonies regarding miracles. Knowledge, he argues, reaches farther than experience, and knowledge of God's power is consistent with violations of natural laws. Thus, miracle testimonies may be credible when they appeal to knowledge of God's power. In contrast with the New Testiment miracles, Rutherforth argues, pagan and Popish miracles are not credible since they do not appeal to the power of God. Rutherforth concedes that he does not solve the question as to the requisite degree of testimony that we need for belief in miracles: "All that I proposed was, to bring the question concerning miracles back to the old state of it." Writing for the *Monthly Review*, William Rose presents a neutral account of Rutherforth's pamphlet, which only summarizes its contents (*Monthly Review*, October 1751, Vol. 5, pp. 358–361). The following is from the 1751 and only edition of Rutherforth's pamphlet.

The Credibility of Miracles defended
Againſt the Author of
Philoſophical Eſſays
IN A
DISCOURSE
DELIVERED AT THE
PRIMARY VISITATION
OF
THE RIGHT REVEREND
FATHER IN GOD
THOMAS
LORD BISHOP OF ELY
IN Sт. MICHAELS CHURCH
CAMBRIDGE
AVG. XXIX.

MDCCLI.

BY
T. RUTHERFORTH D.D. CHAPLAIN TO HER ROYAL
HIGHNESS THE PRINCESS DOWAGER OF WALES.

CAMBRIDGE,
PRINTED BY J. BENTHAM PRINTER TO THE UNIVERSITY;
FOR W. THURLBOURN BOOKSELLER IN CAMBRIDGE; AND SOLD BY
W. INNYS IN PATER-NOSTER-ROW AND J. BEECROFT
IN LOMBARD-STREET, LONDON.

MDCCLI.

TO
THE RIGHT REVEREND
FATHER IN GOD
THOMAS
LORD BISHOP OF ELY.

MY LORD,

As I am encouraged to print the following discourse by the favourable notice, which you were pleased to take of it, in your most excellent charge to your clergy, before whom I delivered it; this alone might be a sufficient reason for me to beg, that I may have the honour of sending it abroad under your Lordship's patronage. But I had another reason for desiring to address myself to your Lordship upon this occasion: it would be, I thought, the most public, and therefore the best, opportunity of testifying my just sense of the many and signal instances of goodness and generosity, which I have received from your Lordship. The favours, which you have been pleased to confer upon me, are great indeed in themselves, and may justly claim the most sincere acknowledgments and the best returns of gratitude, that I am able to make: but the graceful manner, in which they were conferred, has doubled the value of them. Your Lordship's noble and truly christian spirit has in this respect, as in many others, most eminently distinguished you from the rest of the world, by engaging you to seek for opportunities of exercising your bounty, and to prevent, not only the solicitations, but even the wishes of those, who stand in need of your protection and assistance. That they may long be blessed with such a patron and friend, as they are sure of finding in your lordship, and that you may long enjoy all the happiness, which providence can bestow upon one of its best and most faithful instruments in doing good; is, my Lord, the constant and devoutest wish of

> Your Lordship's most obliged
> and most dutiful servant
> THOMAS RUTHERFORTH.

ST. JOHNS COLL.
SEPT. XVIII.
—
MDCCLI.

THE
CREDIBILITY OF MIRACLES
DEFENDED.

—

JOHN XX. 30, 31.

MANY OTHER SIGNS TRULY DID JESUS IN THE PRESENCE OF
HIS DISCIPLES, WHICH ARE NOT WRITTEN IN THIS BOOK: BUT
THESE ARE WRITTEN THAT YE MIGHT BELIEVE, THAT JESUS
CHRIST IS THE SON OF GOD.

The sacred historian hath here informed us with what view he recorded the
miracles of Christ: he designed to convince his readers, that the person, who
could do such mighty works, must have a commission from God, to teach
his will to mankind. And the defenders of christianity have always
imagined, that the miracles, which are related in the new testament, and
are there said to have been wrought by Christ and his apostles, may be
urged as an undeniable evidence in favour of our religion; provided they
can make it appear, that the reality of them is evinced by such testimony,
as would be sufficient to establish the truth of any matter of fact, beyond
all contradiction.

But the state of this question hath been lately much altered. Instead of
being called upon to clear up the testimony, which supports the miracles
of Christ and his apostles; we are now challenged to shew, that any
testimony whatsoever can be sufficient to prove the truth of these, or of any
other miracles.

"A miracle, we are told, is a violation of the laws of nature: for
nothing is esteemed a miracle, if it ever happens in the common course
of things. And consequently; since a firm and unalterable experience hath
established those laws; there must be a firm and unalterable experience
against every miraculous event. But in the judgments, which we pass
upon matters of fact, such an experience as this amounts to a full and
direct proof. We have therefore, from the nature of the fact, a full and
direct proof against the existence of any miracle. If then a miracle, with
such a proof against it, can be rendered credible; it must be by an
opposite proof, which is superior. Therefore no proof from report can
evince the existence of a miracle; unless it over-balances the opposite
proof from the nature of the fact: or, no testimony can be sufficient to
establish the belief of a miracle; unless the falsehood of the testimony

would be more miraculous, than the event, which it endeavours to establish."[11]

The confidence, with which this difficulty is urged against the belief of the gospel, hath made it our duty to examine into the merits of it. I intend therefore, in the following discourse, to employ your thoughts upon this subject, by laying before you some observations upon the measures of credibility, which will assist us in shewing, that this argument is inconclusive, and that no supernatural degree of testimony is necessarily required to prove the existence of a miracle.

Where we have no knowledge or certainty of a fact, by having been eye-witnesses of it; the measures of credibility, make use of to form a judgment upon the truth or falshood of it, are the conformity or consistency of it with our experience; the conformity or consistency of it with our knowledge in general; and the testimony of other men, who vouch the evidence of their senses.

Matters of fact have three different degrees of credibility, in the nature of the thing, arising from their conformity or consistency with our experience.

First; there are some events which we have always found to be brought about steadily and constantly, at stated times, and in certain places, without the least irregularity or exception. The existence of these events is taken for granted; we assure ourselves upon the evidence of such an uniform experience, that they will happen at the usual time and place, without requiring any testimony to prove it. We never think of disputing whether the sun will rise to morrow morning, or of disbelieving, that the tide came in yesterday. The exact likeness between these facts and others, which we have seen and known to be true, induces us to admit them without any hesitation: we take them for truth, because they have, in all respects, a full and perfect resemblance of it.

Secondly; some events have a less exact and less striking likeness of the truth; we find them conformable to our experience in most respects, but not in all. It is most agreeable to what hath commonly been observed to happen, that, in England, there should be frost in some particular week of december, and thunder in some particular week of june. The general resemblance of the truth, which we find in events of this sort, makes us think them likely to be true, and inclines us to believe them. But because they have been sometimes known to fail, and are therefore in some points unlike the truth; the credibility, which they have, in the nature of the thing, does not amount to a full proof of their existence. When we have had no opportunity of observing them ourselves, and cannot ascertain their

---

[11] Hume's Philos. Essays pag. 173–207.

existence by the evidence of our own senses; we are ready to believe, upon the evidence of our former experience, that they have happened: but our belief is never so fixed as to be raised to any degree of assurance or confidence without the help of testimony.

Thirdly; in respect of some events we have equal experience both ways; and in respect of some others we have no experience either way.[12] That it should thunder on a man's right hand, is not more conformable to our experience than that it should thunder on his left. That there lived in Rome such a man as Julius Cæsar; that he was a general, and won a battle against another called Pompey; are facts, about which we have no experience at all. Such events as these are looked upon to be credible in themselves, only because they furnish no cause of doubt from the nature of the thing. They might perhaps with more propriety be called indifferent in themselves: because, as, from the nature of the thing, they furnish no cause of doubt, so neither do they furnish any cause of belief. But whether we call them credible or indifferent; they are confessedly capable of being proved by a fair testimony.

These are the degrees of credibility, which arise from the conformity or consistency of an event with our experience: and we shall find upon inquiry, that the same degrees of credibility arise from its conformity or consistency with our knowledge. For the credibility of events is indeed nothing more than their likeness to the truth. Whenever therefore we find them stamped with this image, it gives them a currency: whether the truth, whose image they bear, is the object of experience or the object of knowledge; whether we came into possession of it by the immediate perception of our senses, or by induction and conclusions of reason.

First; some facts have in all respects an exact conformity with our knowledge: such as these are admitted for true, upon the credit of their full and perfect resemblance of the truth, without any testimony to vouch for them. When by the help of observations, and by reasoning upon such general conclusions as are deducible from them, we have demonstrated, that the moon is retained in its orbit by the force of gravity; the resemblance, which we find, in all points, between the motion of the moon round the earth, and the motions of the satellites round jupiter, determines us to believe, with an assurance little inferiour to certainty, that these bodies are likewise retained in their respective orbits by the same force of gravity.

Secondly; when a fact is conformable to our knowledge in most respects, but not in all; its likeness to the truth makes it credible, and inclines us to believe it. The want of a more exact and minute likeness may, if we consider only the nature of the fact, leave some room to doubt of its

---

[12] Lock's Essay. B. IV. C. XVI. § 8.

existence: but the report of credible witnesses never fails to over-rule this doubt and to establish the belief of it. Whatever probability we may have from experience, that there will be frost, in England, in some particular week of december, and thunder in some particular week of june; we have the same probability from our knowledge of the globe, that, in the opposite southern latitude, there will be frost in some particular week of june, and thunder in some particular week of december. One of these facts is made credible by its conformity with our experience, and the other by its conformity with our knowledge; both of them are so far credible in themselves, that they may easily be established by testimony; and neither of them can be effectually established without it.

Thirdly; some events may happen either way, and yet be equally conformable to our knowledge; others are so far consistent with it, that they may be true, without contradicting any other truth, that we are certain of. Such events as these, being indifferent or credible in themselves, on account of their conformity or consistency with our knowledge, furnish no cause of doubt from the nature of the thing, and are therefore capable of being proved by a fair testimony. When a man plays, with an equal chance against him, his winning or his losing are equally conformable with our knowledge in the doctrine of chances. The planet mars may have a satellite consistently with all our knowledge of the causes, which govern the system of the world. Neither of these facts have such a credibility in themselves as can determine us rather to believe, than to doubt of them: but both of them are so far credible in the nature of the thing, from their conformity or consistency with our knowledge, that a fair testimony would prove on one instance, that the player hath lost, and in the other, that mars hath a satellite.

Perhaps it may be said, that we cannot come at any certainty or knowledge of the real existence of facts, but from the evidence of our senses; that knowledge or experience of facts must therefore be only different names for the same thing; and consequently that conformity with knowledge is not a distinct measure of credibility from conformity with experience. It must indeed be allowed, that all our reasonings, about the laws and order of nature, will be precarious and fantastical, unless they proceed upon experiments and observation. But when we have thus gained some footing, or ground, as it were, to stand upon; our reason can survey from thence many parts of nature, which our senses were unable to discover. Suppose we have determined, by observations, the proportion between the respective distances of the planets from the sun, and the periodical times, in which they describe their orbits: our experience of facts stops here; but our knowledge of them reaches farther. Our reason, proceeding upon these informations of sense, demonstrates the law of that force, which continually urges the planets towards the sun. Thus we arrive at a certain knowledge of this latter fact, though the former only hath been, or indeed can be, the object of experience. But, when I distinguish between experience and knowledge, I would not be understood to mean, that they differ any otherwise, than as the part differs from the whole. Every certain perception of the truth, whether we obtain it by our reason or our senses, is knowledge. All our experience therefore must be allowed to be knowledge. But then I would contend, that all our knowledge is not experience. For as some truths, relating to real existence, are perceived immediately by our senses; so there are others, which we discover by induction and conclusions of reason. And since the resemblance of truth is the inducement of probability, upon which we admit facts to be true; conformity with experience is planely too scanty a measure of credibility; because experience is not the only way of discovering truth.

I designed, by the foregoing observations, to establish these two conclusions; – First; that events are made as credible, in the nature of the thing, by their conformity or consistency with our knowledge, as they are by their conformity or consistency with our experience; – And secondly; that, when events, which are conformable to our knowledge or consistent with it, are supported by a fair testimony, our assent to them is well-grounded.

Allow us the truth of these two conclusions, which we have proved already; and allow us besides, what we can prove, if you deny it, that we have a demonstrative knowledge of the existence, the power, the wisdom, and the goodness of God; and by the help of these principles, we shall be able to unravel all the fallacy of your argument, and to shew you, that miracles do not require any supernatural degree of testimony to establish our belief of them.

A firm and invariable experience amounts, you say, to a full and direct proof. – But no event, for so your argument proceeds, can be called a miracle, unless there is a firm and invariable experience against it. – From hence you conclude, that we must have, in the nature of the fact, a full and direct proof against the existence of every miracle. – The whole stress of your argument rests upon these two fundamental principles, and upon this conclusion, which you deduce from them. Let us therefore enquire into the truth of your principles, and consider how well they will establish your conclusion.

A firm and invariable experience amounts to a full proof; – You would have done well to inform us what it is, which such an experience proves in so decisive a manner. You may have observed the ordinary course of nature, with diligence and exactness, and may have discovered what sort of events are produced, steadily and constantly, in the usual train of causes and effects. From hence you may determine, with the highest probability, that no events, which are repugnant to these, can be produced by the same causes operating in the same manner, or by the ordinary powers of nature, which are the objects of your experience. But your proof from experience can go no farther. When you have observed what events are, constantly and uniformly, brought about by the operation of those laws, which the author of nature originally established; by the qualities, which he impressed upon matter; or by the powers, which he bestowed upon his creatures; you have then acquired a firm and invariable experience. But such an experience will never prove, that no events, which are repugnant to these, can be brought about by the immediate interposition of him, who established these laws, and can over-rule them; who impressed these qualities, and can suspend their operations; who bestowed these powers, and can either control or augment them. For the force of an argument, deduced from experience, can extend no farther, than the experience extends, from whence you deduce it. Your experience of the ordinary powers of nature may be a decisive proof, in respect of those powers, which are the immediate objects of it: but it can be no proof at all, in respect of a power superiour to nature, which is not the immediate object of experience, but of demonstrative knowledge.

Your other fundamental principle is, – That no event can be looked upon as a miracle, unless there is a firm and unalterable experience against it. – The expression here is vague and indeterminate, and we may perhaps mistake your meaning, unless we ascertain it, by looking back to the first principles, from whence this position is inferred. You define a miracle to be a violation of the laws of nature; and, because a firm and unalterable experience hath established those laws, you infer, that there must be such an experience against every miraculous event. You have here shewn evidently, that the experience, upon which we establish our notions of the laws of nature, is repugnant to every miraculous event; or, that every miracle is inconsistent with our experience of the common and visible train of causes and effects. But we must caution you, when you apply this inference, not to confound experience with knowledge, or the common course and laws of nature with the power of him, who is the father of nature, and established its laws. You may certainly infer, from your definition of a miracle, that no event can be called by this name, unless it is inconsistent with our experience of the common course of nature. But the same definition will not justify the only inference, which can serve your purpose; you cannot infer from it, that every miracle is inconsistent with our knowledge of the power of God.

We have now examined your fundamental principles separately, and have seen how far they are true: let us next consider them together, and try what conclusion will come out from them. Suppose then your argument to be thus stated. – A firm and unalterable experience of the common course of nature is a full and direct proof, that no event, which is inconsistent with it, can be brought about by any power, which is the object of our knowledge, or which we know of – But we have a constant and unalterable experience of the common course of nature to oppose to every miraculous event. – Your regular conclusion from hence would be, that we have a full and direct proof, against the likelihood or possibility of bringing about a miraculous event by any power, which is the object of our knowledge. – But such a conclusion, though it is regularly deduced from the principles laid down, is not true: because one of the principles, from whence you deduce it, is false. A firm and unalterable experience of the common course of nature is indeed a direct proof, that no event, which is inconsistent with the usual train of causes and effects, can be brought about by any of the ordinary powers of nature, which are the objects of this experience. But we have already shewn you, that the same experience is no proof at all, against the likelihood or possibility of bringing about such an event by a power, which is superiour to the common course of nature, a power, which we can demonstrate to exist, and which is consequently the object of our knowledge.

Let us try whether your conclusion will succeed better, if the principles, from which you deduce it, are stated in another manner. – A firm and invariable experience of the common course of nature is a full and direct proof, that no event, which is inconsistent with it, can be produced by the ordinary powers of nature, which are the objects of this experience. – But every miraculous event is inconsistent with our knowledge of all the powers, that exist. – The logicians would tell you, that no regular conclusion can be drawn from these premises; because your syllogism will have four terms in it. And common sense will tell you, that no true conclusion can be drawn from them; because one of them is false. We allow indeed, that every miracle must, from the notion of it, be inconsistent with our experience of the common course of nature: but you have not proved, and we think you cannot prove, that it must likewise, from the notion of it, be inconsistent with our demonstrative knowledge of the power of God.

There is still this third shape, in which your argument may be stated. – A firm and unalterable experience of the common course of nature is a full and direct proof, that no event, which is inconsistent with it, can be produced by the ordinary powers of nature, which are the objects of this experience. – But every miraculous event must, from the notion of it, be inconsistent with our experience of the common course of nature. – We grant, that your premises are true, when they are thus stated. But if you would conclude, – that we have a full and direct proof, against the production of a miracle by any powers, which are the objects of our knowledge; – such a conclusion must be false; because it contains more than is contained in the premises. Your premises relate only to the ordinary powers of nature, which are the objects of experience; but your conclusion extends itself to a power, which is superiour to the common course of nature, and is the object of our knowledge. The only regular conclusion, which can be deduced from these premises, is, – that we have a full and direct proof, against the production of a miracle by any of the ordinary powers of nature, which are the objects of our senses, or of common experience. – You must content yourself with this conclusion: for when the principles, from whence you argue, are so explained as to be true, they will justify no other. And this is such a conclusion, as the defenders of christianity have no reason to be afraid of.

In answering this argument, I have laid open the grounds of our assent to the existence of a miracle. Such an event is inconsistent with our experience of the common course of things, and would therefore be, in itself, incredible, and incapable of being proved by any testimony, if we knew nothing of any power existing in the universe, besides those, which are employed in carrying on the visible train of causes and effects. But knowledge reaches farther than experience: reason leads us on from those powers, which are the objects of sense, to another, which is superiour to them, to the power of him, who, as he at first established the laws, and settled the course of what we commonly mean by the word nature, can therefore, when he pleases, suspend or over-rule them. The existence of a miracle hath a general conformity of consistency with our knowledge of such a power: and this conformity or consistency with our knowledge gives it credibility enough, in the nature of the thing, to render it capable of being proved by a fair testimony.

From hence it appears, that when we reject any miraculous event as spurious, which comes to us well attested; our reason for this conduct either is not, or ought not to be, any pretended proof against it, from the general nature of all miracles. For a miracle, considered merely as a supernatural change in the common course of things, is consistent with our knowledge of God's power: and no events, which are consistent with our knowledge, furnish any cause of doubt or suspicion about their existence, and much less any presumption or proof against it, from the nature of the thing. And yet we reject the miracles and prodigies, which we find related in pagan histories, and popish legends; notwithstanding some of them are supported by such a testimony, as might, if we were to give ourselves the trouble of examining it, be found unexceptionable in itself, or sufficient, at least, to establish the truth of any common matter of fact. Upon what grounds then, it may be asked, can we justify our rejecting these miracles; if there is no presumption against them, from the nature of miracles in general, and we either do not examine the testimony, which supports them, or find no exceptions against it, when we do? They, who make this enquiry, might, if they attended to the matter, find a third reason for rejecting many particular miracles, besides the two, which are here suggested. Though we have no objections, from the nature of the thing, that can be urged with any force against miracles in general; yet there are frequently such circumstances appear in the relation of particular miracles, as will afford unanswerable objections to the truth of them. If the circumstances of any particular miracle do either directly, or by necessary consequence, exclude the power of every being, who can change the common course of things; such a miracle, not from the general nature of all miracles, but from its own particular circumstances, becomes inconsistent with our knowledge, and incapable of being proved by any testimony whatever.

"Dionysius of Halicarnassus reports, that in the war between the Romans and the Latins, the Gods Castor and Pollux appeared visibly on white horses, and fought on the side of the Romans; who by their assistance gained a complete victory."[13] It is not any defect in the testimony, when applyed to the miracle, which determines us to reject it; whilst, upon the authority of the same testimony, we admit the battle and the victory: for we reject the miracle, either without enquiring at all into the testimony, by which it is supported; or, if upon enquiry, we should find few or no objections against the testimony, yet we should still reject it. Neither can we reasonably be determined in this case by any general presumption or proof, from the nature of the thing, against the existence of all miracles: for miracles have been shewn to be, in themselves, as consistent with our knowledge, and consequently as credible, as many other matters of fact. But the particular miracle in question is attended with a circumstance, which directly excludes the power of God from being concerned in the production of it. Castor and Pollux have not, that we know of, any power of changing the settled course of things: and for want of such a power in the principal agents, the fact, as it is related, is inconsistent with our knowledge, and incapable of being proved by any degree of human testimony.

The like exception runs through almost all the pagan miracles. And if in any instances we believe what is reported of their oracles; we must first have rendered these facts consistent with our knowledge, by finding out such reasons, as may persuade us, that the great deceiver of mankind, though he is subject to the power of God, who can at any time say to him, – Hitherto shalt thou go and no farther, – hath yet a power, when he is permitted to use it, of changing the common course of things, and of producing such events, as could not have been produced by any of the visible powers of nature, which are the objects of our experience.

Many of the popish miracles are rendered incredible, in the same manner, by having some circumstance connected with them, which directly excludes the power of God. When the miracles, pretended to be wrought at the tomb

---

[13] Middleton's free Enquiry pag. 218.

of Abbe Paris, are found to have been effectually suppressed, only by walling up that part of the church, where the tomb of the saint, who was supposed to work them, was placed;[14] this circumstance cannot be reconciled with our knowledge of God's power: for his purposes, we are sure, could not have been defeated by building a wall.

Many more of these legendary miracles are attended with such circumstances, as exclude the power of God, by necessary consequence, from the production of them. When a set of men have nothing else to recommend them, besides their having devoted themselves to such a way of life, as planely defeats the end, for which they and all mankind were sent into the world, by making them always useless, and commonly burdensom to society: if they should pretend, that God interposes in their favour, and works miracles to establish their credit; a better testimony, than the monks can, for the most part, produce in support of their legends, would not determine a wise man to believe them. Such an interposition would be repugnant to our knowledge of the wisdom and goodness of God, who contrives all his works with a view to the general happiness, and suffers no part of the world to be idle; but requires, as far as reason can teach us his will, that men and brutes, and creatures of what condition soever, should each, in their proper station, concur with him in labouring to promote the same important end. But where the wisdom and goodness of God are thus planely excluded, no testimony can convince us, that his power was concerned.

The truth is; if we study to avoid, as much as may be, the trouble of examining the several popish miracles distinctly, and indolently please ourselves with any thing, which promises to confute them all at once; we shall be easily led to take part with those, who under the specious pretence of defending the protestant religion, would unsettle the foundations of christianity itself, and to maintain, as they do, that there is such a proof or presumption, from the nature of the thing, against all miracles in general, as will make we know not what degree of testimony necessary to establish them. Whereas, if we would contend, as with reason we may, that the popish miracles, which are best attested, are each of them connected with some such circumstances, as render it either directly, or by necessary consequence, inconsistent with our knowledge of God's power; we should then be able both to defend ourselves as protestants, and to give an answer to every one, who shall ask us a reason of our faith in the miracles of Christ and his apostles. For enough hath, I hope, been said to make it appear; that, whatever becomes of these legendary fables, when they are confuted by arguments deduced from the particular circumstances of each of them; yet miracles, considered merely as changes in the common course of nature,

---

[14] Observations on St. Paul's Conversion. pag. 64, 65.

are so far consistent with our knowledge of God's power, as to furnish no cause of doubt from the nature of the thing: and that consequently, when they are attended with none of those circumstances, which either directly, or by necessary consequence exclude his power; more especially if the end, proposed by them, is conformable to our notions of his wisdom and goodness; a fair testimony, though it is not a supernatural one, will be sufficient, not only to fix our assent, but to raise it likewise into assurance and confidence.

It is not my business at present to enquire what precise degree of testimony is requisite for this purpose. All that I proposed was, to bring the question concerning miracles back to the old state of it, by shewing, that there is no proof or presumption, from the general nature of such events, against the existence of them. And if this hath been shewn effectually, the enquiry, in which we are principally concerned, is, whether the miracles of Christ and his apostles are supported by such a testimony, as would be sufficient to establish the truth of any matter of fact, beyond all contradiction. But this question hath been so well examined, and so judiciously settled already, by much more able hands than mine; that, if either my subject would lead me, or your patience would allow me, yet their labours have rendered it needless, to spend any time in enlarging upon it.

THE END.

6
WILLIAM ADAMS

William Adams, *An essay on Mr. Hume's Essay on miracles. By William Adams.* London: printed by E. Say; and sold by R. Dodsley, M. Cooper, and J. Cotton in Shrewsbury, 1752, [4], 134 p.
Complete pamphlet; from 1752 edition.

William Adams (1706–1789) held a number of benefices in the Anglican church before becoming Master of Pembroke College, Oxford, in 1775. He also authored several works in theology and ethics. His *Essay* is a line-by-line attack on Hume's "Of Miracles", against which he aims to defend the miracles in the New Testament. The work is in two Parts, paralleling the two Parts of Hume's original essay. As to Part 1, according to Adams, Hume thinks that miracles are a contradiction in terms, and, hence, impossible; however, Adams notes that a human can propel iron, and "Should the same be done by any invisible power, it would be a miracle". The evidence from natural experience, he believes, "proves a course of nature; but whether this is ever interrupted, is still a question". Since laws of nature are often overturned by single experiments, Adams concludes that "the strongest presumption from experience is of little force against positive evidence". He also contends that the purifying effects of miracles on religion are a presumption in their favour. Thus, "witnesses who have sufficient opportunities of convincing themselves, and give sufficient proof of their conviction, have a right to command our faith". Such is the case, he believes, with the Gospel miracles. Turning to Part 2 of Hume's essay, Adams argues that the gospel accounts rise above Hume's four conditions against miracle testimonies. Adams also maintains that the Gospel miracles differ significantly from modern alleged miracles. Conceding that sick people indeed recovered at the Abbé's tomb, Adams argues that no evidence indicates miraculous healings in this case or with any alleged Catholic miracle. "The disparity, then, between these and the Gospel miracles is infinite." Adams concludes noting that the close of Hume's essay "is little more than a rude insult on the Scriptures.... For fear his readers should mistake his meaning, and not apply his argument where he intended, the author proceeds, with a smiling grimace." William Rose favourably reviewed Adam's *Essay* in the *Monthly Review*:

Among the many useful and valuable productions that have been lately published, this is not the least considerable. The subject is very important, and handled with judgment and accuracy: the full evidence, possibility, and propriety of miracles are distinctly shewn; and the objections of Mr. *Hume*, though urged with great acuteness, proved to be inconclusive. Nor is it the least praise of this performance, that it is written with candour, and in such a manner as shews the author to have enlarged and generous notions of christianity, and a temper free from sourness and bigotry. [*Monthly Review*, January 1752, Vol. 6, pp. 71–74]

Adams's pamphlet was published again in 1754 "with additions" and also in 1767 and 1776.

AN

ESSAY

ON

Mr. *HUME's* ESSAY

ON

MIRACLES.

By *WILLIAM ADAMS*, M. A.
Miniſter of *St. Chad's*, *Salop*,
And Chaplain to the Lord Biſhop of *Landaff*.

LONDON,
Printed by E. Say in *Ave-Mary-Lane*;
And ſold by R. Dodsley in *Pall-Mall*, M. Cooper in *Pater-noſter-Row*, and J. Cotton in *Shrewſbury*.

M, DCC, LII.

AN ESSAY, *&c.*

Mr. Hume hath many of the talents of a fine writer, and hath justly obtained that character by the agreeable *Essays moral and political*, with which he has obliged the world. What he hath wrote well will create a prejudice in favour of his errors; and these will have all their bad influence, when recommended by so able an advocate. The present is a subject of the greatest importance, and the author expresses a particular satisfaction in his performance. These are reasons for considering it carefully, and for guarding ourselves against being deceived by the artifice or eloquence of the writer.

He begins with challenging, a little indirectly, the thanks of the publick, for a discovery, which, he apprehends, will be of universal service to mankind. This is nothing less than an infallible cure for superstition.

"I flatter myself," says he, "that I have discovered an argument, which, if just, will, with the wise and learned, be an everlasting check to all kinds of superstitious delusion, and, consequently, will be useful as long as the world endures; for so long, I suppose, will the accounts of miracles and prodigies be found in all profane history."[15]

The virtues of this specifick are such, that it exterminates all religions alike; as he shews, by trying its strength upon the *Christian*, which, where it prevails, is perhaps more obstinate and hard of cure than any other. Here, however, it has been known to fail. I have given it a fair trial, and known it tried by others, without the least effect, and think I can prove that there is no one ingredient of any virtue or efficacy in it.

The secret itself is contained in the compass of a few lines: and therefore, to give some port and figure to it, the author has thought necessary to introduce it with some preliminary observations.

In the first of these, his meaning seems to be to lay down this as a principle – that all our reasonings concerning matter of fact are founded wholly on experience:

"Tho' experience be our only guide in reasoning concerning matters of fact, it must be acknowledged, that this guide is not altogether infallible, but in some cases is apt to lead us into errors and mistakes. One, who in our climate should expect better weather in any week of *June* than in one of *December*, would reason justly and conformable to experience; but 'tis certain, that he may happen in the event to find himself mistaken. However, we may observe, that in such a case he would have no cause

---

[15] *Philosophical Essays concerning human understanding*, p. 174.

to complain of experience; because it commonly informs us beforehand of the uncertainty, by that contrariety of events which we may learn from a diligent observation."[16]

In illustrating this observation, both here and elsewhere, he seems to confine it to such events as are future:

"An hundred instances or experiments on one side, and fifty on another, afford a very doubtful expectation of any event; tho' an hundred uniform experiments, with only one contradictory one, do reasonably beget a very strong degree of assurance."[17]

Here then I readily allow, that in reasoning concerning future contingencies experience is the best guide we have, tho' in many cases, as will hereafter be seen, a very uncertain one.
This observation is followed by a prudent caution.

"A wise man," he tells us, "proportions his belief to the evidence. In such conclusions as are founded on an infallible experience he expects the event with the last degree of assurance, and regards his past experience as a full proof of the future existence of that event. In other cases he proceeds with more caution: he weighs the opposite experiments; he considers which side is supported by the greatest number of experiments: to that side he inclines, with doubt and hesitation; and, when at last he fixes his judgment, the evidence exceeds not what we properly call probability. – In all cases we must ballance the opposite experiments, where they are opposite, and deduct the lesser number from the greater, in order to know the exact force of the superior evidence."[18]

This logick is very just, and what, I am persuaded, every man of the plainest understanding knows how to practise, without learning it from the schools, or from this author's refinements on the *curious and sublime subject* (as he calls it) of probability.[19]
He then proceeds –

"To apply these principles to a particular instance: We may observe, there is no species of reasoning more common, more useful, and even necessary to human life, than that derived from the testimony of men,

[16] *Philosophical Essays*, p 174.

[17] P. 175.

[18] P. 175.

[19] *Essay on probability*, p. 97.

and the reports of eye-witnesses and spectators. This species of reasoning perhaps one may deny to be founded on the relation of cause and effect. I shall not dispute about a word. 'Twill be sufficient to observe, that our assurance, in any argument of this kind, is derived from no other principle than our observation of the veracity of human testimony, and of the usual conformity of facts to the reports of witnesses."[20]

'Tis difficult to say what the author would here exemplify, there being no clear connexion betwixt this and the preceding paragraphs. But, if I may presume to explain it, his argument stands thus: The principle he set out with, was, that our reasoning about matters of fact depends wholly upon experience. This he hath proved concerning such events as are future: he now wants to prove the same concerning facts that are past. Here he is aware, that, besides experience, we have another guide, which is the testimony of history, that of witnesses, &c. These he does not chuse to distinguish from the former, but insinuates, that the evidence of testimony is included in that of experience, or that every argument from testimony is only an argument from experience, for-as-much as the truth of that depends ultimately upon this.[21] "The ultimate standard," he tells us below, "by which we determine disputes of this kind, is always derived from experience and observation." Now it is true, that the evidence of testimony must be resolved at last into experience: but this experience is of a species entirely distinct from that on which the natural probability of any fact attested rests: nor does it consist, as this author asserts, in our *observation of the veracity of human testimony, and of the usual conformity of facts with the reports of witnesses*. It is built upon other principles, to which the author himself leads us in the words that follow:

"Did not men's imagination naturally follow their memory – had they not commonly an inclination to truth, and a sentiment of probity – were they not sensible to shame, when detected in a falshood – Were not these, I say, discovered by experience to be qualities inherent in human nature, we should never repose the least confidence in human testimony."[22]

[20] P. 176.

[21] It may with more propriety be said, that the evidence of experience is included in that of testimony, than the contrary. Our own experience reaches around and goes back but a little way. But the experience of others, upon which we chiefly depend, is derived to us wholly from history and tradition, that is, from testimony. And it is obvious to observe, that, in a question of fact, the testimony of negative witnesses, how many soever, is, for the most part, no evidence at all; while positive testimony must, more or less, have its weight.

[22] P. 177.

The first of these motives I do not understand. Of the rest I shall observe, that their force we collect, not so much from our observation of other men, as from our own feeling, and a consciousness of what passes within our own breast. We perceive in ourselves, that a love and reverence for truth is natural to the mind of man: and the same self-experience teaches us, that there are certain other principles in human nature, by which the veracity of men may be tried, and the truth of testimony be often put out of doubt, as will be hereafter seen.

The next observation is, that,

> "as the evidence derived from witnesses and human testimony is founded on past experience, so it varies with the experience, and is regarded either as a proof or probability, according as the conjunction betwixt any particular kind of report and any kind of objects has been found to be constant or variable."[23]

Here again the author's meaning is lost in a thicket of words, which it is difficult for a common eye to penetrate. Let the reader try what he can make of the *conjunction varying betwixt any particular report and any kind of objects.* The credibility of an historical fact depends upon the credibility of the fact itself, and that of the historian or witnesses who relate it. These should be always considered distinctly; tho' the author, for reasons of his own, chuses to confound them. The latter of these depends in part upon principles that are fixed and invariable, such as those the author has just mentioned, which are general principles of human nature; and in part too on the personal character of the relator, the interest he has in the fact related, and other circumstances. As these circumstances vary, the evidence varies, and the fact becomes more or less credible. And so, concerning the natural credibility of the fact, this is greater or less, according as our own, and the observation of others, in cases of a similar nature, has been more or less uniform. Something like this I take to be the author's meaning in this place: and this is the amount of all that follows in this and the next paragraph. My design, therefore, in this remark, is, not to contest the author's principles, which, as far as I understand them, are right enough; but to shew that his style and manner of writing tend to embarrass the subject, and perplex the reader.

We are now coming nearer to the matter in question.

> "Suppose," says the author, "that the fact, which the testimony endeavours to establish, partakes of the extraordinary and the marvellous; in that case, the evidence resulting from the testimony receives a diminution greater or

---

[23] P. 177.

less, in proportion as the fact is more or less unusual. When the fact attested is such a one as has seldom fallen under our observation, here is a contest of two opposite experiences; of which the one destroys the other, as far as its force goes, and the superior can only operate on the mind by the force which remains. The very same principle of experience, which gives us a certain degree of assurance in the testimony of witnesses, gives us also, in this case, another degree of assurance against the fact which they endeavour to establish."[24]

Here the author seems to suppose, that a want of experience, in any case, is the same with experiencing the contrary. *When a fact attested hath seldom fallen under our observation,* "*here is,* says he, *a contest of two opposite experiences:*" but, in reality, here is no experience at all; only a fact not observed on one side, and positive evidence, or the fact attested, on the other – a very unequal contest! as we shall presently see; the slightest positive testimony being, for the most part, an over-ballance to the strongest negative evidence that can be produced. I grant, however, all that the author's argument requires, viz. that experience teaches us, of many things, that they are improbable, and not to be hastily believed; of others, that they are naturally incredible: but these are so, not because they are unusual or unobserved, but because there is a known disproportion betwixt the cause assigned and the effect, or because the fact asserted is a contradiction to some known and universal truth.

These premisses he now draws to a point, and makes them center in one conclusive argument against miracles:

"To increase the probability against the testimony of witnesses, let us suppose, that the fact which they affirm, instead of being only marvellous, is really miraculous; and suppose also, that the testimony, considered apart and in itself, amounts to an entire proof: in that case, there is proof against proof, of which the strongest must prevail, but still with a diminution of its force in proportion to that of its antagonist."[25]

I have just allowed, that there are facts which experience assures us are wholly incredible: but of these I shall assert, that no good testimony can be produced in their favour. Truth is always consistent with itself; and no one truth can ever be contradicted by another. The author is, therefore, too kind in supposing that miracles may admit of full proof from testimony. I shall take no advantage of this concession, but readily acknowledge, that, if they are proved *à priori* to be incredible, it will be a vain attempt to prove

[24] P. 179.
[25] P. 179.

them by testimony. Let us see, then, what the author alledges in bar of this proof. His batteries are now mounted, and he begins the attack.

"A miracle," says he, "is a violation of the laws of nature; and, as a firm and unalterable experience hath established these laws, the proof against a miracle, from the nature of the fact, is as entire as any argument from experience can possibly be imagined. Why is it more than probable, that all men must die – that lead cannot by itself remain suspended in the air – that fire consumes wood, and is extinguished by water – unless it be, that these events are found agreeable to the laws of nature, and there is required a violation of these laws, or, in other words, a miracle, to prevent them? Nothing is esteemed a miracle, if it ever happen in the common course of nature. 'Tis no miracle, that a man in seeming good health should die of a sudden; because such a kind of death, tho' more unusual than any other, has yet been frequently observed to happen: but 'tis a miracle, that a dead man should come to life; because that hath never been observed in any age or country. There must, therefore, be an uniform experience against every miraculous event, otherwise the event would not merit the appellation. And, as an uniform experience amounts to a proof, there is here a direct and full proof, from the nature of the fact, against the existence of any miracle: nor can such a proof be destroyed, or the miracle render'd credible, but by an opposite proof that is superior."[26]

I have endeavoured to preserve the strength of this argument entire, by collecting everything that is of any import to it in the observations that precede it: and, that the reader may see it in its strongest light, I shall here repeat it, as it is again summ'd up by the author at the end of his Essay:

"It appears, that no testimony for any kind of miracle can ever amount to a probability, much less to a proof; and that, even supposing it amounted to a proof, 'twould be opposed by another proof, derived from the very nature of the fact which it would endeavour to establish. 'Tis experience alone which gives authority to human testimony; and 'tis the same experience which assures us of the laws of nature. When, therefore, these two kinds of experience are contrary, we have nothing to do but subtract the one from the other, and embrace an opinion, either on the one side or the other, with that assurance which arises from the remainder. But, according to the principle here explained, this subtraction, with regard to all popular religions, amounts to an entire annihilation: and, therefore, we may establish it as a maxim, that no

[26] P. 180.

human testimony can have such force as to prove a miracle, and make it a just foundation for any such system of religion."[27]

This is the author's great discovery. The whole secret is out. And here one cannot but wonder to see a position, which is laid down by all that write in defence of miracles, pleaded as a decisive argument against them, and to find the experience of all mankind brought in evidence against all the religions of the world. An experienced uniformity in the course of nature hath been always thought necessary to the belief and use of miracles. These are indeed relative ideas. There must be an ordinary regular course of nature, before there can be any thing extraordinary. A river must flow, before its stream can be interrupted. It is strange, therefore, that this uniformity, which is implied in the nature of a miracle, should at the same time be inconsistent with it. This is to suppose, that the existence of a miracle is a contradiction in terms; and as such indeed the author seems to treat it: "A miracle supported by any human testimony is more properly a subject of derision than of argument:"[28] And again, "What have we to oppose to such a cloud of witnesses, but the absolute impossibility or miraculous nature of the events?"[29] A modest reader can scarce look such assurance as this in the face: he will be apt to mistrust his own apprehension, and think there is more in these big words than he readily sees. The first reading gave me suspicions of this kind; but, having recovered my self, and taken courage to review it, I fear not to assert, that all the experience the author can bring will amount to neither proof nor argument against the belief of miracles. Let him, if he pleases, plead his own experience – that he has never seen or been witness to any miracle – that he has always found the course of nature to be the same and unchanged: but does this experience teach him, that the laws of nature are necessary and immutable – that there is no power in being sufficient to suspend or alter them – or that there can be no reasons to induce such a power to act? 'Till one or other of these can be proved from experience, it is no evidence in the present case, and, instead of deciding the matter in question, is wholly impertinent and foreign to it. Can the southern climates experience that there is no frost in the north? Or, can Mr. *Hume* experience that I have never seen fire kindled by a touch from ice? This negative evidence, tho' multiplied infinitely, would still be negative: and the fact last mentioned might be true, and capable of very easy proof from testimony, as I shall presently shew, tho' all the world should agree that they had never seen the like.

[27] P. 198.
[28] P. 194.
[29] P. 195.

The uniformity of nature is no way impeached or brought in question by the supposition of miracles. The concurring testimony of mankind to the course of nature is not contradicted by those who have experienced contrary appearances in a few instances. The idea of a miracle unites and reconciles these seeming differences. By supposing the facts in question to be miraculous, the uniformity of nature is preserved, and the facts are accounted for upon another principle entirely consistent with it. Thus, experience teacheth us that lead and iron are heavier than water: but a man, by projecting these heavy bodies, may make them swim in water, or fly in air. Should the same be done by any invisible power, it would be a miracle. But the uniformity of nature is no more disturbed in this case than the former: nor is the general experience, which witnesses to the superior gravity of these bodies, any proof that they may not be raised in air and water by some invisible agent, as well as by the power of man. All that experience teaches is the comparative weight of these bodies. If, therefore, they are seen to float in mediums lighter than themselves, this must be the effect of art or strength: but, if it be done without any visible art or power, it must be done then by some art or power that is invisible; that is, it must be miraculous. This is the process by which we infer the existence of miracles; which is, therefore, so far from being contradicted by that experience upon which the laws of nature are established, that it is closely connected and stands in the fairest agreement with it.

The question then will remain – Whether any such invisible agents have ever interposed in producing visible effects? Against the *possibility* of this, tho' the author is pleased to pronounce it impossible, he hath offered no argument (and, indeed, none can possibly be offered): against the *credibility* of it, the experience which he pleads is no argument at all. This experience proves a course of nature; but, whether this is ever interrupted, is still a question. This experience teaches what may be ordinarily expected from common causes and in the common course of things: but miraculous interpositions, which we are inquiring after, are, by their nature and essence, extraordinary and out of the common course of nature. Miracles, if at all, are effects of an extraordinary power upon extraordinary occasions: consequently, common experience can determine nothing concerning them. That such occasions may arise, both in the natural and moral world, is easy to conceive. The greatest of natural philosophers[30] hath thought, that the frame of the world will want, in a course of time, the hand that made to retouch and refit it. The greatest of moral philosophers[31] hath thought it a reasonable hope, that God would some time send a messenger from heaven to instruct men in the great duties of religion and morality.

[30] *Newton Opt.* ed. *Lat.* p. 346.

[31] *Socrates* in *Platonis Alcibiade* 2°, sub finem.

As to the question of *fact* – Whether any such interpositions have been ever known or observed? this must be tried, like all other historical facts, by the testimony of those who relate it, and the credit of the first witnesses who have vouched it; and not, as this author would have it, by the testimony of others of those who lived in distant times and places. There is mention of a comet, a little before the *Achaian* war, which appeared as big as the sun.[32] If this were well attested by the astronomers of that time, it would be trifling to object against it that the like had never been observed before or since. And just as pertinent is it to alledge the experience of ages and countries against miracles which are said to be wrought in other times and other countries.

But, in truth, were the world to give evidence in the present question, they would, I am persuaded, depose very differently from what this author expects. A great part of mankind have given their testimony to the credibility of miracles: they have actually believed them. By this author's account, all the religions in the world have been founded upon this belief. if this be true, we have universal testimony to the credibility of miracles. How then can there be universal experience against them? The author tells us that we must judge of testimony by experience. It is more certain that we must judge of the experience of men by their testimony.

It is far from true that all religions have been founded on miracles. None but the *Christian* and *Jewish* appear to be so founded. But there is a sort of miracles, which men of all religions have agreed in believing. "A miracle," as this author says, "may be either discoverable by men, or not. This alters not its nature and essence."[33] Many things appear to us to be effected by natural means, the first springs of which may be moved by the immediate hand of God. But every such interposition, in overruling or giving a new direction to the course of nature, is, as the author allows, miraculous. If then Providence ever interposes in punishing exemplary wickedness, or in the support of eminent virtue – in averting evil, or bestowing good – these are miracles. But these have been universally believed. These blessings of heaven have been implored and acknowledged, and these judgments deprecated, in the publick and private prayers of mankind, from the beginning of the world to this time.

We cannot indeed argue, from these supposed interpositions, that therefore Providence will interpose in a visible and sensible manner. But it follows, that such interpositions are possible; it follows, that they are credible. If we believe these miraculous interpositions, when they do not appear to our senses, what should hinder us from believing the like upon the report of our senses, or of credible persons who give witness to them?

[32] *Seneca Nat. Quæst.* lib. 7, cap. 15.

[33] P. 181.

If there are general reasons for concealing these interpositions, may there not too be special reasons for signalizing them at times to the senses and notice of mankind? It is certain, that, if any such reasons can be assigned, all that is difficult of belief in miracles will be removed. Now, though we cannot indeed look into the counsels of Providence, nor, without presumption, pronounce what is fit for God, in any supposed circumstance, to do; yet, in judging of past facts or miracles, that are questioned, we can readily see whether any great end, worthy of God, hath been answered by them: and, if this appear to be the case, it will create a presumption in their favour: and, if, farther–, it shall seem that this end could not have been compassed by any other means, this will amount to some proof of their reality.

To see this matter in the clearest light, it may be proper to consider more distinctly the grounds of that credibility, which we allow, in different degrees, to historical facts. This depends, as I have said, on the credibility of the facts themselves, and on that of the historian or witnesses who relate them.

The credibility of any fact in itself, as this author frequently tells us, depends upon its analogy with the known course of nature.[34] But the powers of nature are so imperfectly known to us, that in most cases we argue with great uncertainty from this principle. A consequence of this is, that testimony is, for the most part, of much greater force to establish the truth of past facts, than experience. It would have been thought highly incredible a few years ago, that an animal might be propagated by cutting it in pieces – that you might, by dividing one living creature, give life to an hundred of the same species. Yet this sort of *Hydra* has been discovered; and the fact, tho' contrary to the whole analogy of nature, was readily believed, when it had been experienced and testified by very few. In like manner, I have no doubt that the magnet loses its polarity in very cold latitudes. I believe this upon the testimony of one man,[35] tho' the experience of travellers in all climates before attests the contrary. Here the most uniform experience is outweighed by a single evidence. The reason is, that the experience of other countries is only a negative evidence in this question. This experience was indeed, before the fact was tried, a very strong presumption against it. The most cautious sailor would have ventured his fortune and life upon it. Yet is this presumption of no weight in the question of past fact, when compared with the slightest testimony.[36]

---

[34] P. 165.

[35] Mr. *Ellis*, in his account of the North-West Passage.

[36] Every proposition or fact asserted is *certainly* true or false. By credible or probable we mean, not any thing real in the character of the proposition or fact, but only its appearance to us, or to the person who estimates this credibility. A thing is said to be

In cases where a sufficient cause is assigned, an effect, however new and strange, may become credible, or even probable, in itself, without any testimony to support it. That fire should be kindled by a touch from ice,

credible, when it wants and is thought capable of proof – to be probable, when there appear more reasons for than against believing it. *Credible* is more than *possible*, and *impossible* more than *incredible*. Again, *probable* is more than *credible*, and *incredible* is more than *improbable*. But these words are used in common language somewhat promiscuously. Thus, what is highly probable is said to be highly credible, and what is very improbable to be very incredible. Hence, there are all degrees of incredible and credible, before you arrive at probability. After this, credible and probable are the same, and admit again of all degrees, 'till you arrive at moral certainty. The same thing then may be credible in all these different degrees to different persons. That the earth is round – that it is constantly spinning about like a top, and travelling with a very swift motion, while the sun and the heavens stand still – This to one part of mankind is wholly incredible, and to another morally certain. The credibility, therefore, or comparative incredibility of any fact is, for the most part, too loose a bottom to ground any argument or inference upon. The same testimony may likewise be variously credible to different persons. But the evidence of this is far more distinct, and its force more easily ascertained. The truth of testimony, where it is doubtful, may be proved many different ways: that of doubtful facts can be made clear only by testimony, which is indeed, after all, the proper proof of facts.

Experience is the general testimony of mankind to general truths. Testimony, as it is here opposed to experience, is the attestation of particular persons to particular facts. The former of these witnesses to the credibility of facts; the latter gives evidence directly to their reality or existence. From the former we collect, that *May* is on this side the line a warmer month than *December*: but the certainty of this in particular instances is only to be proved, and the contrary may be proved, from the latter. We may indeed, as I have granted, in some cases, infer from the former of these the certainty or impossibility of facts. But even here this limitation or condition is always understood – that we know the whole of the case – that no cause intervenes, which is unknown or does not appear to us. And therefore, in the strongest cases that can be supposed, experience is no bar to the evidence of testimony; because it is very possible, in almost all cases, that such cause may intervene. Should I see a stone climb up hill, or a piece of solid iron swim in water, I could not doubt the fact, how incredible soever in itself. Suppose the same to rest upon the testimony of others: I cannot, indeed, see with the eyes of other men; but I can see that they have eyes, as well as myself: and, if their veracity is proved, as I assert it may, even to our eyes and senses (I mean, by sensible and visible facts) I have then nearly as good evidence for the fact, as if I had seen it myself. I might perhaps conclude, that the effect was produced by some invisible agent; but, whether this can be discovered or not, the fact must still be admitted. All this is unwarily allowed by the author himself, in terms as strong as can be desired:

"Suppose all authors in all languages agree, that, from the first of *January*, 1600, there was a total darkness over the whole earth for eight days: Suppose that the tradition of this extraordinary event is still strong and lively among the people; that all travellers, who return from foreign countries, bring us accounts of the same tradition, without the least variation or contradiction: 'Tis evident, that our present philosophers, instead of doubting of that fact, ought to receive it for certain, and ought to search for the causes whence it might be derived." P. 199.

The author of the *Free Inquiry into the miraculous Powers of the primitive Church* has stated this matter in a very different light. He supposes, that we have the evidence is contrary to the experience of some thousand years. But electricity is a cause given equal to the effect. From this time then the fact becomes credible, and even probable, tho' it were not tried and proved by any one witness.

of sense for the natural credibility of facts, and seems to infer, that, when we argue from hence, we go upon surer ground than when we argue from testimony, which he represents as ever dark and doubtful, and amounting only to a reasonable presumption, at best: the contrary to which, in almost every particular, is, I think, the truth. As the principles laid down by this author are very general, and may be easily misapplied, beyond his intention, in the present question, it will not be improper to compare them with what has been said.

"The question concerning these miraculous powers depends," says he, "upon the joint credibility of the facts pretended to have been produced, and of the witnesses who attest them: if either part be infirm, their credit must sink in proportion, and, if the facts especially be incredible, must of course fall to the ground, because no force of testimony can alter the nature of things. The credibility of facts lies open to the trial of our reason and senses: but the credibility of witnesses depends on a variety of principles wholly concealed from us; and, tho' in many cases it may reasonably be presumed, yet in none can it certainly be known: for it is common with men, out of crafty and selfish views, to dissemble and deceive: but plain facts cannot delude us – cannot speak any other language, or give any other information, than that of truth. The testimony, therefore, of facts, as it is offer'd to our senses, carries, with it the surest instruction in all cases, which God, in the ordinary course of his providence, has thought fit to appoint for the guidance of human life." (Preface, p. 9.)

In answer to which, I shall not deny that the credibility of facts may in many cases be tried by our senses; but this is generally learnt from experience, or the common testimony of mankind: And, 2dly, this credibility, however learnt or proved, is no direct evidence of the reality or existence of any doubtful fact; since the fact may be highly credible, and yet never exist – may be in a great degree incredible, and yet certainly true. What the author calls *the testimony of facts offered to our senses* is in this case only the testimony of our senses, or that of other men, to the existence, not of the fact in question, but of other facts that are supposed analogous or similar to it; which, tho' in many cases it may amount to a very high presumption, yet is *in none a direct proof of any doubtful fact*: Whereas, 3dly, testimony is a direct evidence to the existence or reality, not of similar facts, but of the fact itself: and therefore, in judging of past or distant facts, when we cannot have the evidence of our senses, the testimony of those who have this evidence is, not only the surest, but the only *method of instruction which Providence has appointed for our guidance thro' life*. All that we certainly know of such facts is derived from this source. The truth of testimony is always presumed, where there are no particular reasons to suspect it. This presumption alone will give more weight, as we have seen, to a single testimony, and make it better evidence for the truth of facts, than a very high degree of presumption drawn from analogy is against it. 4thly, This presumption may be increased to any degree by the concurrence of other testimony; which concurrence too is itself a distinct proof of the fact attested. Lastly, The veracity of every single witness may be proved by plain and indisputable facts, as will be seen more fully hereafter. If then improbable or incredible facts require stronger evidence to support them, the weight of testimony may be increased, and the proofs that support it multiplied, infinitely; and, consequently, whatever is not absolutely impossible may be thus proved. The force of testimony cannot indeed *alter the nature of things*: but it can make things improbable become probable – it can give credibility, and even certainty, to things that were before incredible.

In moral or intelligent agents we look for moral causes – for reasons or motives to induce them to act, as well as for the natural powers of acting. And, where both a final and efficient cause appear equal to the effect, the effect, however strange in itself, will become credible by testimony, if not probable without it. It is possible for a man to swim across the *Hellespont*. The possibility of this fact will make it credible upon sufficient testimony: but, if a competent reason is assigned for his hazardous enterprize (such as the escaping certain death) this will make it credible upon the slightest testimony, or even probable without any.

The result then is – that whatever is possible, or in the lowest degree credible, is capable of a proof from testimony – that the strongest presumption from experience is of little force against positive evidence – and that, where a cause is assigned equal to any effect, the event is rendered credible upon common testimony, and sometimes probable without any.

But there are, it is granted, many cases, which we may, from nature and experience, pronounce to be impossible. It is impossible that a fact or proposition should be true, when the cause assigned is unequal to the effect. Now, the proportion of causes to effects, the natural powers of agents, and the force of moral causes on the mind, we know, to a good degree, from experience. If we cannot precisely determine the force of natural agents, we can, in most cases, assign limits which they cannot pass. For instance: We cannot precisely mark out the bounds of human power; but we can, in all cases, say to what it does not extend. If the strength of men, at a medium, be equal to one, that of king *Augustus* or *Hercules* may be equal to two; but it cannot be equal to two hundred. A physician may restore a dying man to health; but he cannot restore a dead man to life. Of all such events, as raising the dead, calming the winds or seas, curing diseases, with a word, we may fairly pronounce, that they are impossible to human strength, and therefore, when imputed to it, are incredible; because a force equal to two cannot produce an effect equal to two hundred. In this case experience decides with sufficient authority against the fact. And this, I suppose, the author mistook for an argument against miracles.

But who ever attributed these facts to human power? Those who record, and those who believe, miracles, universally ascribe them to a power superior to man. They agree, that they far exceed all human strength, and therefore are an argument of the concurrence and agency of some superior power. Against the interposition of such superior power, experience, as we have seen, can determine nothing. If common experience does not attest or acknowledge such interpositions, the answer is given – common occasions do not call for them. The common wants of nature are provided for by the common course of nature. Extraordinary occasions only can call for extraordinary interpositions. Of these occasions we are not the proper judges:

but, that many such may arise in the government of free agents, seems obvious even to us.

If men, by a bad use of their liberty, should sink themselves into a moral incapacity of answering the ends of their creation – if they should lose sight of God and religion and all the great motives to holiness and virtue, and this evil should become general and past all natural hopes of recovery – it is very supposeable that God may interpose, by a special act of his Providence, in restoring them to a capacity of serving him, and of attaining that happiness for which they were created. If virtue, and that knowledge which is necessary to it, are worthy the care of Providence – and if these were in danger of perishing out of the world – why should it be thought incredible that God should send a righteous man to recall men to virtue, to teach the doctrines and enforce the duties of religion, with a clear and express authority? This mission of a prophet would be miraculous: but the miracle would not appear; and therefore other miracles would be necessary to attest its truth. Superior knowledge and virtue are not sufficient to characterize a prophet: he must do such things as no man can do, except God were with him, before his mission or character will be acknowledged for divine. Here then is a reason, which, whenever it can be pleaded, will make miracles every way credible, and as capable of proof from testimony as any matter of fact whatsoever.

In the examination of past facts, if no such end appears to have been answered by the miracles alledged, this will be a strong presumption against them. On the other hand, if any great consequences have followed – if, for instance, it should appear from history, that natural religion had, when lost, by the help of these miracles, whether real or pretended, been revived in all its purity, and established in many nations as the will of God – this will be a strong presumption in their favour: And, if there appear no other assignable cause, which could give birth to this great event, but the miracles pretended, this will be a good proof of their reality.

We come next to consider the credibility derived to facts from testimony. This depends in general upon the principles of human nature, which we can argue with the more certainty from, because we experience them in ourselves, as well as observe them in others. We are made naturally to love truth, and to hate and abhor falshood and deceit. The shame of being detected in a lye, and the reproach that ever follows it, is a full proof of this. Even in matters of no moment, in the most transient discourse, where men think it unnecessary to attend to what they say, were there no temptation from vanity or a desire of pleasing, they would never deviate from truth. But this principle will operate far more strongly, where men are called upon to attend, have leisure to consider, and give their testimony deliberately: it will operate more strongly on good men than bad – in cases of great moment than in matters of indifference.

Could we be absolutely certain, in any case, that a man had no interest, real or supposed, in deceiving – that he had no motive to deceive – we might depend with absolute certainty upon the truth of his evidence. Now, this assurance we may have from circumstances that cannot deceive us. Incapable as we are of penetrating into all the reserves and recesses of the human mind, there is yet a certain and infallible test, by which the veracity of men may in many cases be tried. For example: If the person attesting gives up every known interest for the sake of his testimony, without any known prospect of advantage – if he is exposed by it to present sufferings, and is threatened with yet greater – if he persists under all the discouragements that can be thought of, and goes through a long series of evils, which, by receding from his testimony, he might prevent – and, lastly, if he gives up life itself for a painful and ignominious death – this is such a proof of sincerity as cannot be resisted. In this case, we are not only assured that the witness is free from every corrupt biass, but that he has the highest regard for truth. Nothing but a conscious sense of this, with the hope of a future reward from the God of truth, can support men under a loss of all things, and under the actual suffering of all the evils of life. A good man may give up his interest for the sake of truth: a bad man will sacrifice truth to interest: but no man will give up interest and truth together for nothing, or for the sake of falshood, which is worse than nothing.

The maxims we here argue from are the most certain and uncontroverted of any in morality – That men act from motives, and that good, real or apparent, is the object, the motive and aim of every action. The laws by which the moral world is governed are as certain and infallible as those of the natural. The passions, appetites, and senses of mankind act, and are acted upon, with as much uniformity as any powers and principles in nature. That men should love falshood rather than truth – that they should chuse labour and travail, shame and misery, before pleasure, ease, and esteem – is as much a violation of the laws of nature, as it is for lead or iron to hang unsupported in the air, or for the voice of a man to raise the dead to life: but this, I have granted to the author, is, not miraculous, but impossible, and shall therefore have his leave, I hope, to assert, that falshood, thus attested, is impossible – in other words, that testimony, thus tried and proved, is infallible and certain.

It remains, indeed, that witnesses the most upright and unsuspected may be mistaken in their testimony: they may be deceived themselves; and therefore their testimony, even thus proved, is not to be securely relied on. But, happily, miracles, at least all that we dispute with this author, are of such a nature, that it is impossible to be deceived about them. Facts that are visible and palpable to the senses of mankind, that are done in open day-light, that lie open to scrutiny and observation for a long time together, present witnesses must know whether they see or not. They who report them as eye-witnesses cannot be deceived themselves in the belief of them, however they may intend to deceive others.

I conclude then, that miracles, when there appears a sufficient cause for working them, are credible in themselves that, when they come under the cognizance of our senses, they are proper matter of testimony, and, when attested by witnesses who have sufficient opportunities of convincing themselves, and give sufficient proof of their conviction, have a right to command our faith.

And here I accept the author's alternative, without complaining of the insidious terms in which it is expressed.

"The plain consequence," says he, "is (and 'tis a general maxim worthy of our attention) that no testimony is sufficient to establish a miracle, unless the testimony be of such a kind, that its falshood would be more miraculous than the fact which it endeavours to establish: and even in that case there is a mutual destruction of arguments, and the superior only gives us an assurance suitable to that degree of force which remains after deducting the inferior. – If the falshood of any person's testimony would be more miraculous than the event which he relates, then, and not 'till then, can he pretend to command my belief or opinion."[37]

By miraculous it is plain that the author here means, in the popular sense of the word, wonderful or incredible. I assert then, that miracles may be made so credible by circumstances and concurring facts, and so supported by testimony, that, if we reject them, we must believe things more incredible, or, as the author would have us speak, more miraculous than the miracles themselves.

The miracles I shall mention are those in the *Christian* Gospel – healing the sick without any visible means, giving sight to the blind, raising the dead to life, &c. all which are said to be performed by the power of God for ends the most worthy of himself, viz. to restore religion and morality to their true principles, and to establish the practice of them in the world. The character of those who were appointed to this work, and the doctrines which they taught, correspond perfectly with this design: great as it was, they undertook it with alacrity and confidence, declaring from the beginning that their commission was to go and teach all nations: the miracles which they attest, as giving authority to their doctrine, they assert from their own knowledge, as what they saw with their eyes, and handled

---

[37] P. 182.

with their hands: the number of these facts, and the numbers attesting them, were very great: they concurred, without variation, in the same doctrine, and in the same testimony: they submitted, with the same courage and constancy, to the greatest persecutions and afflictions, in confirmation of their truth, and, when called to it (as many of them were) laid down their lives for its sake: they foresaw from the beginning the opposition they met with, and foretold, with the fullest assurance, their success against it; and the event justified their predictions; the religion they taught was in a short time established in a great part of the world.

Here, now, the attempt itself, if not spirited and supported by truth, is wholly strange and unaccountable. That men of low birth and education should conceive a design of new-modelling the religion of all nations, and reforming their manners, by the laws of temperance, purity, and charity – that bad men should concur in an end so great and godlike, or good men in means so impious as fraud and imposture – that men of craft or address should chuse for the hero of their story one who was chronicled as a malefactor, and who had been put to death by the consent of a whole people – one, too, that had abused their confidence, and misled them by false hopes into an endless train of miseries – all this is contrary to nature, and therefore, by the author's rule, impossible.

The zeal with which they carried on this design, traversing seas and kingdoms, without rest, and without weariness – a zeal which could not be exceeded by the most righteous men in the most righteous cause – this, if not prompted by duty and a strong conviction of the truths they taught, is still more incredible.

The excellency of the religion they taught, in its worship and morality far surpassing all human wisdom and philosophy, and the sole end of which is to make men honest, sincere, and virtuous, if it be the work of ignorance and fraud, is equally strange and mysterious.

The success of this design is yet a greater miracle. In this chain of wonders the event is the most miraculous part. The establishment of the Gospel in an hundred different nations, its victory over *Jews* and *Gentiles*, over the power and policy of the wisest and greatest people, over the pride of learning and the obstinacy of ignorance, over the prejudices of religion and those of sin and irreligion, is an event the most wonderful of any in history. But this is a miracle which we see before our eyes: it is a miraculous fact that must be ascribed to a miraculous cause. Even granting the truth of the Gospel miracles, the instruments in propagating it were so unequal to the work, that nothing but the power of God, accompanying and working with them, can account for its success. It was still a miracle that it should prosper in their hands. But, without either truth or providence to support it, this success would be more than miraculous – it would be impossible.

The testimony directly given to these miracles is strongly confirmed by the character of the witnesses, who, as far as appears even from the testimony of their enemies, were unblameable in their lives and manners – men of conscience and religion. Their writings breathe a spirit of piety, a zeal for God and good works, that is not equalled by any writings in the world: they carry in them such marks of candor, truth, and simplicity, as cannot be imitated: all which can never consist with the daring impiety of usurping the most sacred of all characters, and preaching a false religion to the world.

The numbers that engaged in this design, tho' dispersed in different regions, agreed perfectly in the same report. It was in the power of any of these, or of the accomplices that must be concerned with them, to defeat the whole, by discovering the fraud: and it cannot be, that not one should, by fear or interest, persuasion or torture, be prevailed on to discover it.

They put their testimony to the trial, by claiming a power of working miracles themselves: they displayed this power frequently and publickly, and so submitted their truth to the eyes and senses of all about them. This pretence, if false, must have defeated the most probable and hopeful scheme; if true, it was no more than necessary to the difficulties of this. The event was – great numbers were every day converted to the faith. But this conduct cannot, any more than the event, be reconciled to the character or supposition of imposture.

Lastly, They gave the highest proof that can be given to the veracity of testimony, by going thro' the fiery trial of persecution, in all its various forms of imprisonment, torture, and death. This began with the very beginning of Christianity. They saw it evidently before their eyes, and plainly devoted themselves from the first to a life of sufferings and affliction. They gave up ease and security, country, kindred, family, and friends, to be treated every–where with contempt and contumely, to conflict with poverty and want, to be persecuted from city to city, sentenced to imprisonment and stripes, and, at last, to die by stoning, by the sword, or the cross. But this, in support of falshood and wrong, is so contrary to human nature, that it is absolutely incredible.

The supposition then, that the miracles of the Gospel are false, is full of wonders, prodigies, things unnatural, and which experience, the author's criterion in matters of fact, pronounces to be impossible.

And what now is that contrariety to nature, which is pleaded against the possibility of miracles? "A miracle," the author tells us, "may be accurately defined a transgression of a law of nature by a particular volition of the Deity or by the interposal of some invisible agent."[38] But this definition is neither accurate nor consistent with itself. The laws of nature are the laws

[38] P. 181.

of God: and, if God should occasionally change or invert any of these, there is no law, that I know of, against it – no law of God or nature broken by it. But, in fact, where miracles are supposed, there is no change made in these laws. I have shewn, that all that's unnatural in miracles is only appearance. There is nothing contrary to nature in supposing the dead to be raised, or the winds controlled by a power equal to the effect. It was no way contrary to the nature of God to reveal his will to mankind, in order to reform their corruptions, and to conduct them to virtue and happiness. On the contrary, this might be piously hoped for from his wisdom and goodness. It was no way contrary to the nature and condition of men. It appears from the history of mankind, that natural religion was at this time universally corrupted, and that no other probable means were left of restoring it. Reason and philosophy had tried their strength in vain. It was, therefore, on the part of man, highly expedient and desireable. In fact, to this revelation, whether real or pretended, and to no other cause, it is owing, that the great truths of nature, concerning God, a Providence, and a future state, are now so widely spread, and that half the world, instead of dumb idols, are serving the living God: and, if all the good ends, that might be expected, are not yet answered by it, yet the seed of the word is sown, the foundations of true religion are laid, and there is hope that it will in time enlarge its borders, and prevail, where it is received, with more effect and influence. It cannot be denied, that the Gospel is an adequate provision for the wants, a remedy for all the infirmities, of mankind. There is nothing, that can be wished for in a rule of duty, that is not comprehended in it. The miracles, then, that attest it, are accounted for to our reason: we have God, the cause of all things, for their author: and a sufficient reason is assigned for the divine interposition. And this will, at the same time, account for all the wonders that followed: the actions sufferings, and success of the Apostles will, upon this scheme, appear easy, consistent, and natural.

But, if this account be not admitted, these will remain so many contradictions to nature and experience, and it will lie upon the author to reconcile them to our belief. If the common motives to human actions, interest, passion, and prejudice, cannot be pleaded in answer to these difficulties, what other account can be given of them? Some cause must be assigned adequate to the effect. For men to act without motives is as unnatural, as it is for a body to sink without weight – to act against the force of motives is as contrary to nature, as it is for a stone to ascend against the laws of gravity. Hear what this author says himself in another Essay:

"We cannot make use of a more convincing argument, than to prove that the actions ascribed to any person are directly contrary to the course of nature, and that no human motives, in such circumstances, could even induce him to such a conduct."[39]

The author tells us, that in this case we must reject the greater miracle. But miracle is too soft a name for these inconsistencies. Could he shew, that God, or some invisible agent, had interposed in confounding the reason and understanding of all that preached or believed the Gospel, in changing their nature, and giving a contrary direction to their passions, affections, and instincts, they would then be miracles, and proper objects of our belief. But this I shall presume impossible to be proved, because no end can be assigned for such interposition, but merely to deceive mankind – an end so unworthy of God, and contrary to the perfections of his nature, that we may pronounce it impossible for him to promote, or even to permit it to take effect.

Here, then, I may call upon the author, in his own words, to lay his hand upon his heart, and declare, whether the miracles of the Gospel could possibly have been better attested, if true whether there is any one condition wanting that can add credibility to them – whether there is any thing so contrary to nature in these miracles, as in the testimony given, and the belief gained, to them, if false – whether it is not easier to believe the miracles true, than that so many miraculous consequences (a natural effect of true miracles) should arise from them, if false, – or, lastly, whether it be not more credible that God should work these miracles for so great an end as that of giving birth and establishment to Christianity, than that he should work more and greater miracles to confound and deceive mankind. When he has ballanced his account of the impossibility of miracles with the evidence for those of the Gospel, and subtracted the former from the latter, *this subtraction will certainly amount to an entire annihilation.*

Let us now see the poor case which the author puts at last to illustrate and crown his argument:

> "When any one tells me, that he saw a dead man restored to life, I immediately consider with myself, whether it be more probable that this person should either deceive or be deceived, or that the fact he relates should really have happened: I weigh the one miracle against the other, and, according to the superiority which I discover, I pronounce my decision, and always reject the greater miracle."[40]

The author's argument requires him to prove, that no miracles, however circumstanced, can be made credible by any testimony whatsoever. But, in

[39] P. 135.

[40] P. 182.

the case supposed, the miracle has not one circumstance to make it credible, nor the testimony one condition to confirm its truth. A dead man we may suppose raised to life without any reason, use, or end whatsoever: and a dead man may be raised for some extraordinary purpose of Providence, as to give authority and character to the special messengers of God. Now, tho' the former of these cannot be made credible by the naked testimony of one man, the latter may be made credible by the attestation of many, especially, if they give proof, that they were neither deceived themselves, nor intended to deceive others. Tho' one man, unassisted, cannot lift a weight of twenty tuns, twenty men, with the help of engines, may lift the weight of one. I agree with the author, that, when a man is said to rise, like the ghost in *Prince Edward*,[41] only to set again, it is more credible, that the testimony is false, than the miracle true: but, when I see an effect worthy of Providence, in which the religion, virtue, and morality of a great part of mankind are concerned, brought about by the belief of this or such-like miracles, and find, upon inquiry, that this miracle is attested by a great number of persons who lived and died confessors and martyrs to it, the falshood of such testimony appears to me far more miraculous than such a miracle.

The author puts the same case, with the addition of some particulars, in the second part of his Essay:

"Suppose that all the historians who treat of *England* should agree, that, on the first of *January*, 1600, queen *Elizabeth* died – that, both before and after her death, she was seen by her physicians and the whole court, as is usual with persons of her rank – that her successor was acknowledged and proclaimed by parliament – and that, after having been interred a month, she again appeared, took possession of the throne, and governed *England* three years: I must confess I should be surprized at the concurrence of so many odd circumstances, but should not have the least inclination to believe so miraculous an event."[42]

Here, again, the fact supposed is the strangest and most unaccountable that the author could well conceive, because no final cause appears to make it in any degree credible. But when was any such fact attested by historians? If the author thinks the story incredible, I think it as incredible that any good historian should relate it: if he thinks it incredible, because it is a miracle, I think it incredible that God should work such a miracle for nothing.

[41] A late play, called *Edward the Black Prince*.
[42] P. 200.

But the importance of miracles is, it seems, with the author, a thing of no consideration: this, which we considered as a circumstance that gives the highest credibility to the Gospel miracles, is, at last, the very reason why he rejects them as incredible.

"I beg," says he, "that the limitation here made may be remarked, when I say, that a miracle can never be proved, so as to be a foundation of a system of religion; for I own, that otherwise, there may possibly be miracles, or violations of the usual course of nature, of such a kind, as to admit of proof from human testimony, tho' perhaps it will be impossible to find any such in all the records of history."[43]

This concession is very remarkable, and appears to me to be fairly giving up the argument: for, if miracles may be wrought in cases of less moment, why may they not in greater? or, is religion the last and least of all things in the opinion of this author? I confess myself at a loss to guess what can be his intention in this place. If, in compromise for the other miracles which he here grants us unasked, he expects us to give up all that have religion for their object, it will indeed answer his purpose very well. He may grant other miracles possible, and yet make good his argument against them. But these are not so easily dealt with. The surest way not to believe them is not to examine them. And this he wisely recommends as the best expedient that has been tried against them.

"If a miracle," says he, "be ascribed to any new system of religion, men, in all ages, have been so much imposed on by ridiculous stories of that kind, that this very circumstance would be a full proof of a cheat, and sufficient, with all men of sense, not only to make them reject the fact, but even reject it without farther examination."[44]

This indeed, is a short way with religion and miracles; and we must own, that the author hath found out at last a decisive argument against them.

PART II.

Little as it is that the author has done in the first part of his Essay, he seems to think it more than enough, and that half his pains might have been spared;

[43] P. 199.
[44] P. 200.

"In the foregoing reasoning, we have supposed, that the testimony upon which a miracle is founded may possibly amount to an entire proof, and that the falshood of the testimony would be a kind of prodigy. But 'tis easy to shew, that we have been a great deal too liberal in our concessions, and that there never was a miraculous event, in any history, established on so full an evidence."[45]

But, if the author was so sure of his strength, why this corps de reserve, a body of troops that have been for ever harassed, and are yet untired, in the service of infidelity?

The first of these veteran bands is drawn as follows: "There is not," says he,

"to be found, in all history, any miracle attested by a sufficient number of men of such unquestioned good sense, education, and learning, as to secure us against all delusion in themselves – of such undoubted integrity, as to place them beyond all suspicion of any design to deceive others – of such credit and reputation in the eyes of mankind, as to have a great deal to lose, in case of being detected in a falshood – and, at the same time, attesting facts performed in such a publick manner, and in so celebrated a part of the world, as to render the detection unavoidable: all which circumstances are requisite to give us a full assurance in the testimony of men."[46]

The reader will allow me to suppose, that the author has in view, both here and throughout his Essay, the *Christian* miracles, which we have been considering. Now, the objections here made have been so frequently and fully answered by the advocates of Christianity, that it is quite piteous to see the author, after proclaiming a victory, calling in such poor auxiliaries to his relief.

As to the first condition here required, there never was perhaps a fact directly attested by so many witnesses as the miracles in question. We have still upon record the express depositions of many in the writings of the Apostles. The conversion of every single person to Christianity was, in truth, a clear and precise testimony to these facts; for this religion was wholly built upon them. Now, besides the twelve Apostles and seventy Disciples chosen to preach the Gospel, a great number more were converted by the miracles and resurrection of *Christ*. But those that gave this witness to the miracles of the Apostles were without number. Never was there a

[45] P. 183.
[46] P. 183.

doctrine that spread so swiftly thro' the world, or that gained so many present and immediate witnesses to its truth.

The Apostles and first Disciples had not, many of them, the advantages of education and learning. But what learning is required to enable men to see with their eyes and hear with their ears? The miracles they attest were plain facts, the objects of sense. Folly itself could not be deceived in them: and sure folly could never so successfully deceive. These men, illiterate as they were and void of art or eloquence, did what this author, with all his arguments, will never be able to do: they got the better of all the religions in the world about them, and established their own in different and distant countries. They had, therefore, we may hope, sense enough to testify what their eyes had seen and their hands had handled.

They had not perhaps any great reputation to lose. But the good name of a poor man is as dear to him as that of the greatest. If they had no publick character to lose, they had publick infamy to dread: and this they incurred, not by being detected in a falshood, but by persevering in the truth. If it was little that they gave up to follow *Christ*, it was, however, all that they had. And what they gained was a negative quantity, and must be put to the side of their losses: they gained hunger and thirst, toil and labour, watchings and fastings, scorn and reproach, scourgings and death. They lost, then, enough to evidence their sincerity. They gave every proof, that ever was given by man, to the truth of their testimony.

As to the notoriety of the facts, they were done in the most publick manner – in places of constant resort – many of them in *Jerusalem*, at times of the greatest concourse: and, what is more, they were done in direct opposition to the prejudices of all that saw them – before the most vigilant and powerful enemies, who did not, as this author tells us wise men commonly do, "think the matter too inconsiderable to deserve their attention,"[47] but exerted their utmost industry and authority in suppressing this new religion; putting its head and leader to death, suborning false witnesses to discredit him and his miracles, and proceeding immediately, by imprisoning some, and killing others, to deter and disperse his followers. These miracles, therefore, were wrought in the very place where their detection was most certain and unavoidable; and the testimony given to them was given in the same publick manner and in the same place.

The author is well aware, that the testimony of the Apostles and first Christians, if the miracles were false (I mean, the fact of giving such testimony) and the miraculous events that followed in consequence of them, will be thought, upon reflexion, at least as incredible as the miracles

---

[47] P. 198.

themselves; and therefore, to abate our wonder on this head, he observes,

"secondly, that there is a principle in human nature, which, if strictly examined, will be found to diminish extremely the assurance we might have from human testimony in any kind of prodigy. The maxim, by which we commonly conduct ourselves in our reasonings, is, that the objects of which we have no experience resemble those of which we have – that what we have found to be most usual is always most probable. But, tho', in proceeding by this rule, we readily reject any fact that is unusual or incredible in an ordinary degree, yet, in advancing farther, the mind observes not always the same rule; but, when any thing is affirmed utterly absurd and miraculous, it rather the more readily admits such a fact upon account of the very circumstance which ought to destroy all its authority. The passion of surprise and wonder arising from miracles, being an agreeable emotion, gives a sensible tendency towards the belief of those events from which it is derived."[48]

The love of novelty is, indeed, a natural passion; it is no other than the love of knowledge, which God hath implanted in the mind for the wisest reasons: and for the same reasons we may be assured that he hath not laid snares to betray us into error, and much less hath placed in us a principle, as the author here supposes, the tendency of which is to make us believe things, merely because they are incredible. "With what greediness," saith he, "are the miraculous accounts of travellers received, their descriptions of sea and land monsters, their relations of wonderful adventures, strange men, and uncouth manners!" It is true that every new discovery gratifies our love of knowledge, and gives pleasure to the mind: but it must have the appearance of truth to do so. Tho' we love to be informed, we do not love to be deceived. A single miracle would risk the credit of the best-esteemed travels. But, according to this author's principle, the voyage to *Lilliput* or *Laputa* must meet with more credit than that of *Anson* or *Ellis*.

But, if the love of novelty will not reconcile us to miracles, that of religion will make us believe any thing. "If the spirit of religion joins itself to the love of wonder, there is an end of common sense."[49] If the author means, that men are more apt to believe miracles in the cause of religion than in any other case, he is so far in the right. Where should men expect or believe miraculous interpositions, but where it is most worthy of God to interpose? But it does not follow, that religion is a friend to false miracles, or an enemy to common sense. On the contrary, right notions of

[48] P. 184.
[49] P. 185.

the divine nature and perfections, which religion teaches, are a necessary help to distinguish true miracles from false. Now, the *Jews*, in general, were better instructed in these points than the wisest of the Heathens. The men of *Athens* were far more superstitious than the most ignorant of the *Hebrews*. The false wonders of magick, witchcraft, and necromancy, these were taught by their law to hold in contempt, and, consequently, were less liable to be practised upon by appearances of this sort. And, of the Apostles and first Christians, it is certain, that they had all the security against delusion and error of this kind, that a rational piety and the noblest sentiments of God and a Providence could give them. But

"a religionist may be an enthusiast, and imagine he sees what has no reality: he may know his narration to be false, and yet persevere in it, with the best intentions in the world, for the sake of promoting so holy a cause; or, even where this delusion has no place, vanity, excited by so strong a temptation, operates on him more powerfully than on the rest of mankind in any other circumstances, and self –interest with equal force: his auditors may not have, and commonly have not, sufficient judgment to canvas his evidence; what judgment they have they renounce upon principle in these sublime and mysterious subjects."[50]

Here, it is confessed, the author has touched upon a very powerful and fruitful source of error. Men, whose passions are stronger than their reason, will be guilty of excess in religion as well as in other things. A zeal for opinions frequently makes men conclude their own cause to be the cause of God; and, from wishing that Heaven may declare in their favour, they are easily led to believe such interpositions upon the slightest testimony. But, tho' this principle will make men believe false miracles, it will not overpower their senses, or make them see what has no reality. The *French* prophets were extravagant enough to expect that one of their principal teachers would come to life again; but, with all their enthusiasm, none could believe that he saw this miracle: on the contrary, this disappointment opened their eyes, and the pretence to miracle ruined their cause. Nor can I allow, with the author, that men of the best intentions can propagate a known falshood for the sake of truth. An honest man may be hasty in believing; but he cannot be a deceiver or impostor. It is certain, the religion of *Christ* disdains such pious frauds, and his Apostles have forbad and condemned them in terms as severe as language can express: nor is it a principle in this religion, as this writer would insinuate, that men should renounce their judgment in inquiries of this sort: on the contrary,

[50] P. 185.

they are injoined carefully to examine the truth of miracles and doctrines, before they believe them.

But, granting the author's principles in their full extent, the miracles of the Gospel will be no way affected by them: For, first, the Apostles are free from all tincture and appearance of enthusiasm; witness the writings which they have left behind them, and that system of doctrines and morals contained in them: in their piety nothing over-passionate, rapturous, or ecstatick appears, but all is rational, sober, and temperate: their zeal for their master and his religion never transports them into complaints or invectives against his enemies or their own, or into any strained elogiums or panegyricks upon his character: they recite all that is wonderful in his actions, without exclamation, without vehement asseveration, with an undoubting, unguarded simplicity, that is highly singular and remarkable: their whole conduct, in like manner, was void of ostentation, steady, uniform, and regular throughout: they were not only consistent each with himself (which a fanatick spirit seldom is) but all pursued the same plan, without varying or change, with the most perfect harmony and agreement. And, secondly, whatever influence, from passion or prejudice, the witnesses to Christianity were under, this operated the contrary way, and must dispose them to reject, rather than receive, the miracles: the Apostles themselves were *Jews*, and zealous of the traditions and customs of their ancestors: the other converts, whether *Jews* or Pagans, were prejudiced, as strongly as they could be, by religion, against the Gospel: bigotry and enthusiasm rose up every-where in persecution against it: nothing but reason and conviction could induce men to declare for it: every passion, every interest, and every prejudice persuaded against this belief: and, in fact, every single conversion to it was not barely the testimony of an unprejudiced judge, but the testimony of an enemy to its truth.

"The wise," says the author, in another place,

"lend a very academick faith to every report which favours the passion of the reporter, whether it magnifies his country, his family, or himself, or in any other way strikes in with his natural inclinations and propensities. But what greater temptation than to appear a missionary, a prophet, an ambassador from heaven? Who would not encounter many dangers and difficulties to attain so sublime a character?"[51]

Where this character is indeed attended with honour and respect, it will be natural for ambitious men to desire it. But the head and leader of this sect had been every-where reviled and persecuted, and was crucified as a malefactor: his followers every-where shared the same fate. What

---

[51] P. 196.

temptation was there to appear his prophet or ambassador? What vanity or self-interest was gratified by it? But, thirdly, the author tells us,

> "it forms a very strong presumption against all supernatural and mirac-
> ulous relations, that they are always found chiefly to abound amongst
> ignorant and barbarous nations; or, if a civilised people has ever given
> admission to any of them, that people will be found to have received
> them from ignorant and barbarous ancestors, who transmitted them with
> that inviolable sanction and authority which always attends antient and
> received opinions."[52]

This argument, we presume, has been already answered. The miracles of the Gospel were, as we have said, performed where they were most suspected. The *Jews* were by no means a barbarous people, and they were freer from superstition than any other nation in the world. These miracles were immediately canvassed with all the severity that the prejudice of enemies could suggest. Some who were healed of their diseases were sent immediately to the priests, on purpose, as it seems, that they might undergo the strictest inquisition. Others were called before the council, examined, and threatened, and every means tried to refute and silence them. This religion did not get strength in the dark, and then adventure itself by degrees into the light: it was openly proclaimed, from the first, in the temple and in the synagogue, where the *Jews* always resorted: and, when the Apostles had filled *Jerusalem* and *Judæa* with their doctrines, *Rome* and *Athens* were some of the next scenes of their ministry.

Under this head we are entertained with a long story from the *Pseudomantis* of *Lucian*. "It was," saith the author,

> "a wise policy in that cunning impostor, *Alexander*, who, tho' now
> forgotten, was once so famous, to lay the first scene of his impostures in
> *Paphlagonia*, where, as *Lucian* tells us, the people were extremely
> ignorant and stupid, and ready to swallow even the grossest delusion.
> People at a distance, who are weak enough to think the matter at all
> worth inquiry, have no opportunity of receiving better information. The
> stories come magnified to them by an hundred circumstances. Fools are
> industrious to propagate the delusion; while the wise and learned are
> contented, in general, to deride its absurdity, without informing
> themselves of the particular facts, by which it may be distinctly refuted.
> And thus the impostor above-mentioned was enabled to proceed, from
> his ignorant *Paphlagonians*, to the inlisting votaries even among the

---

[52] P. 186.

Grecian philosophers and men of the most eminent rank and distinction in *Rome* – nay, could engage the attention of the sage emperor, *Marcus Aurelius*, so far as to make him trust the success of a military expedition to his delusive prophecies."[53]

But what, if this famous impostor never pretended to miracles? It is said, indeed, that he had his emissaries in distant countries, who reported this, among other things, to his honour: but there is no appearance in his history of his ever counterfeiting or pretending to this power. It was his policy not to hazard his reputation on so dangerous an issue. Ignorant and stupid as his *Paphlagonians* were, it might have been too much for all his art to impose false facts upon their eyes and senses. He had, by a bold and successful cheat of another kind, established his character among this people, who, *Lucian* tells us, differed from brutes in nothing but their outward form. He had the fortune too to gain the ear of a famous *Roman* general, who, by the same author's account, was formed to be the dupe of every pretender. This seems to have got him some name in *Rome*. But I find none, that deserve to be called philosophers, among his votaries. It is certain, that the sight of a *Christian* or an *Epicurean* disconcerted all his management. They were always drove from his presence, having the confidence, no doubt, to deride the prophet and his oracles. Every one must believe, upon the representation here made, that the emperor *Antonine* had undertaken the expedition mentioned at the instigation of the impostor, or, at least, had concerted measures with him for pursuing it. But the oracle given out by this pretended prophet was voluntary and unasked, in order, if the event had happened, as was probable, to increase his own credit. And, superstitious as this great emperor and philosopher was, he did nothing, in pursuance of it, but what the wisest general might have done to humour the superstition and folly of his soldiers, and to inspire them with a confidence of victory. It no-where appears that he hazarded the least point, or altered any one of his measures, in consequence of it. But, if it were true that this impudent impostor had this learned emperor and the schools of *Greece* among his admirers, this would only prove how much the wisest part of mankind were enslaved by superstition, before Christianity released them from it.

The author adds, as a fourth reason which diminishes the authority of prodigies,

"that there is no testimony for any, even those which have not been expressly detected, that is not opposed by an infinite number of witnesses; so that not only the miracle destroys the credit of the testimony, but even

[53] P. 188.

the testimony destroys itself. To make this the better understood, let us consider, that, in matters of religion, whatever is different is contrary, and that 'tis impossible the religions of antient *Rome*, of *Turkey*, of *Siam*, and of *China* should, all of them, be established on any solid foundation. Every miracle, therefore, pretended to have been wrought in any of these religions (and all of them abound in miracles) as its direct scope is to establish the particular system to which it is attributed, so it has the same force, tho' more indirectly, to overthrow every other system: in destroying a rival-system, it likewise destroys the credit of those miracles on which that system was established: so that all the prodigies of different religions are to be regarded as contrary facts, and the evidence of these prodigies, whether weak or strong, as opposite to each other."[54]

This argument, he is apprehensive, will appear too subtle and refined: but the only fault of it is, that it has no foundation in truth. The author cannot name a single miracle, that was ever offered as a test of any of these religions, before their establishment, or to authorise any pretended prophet to teach such religion[55]. *Mahomet* expressly disclaims this power in many places of his *Koran*. It appears, from his manner of speaking of it, that he knew what advantage this pretence would give to his cause, and even felt the want of it: yet, with all the assistance that art and power could give him, he durst not hazard so dangerous an experiment. The author would make us believe that miracles are to be met with in almost every page of antient history:

"When we peruse the first histories of all nations, we are apt to imagine ourselves transported into some new world, where the whole frame of nature is disjointed, and every element performs its operations in a different manner from what it does at present. Battles, revolutions, pestilences, famines, and deaths are never the effects of those natural causes which we experience."[56]

But the truth is, they are very thinly sown in the writings of the heathens. Portents and prodigies I call not by that name. These are to be accounted for from natural causes, or owe their existence to a frighted or disturbed imagination. Of miracles, properly speaking, there are very few upon record: most of these are given up, by the historians who relate them, as

---

[54] P. 190.

[55] There is a wide difference betwixt establishing false miracles by the help of a false religion and establishing a false religion by the help of false miracles. Nothing is more easy than the former, or more difficult than the latter.

[56] P. 187.

vulgar fables, unworthy of belief, and none are so attested as to make them in any degree credible. Of this the author has undesignedly given us a full proof in the story which immediately follows:

"One of the best-attested miracles in all profane history is that which *Tacitus* reports of *Vespasian*, who cured a blind man in *Alexandria* by means of his spittle, and a lame man by the mere touch of his foot, in obedience to a vision of the god *Serapis*, who had enjoined them to have recourse to the emperor of these miraculous and extraordinary cures."[57]

This, the author seems to insinuate, is as well attested as any *Christian* miracle, and may be made as good an argument for the religion of the antient *Egyptians* as any miracle for any religion whatsoever: "Every circumstance," says he, "adds weight to the testimony, and might be displayed at large with all the force of argument and eloquence, if any one were now concerned to enforce the evidence of that exploded and idolatrous superstition." The occasion being so tempting, he has tried his hand, and shewn us how far this miracle may be parallell'd with those of the Gospel:

"The gravity, solidity, age, and probity of so great an emperor, who, thro' the whole course of his life, conversed in a familiar way with his friends and courtiers, and never affected those extraordinary airs of divinity assumed by *Alexander* and *Demetrius* – The historian a contemporary writer, noted for candor and veracity, and, withal, the greatest and most penetrating genius, perhaps, of all antiquity, and so free from any tendency to superstition and credulity, that he even lies under the contrary imputation of atheism and profaneness – The persons, from whose testimony he related the miracle, of established character for judgment and veracity (as we may well suppose) eye-witnesses of the fact, and confirming their verdict, after the *Flavian* family were despoiled of the empire, and could no longer give any reward, as the price of a lye: *Utrumque, qui interfuere, nunc quoque memorant, postquam nullum mendacis pretium.* To which if we add the publick nature of the fact, as related, it will appear, that no evidence can well be supposed stronger for so gross and so palpable a falshood."

As to the character of this wise emperor, *Suetonius*, who has wrote his life, tells us, that he had long before this conceived hopes of the empire, from certain idle dreams and omens, of which he has reckoned up eight or ten, as ridiculous as any in history: that immediately before this, when he was now proclaimed emperor by some of the legions, and had strengthened himself by several alliances, he condescended, notwithstanding his probity

[57] P. 192.

and gravity, to give out a miracle upon his own authority, to make himself considerable in the eyes of the people; pretending that, in the temple of *Serapis*, where he went alone, *de firmitate imperii auspicium facturus*, one *Basilides*, who was known at the time to be far distant and unable to travel, had appeared to him, offering him crowns and garlands – a certain omen (as he and his courtiers interpreted the word *Basilides*) of the royal dignity. As for the credit of the historian, he was no witness of the fact, nor, for ought we know, ever conversed with those that saw it; and the testimony he gives to it does by no means amount to a proof that he believed it himself. To what purpose, then, is the character he gives us of his veracity, penetrating genius, and incredulous turn of mind? But, if the testimony of the historian be not admitted, the witnesses, from whose testimony he related it, were of established character for veracity and judgment. This, indeed, is to the purpose. On this point the whole merits of the cause must rest. How, then, is this proved to us? Why, the author says *it may well be supposed*, and the historian tells us that they persisted in the report, when they could gain nothing by the fraud. But how does it appear that they had never received any reward for their verdict? The emperor, tho' he affected not the airs of divinity, yet was well pleased with his new title, and, no doubt, was well understood to look with a favourable eye on those who contributed to support it. The good uses to which this miracle served are honestly told us both by *Suetonius* and *Tacitus*: *Auctoritas, et quasi majestas quædam, ut scilicet inopinato et adhuc novo principli deeat, hæc quoque accessit*, Suet. *Miracula evenere, queis cælestis favor et quædam in* Vespasianum *inclinatio numinum ostenderetur*, Tacit. The *Alexandrians* could not but have an interest in gaining the favour of this prince: the persons cured are said to be *è plebe* Alexandrina, probably unknown to these witnesses and to all the *Romans* about *Vespasian*: the partisans of the new emperor were prepared to welcome and improve everything that looked in his favour: the physicians, who were consulted whether these disorders were curable, declared that they were: Where, then, is the wonder that two men should be instructed to act the part of lame and blind, when they were sure of succeeding in the fraud, and of being well rewarded (*as we may well suppose*) for their pains?

This story is followed by two other, as marketable proofs of the credulity of mankind, which, having obtained in *Christian* countries, may perhaps be thought more opposite to the author's purpose of discrediting the *Christian* miracles. "There is also," saith he,

> "a very memorable story related by cardinal *de Retz*, and which may well deserve our consideration: When that intriguing politician fled into *Spain*, to avoid the persecution of his enemies, he passed thro' *Saragossa*, the capital of *Arragon*, where he was shewn, in the cathedral church, a

man who had served twenty years as a doorkeeper of the church, and was well known to every body in town who had ever paid their devotions at the cathedral: he had been seen for so long a time wanting a leg, but recovered that limb by the rubbing of holy oil upon the stump; and, when the cardinal examined it, he found it to be a true natural leg, like the other. This miracle was vouched by all the canons of the church; and the whole company of the town was appealed to for a confirmation of the fact, whom the cardinal found, by their zealous devotion, to be thorough believers of the miracle. Here the relater was also contemporary with the supposed prodigy, of an incredulous and libertine character, as well as of great genius – the miracle of so singular a nature as could scarce admit of a counterfeit – and the witnesses very numerous, and all of them, in a manner spectators of the fact to which they gave their testimony: and what add mightily to the force of the evidence and may double our surprize on the occasion, is, that the cardinal himself who relates the story, seems not to give any credit to it, and, consequently cannot be suspected of any concurrence in the holy fraud."[58]

The story is, indeed, remarkable, as the author has told it. First, the relater was *a cardinal and a man of great genius*; and, tho' he had never seen the wooden leg, yet he satisfied himself that the man had now *two natural legs, like another man*. It does not, indeed, appear, that he examined all or any of the cannons, or that he discoursed with any body in town about it: but he found, *by the devotion of the people*, that they believed the man to have had a wooden leg. Then, the cardinal was a man of libertine character, *and, which is still more wonderful, and adds mightily to the evidence, he did not believe the story himself*. This climax of evidence and wonder still rising upon us is very extraordinary. The relater of the story was a *cardinal*, and therefore a good evidence of a *Romish* miracle: he was of *a libertine character*, and therefore had the better right to be believed: but, what puts the evidence out of question, *he did not believe the story himself*; which, again, is *doubly surprizing*, as the author observes, because he was naturally *of an incredulous temper*. This is the first story. The second deserves a more serious attention.

"There, surely, never was so great a number of miracles ascribed to one person, as those which were lately said to have been wrought in France upon the tomb of *Abbé Pâris*, the famous *Jansenist*, with whose sanctity the people were so long deluded. The curing of the sick, giving hearing to the deaf and sight to the blind, were every-where talked of as the usual effects of that holy sepulchre. But, what is more extraordinary, many of

[58] P. 193.

the miracles were immediately proved, upon the spot, before judges of unquestioned integrity, attested by witnesses of credit and distinction, in a learned age, and on the most eminent theatre that is now in the world. Nor is this all: a relation of them was published and dispersed every-where: nor were the *Jesuits*, tho' a learned body, supported by the civil magistrate, and determined enemies to those opinions in whose favour the miracles were said to have been wrought, ever able distinctly to refute or detect them. Where shall we find such a number of circum-stances agreeing to the corroboration of one fact? and what have we to oppose to such a cloud of witnesses, but the absolute impossibility or miraculous nature of the events which they relate? And this, surely, in the eyes of all reasonable people, will alone be regarded as a sufficient refutation."[59]

The author has here asserted many things that he will not be able to support. The miracles pretended were, many of them, refuted upon the spot: a judicial inquest was made by the archbishop of *Paris* into one of the most celebrated, and the cheat was fully detected: the lieutenant of the police brought many to confess that the part they had acted was all artifice and pretence; and an ordinance was hereupon issued from the court for apprehending all that were concerned in such frauds: the archbishop of *Sens* exhibited a publick charge against more than twenty, as palpable and discovered cheats: and Mr. *Montgeron*, the professed advocate of these miracles, of whom we shall have more to say hereafter, does not, in his answer, pretend to defend a fourth part of these: and the author may see his defence of these, and of all the other miracles he defends, *distinctly refuted in the Critiques générale* of Mr. *Des Vœux*. The most usual effects of this sepulchre were not the cures, but distempers – a sort of convulsions, which seized alike the sound and the sick, and were attended with such strange appearances as brought great contempt and ridicule upon the other miracles of this saint. These convulsions, we are told by skilful physicians, are easily counterfeited, and, from being counterfeited, frequently become real and habitual: they are too so communicable, by a sort of sympathy, to persons of weak nerves, that this distemper, it is well known, is for this reason excluded some of our great hospitals; it having been found that, when one is seized, it spreads, like infection, thro' a whole ward. This will account for the great numbers who are said to have felt this extraordinary effect from visiting the *Abbe*'s tomb.

I deny not that there were real cures wrought upon the sick that were brought there: but the same, I dare pronounce, would happen, if a thousand people, taken at a venture, were at any time removed from their sick

[59] P. 195.

chambers in *London* to *St. Paul's Churchyard* or the *Park*, especially, if they went with any strong hope of a cure: in such a number, some are always upon the point of recovery – many only want to fancy themselves well – others may be flattered for a time into this belief, while they are ill – and many more, by fresh air and motion, and especially by forbearing the use of other means, will find a change for the better: but, that the blind received their sight, or the deaf were restored to hearing, by these visits, I deny that we have any competent or tolerable evidence. This sanguine writer does, indeed, take upon him to answer for *the credit of the witnesses and the integrity of the judges.* But these miracles were never proved in a judicial way. The vouchers produced for them are only certificates collected from all sorts of persons, who were neither interrogated by judge or council, nor confronted by other witnesses: they only left their depositions or affidavits in the hands of a notary, who was not concerned to examine, or even to know, the persons who made them, or whether they gave in their own or fictitious names. The credit, therefore, of the witnesses was never proved by any trial whatsoever.

Doctor *Middleton,* who has likewise set out the evidence of these miracles with great parade, is pleased to tell us that

> "the reality of them is attested by some of the principal physicians and surgeons in *France*, as well as the clergy of the first dignity, several of whom were eye-witnesses of them, who presented a verbal process of each to the archbishops, with a petition, signed by above twenty curés or rectors of the parishes of Paris, desiring that they might be authentically registered, and solemnly published to the people, as true miracles."[60]

Any one, who reads this in connexion with what goes before it, will be led to believe that a great number of these miracles had been confirmed by this verbal process:[61] but there never were, as far as I can inform myself, more than four or five thus proved by order of the cardinal *Noailles.* Whether the petition mentioned was presented by physicians and clergy of the first dignity, as the doctor's words seem to import, I will not take upon me to controvert: but, in all that I have read, I find only that it was presented by the twenty-two curés who signed it. The doctor might have told us too that it was rejected as well as presented, and the archbishops reasons for rejecting it, which were nothing less than palpable falshoods and contra-

---

[60] *Free Inquiry,* p. 225.

[61] The verbal process I take to be a narrative of the fact drawn upon the spot by a magistrate (in the present case, by a commissary appointed for that purpose) upon a view of the place and circumstances, an examination of the parties, and the deposition of witnesses.

dictions, legally proved, *par des informations juridiques*, on the witnesses, and even in the depositions taken by order of the cardinal *de Noailles*: he might have told us that thirty of the most eminent *Jansenist* doctors, who were supposed to have an interest in supporting these miracles, protested against the abuse that was made of them, and published many good reasons for not believing them – that, if some physicians of note pronounced the cures in question to be miraculous, many more, who had better opportunities of informing themselves, judged the contrary – that one of the faculty published a treatise to account for the phænomenon of the convulsions in a natural way, and several, who were consulted on the other pretended cures, declared the whole to be fiction and imposture.[62]

All that was real in these phænomena may be accounted for from nature: but a great part was certainly appearance, and owing to art. The *Abbé Paris*, as doctor *Middleton* has told us,

> "was a zealous *Jansenist*, and a warm opposer of the bull or constitution *Unigenitus*, by which the doctrines of this sect were expressly condemned: he died in 1725, and was buried in the churchyard of *St. Medard* in *Paris*, whither the great reputation of his sanctity drew many people to visit his tomb, and pay their devotions to him as a saint; and this concourse, gradually increasing, made him soon be considered as a subject proper to revive the credit of that party, now utterly depressed by the power of the *Jesuits*, supported by the authority of the court."[63]

Half the city of *Paris*, and many among them of rank, took part with the appellants against this bull. The saint was, therefore, sure to have justice done him. Most of these, if they did not believe, yet wished well to his miracles, for the sake of mortifying the *Jesuits* and their party.

"But the evidence of these miracles is still preserved in the pompous volume of *Mons. de Montgeron*, a person of eminent rank in Paris, who, Dr. *Middleton* tells us, dedicated and presented it to the king in person,

---

[62] See letter 7th of the *Critique* of Mr. *Des Vœux*. This judicious writer, who is now minister of the *French* church in *Dublin*, was himself a *Jansenist* and an inhabitant of *Paris* at the time when these miracles were celebrated. This circumstance, which adds to the credit of his verdict, doctor *Middleton*, who had seen his book, and therefore must know it, chuses to conceal, and to represent him only as a *Protestant writer*. This may be excused. But it is too much to assert that "he does not deny the facts, but only endeavours to make the miraculous nature of them suspected:" for near a fourth part of this book, which consists of nine letters, in two volumes, 12mo, is taken up in disproving these facts, and the title at the head of one of the longest letters is *Ou l'on fait voir, per les pieces même que Mr. de Montgeron produit, que les faits qu'il publie ne sont pas vrais*.

[63] *Free Inquiry*, p. 223.

being induced, as the author declares, by the incontestable evidence of the facts, by which he himself, from a libertine and professed Deist, became a sincere convert to the *Christian* faith."[64] As the credit of these boasted miracles rests almost wholly on this book of Mr. *Montgeron*, the reader will not be displeased, if we stop a little to consider the character of the work and its author.

This book was published, as we are advertised at the beginning, to demonstrate, among other things, the justice of the cause of the appellants against the bull *Unigenitus*: but it was so far from answering the purpose of reviving the credit of the *Jansenists* or their miracles, that from this time they sunk into greater disgrace than ever; while the author was cashiered from his employment, sent first to the *Bastile*, and afterwards into banishment. The author declares himself converted to Christianity by the evidence of these facts: but it is strange to observe, from his own history of this conversion, that it was wrought without his either seeing or examining the evidence of any one of these miracles. It appears, from this history, that the author was early impressed with a sense of religion – that, having given himself up to a life of pleasure and debauch, he was, on a certain occasion, so struck with remorse, as to shut himself up in a convent, with design to spend his days in penitence and retirement – that, returning again to his former life, he endeavoured to free himself from the checks of conscience by reading the books of Deists, and persuading himself that religion was a cheat – that the unchristian bull *Unigenitus*, which just then appeared, helped much to confirm him in this belief: but the fears of religion still kept hold of him, and, particularly, on the first report of our *Abbé*'s miracles, his conscience took the alarm, and put him upon inquiring in earnest into the truth of religion – that, upon hearing a second time of these miracles, he resolved to visit the tomb, and make a strict inquiry into their truth – that, coming there, he was immediately struck with the ardor that appeared in the devotion of the people; strongly impressed with which, he fell himself on his knees, and addressed a short prayer to the saint, beseeching him, "That, if indeed he still lived, and had any power with the Almighty, he would pity his blindness and intercede for him, that his mind might be enlightened, and the cloud removed which held him in darkness!" Upon which, immediately, while he continued some hours on his knees, all the arguments for religion, which he had ever heard or read, presented themselves to his mind, and passed in review before him, with such force and conviction, that he became from that moment a zealous and confirmed Christian. Here, you see, the author, without waiting for any miracle, or inquiring into those which he had heard, was not only converted to Christianity, but became a determined believer of all the miracles of this

---

[64] *Free Inquiry*, p. 224.

saint. And from this short sketch we may easily make out his character, which was plainly that of a wrongheaded and violent man, that could think coolly about nothing, changing, as fancy or temper led him, from one opinion, from one extreme, to another, and governed throughout by passion or prejudice, and not by reason.

His book was published ten (or, according to Dr. *Middleton*, twelve) years after the *Abbé*'s death; and 'tis a collection of nine cures, selected out of the great number which are said to have been wrought in all this time; the first of which I shall present my reader with, in a few words, as a specimen of the rest: A *Spanish* youth, at the age of ten years, lost entirely the sight of the left eye by violent rheum and inflammation: a few years after, receiving a blow upon the right eye, he became almost blind for some days, but, by proper remedies, recovered his sight again: at the age of sixteen, this eye was attacked with a fluxion and inflammation like to that which had destroyed the other, but was soon recovered, by the application of a certain water, so far as to allow him for two or three months after to prosecute his studies: but, the disorder then returning, and the same remedy being found ineffectual, he continued in this state, without the application of any remedy, near two months; at the end of which, hearing of the *Abbé Pâris*'s miracles, he resolved, with the consent of his governors, who were zealous *Jansenists,* to apply to the *Abbé*'s tomb: he entered upon a neuvaine, or nine-days devotion, in honour of the saint, and to supplicate his assistance: the effect was, that his pains redoubled, and the inflammation increased; but towards the end of the term these bad symptoms abated, and his eye at last became strong enough to bear the light, and to permit him to return to his studies: and all this without the use of any other means than saving the eye from reading for three months, shutting out the light, and bathing it in the two last days with a little decoction of mallow-roots with laudanum, prescribed by an oculist; and this too owed all its virtue to the manner of applying it, which was not with a common linen rag, but a piece of the shirt in which the *Abbé* died, and some of the earth in which he was buried. A certain *Jansenist* physician, who saw this eye two days before the cure, judging it to be a disorder of the optick nerve, expressed some doubt whether it were curable, and, being told afterwards that no human means had been used, inclined to think the cure miraculous. This, I suppose, is one of the principal physicians, who, Dr. *Middleton* tells us, attested the truth of these miracles. But it is certain that many other physicians and oculists, both in *France* and *Spain,* thought otherwise, and prescribed bleeding, bathing, and use of different medicines for it. The left eye, in the mean time, remained in its former state, uncured; and the eye which was healed relapsed some time after, and was again cured by bleeding. This is the first miracle, as it is related by this author, and attested by many vouchers and certificates printed along with it – a story too contemptible for argument or remark. But, if the reader desires to see the false colouring in which the writer has dressed it, and the inconsistencies and prevarication of the witnesses, detected, he may find this done, to his entire satisfaction, in the letters above mentioned, and in the nineteenth and twentieth tomes of the *Bibliotheque raisonnée*; from which, and Mr. *Vernet*'s *Traité de la Verité de la Religion Chretienne*, most of these remarks are taken.

The evidence, then, for these miracles, tho' set out with much eloquent pomp, when examined, is found to amount to very little. But this is acknowledged, that the credulity of mankind is very fully proved by this and the other legendary miracles of Popery, and that hence an argument of seeming weight still lies against the miracles of the Gospel: for, if so many other miracles have been believed rashly and without reason, it is possible that these may likewise have been received upon incompetent testimony: and, if this be possible, must it not also be allowed more probable, than that events so strange and contrary to the common course of nature should be true? This is the inference, we may presume, the author would have us make from the stories he hath related: and this objection he has incidentally dropped in several parts of his Essay:

"The many instances of forged miracles, and prophecies, and super-natural events, which, in all ages, have either been detected by contrary evidence, or which detect themselves by their absurdity, mark sufficiently the strong propensity of mankind to the extraordinary and the marvellous, and ought reasonably to beget a suspicion against all relations of this kind:"[65]

And again, in the place above cited,

"Should a miracle be ascribed to any new system of religion, men, in all ages, have been so much imposed on by ridiculous stories of that kind, that this very circumstance would be sufficient, with all men of sense, not only to make them reject the fact, but even reject it without farther examination."[66]

As this is one of the most specious and prevailing arguments against the miracles of religion, it will deserve a distinct answer.

To the first consequence, then, which the author here draws from the credulity of men, I readily agree – That miracles and facts of an extraordinary nature may be justly suspected, 'till sufficient evidence of their reality

[65] P. 186.
[66] P. 200.

is produced, and ought never to be received, 'till after a previous examination had into this evidence. But, that all miracles should be rejected without examination, because a great number have been forged, is, sure, a most illogical conclusion. The truth of the Gospel miracles does not imply that all the miracles upon record are true: how then does the falshood of other miracles affect the truth of these? If some men are cheats and impostors, is there no truth in the world? If some have believed upon too slight evidence, must we, therefore, reject all testimony, and disbelieve or doubt about every thing? Is the currency of bad coin a proof that there is none good? The test and assay will always distinguish the true from the false: and it is our own fault, if we are imposed upon by counterfeits. God hath given us reason and understanding to know good and evil, truth and falshood, and, in all things pertaining to life or duty, hath made the difference between them sufficiently clear and discernible, If he speaks to us by miracles, he will, doubtless, cause his voice to be known, and give full evidence of his authority. To those, who are not present witnesses of his power, this evidence will be transmitted with such testimony as cannot be impeached – such as will stand every fair and equitable trial. With such testimony, we assert, the Scripture miracles are delivered down to us. Let them be brought to the trial, and, if they are found wanting, be rejected, but not be condemned, as this supercilious writer would have them, unheard.

I observe, that this author, in common with many others, seems to think every proof of the credulity of mankind a sort of argument against the evidence of the Gospel: they think this sufficient to account for the belief of all miracles, and that it is, therefore, needless and folly to look for any evidence in their favour:

> "When such reports fly about, the solution of the phænomenon is obvious; and we judge in conformity to experience and observation, when we account for it by the known principles of credulity and delusion. And shall we, rather than have recourse to so natural a solution, allow of a miraculous violation of the most known and most established laws of nature?"[67]

But I must deny that there is any such cause or principle in human nature as credulity. If some are more credulous than others – if the same person be more credulous in some points than other – this depends upon other principles: it is a natural effect, and always to be accounted for from natural causes. Interest, when it is opposed by truth, will bias the mind to error: ignorance and indolence will dispose men, the one of necessity, the other of choice, to follow the judgment of others, and to believe as the

[67] P. 197.

world about them does: a deference to authority, whether publick or private – a prejudice to opinions in which we have been educated, or which we have long entertained – has the like effect: where men are, as is frequent, divided into parties by opinion, this prejudice will be heightened by pride and resentment; they will hearken greedily to every thing that favours their system, and be obstinately deaf to every thing that opposes it.

These are principles in human nature of great force and extent; and, where they induce to the belief of any thing, there we may suspect credulity, and that men will be prepared to believe, without evidence, even things the most difficult of belief. If, in these circumstances, it happen, that not the fact itself, but the miraculous nature of it only, is the point that gratifies our wishes, there, the greater the miracle is, the greater are these corrupt reasons for believing it, and, the more strange and incredible it is, the more easily sometimes will it obtain belief: as a stone, the heavier it is, and the more unapt to motion, will descend the swifter, if the plane be sufficiently inclined, upon which it moves.

But, on the other hand, where these or such-like principles have no influence, truth will be fairly heard, and the faith of men will be generally proportioned to the evidence that appears: and, where men believe and maintain opinions contrary to the influence of these principles, it is a fair presumption that their faith is well grounded, and that their assent is extorted by the force of truth. The principles, therefore, of credulity will by no means account for all belief alike. Tho' a stone will descend by its own weight, it does not follow that it can move itself upon even ground; and, if it be seen, contrary to its natural gravity, to ascend a steep acclivity, we are sure that there must be some competent power to impel it. Where miracles are wished for or wanted, the strangest and most unsupported may be believed: but, in other circumstances, the miraculous nature of the fact will hang as a weight upon it, and retard its progress; and, if it make its way, in opposition to the wishes, passions, and prejudices of mankind, there must be truth and evidence to support it.

I have already asserted that it required a stronger faith and more credulity to believe the evidence of the Gospel false, then to believe the miracles true. All the principles that can make men credulous conspired to make the first Christians disbelieve the Gospel. It was not, therefore, credulity, but conviction, which wrought this belief in them. But these principles very naturally account for the miracles of the *Romish* church. Interest, authority, and all the powers of enthusiasm, superstition, and prejudice, forward the belief of these: the power of the church is supported by them, and the countenance of the church, in the opinion of the believer, gives certainty and infallibility to them.

The disparity, then, betwixt these and the Gospel miracles is infinite. The end for which the Scripture miracles were wrought is the greatest that can be thought of, and the testimony, by which they are supported, is confirmed by the surest test of truth. If miracles, therefore, are in any case credible, they are in this; if testimony is in any case to be relied on, it is in this. But what are the ends proposed or answered by the miracles of Popery? More offerings are, perhaps, brought to the shrine at *Loretto*, more gain is made of the relicks of the saints. But are any nations brought to the faith, or is any single infidel converted, by them? Then, the testimony which vouches them is implicitly received, and the veracity of the witnesses confirmed by no proof or trial. There is no one condition here to make miracles credible – no one circumstance to credit the evidence that supports them. There is, therefore, no consequence to be drawn from these to the miracles of the Gospel.

And the same observation will hold, tho' not with equal force, of the miracles recorded in the church before the times of Popery: there were not the same antecedent reasons for working them, nor the same great consequences attending them: and when were any called, at the hazard of their fortunes and lives, to attest them? We are not, therefore, to be alarmed, if the truth of these miracles is sometimes brought in question, or even if many of them should be proved to be false; since the miracles of *Christ* and his Apostles are no way affected by this, and the Gospel wants no miracles, but its own, to support it: nor, indeed, can we do a greater injury to the cause of Christianity, than to parallel these, even supposing them true, with the canonical miracles of Scripture; since, tho' both may be equally true, yet the evidence upon which we receive them, and, consequently, the reasons for believing them, are not equal, but the one, in its weight and force, infinitely transcends the other. Nor is it any reproach to Christianity, or any just cause of offence to pious Christians, if the fathers of the church, men justly celebrated for their piety and virtue, and even for their learning and abilities, are found to have given too easy credit to these miracles. Learning and piety are no security against errors of this kind. On the contrary, men of this character, as they are often less practised in the arts of men, and less apt to suspect design and fraud in others, may lie more open to be deceived. Men may be prejudiced, even by piety and virtue, to such opinions as are thought favourable to piety and virtue, and, where any thing is thought of good tendency, may think it good to believe it. A little acquaintance with history will teach us, if our own observation does not, that men of great abilities and of the most upright intentions may be hasty in believing and zealous in supporting the belief of fables, especially where the cause of virtue or religion is supposed to be promoted by them.

We may, therefore, retain our veneration for the piety and good works of these eminent lights of the church, without believing every thing that they believed: we may believe many of the facts which they have recorded to be false, without hurting Christianity, or in the least impairing the evidence of the Gospel.

I might, under this head, have observed that false miracles are almost a natural consequence of true, and, therefore, their prevalence and reception is rather a presumption of the existence of true miracles than an argument against them. Could we foresee that a series of miracles would be wrought in any country, and a publick worship and religion be established in consequence of it, we might presume that miracles would be there more frequently pretended and counterfeited than in any other place. True miracles, like true money, will give a currency to false: and the authority and character, which they give to those that work them, will excite the crafty and ambitious to imitate them. On the other hand, where no prior miracles are acknowledged, there is less temptation to counterfeit this power, and more difficulty of succeeding in it. In fact, the false pretences of miracles among Christians are no more than might be expected, in consequence of the truth and certainty of the first miracles of Christianity; and, if the number of these has been far greater in the *Christian* world than elsewhere, it is an argument that there, if any-where, true miracles have been wrought. The reader will be pleased to see this argument in the words of Dr. *Middleton*:

"The innumerable forgeries of this sort, which have been imposed upon mankind in all ages, are so far from weakening the credibility of the *Jewish* and *Christian* miracles, that they strengthen it: for how could we account for a practice so universal, of forgoing miracles for the support of false religions, if on some occasions they had not actually been wrought for confirmation of a true one? or, how is it possible that so many spurious copies should pass upon the world, without some genuine original from which they were drawn, whose known existence and tried success might give an appearance of probability to the counterfeit? Now, of all the miracles of antiquity, there are none that can pretend to the character of originals, but those of the Old and New Testament, which, tho' the oldest by far of all others of which any monuments now remain in the world, have yet maintained their credit to this day, thro' the perpetual opposition and scrutiny of ages; whilst all the rival productions of fraud and craft have long ago been successively exploded, and sunk into utter contempt – an event that cannot reasonably be ascribed to any other cause, but to the natural force and effect of truth, which, tho' defaced for a time by the wit, or depressed by the power, of man, is sure still to triumph in the end over all the false mimicry of art and the vain efforts of human policy."[68]

[68] Prefatory Discourse to a Letter from *Rome*, p. 88.

The remainder of this Essay is little more than a rude insult on the *Scriptures* and the *Christian* religion. For fear his readers should mistake his meaning, and not apply his argument where he intended, the author proceeds, with a smiling grimace, to tell us, "that our most holy religion is founded on faith, not on reason; and 'tis a sure method of exposing it to put it to such a trial as it is by no means fitted to endure." This he pretends to make evident by examining the miracles related in the Pentateuch: "Here," says he,

"we are to consider a book presented to us by a barbarous and ignorant people, wrote in an age when they were still more barbarous, and, in all probability, long after the facts it relates, corroborated by no concurring testimony, and resembling those fabulous accounts which every nation gives of its origin. Upon reading this book, we find it full of prodigies and miracles: it gives an account of a state of the world and of human nature entirely different from the present – of our fall from that state – of the age of man extended to near a thousand years – of the destruction of the world by a deluge – of the arbitrary choice of one people as the favourites of heaven, and that people the countrymen of the author – of their deliverance from bondage by prodigies the most astonishing imaginable: I desire any one to lay his hand upon his heart, and, after serious consideration, declare, whether he thinks that the falshood of such a book, supported by such a testimony, would be more extraordinary and miraculous than all the miracles it relates; which is, however, necessary to make it be received, according to the measures of probability above established."[69]

If the *Jews* were thus more than barbarous at the time when these books were wrote, whence, without a miracle, could they learn all the great truths relating to the being and attributes of God, which the most learned part of the world were for many ages after in total ignorance about? Whence could the religion and laws of this people so far exceed those of the wisest Heathens, and come out at once, in their first infancy, thus perfect and entire; when all human systems are found to grow up by degrees, and to ripen, after many improvements; into perfection? The *Jews* had but little commerce with other nations, and, therefore, did not excel in the literary and other arts of *Greece*: but the same Scriptures, which prove that they were earlier in possession of the most useful and sublime parts of knowledge, secured them likewise from ever sinking into that barbarity which the author charges upon them. Let any one compare the book of *Genesis*, which he treats with so much freedom, and which is by

[69] P. 201

many centuries the oldest book in the world, with any of the earliest heathen historians – let him compare the psalms of *David* with the hymns of *Callimachus* or *Orpheus*– let him read the history of *Josephus*, who was just contemporary with *Christ* and his Apostles – and he will incline to judge more favourably of this people.

The great events recorded in this history have no connexion with the argument of miracles, and, therefore, do not belong to this place. But these are corroborated by the strongest concurring testimony that can be desired to facts that are, most of them, older than the use of letters itself. The traditions of every country seem all to point to one and the same original. The late invention of arts and sciences, the foundation of cities and empires, the manner of peopling the world, and the number of its present inhabitants, seem all to prove that the world had its beginning no earlier than the period assigned by *Moses*, and agree perfectly with the account of the deluge. There are no monuments of antiquity which give room to suspect the world of earlier original. The first authors of *Greece* and *Egypt* speak of the chaos, of the abyss of waters that covered the earth, of man's being formed out of the ground, and of his first innocence. From these, one of the *Latin* poets has described the creation, the state of innocence, the gradual corruption of mankind, and the deluge, in a manner very nearly resembling that of *Moses*. The memory of the general flood, which destroyed the whole race of men and animals, except one family, seems to have been preserved for some ages among almost all nations. *Lucian* tells us, the tradition among both the *Greeks* and *Syrians* was, that this was a judgment from heaven on the wickedness of mankind: he describes the manner of the flood, the ark in which some of every kind were preserved, and many other particulars, just as we have them in the book of *Genesis*. *Plutarch*, alluding to the same tradition, mentions the ark, and even the dove that was sent forth to see if the waters were abated. A great number of antient authors, who mention the deluge, and give witness to the building of *Babel*, the burning of *Sodom*, and many other great events in the *Mosaick* history, are reckoned up by *Josephus*, *Grotius*, and others. The present surface of the earth, the shells of fish that are found in midland countries, and even on the tops of mountains, and the remains of land-animals at very great depths in the earth, are still surviving monuments of the deluge.[70] It is almost certain that the world began to be peopled about

---

[70] An universal deluge will, I suppose, be allowed one of the most miraculous facts in the history of the Old Testament. The difficulties that on all sides surround it are as great as can easily be conceived. And hence many *Christian* writers (among whom is the learned Mr. *Wollaston*) have thought it sufficient to believe that this flood was topical, confined to a small part of *Asia*; and that the genius of the language in which the relation is delivered, and the manner of writing history in it, will account for all the rest. But, the more we improve in natural knowledge, the more reasons we see for

the plains of *Babylon* and near where the ark is said to have rested. From the east colonies of men were sent westward; and from thence we can trace pretty distinctly the progress of arts and sciences. The long lives of the first men are spoken of by all the Heathens. This fact is so far from discrediting the *Mosaick* history, that Monsieur *Pascal* reckons it a full proof of the fidelity of the author: "This historian," says he, "has brought the deluge, and even the creation, so near his own time, by means of the few generations which he counts between them, that the memory of them could not but be still fresh and lively in the minds of all the *Jewish* nation." In the line of tradition there are but five steps betwixt *Moses* and the first man. "Therefore, the creation and the deluge are indubitably true. This argument," says he, "must be acknowledged for conclusive by those who apprehend its process."[71] The longevity of men in the first ages seems necessary for the better peopling of the world, the invention and improvement of arts, and for propagating religious and all useful knowledge, when they depended wholly on tradition. And I am persuaded that this author cannot even invent a more probable or rational account of peopling the world than this which he affects to deride.

The other insinuations, which he has thrown out to discredit these books, have been so often refuted, that it is tedious to go over them again. The authority of an historian is not, sure, the worse for his being the countrymen of those whose history he writes. The character of *Moses* is remarkably free from all partiality to himself and his countrymen: he

---

believing this history in the literal and largest sense. One of the latest and ablest writers upon this subject confirms what the best natural historians have observed – that the shells of fishes are found in great quantities in all parts of the world – that the *Lapides Judaici*, which are gathered on the top of mount Carmel, are evidently the remains of a sea-animal – that the *Alps* and *Pyrenæan* mountains abound with others – and that there is not a mountain in the world, in which there have been tolerable opportunities of inquiring, where remains of sea-animals have not been found: he tells us, that many of those which are found in great abundance in our island are natives of other seas – that the horns of Indian deer are found in great clusters, and always at considerable depths, in many parts of *England*, and sometimes under a stratum of sea-shells: and hence, tho' writing upon another question, he concludes, "it is equally certain, that, wherever they are found, water must have at one time overflowed, since there is no other possible means of their being brought there; and, since they are found in every part of the earth, the tops of the highest mountains not excepted, that overflowing of water must have been universal." *Hill's Remarks on Phil. Trans.* p. 53. Here, then, we have one of the most disputable parts of the bible-history confirmed and proved by indisputable fact and experiment. In the mean time, it must be observed that the miracles upon which the *Christian* and *Jewish* religions were built have an evidence of their own, distinct from that of other parts of this history; and that, tho' it were allowed that many errors may have crept into the historical parts of this book, yet the truth of those religions, and the faith of those miracles upon which they are built, would remain unshaken.

[71] *Pascal's Thoughts*, p. 86.

faithfully records all the obstinacy and perverse behaviour of the latter, and frequently reproaches them with it in the severest terms: he spares not his own failings, or those of his nearest friends, and omits many things, which are recorded by others, to his honour: the future government of the *Israelites* he left not to his own tribe, but to that of *Judah*, and, in the appointment of his immediate successor, had no regard to his own family, but left them undistinguished and mixed with the common *Levites*.

As to the arbitrary preference of this people, a distinction in religious privileges is perfectly agreeable to the analogy of God's dispensations to mankind, both natural and moral. But the *Jewish* dispensation ought not to be considered apart, but in connexion with the *Christian*, in which it ended. These are but different parts of one and the same scheme, which naturally illustrate and confirm each other's authority. "And, from this view of them," says Dr. *Middleton*,

> "we see the weakness of that objection commonly made to the *Mosaick* part, on the account of its being calculated for the use only of a peculiar people; whereas, in truth, it was the beginning of an universal system, which, from the time of *Moses*, was gradually manifested to the world by the successive missions of the Prophets, 'till that fulness of time, or coming of the *Messiah*, when life and immortality were brought to light by the Gospel, or the chief good and the happiness of man perfectly revealed to him."[72]

The origin of this people is so far from resembling the fabulous accounts of other nations, that it is quite singular, and in all respects different from any other. They are a numerous people, sprung from the loins of one man, and have continued unmixed with the rest of the world, if we reckon from the time of *Abraham*, when they were first marked out by promise of God to his posterity, near 4000 years – a great part of the age of the world, and approaching very near to the time when it was last peopled by the posterity of *Noah*. Their very existence at this time, taken with all its circumstances, is a miracle, which gives credit to all the miracles of *Moses*.

The books, which record these miracles, were certainly wrote soon after the facts; since the religion, laws, and polity of the *Jews* were wholly built upon them. These books are the great charter by which they were incorporated into a nation. These miracles are the only sanction which gives authority to the laws they contain. The miracles were wrought in the face of all *Israel*, and many of them under observation for a long time together. The books, that record them, were of publick authority and daily resort. It was, therefore, impossible, if false, that they should obtain credit for a

---

[72] Prefatory Discourse to the Letter from *Rome*. p. 88.

day. The very being of these laws is a proof of the miracles connected with
them; since the latter, if false, must have discovered the falshood of the
former. By appealing to these facts, it was put in the power of every one
to see through, or, rather, it was put out of their power not to see through,
the imposture. The memory of these facts was not only preserved in these
records, but they were written, if I may so speak, and recorded in the daily
customs and religious ceremonies of the *Jews*. The *Passover* was instituted
in memory of their coming out of *Egypt* – the feast of *Pentecost* in token
of the law being given upon mount *Sinai* fifty days after – that of
Tabernacles in remembrance of their encamping in the desart – and, in the
form of dedicating or offering their first-fruits, a solemn commemoration
was injoined of the signs and wonders by which they were delivered out
of *Egypt*. The belief, therefore, of the miracles must of necessity be as
antient as their religion; and, indeed, without these, their religion,
government, and even their present existence, as a people, would be more
miraculous than all the miracles recorded in the Pentateuch.

   We are now come to the conclusion of this celebrated Essay: "Upon the
whole," says he,

> "we may conclude, that the *Christian* religion not only was at first
> attended with miracles, but even at this day cannot be believed by any
> reasonable person without one. Mere reason is insufficient to convince
> us of its veracity: and whoever is moved by faith to assent to it is
> conscious of a continued miracle in his own person, which subverts all
> the principles of his understanding, and gives him a determination to
> believe what is most contrary to custom and experience."[73]

   The author, in one of his Essays, complains of a want of politeness and
civility in those who defend religion against the attacks of the Free-thinkers,
"whose moderation and good manners," He tells us, "are very
conspicuous, when compared with the furious zeal and scurrility of their
adversaries."[74] But who can, without some impatience, see a religion
which he holds sacred, and which hath established itself purely by reason
and argument, treated with this open scorn and abuse? Has this author
lived in the time of Sir *Isaac Newton*, Mr. *Locke*, and Mr. *Addison*? Can
he know that these men gloried in the name of Christians, that the first of
them employed many of his best hours in studying and illustrating the
Scriptures, and that the other two have wrote professedly in the defence of
this religion, and yet think himself at liberty to treat all that believe it as
men that are incapable of reasoning or thinking? The charge, which he has

---

[73] P. 203

[74] *Essays moral and political*, p. 62.

here brought against the advocates of *Christianity*, is so far from being true, that I dare rest the whole merits of the controversy upon this issue. Let any one read the authors he mentions, *Collins* and *Tindal*, with *Morgan*, *Gordon*, and the later writers in this cause, and compare them with their antagonists, *Chandler, Conybeare, Leland, Foster*, and judge on which side the temper and moderation lies. And yet, if men claim some authority to opinions which have the publick voice on their side, where is the wonder or the blame? It is nothing unnatural for men thus supported to assume a confidence, and to expect some deference and modesty from their adversaries. But, when men oppose established opinions with an air of authority, and decide against the publick – when they profess to doubt, and yet dictate, about every thing, and act at once the Sceptick and the Dogmatist – this is a character, which, however it may be accounted for, can never be excused.[75] And I here ask my reader, whether he has any-where met with

[75] The author tells us, that, "in all controversies, those who oppose the established and popular opinions affect a most extraordinary gentleness and moderation, in order to soften, as much as possible, any prejudices that may lie against them." (*Essays moral and political*, p. 62.) But the fact is notoriously otherwise. In establishments of every kind, the party which forms the opposition, if they have the liberty to speak out, is usually the most furious and loud in invective. The reason is, the most furious and vehement spirits are the most impatient of control, and the most forward to oppose. A man that is a tyrant in his own temper is sure to complain of tyranny in his superiors; and a proud man will always think you proud, if you differ from him, whatever authority and whatever modesty you may have on your side. Thus the celebrated author of the *Patriot King* pronounces the most candid of all writers to be a *presumptuous Dogmatist* for daring to differ from him in opinion, even before it was known. This consummate writer, not content to shine in his own sphere, assumes the nod, and will give the law in metaphysicks as well as politicks. "I would not say, says he, "that God governs by a rule that we know or may know as well as he, and upon our knowledge of which he appeals to men for the justice of his proceedings towards them, which a famous divine has impiously advanced in a pretended demonstration of his being and attributes: God forbid!" (*Patriot King*, p. 94.) I learn from hence, that the famous divine spoken of has the misfortune to have fallen under the displeasure of this author, and that he has a sovereign contempt for all that do so. But, what his offence is, I am still at a loss to conjecture. I think myself certain, that he has no-where said what the author charges him with, "that we know or may know the rule by which God governs as well as he." He has, indeed, said, "that God himself, tho' he has no superior, from whose will to receive any law of his actions, yet disdains not to observe the rule of equity and goodness as the law of all his actions in the government of the world, and condescends to appeal even to men for the righteousness and equity of his judgments (as in *Ezek*. xviii.); that (not barely his infinite power, but) the rules of this eternal law are the true foundation and the measure of his dominion over his creatures." (Ninth edition, p. 218.) But what is this more than the author himself has said, in terms as free, in the very page that is stained with this censure? "That God is not an arbitrary, but a limited monarch, limited by the rule which infinite wisdom prescribes to infinite power – that he does always that which is fittest to be done – and that this fitness, of which no created power is a competent judge, results from the various natures and the more various relations of things." He adds, "So that, as creator of all systems by which these natures and relations are constituted, he

either a more sceptical, disputatious turn of mind, or a more imperious, dogmatical style, than in the writings of this author? It is remarkable with what ease and alacrity he hath asserted the fact before us. But this cavalier manner is familiar to him. He tells us, in another Essay, "that the Quakers are perhaps the only regular body of Deists in the universe:" And again, "that the leading Whigs have always been either Deists or professed Latitudinarians in their principles, that is," says he, "friends to toleration, and indifferent to any particular sect of Christians."[76] Now, it is certain that the Quakers profess the belief of Christianity as universally as any sect whatsoever. And what right has the author to charge a whole body of men with such flagrant insincerity? As to the Whigs, the principles of toleration are certainly Christian principles, and do by no means imply an indifference to any sect, much less a coldness to religion in general: and, if the best Christians are usually the best subjects and citizens (which I think an

prescribed to himself the rule which he follows as governor of every system of being." This, tho' no candid reader will complain of it, is more crude and perplexed than any thing I remember in the author here arraigned. God does always what is right and fit. But right and fit were not made what they are, when this or any other system of beings was made. The fitness of every action, the same circumstances supposed, was always and ever will be the same. The rule is eternal and immutable as truth itself, and its authority is as universal, extending to all beings and to all possible systems of being; as the author we are speaking of has, with equal modesty and clearness, asserted and proved immediately before the passage here cited. If he has said, farther, that God appeals to men for the justice of his proceedings, he has given his authority for this – an authority which a *Christian* divine must think decisive. And what doth this amount to more than saying that God hath implanted in men a sense of what is just, merciful, and good, and that all his dispensations are agreeable to our ideas of justice, mercy, and goodness? Does not the astronomer try the works of God by the laws of mechanism and geometry, when he pronounces that they are done in number, weight, and measure? And must we not have some measure of justice, mercy, and goodness, when we attribute these to the Deity? To say that we can see the wisdom of God in his works is not saying that we are as wise as God himself: nor does our seeing the fitness and equity of his proceedings in some instances imply that we are competent judges of or can see the reason of his proceedings in all. As the author has not pointed out the passages in the writer he excepts against, I can only guess this to be the place. But, if he has anywhere dropped an expression that may seem less accurate or proper upon this subject, the author might have pardoned it, who confesses, in the same page, that he cannot express himself on this subject properly, and that, when our ideas are inadequate, our expression must needs be improper. To return: We have here a phænomenon, which, to those who have not studied human nature, will appear altogether singular: Lord B——e Complaining of the impiety, pride, and presumption of Dr. *Clarke*. Established opinions and an established character provoked his resentment: Rather than submit to another, he will contradict himself. And this, I take it, is the principle from which most of Mr. *Hume's* philosophy is derived; to whose extraordinary gentleness and modesty that of this writer (to speak in the elegant phrase of the latter) (P. 148) is but as the positive degree to the superlative.

Est genus hominum, qui esse primos se omnium rerum volunt, Nec sunt.

[76] *Essays moral and political*, p. 111.

indisputable truth) I should hope their principles would be no impediment to their faith. I am sure, however, they have no reason to thank this
author for his compliment.

They who believe religion must think that the cause of virtue and the
happiness of mankind are bound up in it: and this will justify a degree of
zeal and ardor in its defence. But what is there to call for or excuse this
spirit in those who oppose it? If the author be a friend to virtue, which,
from his elegance of mind and taste, I scarce can doubt – if he be a friend
to natural religion, which a person of so much thought and reflexion sure
must be – what principles has he in reserve for the support of these, when
Christianity is taken away? The best philosophy, as I have already said,
availed but little in reforming the religions or morals of mankind: and, as
to the philosophy of this author, it is, as far as I understand it, as ill calculated for this purpose as any I have met with.[77] But, indeed, religion can
never be supported, or virtue taught, with any force or effect, by the
reasonings of philosophers. The world will never be governed by
metaphysical ideas of honour and beauty, decency of action, and the
fitness of things. It is the author's own observation, that "an abstracted,
invisible object, like that which natural religion alone presents to us,
cannot long actuate the mind, or be of any moment in life. To render the
passion of continuance, we must find some method of affecting the senses
and imagination, and must embrace some historical as well as philosophical accounts of the Divinity. Popular superstitions," says he, "and
observances are even found to be of use in this particular."[78] The great
thing to be wished, then, for the interest of virtue and the good of mankind,
is, that the maxims of natural religion should be fixed and assured by an
authority that is decisive – that a rule of duty should be taught as the will
and law of God – that the sanctions of this law, a future state and a
judgment to come, should be known alike to all, both small and great – that
the hopes of pardon should be assured to the penitent sinner – that there
should be an institution to propagate this knowledge, and to spread it thro'
the world – that there should be a publick worship set up, and a discipline
and œconomy prescribed, to train men to piety and virtue: but all this, and
much more to the advantage of virtue, we have in the Christian religion.
Can the author tell us where else they are to be found? If he is looking out
a cure for superstition, I venture to assure him, that, with all his researches

[77] The character of this author's philosophical writings, which I should not otherwise
have attempted, may be given in his own words, where he speaks of the *Alciphron* and
other works of the ingenious and good Bishop *Berkeley:* They admit of no answer, and
produce no conviction: their only effect is to cause that momentary amazement and
irresolution and confusion, which is the result of Scepticism." *Essays moral and
political*, p. 240.

[78] *Essays moral and political*, p. 231.

into metaphysicks and morals, he will never find any equal to that religion which he endeavours to explode; which in a few years did infinitely more towards freeing the world from the fear and folly of prodigies, omens, dreams, and oracles, than all the philosophy in the world had done in many ages. If, unhappily, this religion is still corrupted by superstitious mixtures, these I freely commit to the mercy of the author. But Christianity is not to answer for these any more than for the other errors and vices of mankind, which, however it aims to correct, it does not pretend to eradicate. And even these will be better and more successfully opposed by fair argument and civility than with insult and reproach. Where a liberty of debate and free inquiry is allowed, it is unpardonable to insult the publick that allows it. "There is a degree of doubt and caution and modesty, which in all kinds of scrutiny and decision, ought for ever to accompany a just reasoner."[79]

FINIS.

----

[79] *Philosophical Essays*, p. 250.

7
ANTHONY ELLYS

Anthony Ellys, *Remarks on An essay concerning miracles, published by David Hume, Esq; amongst his philosophical essays*. London: printed for G. Woodfall; and C. Corbett, [1752], [2], 5–26 p. Complete pamphlet; from 1752 edition.[80]

Anthony Ellys (1690–1761) was an Anglican churchman who became bishop of St. David's. He was also the author of *A Plea for the Sacramental Test* (1736), and the posthumous *Tracts on the Liberty Spiritual and Temporal of the Protestants of England* (1763–65). Although no publication date appears on Ellys's *Remarks*, the date of 1752 is usually assigned to it, which is consistent with the appearance of an April 1752 review of the pamphlet in the *Monthly Review*. Ellys begins his *Remarks* noting that, although Hume claims to attack miracles only in profane histories, his "true Meaning was not to exempt the miracles in the holy Scriptures". He makes five principal arguments against Hume. (1) In general, fear of divine punishment inclines people to be truthful in their testimonies, which is the case with the Gospel miracles. (2) The experience that we have today of unvaried laws of nature counts only against testimonies of miracles today. (3) As to Hume's claim that natural experience opposes miracle testimonies, Ellys counters that just as the Indian prince's experience against frost does not oppose European testimonies, laws of nature do not oppose miracle testimonies. (4) There is no joint opposition of miracle accounts in rival religions. For, first, God allows miracles in false religions to test the believers of true religion; and, second, we evaluate rival testimonies from various religions on a case-by-case basis, and ultimately the strongest testimony wins. (5) Hume's discussion of the alleged miracles at the Abbé De Pâris's tomb was simply meant to raise prejudices and insinuate that the Gospel miracles are on the same footing as those. William Rose's complete review of the *Remarks* in the *Monthly Review* is as follows:

---

[80] Title page: REMARKS | ON | AN ESSAY | CONCERNING | MIRACLES, | PUBLISHED BY | DAVID HUME, *Esq*; | AMONGST HIS | PHILOSOPHICAL ESSAYS. | *LONDON:* | Printed for G. WOODFALL, at *Charing-Cross*; and C. Corbett, in *Fleet-Street*. | (Price One Shilling).

The author of this small piece is both a sensible and genteel writer: he considers what mr. *Hume* has advanced relating to miracles in a somewhat different light from dr. *Rutherforth* and mr. *Adams*; but as mr. *Adams* has so ingeniously shewn the sophistry of mr. *Hume*'s arguments, (*See* Review *for* January *last*) we shall not detain our readers with a particular account of what he has said. [*Monthly Review*, April 1752, Vol. 6, p. 313]

The following is from the 1752 and only edition of Ellys's *Remarks*.

R E M A R K S

O N

An E S S A Y

CONCERNING

M I R A C L E S,

PUBLISHED BY

D A V I D H U M E, *Esq*;

AMONGST HIS

PHILOSOPHICAL ESSAYS.

L O N D O N:]
Printed for G. WOODFALL, at *Charing-Crofs*; and C. COR-
BETT, in *Fleet-Street*.

(Price One Shilling.)

REMARKS
ON
Mr. *HUME*'s ESSAY
CONCERNING
MIRACLES.

Mr. *Hume* professedly "flatters himself that he has discovered an Argument, which, if just, will be an everlasting Check to all Kinds of superstitious Delusion; and consequently will be useful as long as the World lasts; for so long he presumes will the Accounts of Miracles and Prodigies be found in all *Profane History*."[81] In which Declaration the two last Words may seem designed to give us the Satisfaction of Thinking, that this new Argument, great as it is to be in its Effects, yet will not extend to the Miracles related by the *Sacred Writers*. For if he thought it would take in them as well as others, why did he speak only of profane History, and not of History in general? His Addition of *profane*, which is an Epithet of Restriction, implies an Opposition to sacred History with Regard to the Miracles which it relates, as being unconcerned in what was to be advanced.

But whatever may be inferred from the Propriety of his Expression, the Author's true Meaning was not to exempt the Miracles in the holy Scriptures, any more than others, from the Force of his Argument, which is formed upon Principles that extend alike to all Miracles whatsoever; and his Conclusions from those Principles admit of no Exception. "Upon the whole," says he, Page 202, "it appears that no Testimony for any Kind of Miracle can ever possibly amount to a *Probability*, much less to a *Proof*; and that even supposing it amounts to a Proof, it would be opposed by another Proof derived from the very Nature of the Fact which it would endeavour to establish." Again, Page 203, "we may establish it as a Maxim, that no human Testimony can have such a Force as to prove a Miracle, and make it a just Foundation for any such System of Religion." And a little before, he had expressed himself in Terms yet stronger, but less decent, in Page 195, where he scruples not to say, "that a Miracle supported by any human Testimony is more properly a Subject of Derision than of Argument." Accordingly in Page 205, and 206, he flouts at the Miracles related by *Moses* in the *Pentateuch*; and though, indeed, soon after in Page 207, he says, "that the Christian Religion not only was at first attended with Miracles, but even at this Day cannot be believed by any reasonable Person without one;" yet the Miracles he there means were not those that are delivered to us in the holy Scripture, but some Effects on the

---

[81] Essay, 2d. Edit. *Lond*. M.DCC.LI. page 174.

Minds of Men, which he, in a popular Sense of the Word, is pleased to call Miracles, but which he conceives are far from according either Evidence or Credit to the Gospel.

Now as it is plain, that if this was really the Design of his Essay, it strikes at the Foundation of our Religion, by denying the Truth of all the Miracles wrought by *Christ* to prove that he was sent from God; it seems to be the Concern of all who believe in him, and are able to examine the Arguments of this Author, to satisfy themselves as to what there is in them. And the following Remarks, though at first designed only for *private* Use, are now offered to the Public, because they consider this Essay in Views, somewhat different from those of the learned Persons who have answered it before, and are drawn into so small a Compass, that any Reader, without employing much Time or Pains, may be able to judge how far they answer their End.

The main Design of Mr. *Hume*'s first Argument, is to shew that no human Testimony can be sufficient to prove the Reality of any Miracle, or make it justly Credible; in order to which, he begins with considering on what Grounds the Credibility of human Testimony itself depends. And Page 176 he observes, "that our Assurance of the Truth of any Argument, founded only on human Testimony, is derived from no other Principle than our Observation of the Veracity of that Testimony in general, and of the usual Conformity of Facts to the Reports of Witnesses." And again, Page 177, "Did not Men's Imagination naturally follow their Memory; had they not commonly an Inclination to Truth, and a Sentiment of Probity; were they not sensible to Shame when detected in a Falsehood; were not these, I say, discovered to be Qualities inherent in human Nature, we should never repose the least Confidence in human Testimony. A Man delirious or noted for Falsehood and Vanity has no Manner of Weight or Authority with us."

It is here laid down that these Qualities and Dispositions, known to be inherent in human Nature, will cause Men to speak the Truth, unless accidental and sinister Motives hinder them from doing it. And about *this*, I have no Dispute with the Author: Yet must observe, that he has omitted the principal Thing that ought to have, and no doubt often has, the *greatest Weight* in disposing Men to speak as they think; and that is, *their Sense* of the *Obligation* which *God* lays them under to do it, and their Fear of Punishment from him, if they act contrary to this Obligation. Every one who reflects at all, must be sensible that God was the Author of our Faculty of Speech, and that he gave it, in order to the Benefit and Improvement that Men might receive by imparting their Thoughts and Dispositions to each other. For which Purpose, it is necessary that their Words should express their Thoughts as they really are; because if they did otherwise, their Speech would produce frequently Distrust, Ill-Will and

Disturbance among them. On which Account we may justly conclude, from Reason itself, that God has strictly obliged each Person to speak the Truth; that he has given all others a Right to expect it from him; and that he himself, who always knows how far their Words are expressive of their Thoughts, will severely punish all Breaches of this Duty. This *Sense* of natural Obligation, attended with the Fear of Punishment from him, and of Resentment from Men, in Case of speaking falsely, I say, every one must have in some Degree: It ought to be, and must be, one of his chief Motives to say what he thinks. For this Reason, I cannot easily conceive how the Author came to omit it, and instead of it, to talk of "*Men's Imagination as naturally following their Memories,*" which is a Thing not easy to be understood, if it be at all to the Purpose.

But, taking this Matter as the Author has put it, let us see how he proceeds upon it. He observes Page 177 that

"as the Evidence derived from Witnesses and human Testimony is founded on past Experience, so it varies with the Experience, and is regarded as a Proof or Probability, according as the Conjunction betwixt any particular Kind of Report, and any Kind of Objects has been found to be constant or variable. There are a Number of Circumstances to be taken into Consideration in all Judgments of this Kind; and our ultimate Standard, by which we determine all Disputes that may arise concerning them, is always derived from Experience and Observation. When this Experience is not entirely uniform on any Side, it is attended with an unvariable Contrariety in our Judgments, and with the same Opposition and mutual Destruction of Argument as in every other Kind of Evidence."

He observes farther, Page 178, 179,

"that many Particulars may destroy the Force of any Argument derived from human Testimony. Of this Kind are the Opposition of contrary Testimony, the Character and Number of the Witnesses, the Manner of their delivering their Testimony, or the Union of all these Circumstances. We entertain a Suspicion concerning any Matter of Fact, when the Witnesses contradict each other, when they are but few, or of a suspicious Character, when they have an Interest in what they affirm, when they deliver their Testimony with Doubt and Hesitation, or on the contrary with too violent Asseverations."

But one Thing the Author distinguishes from the others, which diminish the Force of human Testimony; because it is much of the same Nature with the principal Circumstance on which his Argument against that Testimony, in the Case of Miracles, will be founded. He tells us, Page 179,

"that when the Fact which the Testimony endeavours to establish partakes of the *extraordinary* and the *marvellous*, the Evidence resulting from the Testimony, receives a Diminution greater or less in Proportion as the Fact is more or less Unusual. The Reason why we place any Credit in Witnesses and Historians is not from any Connexion we perceive *a priori* betwixt Testimony and Reality, but because we are accustomed to find a Connexion betwixt them. But when the Fact attested, is such as has seldom fallen under our Observation, here is a Contest of two opposite Experiences, of which the one destroys the other as far as its Force goes, and the superior can only operate on the Mind by the Force which remains. The very same Principle of Experience which gives us a certain Degree of Assurance in the Testimony of Witnesses, gives us also in this Case, another Degree of Assurance against the Fact which they endeavour to establish; from which Contradiction there necessarily arises a Counterpoise and mutual Destruction of Belief and Authority."

The Reader, I fear, will begin to be tired with such long Quotations, in which but little of the Argument expected hitherto appears: And, indeed, on that Account, I thought of trying whether the Substance of these and other Observations, to the same Effect, might not be drawn into a lesser Compass. But I quitted that Design upon considering, that an Author's Sense may be misrepresented or weakened by another, even without any Design to do it. On which Account those Readers who desire to form an impartial Judgment, and may not have an Opportunity to see the Author's Book, will probably chuse to have his Sentiments expressed in his own Words. I beg Leave therefore, to proceed with them, as they immediately follow those cited above, and are indeed, a proper Illustration to them.

"The *Indian* Prince, says our Author, Page 179, who refused to believe the first Relations concerning the Effects of Frost, reasoned justly; and it naturally *required very strong Testimony to engage his Assent* to Facts which arose from a State of Nature with which he was unacquainted, and bore so little Analogy to those Events of which he had had constant and uniform Experience. Though they were *not contrary to his Experience, they were not conformable to it.*

But in order to increase the Probability against the Testimony of Witnesses, let us suppose, that the Fact which they endeavour to establish, instead of being only Marvellous, is really Miraculous; and suppose also that the Testimony considered apart, and in itself, amounts to an entire Proof; in that Case, there is Proof against Proof, of which the strongest must prevail, but still with a Diminution of its Force in Proportion to that of its Antagonist."

And now, at length, we come to that important Argument for which all great Preparation has been made. "A Miracle," says our Author, Page 180,

"is a Violation of the Laws of Nature; and as a *firm and unalterable Experience has established those Laws*, the Proof, from the very Nature of the Fact, is as entire as any Argument from Experience can possibly be imagined. And Page 181, there must be an *uniform Experience against every miraculous Event*, otherwise the Event would not merit that Appellation. And as an *uniform Experience amounts to a Proof*, there is here a direct and full *Proof* from the Nature of the Fact against the Existence of any Miracle; nor can such a Proof be destroyed, or the Miracle rendered credible, but by an opposite Proof that is superior."

In order to judge of the Force of this Argument, the first Thing to be considered is, what the Author means by saying that *a firm and unalterable Experience has established the Laws of Nature*. Does he mean that our constant Experience assures us what Laws are *actually settled* for the general Order and Government of the material World? Or does he mean that the same Experience assures us that those Laws are *so absolutely fixed* that they never can be suspended for any Time, or on any Occasion? His speaking of an Experience not only firm, but even *unalterable*, seems to imply that the *latter* was his Opinion. For if our Experience be strictly speaking unalterable, the Laws of Nature themselves must be so too, at least during our Time; and he could not well think that they are more unalterable in this Age, than they have been, and will continue to be in all others. Now if he meant that those Laws are unalterable at all Times, and could make good his Assertion, there would need no other Proof against the Possibility of Miracles. For if the Laws of Nature were *unalterably fixed*, the Consequence is plain, that every Miracle, which implies at least a temporary Suspension of those Laws, or an Effect contrary to them, would be impossible. But I think this can hardly be our Author's Meaning; because a Person of his Capacity must have seen that our Experience cannot be a sufficient Proof that the Laws of Nature are unalterably fixed. It does, indeed, prove that certain Laws are settled by God for the Government of the material World, and that they are highly expedient to it. From whence it is certain that he will not alter nor break in upon them without some Reason of great Importance. But that he will never suspend those Laws on any Occasion, nor permit that any other invisible Beings should ever act so as to interrupt them in their ordinary Course, our Experience is far from being able to prove; unless it could discover that either he has made an absolute Decree against all such Proceedings, or that they must have Consequences some Way repugnant to his Perfections; both which, are Discoveries that neither our Experience, nor even our Reason will ever make.

Indeed, Mr. *Hume* appears to have been so far sensible of this, that he does not attempt to prove directly against the *Possibility* of any Miracle considered in itself, but only against the *Possibility* of its being *sufficiently proved by any human Testimony.* This latter Point he knew would serve his Purpose as well as the former, and he thought it might be more easily maintained. He therefore attempts it by comparing our Experience upon which the Credibility of human Testimony depends, with an opposite Experience which he supposes us to have against Miracles; and imagining that this latter Experience is much the more uniform and constant of the two, he, according to his Rule before laid down, that in our Judgments of Things we are to be governed by our strongest Experience, determines that Miracles can never be rendered credible by any human Testimony whatever.

But in order to see the Weakness of this reasoning, let us enquire what the Author means by *Experience against Miracles.* The Word Experience supposes the Existence present or past, of some Facts or Events as the Objects of it; for Experience of Things that have never been, is a Contradiction in the Terms, and therefore it cannot be properly said that we have had, or can have, any *Experience against Miracles.* Mr. *Hume* perhaps will say, that an Experience of the unvaried Continuance of the Laws of Nature is, in Effect, the same Thing as an Experience against Miracles, though the latter Expression may not be quite proper. I answer, that it is not the same Thing as to the Force of his Argument; for *that* requires an Experience which can yield such an *Evidence against Miracles* as may justly be Opposed to, and in Strength will exceed the *Evidence for them,* which arises from the Credibility of human Testimony grounded on Experience. But our Experience of the unvaried Continuance of the Laws of Nature cannot yield any such Evidence against Miracles; for, as I have before said, it can only prove that no Miracles have been in our Time. But from thence it does not follow, nor can it possibly by this Medium be proved, that no Miracles have been, or can be, at all. Now, if our Experience, with regard to Miracles, is no Proof that there cannot be any such, then this Experience can neither be superior in Strength, nor be any way *Opposed,* to the Experience for the Credibility of human Testimony, which affirms that there have been frequent Miracles. And if our Experience for the Credibility of human Testimony be *not Exceeded,* nor even *Opposed* by any other Experience with regard to Miracles, then, the former of these Experiences remains, in its full Strength, on Behalf of the Credibility of human Testimony with regard to Miracles. From whence it follows that when that Testimony is given by Persons fitly qualified, by their Knowledge, and their Veracity, we ought to believe it with regard to Miracles as well as to other more common Events.

Mr. *Hume* allows this to be true, in the Case of the *Indian* Prince above-mentioned, with regard to the Accounts given him of the Effects of Frosts in cold Climates. That Prince might have argued against the Credibility of those Accounts, exactly as our Author does against the Credibility of Miracles. He might have alledged his own Experience, and that of all other Persons in his Country, to prove that the Fluidity of Water was a constant unvaried Phænomenon or Law of Nature. It had never been known to become a solid Body, on which Men, unsupported by any thing else, might walk without sinking; nor did it seem *capable* of becoming such a one. Now this their constant Experience about it, was of much greater Force to prove that it never could become solid, than any human Testimony, the Credibility of which is grounded on a *lesser* Experience, could be to prove that it ever *had been* solid: And therefore, this Prince, according to Mr. *Hume*'s Way of Reasoning, might have justly refused to believe that Water had ever been actually frozen into a solid Body, though this Fact had been affirmed to him by any Persons, however numerous, or however great seeming Probity.

Yet this Author intimates plainly enough, that *very strong Testimony might justly* have engaged the Prince's Assent to these Accounts of the Effects of Frost: For though they were not conformable to his Experience, *yet they were not contrary to it*. The last Expression, as it came from Mr. *Hume*, has, indeed, a little different Turn, but is, in effect, the same with *this*. And his Observation is certainly right; for the Prince neither had had, nor could have, any Experience that Water could not be frozen to Solidity. All that his Experience amounted to, was, that Water *had never been* actually solid, within his Knowledge or Observation; but this was no Proof from Experience that it could not ever have been so. There was no Experience in this Case that *could be Opposed* to the Experience for the Credibility of human Testimony. And therefore such Testimony, when strong, as it ought to be, in Proportion to the extraordinary Nature of the Fact related, must remained in its full genuine Force, and was therefore justly credible, and capable of rendering the Fact related credible to the Prince. Now as Mr. *Hume* saw the Justness of this Reasoning in the Case before us, so he ought to have seen it, with regard to the Credibility of *Miracles* upon sufficient human Testimony. For the Reasoning is exactly the same in both. There is *no more Experience* to any one *against Miracles*, than there was to the *Indian* Prince *against the Effects of Frost*. And since there is no such *Experience* to be *Opposed* to that *Experience*, upon which the Credibility of human Testimony is grounded, that Testimony ought to have its *full Force* in the Proof of *Miracles*, as well as of any other Events.

Having made these Remarks upon the only Argument which Mr. *Hume* has urged against Miracles in the first Part of his Essay, I proceed to the second, in which we meet with another Argument of the like Kind, in the following Words: "There is no Testimony," says he, Page 190,

> "for any Prodigies, even those which have not been expressly detected that is not opposed by an infinite Number of Witnesses; so that not only the Miracle destroys the Credit of the Testimony, but even the Testimony destroys itself. To make this the better understood, let us consider that in Matters of Religion whatever is *different* is *contrary*, and that it is impossible that the Religions of ancient *Rome*, of *Turkey*, or *Siam*, and of *China* should all of them be established on any solid Foundation; every Miracle therefore pretended to have been wrought in any of these Religions, (and all of them abound in Miracles) as its direct Scope, is to establish the particular System to which it is attributed, so it has the same Force, though more indirectly, to overthrow every other System; in destroying a rival System, it likewise destroys the Credit of those Miracles on which that System was established; so that all the Prodigies of different Religions are to be considered as contrary Facts, and the Evidences of these Prodigies whether weak or strong, as opposite to each other. According to this Method of reasoning, when we believe any Miracle of *Mohamet* or any of his Successors, we have for our Warrant the Testimony of a few barbarous *Arabians*, and on the other Side, we are to regard the Authority of *Titus Livius*, *Plutarch*, *Tacitus*, and in short, of all the Authors and Witnesses *Grecian*, *Chinese*, and *Roman-Catholick*, who have related any Miracle in their particular Religion, I say, we are to regard their Testimony in the same Light as if they had mentioned that *Mahometan* Miracle, and had in express Terms contradicted it with the same Certainty as they have for the Miracles they relate. This Argument may appear over subtle and refined; but it is not in Reality different from the reasoning of a Judge, who supposes that the Credit of two Witnesses maintaining a Crime against any one, is destroyed by the Testimony of two others who affirm him to have been two hundred Leagues distant at the same instant when the Crime is said to have been committed."

At the Beginning of this Argument there are some Propositions about which I shall not dispute with the Author: They are, First, That in Religion whatever is different is contrary, and that, therefore no two opposite Religions can be both of them true. Secondly, That every Miracle wrought in Support of any Religion, not only tends directly to prove the Truth of that Religion, but also tends though more indirectly, to disprove all other Religions. Thirdly, That every Miracle, while it tends to disprove the

Truth of any different Religion, does likewise disprove the Truth of all the Miracles pretended to have been wrought on Behalf of that Religion. The last of these Propositions indeed, ought not to have been advanced without some Proof; for the Author must have known that both the *Jewish* and *Christian* Religions[82] suppose that some Miracles have been, and may be wrought in Religions opposite to them; and of consequence, must suppose, that their own Miracles do not effectually disprove the Reality of those other Miracles. The Reasons they give why God sometimes permits Miracles to be wrought in false Religions, are, that he does it to try the good dispositions of Men in the true one, and to put them upon a more careful Examination of the Nature and external Evidences of it; which Reasons this Author would not have been able to confute; and on that Account, perhaps has declined to consider them, as he likewise has forborne attempting to prove that all Miracles in opposite Religions *are incompatible with each other*; though this is the necessary foundation upon which his present Argument is raised, and without it, must immediately fall to the Ground.

However, that we may see what a Structure he can make if this Foundation be allowed, let us pass over his third Proposition as well as the two former without any Dispute. Now his reasoning from them is to this Effect: Because the Testimony for the Miracles in any Religion tends to disprove, as far as it can, all the Testimonies for the Miracles in every one of the different Religions, the Consequence is, that the Testimony in Behalf of the Miracles in every particular Religion is opposed by an *infinite* Number of Witnesses, whose Testimony being very much stronger than the Testimony for the Miracles in any such particular Religion can be; on this Account, no Testimony of this Kind can ever make the Miracles pretended to have been wrought in any such Religion be justly credible. To illustrate this Doctrine, our Author supposes us to have an Account of a Miracle performed by *Mahomet*, or one of his Successors; and that for our Warrant in believing it, we have the Testimony of a few barbarous *Arabians*; while, on the other Hand, we have, against it, the Authority of *Titus Livius, Plutarch, Tacitus*, and in short, of all the Authors and Witnesses, *Grecian, Chinese*, and *Roman Catholic*, who have related any Miracle in their particular Religion: For the Testimony of all these, "must be regarded," says he, "in the same Light, as if they had mentioned that *Mahometan* Miracle, and had in express Terms, contradicted it, with the same Certainty, as they have for the Miracle they relate."

These Suppositions and Assertions may, at first Sight, appear very unaccountable: For how can *Livy, Plutarch* or *Tacitus* be regarded as

---

[82] See *Deuter.* xiii. 1, 2, 3. *Matt.* xxiv. 24, 25. 2 *Thess.* ii. 9, 10, 11, 12. *Rev.* xiii. 13, 14.

Witnesses against a *Mahometan* Miracle, which, if such a one had ever been, could not have been wrought till some hundreds of Years after they all were dead? Or how can even the *Grecians*, the *Chinese*, or *Roman Catholics* be considered as giving Testimony against the same Miracle, of which our Author does not seem to suppose that they had ever known or heard any Thing at all? But in order to do him Justice, the Reader must observe, that all these Persons are, and great Numbers of others might have been alledged as Witnesses against it, in Consequence of his Reasoning here before mentioned; which is, that because no two Miracles in different Religions can, both of them be true; therefore, the Testimony of the *Grecians*, the *Chinese*, and all the rest, for the Miracles, in their several Religions, must really opposed, and, as far as the Strength of their Evidence will go, must tend to disprove the Testimony of the *Mahometans* for the Miracle pretended to be wrought in Behalf of their Religion. And, indeed, since this Reasoning proceeds upon the Author's third Proposition at the Beginning of this Argument, which I have passed over without disputing it, I am now obliged to allow the Reasoning to be so far *conclusive* as it aims at proving that the Testimony in every particular Religion, the *Mahometan* for Instance, is virtually opposed by the Testimony for the Miracles in all other Religions, whether these latter Witnesses ever *knew* any Thing against the *Mahometan* Testimony or not.

But such a merely consequential Opposition of all the Testimonies for the Miracles in all the different Religions, will not be sufficient for our Author's Purpose of disproving the *Mahometan* Miracle. He must go somewhat further, and shew, either, first, that some one of the opposite Testimonies is really, in itself, stronger than what there is for the *Mahometan* Miracle: Or, secondly, that since all these several Testimonies, are alike virtually opposite to the Testimony for that Miracle, there may, by an Alliance or Union of them, be a Testimony formed against it, of much greater Strength than its Testimony has; and which, therefore, will destroy the Credibility of it.

Our Author seems to have declined insisting on the former of these Points; because though he might have shewn in some one of the Religions opposite to the *Mahometan*, a Miracle that had a Testimony *for it* stronger than this has; yet he might not be able to shew so much in the Case of *another* Religion which seems to have been chiefly in his View, though he would not here mention it. He could hardly hope to find in any of the Religions opposite to this latter, a Testimony superior to that by which a very remarkable Miracle in it is supported. And therefore he chose a Way of arguing that he thought would not fail to prove as well against *this* Religion, as against the *Mahometan*, and, indeed, would prove, in general, against all that pretended to be grounded on divine Revelation. To this End, he had Recourse to that *infinite Number of Witnesses* which might be drawn together from all the Religions opposite to the *Mahometan*, or to any other that he should have a Mind to disprove; in order, from this Collection of them, to make up a united or aggregate Testimony that should be plainly superior in Strength to any Testimony that could ever be alledged from the Miracles in any single Religion.

But however plausible this Scheme may have appeared to Mr. *Hume*, it is nothing but a Fallacy, and can have no Effect. We shall plainly see this, if we consider that, supposing, a Miracle related to us has been *possible* in itself, the *Credibility of the Persons* by whom it is attested, must always depend, on the Opportunities they have had to know the Nature and Circumstances of the Fact; on their Abilities to judge well of it; on their Character for Veracity, in declaring exactly whatever they know or believe about it; and on their Number and Agreement with each other. In Proportion as these Circumstances appear to have been more or less in their Case, they will be more or less credible. But whatever the Degree of their Credibility is, common Sense plainly dictates that it must depend solely *upon themselves*, and cannot be either increased or diminished by the Testimony of any other Persons who have never known or heard of the Miracle in Question, but only attest some other Miracles different in all Respects from this. The Credibility of the *Persons* who relate a Miracle supposed to have been done in *China*, can neither be impaired, nor can it be increased, by the Credibility of any other Persons who relate a Miracle done in *Italy*. As each of these Credibilities has been derived merely from the Circumstances and Dispositions peculiar to the Persons concerned in each Testimony, and who on either Side are supposed to be quite Strangers to the others, and to the Fact attested by them, it is therefore, impossible that either of these Credibilities can be rendered greater, than it is in itself, by any Conjunction it can have with the other. For no Man can imagine that personal Circumstances, Abilities, and Dispositions can be trans-ferred, or in any Degree imparted from the one Set of these distant Witnesses to the other. You might as well think of adding to a Number, by putting Cyphers to the left of it, or of lengthening a Line, by adding a Sound or a Colour to it, as of increasing the Credibility of the *Chinese* Witnesses, by adding the Credibility of the *Italians* to it.

Which Consideration plainly shews, that though indeed the Testimonies for *both* these Miracles may be, in *one Respect, opposed* to the Testimony for the *Mahometan* Miracle; yet neither of those former Testimonies can ever receive, *except in one Case only*, any increase of its Credibility from the other of them, so as that both will, on that Account, become more credible, in Opposition to the *Mahometan*, than either of them would have been alone. The case that I except is, when any of the Witnesses for each of these two opposite Miracles are supposed to have known Circumstances of the same, or a like Nature, that concern the *Mahometan*, or the

Witnesses to it; and tend to detract from the Credibility of either of them. In that Case, indeed, the Credibility of each of these two Sets of opposite Witnesses would be *increased* by the Addition of the other, considered as being *opposed*, in *Conjunction with it*, to the Testimony for the *Mahometan* Miracle: And the Credibility of this latter would be impaired more by such an Alliance or Union of those Testimonies, than by either of them singly, in Opposition to it: And so, more still, in Proportion, if there were a greater Number of Testimonies, *of this Nature*, against it.

But if no one of the opposite Witnesses declares any Thing, in particular, against the Credibility of the *Mahometan* Miracle, or appears to know any Thing of it, or of the Witnesses on its behalf; in this Case, how many soever these opposite Witnesses may be, their Number will avail nothing against it; in Regard that their Testimonies can not be united, nor their Credibility by that means, be increased. They can only act by the single Weight of each, compared, as to its Credibility, with the Testimony for that *Mahometan* Miracle. Upon which Comparison, indeed, any one of them that is found its superior in Credibility, will prevail and disprove it. But in doing this, it can receive no Advantage from the *infinite Number* of the *Witnesses* that, merely by Virtue of our Author's Reasoning, are joined with it in a virtual Opposition to that Miracle: For a Conjunction of this Sort can have no Effect at all, either upon the Credibility of the several Testimonies so drawn together, or on that of the *Mahometan* Miracle whose Testimony they oppose.

It is evident, therefore, that this supposed *infinite Number of Witnesses*, raised by Mr. *Hume*, in Opposition to that Miracle, and by a Parity of Reason, to any other which he intends to disprove, is mere Amusement. Whatever Witnesses there are who really know any Thing against such a one, they would be of as much Force as they can ever be, without this consequential joint Opposition; and those that know nothing of *this* Miracle, will do it no harm, however, great Numbers of them may be brought to make their Appearance for that Purpose. They are like separate Parties of Troops which make a great Shew in the Field of Battle, by appearing all on the same Side; but can never be drawn into one Body, nor made to charge the Enemy together, but act singly by themselves, with only their own unassisted Force; and therefore, if each of them be weaker than the Enemy, there can be no Prospect that they will ever prevail. But quitting this Simile, and the Argument itself, which I hope has been set in its proper Light; I only beg leave, on this Occasion, to make one general Remark: It is, that the Interests of Truth and Virtue, which undoubtedly are the most valuable Blessings in human Life, would be in a much better State than they are, if Men of Letters would be more cautious how they lay a Stress upon novel Arguments of their own Growth, against any Points of Moment in Religion; and especially how they, by making them public, throw them into the Hands of Persons of all Ranks, who are Dabblers in Reading. There are, in the present Age, great Numbers of People who answer to the Character given by St. *Paul*,[83] 2 Tim. iii. 7. *That they are ever Learning, and never able to come to the Knowledge of the Truth*; because indeed they are not disposed[84] to receive it. These Persons are always ready to be taken by any new Conceit, especially if it be to the Disadvantage of Religion. But to consider, with proper Care, what is said in answer to such Objections, is a Talk for which they seldom have any Inclination, or at least not enough to make them go through with it; and so, the ill Impressions they have received continue upon them: Their Faith is subverted, and their Morals often ruined in consequence of it.

This was an Effect that generally followed upon the sceptical Discourses of some Philosophers among the *Greeks*, in Opposition to the great Principles of Religion and Morality. *Socrates*[85] observed it with very much Concern; and accordingly declared, that every one ought to be extremely cautious how he treated Points of such high Importance, especially in publick. And he himself gave an Example of it, expressing great Diffidence of his own Abilities when he was to speak of the *chief Good*,[86] of the Nature of the *supreme Being*, or of any other such Subjects. And in Pursuance of his Advice, one of his Friends, before he entered on a Discourse of this Nature, expressed himself in these following Terms. ΘΕΟΝ – ΣΩΤΗΡΑ, ἐξἀτόπου κὶ ἀήθους δεηγήσεως, πρός τὸ τῶν ἐικότων δόγμα διασώζειν ἡμᾶ, ἐπικαλεσάμενοι, πάλιν ἀρχόμεθα λέγειν.[87] *Plat. in Timæ*, p. 1059. If some of our modern Authors had taken a Course like this, before they fate themselves to write or publish their Thoughts upon Matters of Religion, the World perhaps would not have been troubled with so many of their crude and false Notions; which, though sufficiently answered, have yet had a pernicious Effect in corrupting the Principles and Morals of our Nation.

---

[83] *Terence* describes such People with some Humour, in prolog. *Andr. Faciunt næ intellegendo ut nihil intellegant.* They really come to understand so, as to know nothing of the Matter.

[84] *Socrates* used to say, as *Tully* quotes with Approbation, *de Orat.* lib. i. *Quibus id persuasum est ut nihil mallent se esse quam Bonos Viros, iis reliquam facilem esse [Virtutis] Doctrinam.* They who have nothing more at heart than to be Good Men, will easily learn the Way to be so. One sees how agreeable this Observation, made by two of the greatest Men among the antient Heathens, is to what was delivered afterwards by the highest Authority, *John* vii. 17. *If any Man will do His [God's] Will, he shall know of the Doctrine, whether it be of God, or whether I speak of myself.*

[85] *Plato, de Repub.* lib. vii. p. 708. Edit: Francof. M.DC.II.

[86] *Plat. de Repub.* lib. vi. p. 506.

[87] *After an address to* God the Saviour, *that he will preserve us from saying any thing absurd or immoral, [and lead us] to fit Opinions of Things, we begin again to speak.*

But to return from this Digression to Mr. *Hume* and his Essay, I have considered all that Part of it which contains any Argument; the rest of it consists either of Assertions destitute of Proofs, or of Observations from which nothing can be justly concluded, and which tend to nothing but to raise undue Prejudices in the Minds of weak Readers. Of this latter Kind are our Author's Observations, from Page 184 to Page 199. He acquaints us in a great Number of Words, that Men are generally apt to be pleased at hearing extraordinary and wonderful Things; that some may be Enthusiasts; others may think they do right in telling Lies for the Advantage of their Religion; Vanity and Interest may be to others, their Motives for endeavouring its Propagation; they may be encouraged in attempting to do it by the Credulity and Weakness of those Persons to whom they apply. That if they have Eloquence, Craft and Address, they may be likely to work upon illiterate and barbarous People, as *Lucian*'s *Alexander* did on the *Paphlagonians*. That Accounts of Miracles have chiefly abounded among ignorant and barbarous Nations, and after they have received there for some Time, it has been difficult to detect the Falsity of them; that Men are disposed to say Things, which tend to the Honour of their own Country or Families; that if they have Opportunities, they may easily be tempted to assume the high Character of Missionaries from Heaven; and when they have done so, may bear many Distresses in order to maintain it.

Most of these Observations, may in some Cases, have been true. But what just Consequences can be drawn from them against the Credibility of *all* human Testimony when alledged in Proof of Miracles? If *some* Men be weak or ill-disposed, must *all* therefore be so? Were there never any Men of good Sense or Probity? Is there not very great Reason to believe that some such there have been in every Age, as there are in the present? Have not indisputable Proofs been given by Witnesses, in some Cases, of their Integrity, their good Judgment, and their perfect Knowledge of the Things they related? If these Facts are beyond Question, what Advantage can our Author gain, by observing that there have also been great Numbers of *Knaves* and *Fools* in the World? His Design is to insinuate, that the *Witnesses* to *all* the *Religions* that have pretended to be divine Revelations, were Persons of one or other of the last mentioned Characters. But every Eye must be able to discern that there is not the least Consequence in this Sort of Reasoning, which really does not deserve that Name.

And this Author's *Assertions* are not better grounded; of which we have an Instance in Page 183. He affirms, "that there is not to be found in all History, any Miracle attested by a sufficient Number of Men, and with such other Circumstances as are requisite to give us a full Assurance of the Truth of their Testimony." This is an Assertion which is hardly *capable* of a *due Proof*. For in order to a compleat one, this Author is obliged to consider and disprove *all* the several Evidences that have ever been given for *all* the

Miracles of which we have any Account. And this, I think, he has hardly yet done, or is likely to do soon. At least in this Essay, he has not attempted any Thing material to this Purpose. His Assertion remains entirely *unproved*, and therefore, cannot, with Reason, be allowed any Weight.

However, as it is an express Declaration of his own Opinion about the Testimony for *all Miracles*, which, without any Exception, he reckons insufficient to prove, or render them credible; we may from thence be led to ask, For *what Purpose* he has mentioned the Miracle related by *Tacitus*, as having been wrought by the elder *Vespasian*; or the marvellous Creation of a new Leg, to a Man at *Saragossa*, by the Use of the holy Oil; of the numerous Miracles ascribed by the *French* Jansenists to their *Abbè Paris*? Since *he* plainly looked upon all these, as false Stories and Impostures, why did he trouble his Readers with Accounts of them? I must be so free as to tell Mr. *Hume*, that the Respect due to *Mankind*, and much more to GOD and his sacred Truth, ought to hinder an Author from publishing any Thing, especially on Subjects that concerns Religion, but what he either knows, or on reasonable Grounds, believes to be true. He ought not to make Use of that very unfair, though sometimes indeed too effectual Method, of raising *Prejudices* in weak Minds, against a Thing which cannot, by Reason, be confuted. If he thinks that the Testimony given for the *Mosaic* or the *Christian* Miracles is not sufficient to satisfy any reasonable Man, let him endeavour to disprove both it and them. To those Objections which he has raised against the History of *Moses*, let him add what others he can find or Form of a more solid Kind. But let him not take the low Way of *insinuating*, quite without Proof, that the Evidence for the Miracles of *Moses* and of *Christ* is not at all better than what has been given for those other Miracles that he has mentioned; which is plainly his Design in relating, with such an Air as he does, those notable Stories. There is no Sort of Reasoning, or Justness of Consequence in such Comparisons or Insinuations. They tend only to raise Prejudices against the Truth, and to throw discolouring Lights upon it. They are therefore, unworthy of any Man who pretends to Religion, or even to ordinary Probity and Candour.

Which Censure I must, with Concern, affirm, is yet more due to that Treatment almost beyond Parallel, which is given, soon after, *more openly*, by this Author, to the *Christian* Religion and to all who believe it. At the 202d Page, he briefly resumes the Arguments, by which he has attempted to prove, that "no Evidence for any Miracle can amount to a Probability, much less to a Proof; and that, even supposing it amounted to a Proof, it would be opposed by another Proof derived from the very Nature of the Fact, which it would endeavour to establish, *&c.*" After which, he insists on his Conclusion, and even establishes it as a *Maxim*, that no human Testimony can have such Force as to prove a Miracle, and make it a just Foundation for any System of Religion, And "he is the better pleased," he says, Page 204, "with his own Reasoning, as he thinks it may serve to confound those dangerous Friends or disguised Enemies to the *Christian* Religion who have undertaken to defend it by the Principles of human Reason." He himself affirms, "that *our most holy Religion* is founded in *Faith, not in Reason*, and that it is a sure Method of *exposing it*, to put it to such a Trial as it is by no Means fitted to endure." His Meaning is, that *they* will indeed *effectually expose it* who aim at proving, by the *Means* of *credible Testimony*, that the Miracles said to have been wrought on its Behalf, were rational and sufficient Proofs that it came from God. For that, he pretends, is a Thing to be received by Faith alone, without any Proof or Reason whatsoever.

Yet presently afterwards, in Page 207, this Author Affirms, "that the *Christian* Religion was not only at *first attended with Miracles*, but even at this Day cannot be believed by any reasonable Person without one. Mere Reason is insufficient to convince us of its Veracity; and whosoever is moved by Faith, to assent to it, is conscious of a *continued Miracle in his own Person*." Does there not appear to be some Inconsistency in these Declarations? No. He represents very plainly, all those who at first embraced what he calls, with a Sneer, *our most holy* Religion, or who now believe it, since they must do it entirely *without Reason*, "*to have subverted all the Principles of their Understanding*," and says, "that by believing what is most *contrary to Custom and Experience*, they are Instances of *Miracles in their own Persons*." Now what *other Miracles* could *he* think *these* to be, after what he has said through the whole Course of this Essay, but *prodigious Effects* of Credulity and Folly?

These last indeed, are not *his* Words; but that they express his real Sense, an impartial Reader will easily perceive: And when such a one considers by WHOM, in this Nation, the *Christian* Religion is publickly established, as well as professed, he will know what to think of an Author, who *could* treat THEM in such a Manner; and make such an Use of the valuable Liberty they are pleased to allow Men of publishing their Thoughts on Religion itself, as well as on all other Matters of Importance. He will not think it strange if a Person so disposed, should not be affected either with the Doctrines of the *Christian* Religion, or the Evidences for it. Nor if another, to whom the Promises of the Gospel are Objects of very pleasing Hopes, should have shewn some Concern for its Vindication, when it has received such unworthy Treatment.

The END

8
GEORGE ANDERSON

[George Anderson], *An estimate of the profit and loss of religion personally and publicly stated: illustrated with references to Essays on morality and natural religion*. Edinburgh: 1753, iv, 392 p.
Selections from Section 6; from 1753 edition.

George Anderson (1676–1757) had been an army chaplain and was later master at Watson's Hospital in Edinburgh. In the last few years of his life, Anderson and others made a concerted effort to have the Church of Scotland excommunicate Hume and Henry Home, later Lord Kames. Anderson's *Estimate* consists of eleven religious and moral essays, most of which contain criticisms of Kames's *Essays on the Principles of Morality and Natural Religion* (1751), with occasional parallels from "his assistant" Hume – specifically from Hume's two *Enquiries* and *Political Discourses*. In view of the fact that Kames published his work anonymously, Anderson dubs Kames "Sopho" after Sophos, the wise, dropping the final "s" to avoid "a disagreeable hissing". Other writers followed Anderson's convention by referring to Kames as "Sopho". In Section 6 Anderson examines Kames's and Hume's attacks on theistic arguments; he focuses on Hume's "Of a Particular Providence" and Kames's gloss on Hume (selections from Kames are contained earlier in this volume). Contrary to Hume, Anderson argues that we may infer beyond the imperfections of the world to a perfect cause since "there must be more perfection in the cause than in the effect". Further, according to Anderson, creating something from nothing is an infinite obstacle, which requires an infinitely perfect cause. Although a conservative evangelical, Anderson was far more widely read in philosophy than most of his associates. Anderson's *Estimate* was favourably reviewed in the *Monthly Review*; for excerpts from this and a discussion of Hume's reaction to Anderson see *Early Responses to Hume's Moral, Literary, and Political Writings*. The following is from the 1753 and only edition of Anderson's *Estimate*.

SECT. VI.
Arguments for the Being of GOD, *supported against* MODERN EXCEPTIONS.

...

DAVID HUME, Esq; in his eleventh essay concerning human understanding, hath said that we have no foundation for ascribing any attribute to the Deity, but what is precisely commensurate with the imperfection of the world. For the improvement of this, SOPHO says,

"That, supposing reason to be our only guide in these matters, which is supposed by this philosopher in his argument, I cannot help seeing his reason to be just. It appears to be true, that by no inference of reason, can I conclude any power or benevolence in the cause, beyond what is displayed in the effect. But this is no wonderful discovery. The philosopher might have carried his argument a greater length. – There is still a wider step, which is, that reason will not help me out in attributing to the Deity even that precise degree of power, intelligence, and benevolence, which appears in his workmanship. I find no inconsistency that a blind and undesigning cause may be productive of excellent effects. It will, I presume, be difficult to produce a demonstration to the contrary. And, supposing, at the instant of operation, the Deity to have been endued with these properties, can we make out, by any argument *a priori*, that they are still subsisting in him? Nay, the same philosopher might have gone a great way further, by observing, when any thing comes into existence, that, by no process of reasoning, can we so much as infer any cause of its existence."[88]

Upon perusing these passages, one might be apt to think that they had been collected from different authors, and of very different principles: And, if they were the production of one head, they must have come forth at different times, and in different seasons of life; some in the beginning, and some in the decay, of understanding. And, if they do proceed from a man in the maturity of his judgment, it must have been when his thoughts, like the epicurean and lucretian atoms, run at random in to endless contradictions. Tho' these contradictions are obvious to the attentive reader, yet, since there may be headless readers, as well as false and deceitful writers, I think it my duty, not to pass them over without some particular observations; and the rather, because all the arguments for the being and attributes of ALMIGHTY GOD are resolved and dissolved into *sense* and *feeling*. What I have already said, and what every reader must observe, gives me a right to conclude that SOPHO's *feelings* are only a *salvo* for

[88] Page 355.

something not yet to be named. It is as the shiboleth, or as the mason word, among a certain set of men.

SOPHO makes the knowledge of the Deity both natural and easy. Though it is not *solely* founded on reason, yet, from the effect, he concludes a cause; but this, he says, he doth not by reasoning, but merely by perception and feeling. By the word *solely* he reserves a place for reason, and immediately fills it up with *perception* and *feeling*. For, as it is merely by feeling, it is neither, in whole or in part, owing to reason, that we come to the knowledge of the Deity. *We discover his Being and attributes in the same manner we discover external objects.* Well said! We discover external objects by our external senses: and, if it is true that SOPHO hath discovered GOD the same way, how is it possible the most solitary savage can be ignorant of this great and good and glorious truth? This is altogether inconsistent with his assertion, that it is to society we owe all the blessings of life, and particularly the knowledge of the Deity. But how are savages disciplined into the belief of a divine Being without reasoning? In their savage state, they had the use of all the external senses, and, in some cases, they had the exercise of their reason; they consulted with themselves, and made choice of the proper means for the preservation of life, and for the gratification of their desires. And, in their social capacity and state, if reason is laid aside, they will have as few means of coming to the knowledge of GOD, as they had before.

A thing, saith SOPHO, that can be conceived, can never be proved inconsistent or impossible. And it is in his power to conceive, but it is not in his power to believe. To conceive that a fine piece of painting, a well wrote poem, etc. may be the effect of chance or blind fatality, is possible; but it is not in his power to believe, that this *can ever* be the effect of chance or blind fatality. If he cannot believe his own conceptions, how can he believe any thing? Sure, what he conceives, he considers as possible, and yet this possibility cannot be; and, what cannot be, is impossible. I acknowledge that many things are possible, that are not actually in being; for possibilities are infinite. But, to assert that a thing possible cannot be, is to make *possible* and *impossible* the same.

The possibility of chance or blind fatality being the cause of the most curious and exquisite productions, is limited by Sopho with *so far* as *we can discover*, and *for any reason we have to the contrary*. But such reserves, in the case of *possible* and *impossible,* are highly impertinent. What, to my judgment, doth not involve an inconsistency, must, in my judgment, be consistent, and consequently possible. And, as I judge by my own ideas or perceptions, if I know them, (and, every one must know his own, or he hath none); I must conclude and determine peremptorily. His blind chance or fatality, with this qualification, *so far as he knows*, being the cause of exquisite productions, amounts only to this, that he knows nothing of the matter. Of this blind and undesigning cause we hear again in the forecited passages, which I shall very soon take into consideration.

SOPHO, who plays fast and loose with reason, attempts to prove the existence of the Deity from the principles which he both acknowledges and denies. He says that he hath made out, first, that every thing, that hath a beginning, is perceived as a production or an effect. Secondly, that, we necessarily ascribe to the cause whatever a contrivance or design is discovered in the effect. If the production or effect exceeds the known powers and faculties of man, we determine upon some superior power.

"Attend, saith he, to the anatomy of the meanest plant, so much of the art and curious mechanism is discovered in it, that it must be the production of some cause far surpassing the power and intelligence of man. The scene opens more and more, when, passing from plants to animals, we come at last to man, the most wonderful of all the works of nature. And when at last we take in at one view the material and moral world, full of harmony, order and beauty, happily adjusted in all its parts to answer great and glorious purposes, there is in this grand production *necessarily* involved the perception of a cause unbounded in power, intelligence and goodness."[89]

Ever since logic was logic, such discourse hath past for a piece of reasoning. There are premisses laid down, and a conclusion drawn from them, and that in the strongest terms. *There is in this grand production necessarily involved the perception of a cause.* All necessary conclusions are demonstrations; because the highest evidence, that can be given, or required. "The Deity cannot be long a secret to those who are accustomed to any degree of reflexion." But there is no reflexion without reasoning; and therefore, by reason, we come to the knowledge of the Deity. Sopho, notwithstanding, by one of his usual axioms, says, "And this we do, not by any process of reasoning, but merely by perception and feeling."[90] Never did a reasonable man treat reason with so much rudeness and contempt!

After he had stated and formed his argument for the being of God, from the production of the material and moral world, he demolishes that and all arguments *a posteriori*; "for they are generally defective. There is always wanting one link in the chain." And, if there is *always* wanting one link in the chain, they are not only *generally*, but *always* defective; and this defect is, "That by no process of reasoning, can we demonstrate this proposition to be true, that order and beauty must needs proceed from a designing cause. For, reason cannot make out, that the thing which we name an effect, may not exist of itself, as well as what we name a cause."

[89] Page 327.

[90] Page 328.

The propositions which he says he hath made out, (and he must have made them out by reason and argument), and upon which the grand argument *a posteriori* is founded, are, that every thing that begins to be must be an effect, that every effect must have a cause, and that to the cause we transfer all the contrivance and design that is to be found in the effect. With this, reason, saith he, hath nothing to do; "For, laying aside perception and feeling, I should be utterly at a loss, by any sort of reasoning, to conclude the existence of any one thing, from the existence of *any* other thing."[91]

That he should be at a loss to make out this proposition, is not surprizing: for, I believe, never one attempted to prove the existence of a thing, from the existence of any other thing; for that is equivalent to this universal proposition, *every thing infers the existence of all things*. But, I am at no loss to prove the existence of some certain cause, from the existence of any effect; but if, in complaisance to the author, I should lay aside perception (for feelings, he says, are deceitful, and, for that and other reasons, should be laid aside); I acknowledge I can prove nothing: apprehension, perception, and idea, are used by philosophers old and new, to signify the first and simplest operation of the understanding; lay aside then perception and understanding, and sure I am, that SOPHO, with all his acuteness, can understand and demonstrate nothing.

If "reason cannot make out, that the thing we name an effect, may not exist of itself, as well as what we name a cause;" it must be, because we cannot distinguish the one from the other. And, in this case, I must conclude, that SOPHO and I are both of us very unfit for essays on morality and natural religion. I am well convinced that SOPHO himself is an effect; for an effect is what begins to be: and he hath not always been, as can be proved from the parish-register of births and baptisms. An effect he is, with respect to an anterior cause, and all backwards are effects as he is, until we come to the first cause, a self existent and uncaused Being.

His most formidable and his final attack upon all arguments *a posteriori* for the being of GOD, is to be found in his improvement of an exception, suggested by a writer near as wonderful as himself. The exception is, that we have no foundation for ascribing any attribute to the Deity, but what is commensurate with the imperfection of the world; but neither he nor his author had any right to put the argument in the mouth of an *Epicurean*; for *Epicurus* believed not the gods either made or meddled with the world. However SOPHO approves of the argument so far as it goes, and wonders he did not carry it a greater length; I take upon me to say, with or without their leave, that *David Hume*, Esq; hath carried it too far; for there may, and there must be more perfection in the cause than in the effect: for instance, when I perceive a piece of marble, cut into the form of a human

---

[91] Page 337.

head, I immediately conclude that the artificer was himself not such a blockhead. A fine piece of painting, a picture drawn to the life, is far from being equal in perfection to the painter: the workmanship is an evidence that the workman is the more excellent being. This, with respect to the power and knowledge of man, will pass without being quarrelled. But, when from this we ascend to the harmony, beauty, and order of the universe, to conclude the unbounded power, wisdom and goodness, of the supreme cause; SOPHO retracts his concession, and will not allow that reason can help him out in attributing to the Deity, even that precise degree of power, intelligence and benevolence, which appears in his workmanship: because he finds no inconsistency that a blind and unintelligent cause may be productive of excellent effects. But my reason helps me to find out, that this is a mistake of the case, as stated by his author, and by himself. For, after supposing a production to be the work of the Deity, he cannot assign it to a blind and unintelligent cause. Whatever effects this blind and undesigning cause may produce, it produces none of these that are the workmanship of the Deity; and he hath not yet said that the Deity is a blind and undesigning cause. He next supposes, though, at the instant of the operation, the Deity might have possessed those properties; he then asks, if, by any arguments *a priori*, it can be made out that they still subsist in him. Because, I believe, he is the first that ever asked the question, it were a pity to send him far for an answer: I therefore refer him to himself, where he proves that GOD is a necessary and self-existent being; and therefore, the same from everlasting to everlasting. Though he hath said, and said again, and laid it down as one of his principles, that, whatever begins to be, must have a cause; still, for fear the argument *a posteriori* should take place, he concludes his improvement, "Nay, the same philosopher might have gone a greater way further, by observing, that when any thing comes into existence, that by no process of reasoning can we so much as infer any cause of its existence." Had *David Hume*, Esq; made this observation, he must have made it against his supposition, that the world is the workmanship of God.

But this poor tale, which in this place is not to the purpose, is not a whit the better for being twice told. That nothing can begin to be without a cause, is in itself so evident, that it needs no proof: and he that wants a proof, cannot understand it when finished; as appears by SOPHO's misrepresenting what Mr. *Locke* and Dr. *Clark* have said upon the subject. The gentleman hath adopted it as one of his first principles, "that the force of our conclusions from beauty and order is not from reason, but from inward light, which shews things in their relation of cause and effect." If this is true, then it is a certain, and self evident truth, that, whatever comes into existence, must have a cause; and this rather supports than destroys the argument *a posteriori*.

The Esquire's *hypothesis*, is, that admitting the world to be the workmanship of GOD, and that it is proved by an argument *a posteriori*, and that we know no more of him than what is discovered by this grand production, such as it is; we have no foundation for ascribing any attribute to the Deity, but what is precisely commensurate with the imperfection of the world. It is scarcely to be imagined, that his meaning is that; for all that we can learn from this discovery, we cannot say that GOD is more perfect than his work: I rather suppose that he means that this cannot afford us reason to conclude any perfection in the Maker of the world, but what follows from this single operation. To which I say, first, that, it is not *only* from the works of GOD, that we know him; but that there are other arguments, and other ways, whereby the divine Being is made manifest to us. Secondly, that, admitting the works of the Deity to be the only way we arrive at the knowledge of him, even such a knowledge will furnish us with proof of his infinite perfection.

A curious piece of clock-work is an evidence that the artificer was a man of understanding, and a being as far superior to the machine, as the rational exceeds the mere material part of the universe: then it follows, that he that made the clock-maker, must, in proportion (if proportion can take place) surpass the artificer in perfection. Part of him GOD hath made without materials, by bestowing upon him reason and understanding. But, to make a thing without materials, is immediate creation. It is raising a new being out of nothing; which, in my conception, is an act of greater power than to form the sun, moon, and stars, and this earth, from pre-existent matter; and a greater power cannot be conceived, and therefore we must conclude it infinite. Betwixt *being* and *nothing*, there is an infinite distance, and, to commensurate which, infinite power is necessary. A limited power can never surmount an infinite obstruction.

It follows, from the world's being the work of GOD, that he is the first cause, and consequently a necessary, eternal, and self-existent Being. A self-existent Being is a self-sufficient Being; and therefore he is infinite in duration, and infinite in happiness: and that Being, to which any infinite attribute belongs, must be possessed of all perfection, because nothing can be both finite and infinite.

...

9
GEORGE PSALMANAZAR

[George Psalmanazar], *Essays on the following subjects: I. On the reality and evidence of miracles, ... Written some years since, ... By an obscure layman in town.* London: printed for A. Millar, 1753, xxxi, [1], 360 p.
Essay 1, Letter 1, complete; from 1753 edition.

George Psalmanazar (1679?–1763) is the assumed name of a French author who spent much of his life in London. His most noted work is *An Historical and Geographical Description of Formosa* (1704); his *Memoirs* appeared a year after his death. In the Preface to his anonymously published *Essays*, Psalmanazar explains that the five essays in this work were originally part of a series of letters that he wrote a few years earlier. The letters, he notes, aimed to defend a young clergyman who was being ridiculed by several of his sceptical neighbours. The first letter of the first essay defends biblical accounts of miracles against attacks by Hume. Psalmanazar argues that Hume does not give adequate weight to testimonies of the biblical miracles, and gives too much weight to our supposedly constant experience. He also criticizes Hume's "Of a Particular Providence" for limiting divine attributes to what falls within our observation. Writing for the *Monthly Review*, William Rose praises Psalmanazar's work as a whole:

> In the essays now before us, the learned author has shewn an extensive acquaintance with the laws and policy of the *Jews*, and thrown new light on most of the subjects treated in them.

As to Letter 1, Rose finds Psalmanazar's efforts less original than other parts of the work:

> As he has scarce advanced any thing new in this part of his work, we shall not detain our readers with any abstract of what he has said, and shall only acquaint them, that he has fairly represented the arguments urged by the deists against miracles, and given, in our opinion, a clear and satisfactory answer to them. [*Monthly Review*, November 1753, Vol. 9, pp. 321–330]

The following is from the 1753 and only edition of Psalmanazar's *Essays*.

ESSAY I.

LETTER I.

On the real Evidence of Miracles in general; and more particularly of those which were wrought in Confirmation of the Jewish *and* Christian *Revelation.*

Reverend Sir,

I am not a little concerned to hear, that your Lot is so unluckily fallen into a Parish where you are so frequently attacked by your sceptic Neighbours; who take an ungenerous Delight in pressing you upon those difficult Points of Scripture, in which they know you to be least versed; such as particularly the *Hebrew* and other Eastern Tongues; the *Jewish* Oeconomy, Antiquities, Laws, and Customs. And it is greatly to be wish'd, either that there were not so great a Number of our Clergy, who have, like you, been misled into a Neglect of so necessary a Branch of Learning, or that they would, as often as they fall under the like Difficulties, make use of the same Method you have condescended to take, of supplying that Defect, by appealing to some more proper Judge of every Point in Dispute, rather than to suffer the Authority of the sacred Historians to be impaired thro' your want of Ability, as you modestly word it, of defending them. And I no less applaud your Prudence in the Choice of a Layman, who will, in all Probability, be thought less exceptionable than a Clergyman, in a Controversy of this nature: But why you should single me out for the Task, when you might so easily have pitch'd upon one of much superior Ability, to answer the End, I can only ascribe to that partial Satisfaction you lately expressed, in reading some of my former Observations on several obscure and controverted Points of the Old Testament. I shall therefore the more readily accept of your Offer, as it will afford me an Opportunity of communicating to you, and your Neighbours, some more of the same kind, which I have had occasion to make during my long Recess from the World; and which, in all Likelihood, must otherwise have lain neglected and useless by me. And I own myself highly obliged to you, for having engaged yourself to conceal my Name, unless permitted by me to do otherwise; which I cannot by any means consent to, upon several Considerations I need not trouble you and them with; one of which will, however, easily occur to you, that it is too obscure, and too little known, to add any Weight to what I shall transmit to you. On its own Merit let it stand or fall. One thing you may indeed acquaint them with, because it may, in all Probability, make a favourable Impression on them; *viz.* That the Writer is a Layman, who, tho' neither designed for, nor ever intending to enter into Holy Orders, hath yet chosen to dedicate the greater Part of his latter Life to this kind of Study; but hath still, for some not unworthy Reasons, carefully concealed his Name; altho' some of his Productions have met with a good Reception from the Public. And as you are sufficiently apprised, that this is my case, so it can hardly fail of meeting with a ready Belief from a Person of your singular Integrity. Thus much in Answer to the former Part of your Letter.

As to the Objections and Difficulties raised by them against several miraculous and other historical Facts, recorded in the Old Testament,[92] as I have long ago had occasion to examine them at my leisure Hours, so I doubt not to convince them in the subsequent Essays, that they chiefly arise either from their not being sufficiently acquainted with, or their not having given sufficient Attention to, the peculiar Genius of the *Hebrew* Idiom, the Laws, Discipline, and Customs, of the *Jews*, and the uniform and general Design of Providence towards them; and more particularly to a Misapprehension of their being calculated solely in favour of that Nation; whereas, in fact, they were no less designed and fitted for the Benefit of the rest of the heathen World. So that if your sceptic Neighbours are the Persons of the Sense and Candour you represent them, I flatter my self I shall find no great Difficulty in removing all that Heap of Doubts and Difficulties which they have thrown in your way, with respect to the Facts in question; and, at the same time, make it appear to their Satisfaction, that this admirable and long Series of Miracles which were wrought both in *Egypt*, and in the Land of *Canaan*, were so far from being calculated in favour of the *Jewish* Nation only, that they are no less than a gradual and uniform Sequel of that divine Scheme, which had been laid ever since the Creation, for the Benefit of all Mankind, and was to be fully completed in the Person of the *Messiah*, when the Fullness of the Time was come.

In the mean while, as you inform me, that some of your Antagonists are great Admirers of the noble Author of the *Characteristics*,[93] of *Collins*, *Tindal*, the late Writer of the *Moral Philosopher*,[94] and other professed Opposers of Divine Revelation, and of the Miracles on which the *Jewish* and *Christian* Religion are built, it will be highly requisite, before I proceed farther, to take a short Examen of the Arguments by which those Authors pretend to prove, not only the Incredibility, but likewise the Impossibility,

---

[92] These are particularly mentioned in the Title-page and Preface.

[93] [Anthony Ashley Cooper, Earl of Shaftesbury (1671–1713).]

[94] [Thomas Morgan (d. 1743), *The moral philosopher, in a dialogue between Philalethes a Christian Deist, and Theophanes a Christian Jew*. London, Printed for the author (1737–1740).]

of all Miracles in general, as well as of those which are urged in Confirmation of the Law and Gospel. Were a mere Stranger to guess at the Merit of the *Christian* Revelation, by the indefatigable Pains which these pretended Well-wishers to Mankind, and public Society, have taken to overthrow it, he must of course conclude it to be one of the worst, and the most dangerous, instead of the most beneficial and comfortable Systems of Religion in the World. And if we were to measure the Success of their Labour, either by the Number of their Admirers, or by the victorious Applauses they assume to themselves, or have received from them, we could not hardly suppose any thing but that they had long since gained their Point, and silenced all Opposers, by the most irrefragable Arguments, and clearest Demonstration.[95] And yet we plainly see, that as on the one hand they have never dared yet openly to impugn the excellent Morality of its Precepts, so neither have they been able, on the other, to undermine its Foundation, by all the Variety of Engines they have set on work for that purpose. They have all, indeed, made strong Efforts to cry down the Validity, Truth, Probability, and some of them even Possibility, of those numberless Miracles on which its Evidence is chiefly founded: They have left no Art untried, to expose them as contrary to Reason, and the Experience of Mankind, and what they know of the stated Laws and Course of Nature: They have represented them as inconsistent with the Immutability of the Supreme Being, and as insufficient Evidences of the Doctrines they are urged in Proof of. Some of them have endeavour'd to expose the Law, and the Gospel, as unnecessary and impertinent Revelations; *Mens natural Faculties being able to teach them the most excellent Morals, to furnish them with the most effectual Incentives to the Observation of them, and to inspire them with the truest Notions of the Divine Nature, and a well grounded Belief of a Supreme Being, and his Providence:* Which, if true, overturns at once the Necessity of a Revelation, and of the Miracles urged in Proof of it. Others again as positively affirm, that such Revelations were not only needless, but that the admitting of any such, implies some extraordinary Defect in the moral World, which requires a Divine Interposition to amend it: Whereas all God's Works, being the Result of infinite Wisdom, Power, and Goodness, can never be supposed to stand in need of any Amendment, much less of a Divine Interposition to rectify them. Lastly, they affirm, with the same Assurance, that if such an Interposition of the Divine Power was ever requisite upon that, or any other Occasion, it must

---

[95] *De his vid. int. al. Spinos. Leibnit. Dissert. de Fid. & Ration. Collins. Tindal. Moral Philosopher. Considerations on the Resurrection, against The Trial of the Witnesses, & al.*

have been always, and ever continue to be so. If Miracles, therefore, were thought necessary or expedient at any time, they must be so at all times; because, say they, whoever supposes God to have wrought them in one Generation, and not in another, must of course look upon him as a partial Being,[96] This is the Sum and Substance of all their Arguments against the Reality, Evidence, and Possibility, of Miracles: In consequence of which, they have made no Scruple to condemn them all in the Lump, as Delusions and vile Impositions upon Mankind; and the Recorders of them, be their Character what it will in other respects, as Dealers in Forgeries and Monstrosities, and unworthy any Credit or Regard.[97]

From this short Scantling I have given of the Premises and Conclusion, you, and your sceptic Neighbours, may clearly see what Pains those Authors have taken to eradicate, as far as possible, the very Notion of a Divine Revelation, founded on Miracles, out of the World. And it was natural for them to prefer that expeditious Way to any other: And since they could not stand against the Shafts that galled them from the Battery, to endeavour, by any means, to blow it up. And if their sanguine Hopes have hitherto failed of Success, the World will at least say thus much in Justice to them, that their Disappointment is owing to some other Cause, than to the want of Zeal, or hard struggling for it, on their Part: Whilst those who reflect more justly upon it, will, probably, be reminded of *Christ's* infallible Promise to his Church,[98] that he would protect it to the End of Time, and against much more powerful and dangerous Attempts than any of these Gentlemen can make against it. But this more properly belonging to your Province, I shall leave to you to take notice of, and urge against your Opponents, as occasion offers. And as I doubt not but you are by this time thoroughly acquainted with those excellent Authors, who have written in Defence of the *Jewish* and *Christian* Revelation,[99] it will not be improper to observe to them, how short those of the opposite Side are from having completed their Task, were even their Arguments against Revelation more solidly founded, and their Inferences more fairly drawn, than they will be found, upon closer Examination, to be: For, even in such

---

[96] *Consider. ubi. sup.* p. 98. Edit. 3. p. 82.

[97] *Hume's Essay on Miracles*, p. 179, & *seq.*

[98] *Matth.* xvi. 18.

[99] I shall here insert some of the principal of them, for the sake of the younger Sort of Readers. See *Grotius*, and *Labadie de Verit. Limborch's Theolog.* & *Amica Collat. cum erudito Judæo. Lesley's Short Method with the Deists. Bentley's Boyle's Lectures, and Philo-Luther. Lipsiens.* Dean B.'s *Alciphron*, Dr. *Sam. Clark, Saurin, Calmet,* & *al.* on the most difficult Places in the Old Testament.

case, the Merit of the Controversy, at the best, will be still left in Suspense, until they have fully consulted all that hath been urged in Defence of it; and all that a Reader of a moderate Capacity could conclude, after a careful Perusal of both Sides, would be only this, that it was a Point about which much might, and had been urged *pro* and *con.*; but on which Side to fix, he was still at a Loss. 'Tis true, one thing must greatly help to determine him in favour of our Side, who are the Defendants in Possession; *viz.* our Readiness, at all times, to enter the List with them on the fairest Terms, and to give their Arguments a candid Hearing, as well as the most solid and pertinent Answers; whilst they, without paying the least Regard to them, take all Opportunities they can, to appear in the Field with the same Air of Triumph, tho' so often repulsed, and with the same old weather-beaten Invalids, kept up, it seems, in Reserve, upon every fresh Occasion, to make a short-liv'd Parade in some new modish Dress, and be laid up again till farther Orders. It would be no difficult Matter to discover the Grounds of these so frequent and indecent Insults on a Revelation that hath the Seal of Heaven for its Credentials; the most excellent and exalted Morality for its Voucher; the Testimony of all Antiquity, Foes as well as Friends, for its Evidence; the most considerable Men of all Ages for Learning, Judgment, and Integrity, for its Defenders; and the Legislative Power for its Support. But I shall leave that to you, and others, to infer from the plain Tendency and Spirit of their Writings, and the Nature of the Religion which they would substitute in its stead. There you'll likewise see, with Ease, the true Motive of their singular Contempt for the Clergy, especially of those who have written most clearly and powerfully in Defence of Christianity, and most effectually detected and exploded the Sophistry and Fallacy of their Arguments against its Evidence from Miracles. This last is indeed an Affront, or Injury, perhaps, in their Sense, they will not easily forgive them; as it hath cast no small Reflection on their Integrity, as well as Judgment; and, by that means, prevented their favourite Scheme from going so swimmingly on, or meeting with so general an Approbation, as they seemed to expect.[100] It is not unlikely neither, that your sceptic Neighbours, and others of their Admirers and Disciples, may flatter themselves with the Hopes of better Days, and an happier World, should these Demagogues prove so successful as to become the only Instructors and Reformers of it; and, by procuring their so much boasted System of natural Religion to be adopted instead of the Christian, which is now establish'd, set human Reason at once free from the Oppression of mysterious Creeds, and their Fellow-subjects from the Dominion of Priestcraft, and other religious Impositions: So that every one might live peaceably

---

[100] See *Rights of the Christian Church defended. Christianity as old as the Creation. Independent Whig. Moral Philosopher,* & al. *pass.*

under his own Vine, and under his own Fig-tree: And I may add, in his own Way, without Fear or Danger of Coercion, or other Disturbance from those hot Zealots for Revelation. But were that more likely to be ever the case than it is, I can see but little Reason to expect, that we of the Laity should meet with better Quarter, by becoming the Disciples and Catechumens of these New Guides, than we enjoy under our present ones; or that Men that betray so much Subtilty and Sophistry in their Reasonings, and shew themselves, in the highest Degree, either sceptical or dogmatical, as best suits with their Purpose, could much better agree in any one System of Morality or Religion than ours do, or indulge their Disciples in a greater Freedom of thinking and acting than these do their Flocks. Hitherto they have been only endeavouring to undermine and pull down an old Structure they do not like: But if we may guess from thence, how they will act when they come to build their new one, it is much to be feared, that, let them split themselves into ever so many Systems about it, they will agree in this one Canon, to turn Scepticism over to their Hearers, and to allow of none to act the Dogmatists but those that sit in the Chair. But, not to create to ourselves needless Fears from their ill-grounded Hopes, let us now take a short Survey of those pretended irrefragable Arguments they have hitherto urged against the Credibility and Possibility of Miracles; and on the Strength of which one of their latest Writers hath made no Difficulty to affirm they may, and ought to be, rejected, as Delusions and Forgeries, merely on account of their being Miracles, let the Authority of the Recorder, or Evidence of the Fact, be what they will; because, according to him, the Evidence of the Testimony must naturally rise or fall, according as the Fact related is more or less agreeable to our common Experience and Observation: The Consequence of which must be, That *where the Fact attested hath seldom fallen under Observation, there is a Contest of two opposite Experiences, of which the one destroys the other, as far as its Force goes.*[101] This strange Way of Reasoning, which seems to imply, that *want of Observation, and contrary to observation, are the same Thing,* hath been already so clearly confuted by a learned Author,[102] that it were superfluous to add any-thing to it: Only I cannot but observe, that it is much the same with that which a witty *French* Writer[103] supposes Roses would be apt to make, concerning their Gardener, and conclude him to be some eternal and unchangeable Being, because they had never observed any Alteration in him, either with respect to Age, Dress, &c. Now, if I may be permitted to carry the Allusion a little farther, Let us suppose, that they had

---

[101] *Hume's Essay on Miracles*, p. 179.

[102] *Adams's Essay on Miracles*, p. 10. & *seq.*

[103] *Font. World in the Moon.*

some authentic Records, that this same Gardener had, many Generations before, made a much finer Appearance for some time, that is, in his *Sunday*'s Dress; or that in some Corner of the Rose-bush there had been kept a constant Tradition, and very authentic Monuments and Records, that the same Gardener, in some Ages still more remote, had been so kind to the whole Shrub, as to cut down a Tree which greatly incommoded it by its Shade, and frequent dropping of Rain; or that he had planted a very convenient and comfortable Fence to shelter them against the cutting North-winds. In this case, if that Author reasons justly, it is plain, that all these Facts must be rejected as fabulous, or mere Forgeries, because they could not find, either by Observation, or Experience, that they had been ever incommoded by any such Tree on the one Side, or had ever wanted such a Shelter on the other, or that ever the Gardener had been seen in any but one and the same Dress.

But is there no Disparity between the Facts recorded of the Gardner, and those which the Sacred Writers ascribe to the Supreme Being? Yes, doubtless, a vast one: But as the Want of Observation could be no sufficient Argument against the Authenticity of the Facts in one Case, so neither can it be against that of the other, unless either of them can be demonstrated to be above the Power of their respective Agents, or to have implied a palpable Contradiction. An hard Point this, one would think, to prove, with respect to the Deity: Let us therefore see now how they have succeeded in their Attempt to do it. But here you will, I doubt not, easily excuse me, if, for Brevity and Clearness sake, as well as to avoid troubling you with a Multitude of Quotations, I choose to link the Sum and Substance of all their Objections and Reasonings, together with my Answer to them, in one Chain; and to contract both in one short View, rather than as they lie scattered in the Works of the Writers on both Sides of the Controversy. And you will do me the Justice to think, that as I would not charge them with any thing but what is expressly found in their Writings, much less would I omit any thing they have said on this important Head, that caries any Weight with it: For tho' your Antagonists at P. – may not perhaps carry their Opposition so far as the Authors I am going to examine; in which case they can easily disculpate themselves from it to you; yet would it by no means excuse my omitting any material thing that hath been urged by others on so momentous a Point.

First, then, as to that old and trite Objection against Miracles, that they are no proper Proofs of any Doctrine, I have already shewn some Instances in which they really are; and that the Raising of the Dead is as full and proper Evidence of the Doctrine of the Resurrection, as any that could be possibly given, or reasonably required.[104] Again, the miraculous Cures

---

[104] See the Preface.

wrought on the Blind, Lame, Lepers, Lunatics, Paralytics, and other Diseases, were no less proper, as well as pregnant Proofs both of the universal Depravity of Mankind, and of the Guilt incurr'd by it, when the same miraculous Power that delivered them from the dire Effects of the former, pronounced them absolved from the latter.[105] What greater Proof could any one require to convince him, that his Guilt or Sin was really remitted to him with respect to the Penalty or Punishment of it in the next Life, than such a miraculous Deliverance from that only Part of it which was the Consequence of it in this? With respect to the monstrous Idolatry, and abominable Superstitions, which had over-run the greatest Part of the heathen World, and the time when *Moses* made his second Appearance in *Egypt*, could any thing be more proper or pertinent to convince that Nation of the Absurdity and Impiety of their worshipping, and putting any Confidence in, the false Deities of their own creating, or of the God of *Israel* being the Supreme Governor and Disposer of all sublunary things, than that long and wonderful Contest, which he condescended to enter into with them; wherein every Miracle wrought under his Direction and Auspices, by his Servant, was so exactly levelled against some one or other of their pretended Deities, and every other Branch of their superstitious Worship, as will be more fully shewn in the next Essay? And if *Egypt* was at that time the chief Seat of Learning, from which every Branch of it, together with that vast Variety of Extravagancies which related to their Worship, flowed into most other Countries about it, far and near; if their Priests and Doctors were allowed to excel all others, not only in the Knowledge of their profound and mystic Theology, but in their Skill in Astronomy, Astrology, Natural Philosophy, Magic, Divination, and other pretended occult Arts and Sciences; where could there be a more proper Scene for this Display of his supreme and irresistible Power, than that? What Means more likely to convince, not only *Pharaoh*, and his Subjects, but all other Nations which had received their false Theology from thence, of the Vanity and Impotency of their imaginary Deities, than the constant Defeat which was given to them at every new Tryal? What Time more proper than this for it, when the Infection was grown so universal, and become incurable by any other Means, by its reigning under the Pretence of a Divine Sanction, whilst those who alone had the Power of suppressing, made it their Interest and Glory to support and propagate it? Lastly, What Occasion more worthy of the Divine Interposition, than the reducing such a Number of Nations from the most destructive and abominable Errors in Faith and Practice, to such a Sense of his unerring Providence, such an Obedience to his Will, and such pure and undefiled Worship of him, as could alone intitle them to his Favour and Blessings in this, and the next Life?

[105] *Matth.* ix, 2, & *seq.*

Hence then we may safely conclude, that Miracles were so far from being such improper Evidences of God's gracious Design of reclaiming a degenerate World from that Multitude of Errors and Enormities, into which it was irretrievably immerged, that they appear to have been the most effectual, if not the only Means, that could bring about so desirable a Change; as they were most apt to awaken the Attention of Mankind; appealed to their rational Faculties, without offering any Violence to their freedom; and gave them the strongest Assurances of his over-ruling Providence over the whole Creation; and, what still more nearly concerned them to know, over all those imaginary Deities, whether the Luminaries, Planets, Stars, Elements, or any other mistaken Object of their Worship and Confidence. Hence also we may judge, how worthy of the Divine Goodness and Justice such a miraculous Interposition ought to appear to every serious Thinker, that is, not as merely calculated in Favour of the poor and despicable Nation of the *Jews*, as our Opposers falsely suggest, but for the Benefit, both present and future, of the heathen World; and ultimately, as a Part or Prelude to the grand System of the Redemption of Mankind.[106]

Against all this, how reasonable soever, they have, as I observed to you a little higher, levelled a new Set of Arguments, which, in their Judgment, amount to no less than so many Demonstrations, not only against the *Credibility*, but the *Possibility of all Miracles*, how firmly soever attested, and on what occasion soever pretended to have been wrought; how justly, we shall now examine.

First, then, with regard to the universal Disaster, which we lately observed had overrun the moral World, and stood in need of nothing less than the divine Interposition to rectify, they peremptorily object, *That both the material and moral World, being alike the Production of infinite Wisdom, Power, and Goodness, cannot be otherwise than perfect, each in their Kind; and consequently out of all Possibility of ever standing in Need of any such Interposition to amend it.* This is one of their fundamental Axioms; which whosoever can admit, without any farther Proof (for none they have, or can give of it), must of course give up the Cause of Miracles as absurd, and utterly exploded. What they affirm of the material World being less pertinent to our present Controversy, I shall content myself with reminding them, that a much greater Natural Philosopher, than they can produce out of their Class, made no Scruple to declare himself of a contrary Opinion; *viz. That the Frame of it would, in Course of Time, require the same divine Hand to re-touch and refit it, that had at first created it.*[107] With respect to the moral World, it is no less certain, that two

---

[106] See *Grot. de. Verit. Lib.* I. *Comm. In Exod. L'Abadie Verit. de la Religion Judaique. Bate's Harmony of the Divine Attributes. Bray's Covenant. Hammond,* and other Commentators on *Exod. Sam. Clark's Lectures, & al.*

[107] Sir *Isaac Newton's Optics.* P. 346. last Edit.

as great Moral Philosophers, as ever Antiquity, or the World, could boast, were so far from dreaming any thing like its having been created in such pretended Perfection, as to be above all Possibility of ever wanting the Divine Interposition to reform it, that one of them, *Socrates*,[108] *thought it highly reasonable to hope, that God in time would send some proper Messenger from Heaven, to instruct Mankind in the great Duties of Religion and Morality.* The other, the celebrated *Confucius*, who flourished in *China* above a Century earlier than that of *Athens*; that is, about 530 Years before the Christian Æra; used to comfort himself, and his Disciples, under the then reigning Degeneracy, with a prevailing Tradition they had among them, that the SAINT, or HOLY ONE, so he stiled the extraordinary Person, who was expected to work a signal Reformation in the World, would, in time appear in the *West*;[109] meaning, doubtless, *Christ*, the promised *Messiah*, and Divine Lawgiver.[110] We may indeed safely leave it to them, to make out this pretended Impossibility of the World's ever wanting to be amended, against the known Sentiment of the rest of the World, and the constant Experience of all Ages and Nations; and to shew in what Sense such a Divine Revelation, as that we are defending, can be said to amend God's original Work, except that in which a good Education, or Instruction, is known to do; for what doth a Divine Revelation else, than afford Mankind a clearer and more certain Knowledge of his Divine

---

[108] *Vid Plut. in Alcibiad. ad fin.*

[109] *Martini. Hist. Sinens.* p. 413. *Du Halde in vit. Confuc. & alib.*

[110] This Notion of an holy Lawgiver, or Reformer, together with his Character of a peaceable Prince, and the very Year of his coming into the World, if we may believe the *Chinese* Missionaries, was so well known, and strongly believed, not only in *Confucius*'s Time, but for several Ages after him, that on the very Year in which it was foretold he should be born, which was exactly that of *Christ*'s Birth, the then reigning Monarch, a Prince otherwise of no great Character, is recorded to have changed his Name of *Ngay*, which signified a Conqueror, into that of *Ping*, or *Peaceable*, in Memory of that remarkable Event (*Martin Du Halde, & al. ub. sup.*).

How they came by this Tradition, or could be so exact as to the Year, we are not told; but it is not unlikely, that the *Chinese* received it from *Noah*, or some of his immediate Descendants, as they were settled in those remote Parts some few Ages after the Flood: And as to their being exact, with respect to the very Year, it is probable, that they kept their Records more carefully, as living separate from other Nations, who were continually at War with each other, whilst they enjoyed a constant Peace among themselves, and Freedom from Invaders without: so that the Tradition being, in all Probability, the same which was likewise preserved in the Family of *Shem*, and descended from thence to the *Israelites*, importing, that the *Messiah* or promised Seed, should appear at the Close of the Fourth, or Beginning of the Fifth Millenary, *Confucius* might more easily determine the precise Time from their Records, with which he was perfectly acquainted: But as to the precise Coincidence of the Year with that of *Christ*'s Birth, it wholly depends on the Credit of the Jesuits above mentioned.

Nature and Attributes, than bare unassisted Reason could do, in order to render us more conformable to his Will, and to the Ends for which he made us? We may therefore pronounce the moral World perfect, when every Part of it is endowed with Faculties answerable to those Ends. And it is in this very Sense, that the wise Man[111] tells us God made Man perfect, or upright; yet adds, that they sought out many Inventions, or, as the Original imports, vain Imaginations. He was endowed with sufficient Faculties to know what is right or wrong, and a free Power over his own Actions; that is, of making a good or bad Use of those Faculties; without which he would have been only a mere Piece of Machinery, instead of rational free Agent; and consequently incapable of Virtue or Vice, of Reward or Punishment. But as this doth not exclude, but rather enforces, the Necessity of Tutors to instruct and direct, and Monitors to encourage or deter, to reprove or reclaim Individuals, so much more will it do so with respect to the whole moral World. And since the Experience of every Age and Nation shews it to be in a continual Fluctuation, one while making vast Advances and Improvements in Virtue and Knowledge, and, by-and-by, sunk into the grossest Ignorance and Immorality, Superstition and Idolatry; if such has been the State of the Moral World, that the far greater Part of it hath preferred Falshood to Truth, Vice to Virtue, Superstition to a pure Worship, with what Face can these Pretenders to Reasoning and Philosophy affirm it out of all Possibility of wanting any Amendment? They may indeed pronounce those Disorders to be incurable; and so they do, in fact, by excluding the only Means that can possibly rectify them. But what Reason can they give us, the Disease being thus far above all human Remedy, to believe that Divine Goodness too unconcerned to interpose, in our behalf, and furnish us with a more suitable, powerful, and effectual one; *viz.* a more perfect Revelation of himself, and a system of morality more suitable to his Divine Will? But here they tell us again, that we assume too much, when we pronounce the disastrous State of Mankind to be beyond all human Power to rectify, seeing *the Faculties with which he hath endowed Mankind are abundantly sufficient to recover Mankind from any Miscarriage, and to furnish them with such a System of Religion and Morality, and such a competent Notion of God, and his Providence, as will answer all the Ends of such a supposed Revelation.* This they positively affirm; and tho' none of them hath hitherto dared, as they have in other Cases, to appeal to common Experience and Observation for the Truth of so bold an Assumption, they being point-blank against it; a small Retrospection on the brightest Ages of the most polite antient Nations, the *Egyptians,*

---

[111] *Eccles.* vii. 29.

Chaldeans, Babylonians, Greeks, Romans, &c. will soon convince us how few there were amongst their wise and learned Men, that had any true Notion either of the Deity, or of Religion and Morality; how fewer still, those who had either Credit, or Courage, to stem the Current of Superstition and Degeneracy, in Comparison of those who suffered themselves to be hurried away with it; to say nothing of the small, if not rather ill Success, of such an Opposition against such powerful Supporters as the Civil Power, the Priesthood, and an headstrong Populace. Our Antagonists therefore, being conscious how little able that vain Assertion was to stand against two such powerful Witnesses, have thought it more expedient to endeavour to prop it up by some far-fetch'd Arguments, which, how inconclusive soever, might at least bear the specious Face of Reasoning. And first, they tell us, that *such a miraculous Revelation is inconsistent with God's Immutability, one of his most essential Attributes;* that is, according to their Logic, if God is immutable in his Nature, he must be likewise so in his Actions. Wild Conclusion this! and of no Force, unless they can also prove all his Creatures to be as unchangeable as himself, than which nothing is more contrary to all Observation and Experience, nor more absurd and unreasonable to suppose, and much more so with respect to the moral World: For if the Experience of all Ages shews it to have been in a constant Fluctuation; if whole Nations appear to have sunk from a good Pitch of Learning, to the lowest Dregs of Ignorance; from the truest and sublimest Notions of the Supreme Being, and of the pure Worship that is due to him, to the basest Degrees of Idolatry and Superstition; and from the noblest Sentiments of Virtue and Morality, to the most shameful Degeneracy and Corruption, both in Theory and Practice; what Reason can there be to suppose, much less to affirm so peremptorily, as our Opposers do, that a *Divine Interposition must necessarily be contrary to his Immutability?* Is it not rather more just to infer, that the very Immutability of his Nature and Counsels must incline, I might say, oblige him to alter his Measures with his Creatures, as often as he sees them deviate from, or go contrary to them, or abase those Faculties, and that Freedom of Choice, with which he had endowed them, to Purposes quite opposite to the Ends for which he had created them? Can a Clock-maker be said to change his Mind or Design, when he goes about mending what is amiss in a Clock; or a Physician, when the Irregularity of his Patient obliges him to alter his Prescriptions, and Method of treating him, in order to his Recovery? Much more absurd, if not impious, will it be, to infer a Mutability in the Supreme and All-wise Being, who, foreknowing from all Eternity all the possible Exigencies of his moral World, and the ill Use Men would make of those Faculties, and the Liberty, with which he had endowed them, must necessarily be thought to have decreed likewise, in his eternal Counsel, a proper Supply for every Want, and Remedy for every Disorder: So that every such extraordinary Interposition, as we are contending for, that is, where the Subject is worthy of it, is so far from implying any thing like a Mutability in the Godhead, as our Opposers would infer, that it is in Reality no other than an Effect of his eternal and Unalterable Decrees. I dare venture to appeal to every considering Man, whether Immutability, in this Sense, is not more truly, and every way, worthy of the Divine Nature, than that which our Opposers attribute to him, and which represents the whole Creation as a mere large Piece of compound Mechanism; which, having been once set in Motion by its Maker, is left to go on its own Way, without any farther Care or Regard from him, notwithstanding that great Variety of Disorders and Irregularities which is seen and felt in our moral Part of it?

But here, again, we are strangely stopped on the sudden, and are boldly arraigned, as entertaining too high Notions of the Divine Nature and Attributes; and all our Reasonings, from the Effects to the Cause, and ascribing those Perfections to the latter, in an infinite Degree, which we observe in the former, is, it seems, all false Logic: And whatever Degrees of Wisdom, Justice, Goodness, Power, &c. we ascribe to the Creator, *beyond what hath immediately fallen under our Observation on the Works of Nature, being all together unsupported by any Reason or Argument, can never be admitted, but as mere Conjecture and Hypothesis.*[112] So that, according to this Author's Reasoning (which is, for Form's sake, put into the Mouth of an *Epicurean* Philosopher, supposed to defend his Doctrine before an *Athenian* Senate), as many as have ascribed *any higher, or any other kind of Attributes or Perfections, to the Deity, than actually appear to have been exerted to the full, in his Works, have been guilty of Flattery and Panegyric, rather than Masters of just Reasoning and Philosophy; which can never be able to carry us beyond the usual Course of Experience, or give us different Measures of Conduct and Behaviour from those which are furnished by Reflection on common Life.*[113] Whence we are taught these two special Lessons; *viz.* First, to take care, for the future, how we launch out in the Praises of the Supreme Creator, at that extraordinary rate the greatest Divines, and Moral Philosophers, have hitherto done, seeing the Notion of his infinite Wisdom, Power, Justice, &c. is no better than absurd Nonsense, an absolute Contradiction to Experience and Reason; the one plainly shewing, that he never did, and the other, that it is impossible for him ever to exert any of his Perfections or Attributes, were they ever so truly infinite, in any such Degree as we may safely pronounce to be such, from any effectual Appearance, or Impression, they can make upon a

[112] *Hume Essay*, xi, p. 228.

[113] *Ibid.* p. 230.

finite Mind: The other Lesson we may learn from it is, not to suffer ourselves to be any more imposed upon, by any Pretence, how specious soever, that he ever did, or ever will, interpose his Power, or furnish us with any new Means to amend his moral World; since, if our Author's Logic is good, we have no Reason or Argument to convince us, that, bad or corrupt as it may appear to us, it is not in as good and perfect Condition as he could, or knew how to, make it; and contrary Supposition, that he might, if he would, is at best but mere *Conjecture and Hypothesis.*

I shall readily leave it to him to make the most of all this bold assuming Stuff against the clearest and most convincing Reasonings of those great Divines, and learned Philosophers, who have hitherto argued in Defence of God's infinite Perfection. If such dogmatical Assertions as his may pass for Demonstrations with any Set of Men, not only the Notion of the divine Attributes, but that of the divine Nature, may be in some Danger of dwindling into a mere imaginary Shadow, in their Estimation: And we may plainly see, by the Topics they have hitherto made use of, to explode the bare Possibility of its interposing in human Affairs, upon any Account or Exigence whatsoever, how much they have already ventured to sink it below the Mark to which most other Schools, except their own, had so universally raised it.

But since this Author not only makes Experience and Observation the sole Touchstone by which we may judge of the Truth of any historical Facts, but seems to engross the sole Property and Evidence to his own Side, whilst he absolutely excludes ours from challenging any Benefit from it, merely because those we challenge in Defence of the divine Revelation are of a miraculous Kind, it will not be improper here to examine which of the Two hath the better Claim to it, even according to his way of Reasoning: For if that Experience may be most safely depended upon, which is founded upon the best Testimony, it is plain, that ours hath produced the amplest, the most positive, unquestionable, and universal, from the Friends and Foes, and been confirmed by other authentic Monuments, in Proof of the Miracles recorded in our sacred Books;[114] whereas all the pretended Experience he objects against them, being of the negative Kind, and implying no more than a Want of Experience and Observation, and not a Contrariety to it, can never be allowed to outweigh the Evidence of a single well-attested Testimony, much less of such a Number and Variety of them as we allege against him. This he could not but be sensible of; and that, as he could not object any thing against the Sufficiency of them, either on account of their Paucity, or of the Character of the Witnesses, but what had been fully answered long ago, and by many able Pens, he must likewise

---

[114] *Vid. Grotius, & L'Abadie de Verit. Lesley's Short Method, & al. sup. citat. vid. & Un. Hist. Octavo,* vol. 3. p. 390, *& seq. sub not.* p. *& alib. pass.*

think, that his confining his negative Experience to such Periods of Time, in which no such divine Interpositions were become unnecessary, and, consequently, could not fall under our Observation, is but a weak Argument against the Credibility of their having been displayed in former ones; when the Exigencies of the moral World did more immediately require them, and the Occasion of them was altogether worthy of them. And when could there be a more worthy one, than when Mankind were not only sunk into the most dishonourable Notions of the Deity, and the most abominable Rites in his Worship; but had even degenerated so far, as to shelter them under the Sanction of his Authority and Institution, barring up by that means, all possible Avenues against Conviction, and rendering the Distemper incurable by any other Means, but that of a new Revelation of himself, and his divine Will? If in such a Case we have sufficient Testimony, that the divine Providence interposed, and, by a long Series of Miracles the most apposite, strove to convince the *Egyptians*, who were the first Broachers and Propagators of that detestable Theology and Worship, of the Vanity of their false Deities, the Impiety of their religious Rites, and of his alone and absolute Superintendency over all his Creatures (and our Author is not above supposing, that *the Testimony for those Miracles, considered apart, and in itself, may amount to a full Proof*), I would gladly know of what Evidence his negative Experience of latter Ages, when no such Exigence called for them, can be, against that of the former ones, when there was such a visible Necessity for them? Or how the want of Observation in the former can invalidate the Testimony which we have of their having been so frequent, and so signal, in the latter? At this rate of Reasoning, an Inhabitant of *Lower Egypt* must never believe, that *Palestine*, and other Countries, enjoy the Benefit of the former and latter Rain, let ever so many credible Eye-witnesses assure him of it; because such a Blessing is seldom or never observed in his own: And, for the same wise Reason, those that live within the Tropics, ought not, on any Account, to believe that there is either Snow or Ice without, because there is no such Thing to be seen within them: And one-half of the Moon's Globe must not believe, that our Earth is a Planet to it, because it can never be observed by those of that Side, by reason of its being constantly turned from us.

But here it may be asked, How doth all this affect our Author's Argument, drawn from Non-experience, and Non-observation, against Testimony? which is not here levelled against a few rare Phænomena of Nature, but against Miracles, which are a plain Deviation from, or (as he pleases to stile them) a Violation of, the Laws of Nature? Is not this single Consideration sufficient to discredit it, and explode the bare Possibility of them, against any Testimony whatever, *tho', considered apart, and in itself, amounting to a full Proof?* I grant that the Charge of Violation of Nature's Laws, were Miracles really such, as is here so boldly affirmed, carries an Absurdity sufficient to discourage any thinking Person from admitting the bare Possibility of it, let who will be Violator of them, whether the Supreme Author of those Laws, or any other subordinate Power. But here the Absurdity lies, in the Supposition of either being possibly chargeable with it; for in what Sense can the former be possibly taxed with violating his own Laws, whenever he sees fit, for Motives worthy of himself, to suspend or dispense with them? Or how can the latter, who only act as Instruments under him, and by his sole Direction and Power? That Nature would act constantly, and uniformly, to the Laws that were first impressed upon it by the Supreme Being, is out of all Question; but what less, than being of his own eternal Council, or having it revealed to him, can embolden any Creature to affirm, or even imagine, that he divested himself of all Power of ever suspending, or dispensing with them, upon any Occasion whatsoever? much less, that such a Suspension of, or dispensing with, was a Violation of them; especially as we still see the same Laws constantly observed in every Instance, but where the Exigences of the moral World rendered such a casual Interposition necessary or expedient: In which case it[115] cannot be deemed any other than an Effect of his divine Wisdom and Prescience, and a Part of his eternal Decrees, in consequence to it, as I observed a little higher to you.

Here, again, therefore, the Author last-quoted hath greatly overshot himself in making what he calls Experience, or Observation, the common Standard of the Laws of Nature,[116] which, were it ever so truly such, as in many Cases it is plain it is not, yet hath nothing to do with Miracles; the very Notion of which supposes a Deviation from those Laws; the Impossibility of which can never be, with any Justice, pleaded against Testimony, until it hath been fully demonstrated: But that is what our Opposers could never yet do, nor, I may add, ever will: For where is the Absurdity or Impossibility of the Supreme Lawgiver's suspending his own Laws, or even of his decreeing, in his eternal Counsel, the Dispensing with, or Suspension of them, for some wise Ends, towards his rational Creatures? that is, either to convince them of his Omnipresence, Prescience, Providence, Mercy, Justice, and absolute Government over the whole Creation; or to inspire them with the deeper Regard to him; or to revive it in them, when obliterated or extinct, thro' the Depravity of human Nature; or to answer any other Designs of his unerring Will. If a true Sense of those divine Attributes is so beneficial, or necessary, as having a most powerful Influence upon Mankind, surely such a constant, uniform, and universal Observation, of what they stile the Laws of Nature, was the most unfit Means to revive it in their Minds, after it had been once obliterated;

---

[115] [In place of "it" the original text reads "in", which is probably a printer's error.]

[116] *Hume ibid.* p. 180.

and the Experience of all Ages plainly assures us, that the very Hypothesis of it hath only served to extinguish, instead of rekindling it: For what are the wild Systems of the *Stoics* and *Epicureans*, to name no others, but the genuine Off-spring of that unphilosophical Supposition, which hath been ever observed to be the constant Shelter of the most licentious and abandon'd of Men, and the most effectual Means to harden them against all Remorse and Reproofs? In a Word, have not all the enormous Disorders that have ever infected the moral World, both with respect to Theory and Practice, been chiefly owing to the destructive Notion of the World's for ever continuing in the same unalterable Course, and without all Possibility of its ever wanting, or receiving, any Amendment from its Supreme Architect? But enough hath already been said before, against the monstrous Absurdity of excluding the Divine Providence from interposing in the extraordinary and miraculous Way we are told, from sufficient Testimony, he did in favour of his moral World, especially as that was the only one consistent with the Liberty of rational Creatures, that could possibly reclaim it, and the doing of it, by such means, every way worthy of the divine Goodness and Wisdom.

It is plain then, notwithstanding all the dogmatical Parade of the Opposers of Miracles, that they have not hitherto produced one fair Argument against their Probability and Possibility, that can outweigh, or even affect, the contrary Evidence we have of them, from Reason and Testimony: I shall therefore hasten to the last Argument they urge against us, and which, tho' no less illogical and unphilosophical than any of the former, must by no means be passed by, especially as it hath been ushered in by some of them, with such a seeming Confidence and Triumph, as if it carried the most irresistible Demonstration.[117] I shall content myself with giving you the Substance of it, which is to this Amount; That if God be supposed to have thus miraculously interposed his divine Power in any Age, or to have made use of that extraordinary Method, to reveal his Will to any People, he must of course be concluded to do so in all Ages, and towards all Nations: So that, according to their Way of Reasoning, if Miracles were ever necessary or expedient to answer any of the Designs of the divine Providence, they must be ever so; because, whether the Nature of Things, or the Laws of Nature, be allowed to be changeable, or not, yet God, being unchangeable in his Nature, must still pursue the same Methods, whether we allow the State of the moral World to require it or no; that is, in other Words, if God ever wrought any Miracles, when the State of Mankind made them expedient or necessary, he cannot but continue so working of them, when they cease to be so. This Inference, wild as it is, they draw not

---

[117] See the *Considerer of the Trial of the Witnesses*, p. 96. *Hume Essay on Miracles, Tindal, Collins, & al.*

only from his Immutability, which hath been already proved to be out of the present Case; but back it by another Argument, no less assuming and inconclusive; *viz.* That he cannot cease to do so, without being chargeable with Partiality towards one Age or Nation, above another. I shall forbear reflecting on the Boldness of such a Charge, as well as on the Presumption of these Writers, who dare thus freely to cavil at the Counsels of infinite Wisdom; which, extending to all Ages, cannot but be above all possible Comprehension: Let it suffice to observe here, that as God will ever act with the same unalterable Wisdom, Goodness, and Justice, toward his Creatures, so he will always display the same miraculous Interposition, whenever the State and Circumstances of the moral World make it expedient or requisite; but at no other time doth it follow, that he must or can do so, because, according to their own Confession, he can do nothing in vain. That he condescended to act in this miraculous manner, upon some particular Occasions, at some particular Times, when nothing less than such an extraordinary Interposition, could reduce Mankind from those Enormities into which it was plunged, both with regard to their Religion and Morals, as both were then established and upheld by the civil and priestly Power, and under the Pretence of the divine Sanction, we have such sufficient Evidence, as they have not been able hitherto to overthrow. But after he had, by a long Series of Wonders, made so ample a Manifestation of his Will, Nature, Attributes, given them the most sensible Proofs both of his over-ruling power, and of his high Displeasure at their abominable super-stitious Idolatries, inhuman Rites, by the severest Punishment of those whom the milder Displays of his Arm could not soften into an Acknowledgement of his Almighty Power and Sovereignty, as in the Instance of the *Egyptians* and *Canaanites,* of which see the next Essay; lastly, after he had caused those Wonders to be recorded in such indelible Characters, both under the *Mosaic* and much more so under the Christian Dispensation; where could there be any occasion for renewing and repeating them in every Age and Nation, when the Memory of them, if duly preserved, was of itself sufficient to answer all the Ends for which they had been wrought? Now, that they had been so preserved in the sacred Records of the Old and New Testament, the frequent and vain Efforts, and illusory Shifts, the Opposers have hitherto used to discredit those sacred Books, in which they are recorded, would of themselves afford us a sufficient Proof, had we no other Evidence of their divine Authority, or were those Facts which they relate destitute of that Cloud of Testimonies which we have of them, from all Antiquity, and from Foes, as well as Friends, of the *Jewish* and *Christian* Revelation. But I have already said enough on this Head; and may have occasion to resume and back it with some fresh Proofs, in some of the following Essays. But before I take my Leave of them, and the Subject of Miracles, I cannot pass by a new illusory Argument, or rather an old one, in a new Dress, they have started to invalidate this pressing Testimony we urge against them; especially, because it may, tho' a poor one, chance to impose on such of their Readers as are either bypassed in their Favour, or too indolent to look beyond the Surface of it. One of the last Writers gives it to us, in Words to this Purpose: Most Religions, whether antient or modern, and how different soever from one another, were at first established on the like pretended Evidence of Miracles; which, if of any Weight, would argue them to be all alike true, and to stand alike on a solid Foundation; which yet must appear to be absolutely impossible, to every one who considers their vast Contrariety. To make this Assertion appear more plausible, we are reminded of an *Apollonius Tyaneus* at *Rome,* a *Simon Magus* at *Samaria,* an *Alexander* in *Paphlagonia,* a *Titus* at *Alexandria,* and many others, who are recorded to have wrought much the same Miracles which are urged in Confirmation of the Christian Revelation. Next to these are brought in sundry Legends, both new and old, of Popish Miracles; to which the Essay writer lately quoted hath added a Catalogue of others published some time since at *Paris*; and affirmed to have been wrought at the Tomb of a *Jansenist* Saint; all which, if we will take his Word for it, are as fully attested, and as universally believed, as those recorded in the Gospel:[118] In consequence of which, he makes no Scruple to put them all on the same Level, and to pronounce them mere Delusions, and Impositions upon Mankind. A modest Inference this, and of a Piece with the Premises; but of which I shall take no farther Notice, than to observe, from the Whole, what impartial Regard these great Pretenders to Reasoning pay to that vast Number and Variety of irrefragable Arguments, which have been urged by much abler Pens, in Confutation of so odious and unjust a Parallel; and to shew, beyond all Contradiction, the vast, and almost infinite Disparity there is between the Miracles recorded in our sacred Books, and those which are opposed to them, either with respect to their Nature or Evidence. Instead, therefore, of treading the same irksome Road, of proving afresh what hath been so fully and clearly demonstrated by so many learned and judicious Men,[119] I think we may fairly challenge them to prove that pretended Parity, by some stronger Arguments than those that have been hitherto used to confute it, before they venture to urge it again on their own bare Word, and against such Evidence to the contrary. As for those of more modern Date, which the same Author hath mustered up in his Essay on this Subject,

---

[118] *Hume Essay on Miracles,* p. 192, *& seq.*

[119] *Vid. Grot. de verit. L'Abadie, Limborch, Bentley, Clark, Bullock, Middleton, Lesley's Short Method with the Deists, & al. sup. citat.*

they have been so fully and judiciously exploded by one of your Reverend Brethren,[120] that you will easily excuse my taking no farther Notice of them here. Upon the Whole, I shall readily submit to the Judgment of every candid Reader, Who hath the juster Claim to impartial Reasoning, they who from this general, tho' false Pretence to Miracles, conclude that some real ones must have been wrought, to give Rise to it; or those, who from the Uncertainty and Absurdity of some, pronounce all the rest, how reasonable or well soever attested, to be equally false?

By this time, I hope I have sufficiently answered all the Objections which have been hitherto raised against the Reality and Evidence of Miracles; and by that means cleared, in some measure, the way to the subsequent Essays; in which I am to remove the Difficulties which your neighbouring Antagonists urge against those which were wrought in *Egypt,* and in the Land of *Canaan.* And if the Subject I have been upon hath been so far exhausted, by much better Hands, that it was scarcely possible for me to add any new Thing to it, I hope you'll find the subsequent ones treated in a more untrite, tho' no less clear and satisfactory way, than they have hitherto been: And if I have taken the Liberty to suspend the taking Notice of those which they have raised against those two celebrated Transactions, the miraculous Passage of the *Israelites* thro' the *Red Sea*; and the supernatural Solstice obtained by *Joshua's* Prayer, in Favour of the *Gibeonites,* his new Allies and Proselytes; it is for no other Reason, but because they are so fully, and, in my Opinion, so satisfactorily cleared up in that Book, which I had once the Pleasure to recommend to your Perusal;[121] and which hath since met with such Approbation, that I am highly pleased to hear, by the public Proposals and Advertisements given about, it is now ready for a third Edition: For if what I have hitherto said on the Subjects of Miracles, be thought sufficient, by your sceptic Neighbours, to answer all the Objections that have been urged against their Reality and Evidence, as well as against the Character and Authority of the inspired Historians; as I can hardly question but it will, if they are the judicious and candid Opponents you represent them to be; you may safely refer them to the Book for a full Satisfaction to all that they, or any other Objectors, have said or written against them: Tho', if there should still be any Doubt or Difficulty left, which they think not sufficiently cleared up; or if they should chance to start up any new ones against either of those two extraordinary Events; I shall not be wanting in my Readiness and Endeavours, according to my small Ability, to remove them, as soon as you shall be pleased to apprise me of them.

[120] *Adams's Essay against Hume,* p. 72. *& seq.*

[121] *Universal History,* Folio Edit. Vol. i. Chap. 7. Sect. 6, 7. Octavo Edit. Vol. iii. Page 390, & *seq.* 404–419.

If the following Essays have the good Fortune to answer the End proposed with your sceptic Friends, I shall readily embrace any Opportunity you shall afford me, of pursuing hereafter the same laudable Tract; especially as they pretend to you, that these you have sent me, in this first Packet, are but a small Sketch, in Comparison of what they can muster up against the Authority of our sacred Books. But on the other hand, if you should find our Endeavours, as far as they have gone, to come short of our Expectation, I beg you will apprise me of it, by a Line, seeing you and I can spend our time to a much better Purpose, than in vainly trying to wash a Blackmoor white. I rest, dear Sir,

Your ever affectionate
and obliged, &c.

10
JOHN DOUGLAS

[John Douglas], *The criterion: or, miracles examined with a view to expose the pretensions of pagans and Papists*. London: printed for A. Millar, 1754, [4], 402, [2] p.
Selections; from 1807 edition (pp. 1–37, 94–131).

Born in Aberdeenshire, John Douglas (1721–1807) became an Anglican clergyman and was later Bishop of Carlisle. He authored several theological and literary works. In 1754 his lengthy *Criterion* appeared, which defends New Testament miracles by showing how they differ from other alleged miracles. Two sections of the work discuss Hume's essay "Of Miracles". The first, at the opening of the book, attacks Hume's central philosophical argument. According to Douglas, Hume ultimately holds the narrow and erroneous view that no testimony can establish any event for a given person, unless that person first has direct experience of that event – a view that Douglas extracts from sections 4 and 5 of the *Enquiry*. In his second discussion, Douglas disputes Hume's examples of alleged miracles, which Douglas believes are not supported by sufficient evidence. William Rose favourably reviewed Douglas's *Criterion* in the *Monthly Review*:

> The author's design, in this sensible performance, is, as appears in the title, to compare the miracles of pagans and papists with those wrought by Christ and his apostles; and by the comparison to shew the vast superiority of the latter in point of evidence. In the execution of this design, he has shewn no inconsiderable share of judgment and learning; and tho' he advances little that is new, yet he writes like one who is master of his subject, appears capable of managing an argument to good advantage, expresses himself in a plain and easy, and often in an elegant and spirited manner. [*Monthly Review*, June 1754, Vol. 10, pp. 463–471]

In his *View of the Principal Deistic Writers* (Postscript to Letter 21, included in this volume), John Leland also gives a favourable evaluation of Douglas's work. Hume was pleased with Douglas's treatment of him and the two exchanged letters on several occasions. Three of the surviving letters from Hume to Douglas relate to papers of Henry Earl of Clarendon – as Douglas oversaw the publication of Clarendon's letters and diary in

1763. Douglas's *Criterion* was republished in 1757, 1807, 1824 (abridged), and 1832. The following is from the 1807 edition.

THE
CRITERION,
&*c.*

Sir,

My surprise has not been greater than my concern to observe that a person of your good sense, candour, and learning, should have reasoned himself, as you say you have done, into an unfavourable opinion of the evidences of Christianity. Ever since our last conversation on this subject, my thoughts have turned principally on your scruples, and on the unreasonableness of them; and the result of my reflections you shall have in the present sheets. Nor do I think that this address needs any apology. The importance of the subject, and my repeated promises that I would give you my thoughts concerning it, sufficiently plead my excuse. And happy should I esteem myself, if any thing I suggest, prove a means of bringing you back to the religion which you seen to have forsaken, and of satisfying you that the reasons you assign for *rejecting* the miracles recorded in the New Testament, ought not to weigh with one of your discernment.

Unskilled in controversy, it may seem presumption in me to offer my opinion on a subject, already so fully and frequently canvassed by the most eminent writers; and it may be thought that if *their* arguments have proved ineffectual to satisfy your doubts, it will be a vain attempt in *me* to aim at your conviction. But when I consider the nature of many of your objections, which are peculiar to yourself, and not borrowed from books; when I reflect, farther, that controversy, with regard to the credibility of the *Gospel miracles,* has, of late, taken a turn somewhat new, it is obvious, that to refer you to the many excellent defences of Christianity, already in the hands of the public, would be entirely unsatisfactory; for these treatises having been adapted to the prevailing objections of unbelievers, at the particular periods when they were written, it becomes necessary that the Friends of our religion should change their method of defence, since the attack is not carried on in the old way.

You may remember what points you have chiefly insisted upon in our debates on this subject. You granted (as every thinking person must grant) that a power of working miracles, vested in one assuming the character of a *Teacher* from God, would sufficiently establish the truth of his claim;

"but you urged, withal, that there was no solid foundation to believe that any such person was ever vested with such a power; for that the miracles of *Jesus* and his Apostles, related in the New Testament, were not supported by stronger evidence than were the prodigies that disgrace the pages of *Livy*, and Legendary Tales that swell the lives of the *Romish* saints. Now these latter accounts are, on all hands, justly rejected as false, but the former, it seems, are admitted as true: but then, how, you say, can we fairly dispute the authenticity of the one, and insist so much on the credibility of the other? For, as the testimony in both is equally strong, the miracles recorded in both the accounts must be equally credible. That, therefore, you had no way of extricating yourself out of this labyrinth, but by rejecting, at once, all miraculous pretensions whatever."

The whole dispute subsisting between us may be stated thus. – The Protestant Christian thinks himself obliged, from all the principles of reason, to believe *that* evidence true which is brought to support the Gospel miracles; but is at liberty, he thinks, from the same principles of reason, to doubt or disbelieve the miracles ascribed to the *Pagans* of old, or to the *Papists* of later times, or, indeed, to any other person since the publication of the Gospel. But, herein, you are pleased to charge us with a strange and inconsistent belief, because, you say, the evidence for the truth of the miracles in each case, is either the very same, or equally strong.

I have not the least hesitation when I pronounce this charge to be groundless. And I trust, that I shall be able to convince every candid reader of this treatise; addressed to you, that base metal is not more easily detected, when an attempt is made to pass it for gold, than are the false pretensions of *Paganism* and *Popery*, when an attempt is made to put them on the same footing of credibility with the miracles of *Jesus and his apostles*.

I most readily admit that the credibility of such extraordinary performances, as are miracles, will not be sufficiently ascertained, unless the accounts of them be authenticated by such a weight of unexceptionable testimony, as must satisfy every candid and capable inquirer after truth.

You cannot, surely, refuse to join issue with me here. For, with all your unfavourable notions about miracles, I see not how you can require a greater concession than this. And yet, however great it be, I am confident I shall not endanger the cause for which I am an advocate, by setting out with it. For if we can prove (and my design in the following pages is to prove) that the evidence brought for the Gospel miracles, is full as extraordinary as the facts themselves, and that no just suspicion of fraud and falsehood appears in the accounts, while every thing is the reverse with regard to the evidence brought for the *Pagan* and *Popish* miracles, if we can prove this, I say, our reason will tell us that we safely may, and that we ought indeed, to make a distinction, and to believe the former while we reject the latter.

But before we proceed, give me leave to observe, that it is in vain to begin this important dispute, unless you are agreed to decide it by the only kind of evidence that can possibly be had – namely, by the credit that is due to those who appear as witnesses, or, in other words, by examining the facts with all the circumstances of them, and considering, at large, the characters, the views, and the conduct of those who reported them.

Writers, on the side of infidelity, have very rarely ventured to assert the absolute incredibility of miracles; and their precaution seems very prudent. For a miracle being an event brought about in a way contrary to the course of nature, and the course of nature being the establishment of God, every believer of his existence, it should seem, must admit, that it is in his power to reverse it. But this, we know, has been denied by a late very ingenious, but very sceptical author,[122] who has not scrupled to give us *his* reasons, why he makes *the impossibility and miraculous nature of events,*[123] synonymous, and why he gives his decision, *that a miracle supported by any human testimony, is more properly a subject of derision than argument.*[124] It may not, therefore, be improper, to take some notice of this author's favourite nostrum against miracles, which he himself is so fond of, as to boast *that it will with the wise and learned, be an everlasting check to superstitious delusions;*[125] for to him it seems that all miracles are superstitious delusions.

"A miracle," says he, "is a violation of the laws of nature, and as a firm and unalterable experience has established these laws, the proof against a miracle from the vary nature of the fact, is as entire as any argument from experience can be possibly imagined."[126] – Now it is obvious, from this quotation, that our author's argument against the credibility of miracles, depends entirely upon this, of their being events contrary to firm and unalterable experience. But why an event should be incredible, and incapable of being proved by testimony, because it is contrary to our experience, this point, on the certainty of which alone our author's boasted argument is built, I did not, upon perusing the *Essay on Miracles*, find any attempt made to prove; but upon examining the other essays in the collection, it appeared that this point had been the subject of two

---

[122] Philosophical Essays concerning Human Understanding, by David Hume, Esq.

[123] P. 195. – where the author speaking of Abbé Paris's miracles says; what have we now to oppose to such a cloud of witnesses but the absolute impossibility or miraculous nature of the events they relate?

[124] P. 194–5.

[125] 174.

[126] 180.

foregoing ones;[127] and that having established its truth there, as he supposed, he thought himself warranted in his subsequent *Essay on Miracles*, to lay it as the foundation of his reasoning.

What then is this grand principle of our author's new philosophy?[128] – He begins with observing, that

> "all reasonings concerning matter of fact, seem to be founded on the relation of cause and effect, and that by means of that relation alone, can we go beyond the evidence of our memory and senses. If you were to ask a man, says he, why he believes any matter of fact which is absent; for instance, that his friend is in the country, or in *France*; he would give you a reason, and this reason would be some other fact; as a letter received from him, or the knowledge of his former resolutions and promises. A man, finding a watch or any other machine in a desert island, would conclude that there had once been men in that island. All our reasonings concerning fact are of the same nature: and here it is constantly
> supposed that there is a connexion betwixt the present fact and that inferred from it."

Thus far his doctrine is unexceptionable; but when he proceeds to enquire how we arrive at the knowledge of causes and effects, here we must leave him, unless we would, with him, contradict first principles, and strike at the foundation of all certainty. For he lays it down

> "as a general proposition, which admits of no exception, that the knowledge of this relation of cause and effect is not, in any instance, attained by reasoning, *a priori*, but arises entirely from experience, when we find that particular objects are constantly conjoined with each other. Let any object be presented to a man of ever so strong natural reason and abilities; if that object be entirely new to him, he will never be able, by the most accurate examination of its sensible qualities, to discover any of its causes and effects. *Adam*, though his rational faculties be supposed, at the very first, ever so perfect, could not have inferred, from the fluidity and transparency of water, that it would suffocate him, or from the light and warmth of fire, that it would consume him. No object ever discovers, by the qualities which appear to the senses, either the causes which produced it, or the effects which

---

[127] The 4th and 5th.

[128] P. 49.

will arise from it; nor can our reason, unassisted by experience, ever draw any inferences concerning real existence and matter of fact."[129]

It is on the truth of these assertions that the argument depends, by which our author would prove that miracles are incapable of being made credible by human testimony. For thus they seem to be connected together. Previous to our own experience, we can discover no connexion between cause and effect, nor assure ourselves, by reasoning, *a priori*, that a cause has an aptness to produce one effect rather than another. From this position then it follows, that unless our own experience has connected a cause with a particular effect, no testimony of witnesses can induce us to believe that this effect was produced; but miracles being events *contrary to firm and unalterable experience, the proof against a miracle, from the very nature of the fact, is as entire as any argument from experience can possibly be imagined.* – I have endeavoured, with all the impartiality I am master of, to give you a fair representation of this argument; and I hope I have not mistaken it, though a mistake here might be very pardonable, considering the obscurity of this writer, owing more to the singularity of his matter than to any defect in his style. I shall now endeavour to satisfy you, that one who can insist on such points has no pretensions to be followed as a guide.

For it should seen, that the very proposing of his opinion will, to every one who has not renounced the first principles of human knowledge, be a sufficient confutation of it: and though we could not point out any inconsistencies or contradictions in the reasoning by which it is supported, yet as it is apparently sceptical, nay, as the author himself tells us it is so,[130] his arguments, for this one reason, merit no answer, because they can scarcely meet with advocates; they may puzzle, but they cannot convince; they may confound, but will never convert the reader. And it is no inconsiderable proof of the weakness of a cause, when it cannot be defended but by running counter to the general sense of mankind, and contradicting truths looked upon as self-evident.

If no event, however well attested, be credible, which contradicts experience, then there can be no certain standard of the credibility of facts; but this will vary as does the experience of those to whom they are proposed; for all men have not the same opportunities of seeing the same events; and a thing may be familiar to one, and never heard of by another. That there are many events true, which men can have no experience of, is certain. But were the doctrine which we are now opposing to be admitted, no such thing could ever be made credible to one who has not seen it: but

---

[129] P. 50–51.

[130] The fourth Essay he calls *Sceptical Doubts*, and the fifth, *Sceptical Solutions of these Doubts*.

what strange work would this make in life? and how ridiculous would a man make himself if he rejected matters of fact, indisputably true, and confirmed to him by the most unexceptionable testimony, – merely because they were contrary to his experience. For instance, what could be more contrary to experience, *to firm unalterable experience*, within these three or four centuries, than that a small iron bullet, of a few pounds weight, should be able to batter down the thickest and strongest walls? At the first invention of fire arms, suppose that this fact had been attested to a person at a distance, who was entirely unacquainted with the principles and mechanism of the new machine; suppose it attested in the strongest and most unexceptionable manner, by thousands of witnesses, persons of credit and reputation, persons who were spectators, and who could not be suspected by any design to impose a lie – would it be enough for the person to whom this matter of fact was proposed, to say I will not believe it, because you tell me a thing contrary to uniform and constant experience? would he not be looked upon as a whimsical sceptic, if he refused to believe it on this evidence? – Certainly he would, with every body except the author of *Philosophical Essays*, according to whose principles this evidence must be resisted. So that this doctrine, that no event, however well attested, is to be believed, unless it be warranted by experience, excludes from being credible, events deducible from the laws of nature, and which are to be accounted for on mechanical principles, as well as it does miracles. It therefore proves too much, and consequently proves nothing at all. This will be farther illustrated by putting the following case: It is contrary to the uniform, constant experience of the inhabitants under the torrid zone, that water should become solid as the dry land. Suppose, then, what we know must have happened, that persons from our part of the world should go into these sultry regions, and affirm there, to the natives, that water frequently became thus hard in the countries they came from; suppose that vast numbers of witnesses agree in the same attestation, and that this matter of fact is affirmed by every one who arrives from our climates; must all this weight of testimony go for nothing, merely because they assert what is contrary to firm and unalterable experience? This would be very absurd, yet, upon our author's principles it must. – Nor will it make any difference to say, that such events alone are incapable of being rendered credible by testimony, which are contrary to uniform experience in all different parts of the world. For if a person be ignorant what is usual in other climates, then a thing contrary to the settled course of nature in the country where he lives, is as much a miracle (to him I mean) as a thing contrary to the settled course of nature in all parts of the world. That a dead man should be again brought to life, is an event contrary to the settled course of nature in all parts of the world: and supposing such an event attested in the most unexceptionable manner to the inhabitants of any country whatever, they could have no greater reason to look upon it as incredible, than the inhabitants of the torrid zone have to look upon the freezing of water as incredible.

Again – if no event, however well attested, is to be believed, unless we have experience for it, then would it follow that we could never infer the possibility of any events by arguments drawn from reason, or from the nature of the thing. Our author was aware of this, and, therefore, to obviate such an objection, he endeavours to prove that the distinction usually made betwixt arguments drawn from experience, and those drawn from reason is, at the bottom, erroneous; and asserts, "that all those arguments, which are supposed to be the mere effects of reasoning and reflection, will be found to terminate, at last, in some general principle and conclusion, for which we can assign no reason by observation and experience."[131] But is it possible for any serious man to reason thus in earnest? For, if reason, antecedent to experience can, in no instance, point out a connexion betwixt cause and effect, then must we say that there is no foundation in reason for believing that a fabric, consisting of a variety of parts, nicely and regularly put together, is the effect of a *designing cause*, rather than that it sprang from *blind* chance. – We universally assent to the truth of this proposition, that whatever had a beginning arose from a cause prior to it, and producing it. But will our author assert that we could never have known the certainty of this, unless we had drawn it from experience? Will he assert that experience is our sole ground for concluding that life, consciousness, and reason, could not be communicated but by a cause vested with such perfections? Strange as these doctrines are, they are the obvious consequences of the position that experience alone points out the connexion between cause and effect. Nor indeed are these consequences such as our author will disown; for he expressly tells us, *that if we reason* a priori, *any thing may appear able to produce any thing, the falling of a pebble may, for aught we know, extinguish the sun, or the wish of a man control the planets in their orbits*: and again, *that not only the will of the Supreme Being may create matter, but for aught we can know, a* priori, *the will of any other being might create it, or any other cause that the most whimsical imagination can assign.*[132] – I need say no more to you I am sure, nor indeed to any person of sound judgment, to make you disclaim this author as a guide, whose argument against *miracles*, if it has any weight, is equally an argument against the existence of an intelligent *first cause*.

The sophistry of our author's argument, by which he would prove, that without experience, we never can discover the connexion between cause

[131] P. 74.
[132] P. 254.

and effect, lies here, that he brings his instances from the laws of matter and motion established in the world: which laws being, confessedly, arbitrary constitutions of the Creator, the manner of their operations cannot, to be sure, be deduced from any previous reasoning, but must be drawn solely from experience; and from these particular instances he infers his universal conclusion; which is evidently false. For does it at all follow, that, because there is no connexion discoverable *a priori* betwixt cause and effect in some cases, there is no connexion discoverable *a priori* in any case? Because God (and I pretend to reason with none but believers of a God) has established such and such laws in the universe – for instance, that fire should consume, and water suffocate, and a heavy body descend – will it follow that, in this case, we cannot discover from reason, independent of all experience, that God could have established laws different from these at first, and can, when he thinks fit, suspend them now that they are established? This was what our author ought to have proved, and for this plain reason: – every one who has admitted the existence of a God, will be apt to urge that we can discover, by reasoning, *a priori*, that there is a connexion between and Omnipotent Being and Almighty cause; and *every* effect that is the object of power, and, consequently, that we can discover, by reasoning, *a priori*, the possibility of miracles, because it requires the exertion of no greater power to reverse the established laws of nature (in the doing of which consists a miracle) than, at the beginning, to establish them. Our author foresaw some such objection as this might be urged; for he tells us that "though the Being to whom the miracle is ascribed be Almighty, it does not, upon that account, become a whit more probable; since it is impossible for us to know the attributes or actions of such a Being, otherwise than from the experience which we have of his productions in the usual course of nature." Here he presents us again with some of his paradoxes. Who would not have thought that an Almighty Being could produce every possibility, and consequently depart from *his productions in the usual course of nature?* A person of a plain ordinary understanding would have thought, that the very idea of Omnipotence implied the power of doing this: and will expect to hear it demonstrated, that nothing is possible but what is established in the usual course of nature before he alters his opinion. – Unless, therefore, our author can demonstrate this, which, however enterprizing, he has not pretended to do; unless he can shew that an event, contrary to the usual course of things, is not an object of power; the idea of the omnipotence of God will lead us to admit the possibility of such events, and if once their possibility be admitted, in spite of all the quibbles of the sophist, all the art of the sceptic, common sense will teach us, that such events, which are what we call miracles, may be made credible by testimony; because they are supposed to be matters of fact, of the certainty of which spectators may have all the assurance they can have for the certainty of the most common events.

But why need I take so much pains to prove that miracles may become credible by testimony, when I can bring in our author as concurring in the same conclusion? It is frequently the fate of writers, especially of such as aim at something new and singular, to confute themselves in their own works: and that the author of the *Essay on Miracles* has done this, will appear from the following quotation: –

"I beg the limitation here made may be remarked, when I say that a miracle can never be proved so as to be the foundation of a new system of religion. For I own that otherwise there may possibly be miracles, or violations of the ordinary course of nature, of such a kind as to admit of proof from human testimony, though, perhaps, it will be impossible to find any such in all the records of history. Thus, suppose all authors, in all languages, agree, that from the first of *January* 1600, there was a total darkness over all the earth for eight days: suppose that the tradition of this event is still strong and lively among the people; that all travellers, who return from foreign countries, bring us accounts of the same tradition, without the lease variation or contradiction; it is evident that our present philosophers, instead of doubting of that fact, ought to receive it for certain, and ought to search for the cause whence it might be derived."[133]

Not to insist on the obvious inconsistency of recommending it to the philosophers, to search for the cause of an event contrary to uniform and constant experience, when, according to our author's doctrine, such a search would be absurd and useless, *Because experience alone points out the connexion between cause and effect*, not to insist on this, I shall beg leave to observe, that in the above quotation, he himself pulls down his own favourite scheme. – For I appeal to every reader, whether we have not here a confession, that human testimony may, in some cases, give credibility to miracles, or violations of the laws of nature? He forgets then that he had laid it down as a principle "that *no* testimony for *any* kind of miracle can ever possibly amount to a probability, much less a proof;[134] that it is experience *only* which gives authority to human testimony,[135] – that a miracle supported by *any* human testimony is more properly a subject of derision than of argument;"[136] – for here he allows that testimony, under

[133] P. 199.
[134] Ibid.
[135] P. 198.
[136] P. 194.

certain circumstances, may give credibility to a stranger prodigy than ever happened. Perhaps he will say, that the universality of the miracle and of the testimony, in the instance assigned by him, makes it different from all others. I answer, that admitting it does, still he stands charged with a contradiction of his own principles, which, how he can get clear of, I see not. His general opinion, as is evident from his own words just quoted is, that human testimony, in no instance, can prove a miracle; how, therefore, can this position be maintained, and it be granted, at the same time as he does grant, that such a testimony as he describes will give credibility to the miracle of the eight days darkness? In the one place he rejects human testimony *absolutely*, and *without any restrictions*, when reporting a miracle; and, in the other place, he gives us leave, provided human testimony have certain qualifications mentioned by him, to admit it, however miraculous the fact attested be.

But I see no reason why a *local* violation of the course of nature – a darkness, for instance, of eight days in one country only, if attested by those who lived near the place where it happened, and confirmed by the tradition of those who had opportunities of knowing the fact, should not be looked upon as equally credible with the universal darkness instanced by our author. The possibility of a *local* miracle cannot, surely, be denied by the person who admits the possibility of so strange a miracle as one extending over the whole earth. Now, if a local miracle be possible, nothing more can be requisite to establish its credibility, but that we have all the evidence for it that the nature of the fact can admit of; and as it was not universal, universal testimony must not be expected. For the nature of the proof from testimony is the same, whether we have five hundred or five millions of witnesses. If the lesser number have equal opportunities of knowing what they attest, and are equally credible in other respects with the greater number, we have equal reason for admitting the testimony of both.

You see, sir, that the great champion against miracles, does himself admit, that human testimony may prove a miracle of as extraordinary a kind too as we can suppose ever to happen.

But, upon a closer attention, I begin to think I have injured him, by supposing that he could ever deny that miracles, in general, can be made credible by testimony; for, it seems, his opinion is that only such miracles cannot be made credible by testimony, as are urged *to be the foundation of a new system of religion; and he desires us to understand him with this limitation.*[137] Not to misrepresent him, therefore, this limitation shall be allowed him. But, at the same time, I would ask him this plain question, if this be allowed him, will it not involve him in a labyrinth of contradictions? For it matters not, whether a miracle be wrought in support of a

[137] P. 199.

religion or no – our author's boasted argument strikes at all miracles; and, according to his principles, *all* miracles must be rejected, because *all* miracles are events contrary to firm and unalterable experience. Before, therefore, he had admitted that human testimony may give credibility to such miracles as are not *ascribed to a new system of religion,* he should have taken care to have weighed the obvious consequences of his own arguments, which expressly forbid him to believe *any* miracles at all. – But not to carry this charge of inconsistency any farther, we have here a clear view of the principles of this gentleman. He will believe any thing when religion is out of the question, let it be ever so strange; but whenever religion is concerned, he is so scrupulous, that he will admit nothing. He grants that the most extraordinary prodigies may be proved by testimony, provided no body can assign any end or purpose they could be designed to answer; but whenever miracles are appealed to as *the foundation of a new system of religion,* that is, when ever a wise and important end can be served by them, then, he would have us believe, that we have been imposed upon, and that no such miracles were really performed. How wild and inconsistent this way of talking (for I cannot call it reasoning) is, I appeal even to yourself; which, while it absolutely refuses credibility to the miracles of the Christian scriptures, allows us to believe such miracles and prodigies as are to be met with in *Livy* or *Dion Cassius.*

But what is the reason assigned for the incredibility of miracles, when they are made the foundation of a new religion? "Because," says our author, "men, in all ages, have been so much imposed upon by ridiculous stories of that kind, that this very circumstance would be a full proof of the cheat, and sufficient, with all men of sense, not only to make them reject the fact, but even reject it without farther examination."[138]

Are we then brought back, after all the efforts of metaphysical scepticism, to this weak and childish argument – That, because some men have been knaves and fools, therefore, all must be such: that because some men's testimony in relating miracles has been false, no testimony whatever for a miraculous fact ought ever to be taken? – To infer from the world's having been sometimes imposed upon by false miracles, that no miracles have ever been true, is as absurd as if one should deny that there is any real virtue among men, because there is much hypocrisy; or as if he should refuse to take any coin, because it sometimes has been counterfeited. Counterfeit coin, supposes that there is such a thing in the world as good money, and no body would pretend, outwardly, to be virtuous, unless some were really so. In the same manner, the false miracles, about which so much work is made, suppose the existence of real ones; and the cheats that have been imposed upon the world, far from furnishing us with reasons to

[138] P. 200.

reject all miracles in general, are, on the contrary, a strong proof that *some,* of which they are imitations, have been genuine. By what criterion we can distinguish the true from the false, is indeed a most important enquiry, and will be the subject of the following sheets.

I shall not prosecute my examination of this author's boasted argument against miracles any farther, both because it has been fully and effectually answered by others,[139] and because what I have just thrown out must satisfy you that events contrary to firm and constant experience, may become credible by human testimony, especially as you have *his* word for it; and he was the first, I know of, who ever denied it, giving us his reason for doing so. In this acting the part of a fair adversary, and at the same time, in my opinion, giving the severest blow to the enemies of the Gospel miracles that they ever received; because he has shewn that he could not (and if he could not, I am sure no other person can) establish the incredibility of miracles, but by calling in question the first principles of human knowledge; but by introducing the most extravagant scepticism, that ever made its appearance under the venerable name of philosophy. – I shall only add, that an author who espouses such opinions, can never be a dangerous enemy to religion. His arguments having novelty, may please for a while; but so opposite are they to every one's settled notions, that their influence cannot be lasting. Sorry I am to say, that the author of the *Philosophical Essays* seems to have a right to this character, – a character which must sink the value of his writings, in spite of the most eminent abilities.

Though I have sufficiently exposed the weakness of Mr. Hume's sceptical subtilties, the advocates of infidelity, in general, not having adopted them, it is incumbent on me to take notice of a more popular objection to which they usually have recourse. It is this, that man has a light within, which answers, to the full, all the purposes of religion, and that a due attention to his rational faculties, will, without the assistance of supernatural instruction, enable him to know and to act in conformity to the divine will, as the means of securing the favour of heaven and the happiness of a future life.

...

The same way of reasoning will overturn the credibility of the miraculous cures attributed to *Vespasian.* The author of the *Essay on Miracles,* speaks of them in the following manner:

"One of the best attested miracles in all profane history is that which *Tacitus* Reports of *Vespasian,* who cured a blind man in *Alexandria* by

---

[139] By Dr. Rutherforth in a sermon; by an anonymous author of Remarks on an Essay concerning Miracles; supposed to be a worthy prelate; but more at large by the Revd Mr. Adams of Shrewsbury, and by Dr. Campbell of Aberdeen.

means of his spittle, and a lame man by the mere touch of his foot, in obedience to a vision of the god *Serapis*, who had enjoined them to have recourse to the emperor for their miraculous and extraordinary cures. The story may be seen in that fine historian, where every circumstance seems to add weight to the testimony, and might be displayed at large, with all the force of argument and eloquence, if any one were now concerned to enforce the evidence of that exploded and idolatrous superstition. The gravity, solidity, age and probity of so great an emperor, who, through the whole course of his life, conversed in a familiar way with his friends and courtiers, and never affected those extraordinary airs of divinity assumed by *Alexander* and *Demetrius*. The historian, a contemporary writer noted for candour, and veracity, and withal the greatest and most penetrating genius perhaps of all antiquity, and so free from every tendency to superstition and credulity, that he even lies under the contrary imputation of atheism and profaneness; the persons from whose testimony he related the miracle, of established character for judgement and veracity, as we may well suppose, eye-witnesses of the facts, and confirming their verdict after the Flavian family, were despoiled of the empire, and could no longer give any reward as the price of a lie – *utrumque, qui interfuere, nunc quoque memorant, postquam nullum mendaciis pretium.* To which if we add the public nature of the fact as related, it will appear that no evidence can well be supposed stronger for so gross and so palpable a falsehood."[140]

It seems to me that the ingenious essay writer, in the above quotation, confounds two things very different from each other – The evidence that this transaction happened, and the evidence that there was any thing supernatural performed. The circumstances which he expatiates so much upon, the character of the emperor, the veracity of *Tacitus*, the testimony of eye-witnesses, and the public nature of the facts do, indeed, prove unexceptionably, that the two men in question did apply to *Vespasian*, in the manner related.[141] But that there was any truth either in the vision of

---

[140] Essay on Miracles, p. 192, 193.

[141] For the satisfaction of the reader I have subjoined Tacitus's account of this matter. Per eos menses quibus Vespasianus Alexandriæ statos æstivis flatibus dies, & certa maris opperiebatur, multa miracula evenere, *quis cælestis favor, & quædam in Vespasianum inclinatio numinum ostenderetur.* Ex plebe Alexandrina quidam oculorum tabe notus, genua ejus advolvitur, remedium cæcitatis exposcens gemitu, monitu Serapidis Dei; quem dedita superstitionibus gens ante alios colit: precabaturque principem, *ut genas,* et *oculorum orbes dignaretur respergere oris excremento.* Alius manu æger eodem Deo auctore, ut pede ac vestigio Caesaris calcaretur, orabat. Vespasianus primo irridere, aspernari, atque, illis instantibus, modo Famam vanitatis metuere; modo obsecratione ipsorum, & *vocibus adulantium* in spem induci, postremo æstimari a medicis jubet, an talis cæcitas, ac debilitas, ope humana super-

god *Serapis,* or in the cures pretended to, we are so far from having the strongest evidence, that no evidence can well be supposed weaker.

It is certain in the first place, that both the complaints said to be cured, could easily have been counterfeited.[142] The lame and blind who infest our streets, can see, and use their decrepid arms or legs, when the business of the day is over. Cures, therefore, may in such cases be pretended to be performed, while the spectators are the dupes of a concerted scene of imposture. The lame need only move that member which, before, he did not use, and the blind open his contracted eyelids, and the work is done. To have recourse therefore to a supernatural interposition, in this case, when the whole transaction can be so easily accounted for by supposing a collusion to subsist, between the men who were to pretend a cure, and the emperor, or at least his courtiers, would be highly superstitious. But the possibility of there being such a collusion, is not all that we have to urge; for the relation of these pretended miracles, as given us by *Tacitus,* suggests strong suspicions that such a collusion actually subsisted. The eagerness of *Vespasian's* courtiers pressing him to make trial of his healing power, and particularly of his physicians, who flattered him with a compliment of his being, perhaps, chosen by the gods as their instrument in this affair; these circumstances, added to this consideration that the whole transaction was calculated to do honour to the emperor, and to add lustre to his imperial dignity lately assumed, authorize us sufficiently in our suspicions of fraud. – And when we consider, that the superstitious *Alexandrians,* who were the persons immediately imposed upon, would eagerly believe miracles ascribed to *Serapis,* the god whom, we learn from *Tacitus,* they honoured before all others; and at the same time, observe that they who had all the means of detection, were the contrivers and actors of the fraud, we shall

---

abiles forent. Medici varie disserere; *huic non exesum vim luminis, & redituram si pellerentur obstantia; illi elapsos in pravumartus, si salubris vis adhibeatur, posse integrari.* Id sortasse cordi deis & divino ministerio principem electum. Denique patrati remedii gloriam penes Cæsarem; irriti ladibrium penes miseros fore. Igitur Vespasianus cuncta fortuna patere ratus, nec quidquam ultra incredibile, læto ipse vultu, erecta, quae astabat, multitudine, jussa exsequitur. Statim conversa ad usum manus, ac cæco reluxit dies. – Utrumque qui interfuere nunc quoque memorant, postquam mullum mendacio pretium. Tacitus Hist. Lib. 4.

[142] The report of the physicians, as Tacitus relates it, confirms this. According to them, *the blind man's organs of vision were not destroyed, and that his sight might be restored on the removal of some obstacle.* But what this obstacle was, and whether there was any obstacle but what the patient could create or remove himself, is not mentioned. – Equally ambiguous doth their report represent the case of the lame man to be – for they tell us *that the disorder was in the joints, and might be remedied by the application of a healing power.* Now, such a lameness has seldom any external marks of it discernible by the eye: so that here, also, there was wide scope for imposture.

then be warranted to conclude, that *Vespasian's* pretended miracles were not *examined*, in the time and at the place where they were published, and that therefore they will not bear to be tried by the rule I last laid down.[143]

I shall only add, that the manner in which, as *Tacitus* relates, one of these pretended cures was performed by *Vespasian*, so exactly resembles that which *St. John*[144] informs us our Saviour adopted in the cure of the man born blind, as to afford a fair presumption, that the contrivers of the *Pagan* imposture having it in their view to check the rapid progress of Christianity, produced by an appeal to the miracles of its great founder, fabricated similar powers for their emperors; – And it is very remarkable, that this honour was also conferred on *Adrian*, another of them, who is represented as having cured blindness by the same mode of operation.

The same insufficiency of evidence which destroys the credibility of the *Pagan* miracles above-mentioned, equally affects the credibility of such of the *Popish* ones that can be traced up to the times when they were said to be performed, and were published on the spot. For, on trying them, as I have done the former, by the test of the third rule laid down by me, we shall invariably find, that the circumstances attending them are such as must satisfy us that the evidences on which they were supported, had this most capital defect of having never been carefully examined, as the means of removing the suspicion of fraud being practised on the credulous believers.

---

[143] It cannot be thought I go out of my way, when I take notice here of a remarkable instance of the incorrectness, not to say of the unfairness of Dr. *Middleton*, whose abilities as a writer, however admired, can never atone for those deviations from truth, with which, especially in his quotations, he has been so frequently charged. In his *Free Inquiry*, p. 171, speaking of the miracles in question, he says "The same writers (Suetonius and Tacitus) also "declare that this good emperor by a divine admonition from the god Serapis, publicly restored a blind man to his sight," *&c. &c.* – Now would not one who reads this, imagine that the divine admonition, mentioned by the two historians, was pretended to be made to Vespasian himself? – The Doctor's words can bear no other meaning; and yet it is told us, as plainly as could be, both by Tacitus and by Suetonius, that the admonition was pretended to, by the men themselves, who were to be cured. Tacitus's words I have already quoted, and Suetonius's account is as follows. E plebe quidam luminibus orbatus, item alius debilicrure, sedentem pro tribunali pariter adierunt, orantes opem valetudinis demonstratam a Serapide per quietem. – I shall only observe that if the author of the Essay on Miracles had read Tacitus and Suetonius, as misinterpreted, or rather misrepresented, by Dr. Middleton, he might have pledged the veracity of Vespasian himself for the truth of this vision from the god Serapis, for which, at present, no other evidence can be alleged, but the affirmation of two unnamed wretches from the dregs of the people, fit tools to be employed in acting a part in an imposture.

[144] John 9, p. 6.

What then hath been the nature and tendency of the miracles that have at any time been appealed to by the *Papists*? They were always invented to propagate the belief of certain rites and doctrines, and practices, which had crept into the church; to advance the reputation of some particular chapel;[145] image;[146] or order[147] of religious; or to countenance opinions

[145] One of the most boasted miracles amongst Papists is the transportation of the *Virgin Mary's* house from Palestine, first into Dalmatia, and then after several changes of situation, to Loretto in the Pope's dominions. A story, which, from the amazing riches heaped up in the treasury of the church built over the Holy house, the presents of votaries who croud from every part of Europe to Loretto, appears to have answered the designed end, though it be so big with absurdities, and the imposture be so glaring, that one could scarcely suppose it possible that the most lamentable ignorance, and the most stupid credulity, could believe it. Tursellinus, the same who displayed his talents in celebrating Francis Xavier, his bestowed a book on the *wonderful migrations of the Holy house.*

[146] The gain arising to the possessors of an image which has a reputation of working miracles, has contributed wonderfully to enlarge the catalogue of such boasted facts. The miraculous images of the blessed Virgin are most frequent. Amongst many others, our lady of Atocha, near Madrid; our lady of Montserrat in Catalonia; our lady of Saragossa; and our lady of Halle in Brabant, are remarkable. The last mentioned image performs daily, so many miracles, that the printed list of them is greatly augmented, from time to time, and now is swelled to a large pamphlet. Nay, whoever visits her church at Halle, may see a *standing miracle* with his own eyes. There is placed in a corner, a heap of stone bullets, which, as the infallible legend sets forth, being fired into the town when it was besieged by the Saracens (no matter in what age or year) the Virgin left her place in the church, walked the ramparts, and having caught the bullets in her lap, deposited them where they now lie. Should you disbelieve this, you will be told as a proof of its being true, that, if you attempt to count these bullets, you cannot reckon the same number twice, and that if two persons count, at the same time, they cannot agree in their report. That it should be difficult to reckon, merely by the eye (for you are debarred touching, by the interposition of iron bars) between thirty and forty bullets heaped one upon another, is easy to be imagined. But that there is any thing supernatural in this, I should have scarcely thought there could be any body so credulous as to believe, had I not been upon the spot, and met with such believers.

[147] The miracles of monks and friars, calculated to promote the interests of monkery in general, and of the respective orders of religious in particular, and equally numerous as they are silly and ridiculous. For a specimen of them, the reader may peruse Dr. *Geddes's* View of all the Orders of Monks and Friars in the Roman Church, with an Account of their Founders, &c. in the 3d vol. of his Miscellaneous Tracts.

either such as were[148] contested amongst themselves, or such[149] as the whole church did teach and require as points of faith. To descend to

[148] Of this kind are the miracles of the *Dominicans* against the *immaculate conception of the blessed Virgin*, and the miracles of the *Franciscans* for this tenet, the former listed under the banner of Thomas Aquinas, the latter under that of Duns Scotus. A very remarkable scene of forgery detected amongst the Dominicans in a convent at Berne, 1057, may be met with in *Burnet's Travels*, from p. 31, to p. 41. It is an observation which I believe upon examination will be found to hold good, that whenever any pretences to miracles have been detected, by those who are in power, amongst the Papists, these have always been facts alleged in confirmation of doctrines about which Papists themselves have been divided, and the belief of which has not been calculated so much to be beneficial to the Holy church in general, as to serve the interested views of jarring ecclesiastics. This has arisen from the following reason, When a miracle pretended to, was of such a nature as to confirm a doctrine, in the belief of which *all* the orders of ecclesiastics, that is, all the ruling part of the church, equally concurred and were equally interested, in this case, it is easy to conceive that all would join in confederacy to propagate the fact among their credulous votaries. But when a miracle has been alleged by one order of ecclesiastics to confirm a doctrine admitted by them, but opposed by other orders, in this case, as there was an opposition of interests there could be no general confederacy. The rulers of the church being divided among themselves, they were spies on each other; and being bound in honour to support the doctrines of their respective parties, no pains were spared to examine into the miracles appealed to, by their antagonists; which, of course, has produced many detections of gross impostures, and particularly, occasioned the detection and punishment of the actors in the scene of villainy at Berne. A very similar instance of imposture, attempted by the Franciscans at Orleans, in 1534 was detected and punished by banishing these contrivers. This pretended miracle not having any references to the general interests of the church, the civil magistrate's interference was readily obtained, and easily became effectual. See *Gaillard*'s Life of *Francis I.* vol. 6. p. 460. to 466.

[149] The confirmation of relique and saint worship has been a fruitful source of miracles, from the fourth or fifth century downwards. The more modern corruptions of image worship, purgatory and transubstantiation, have had their truth attested by a variety of wonderful visions, revelations, and prodigies. Transubstantiation, in particular, has been often proved by the springing out of blood from consecrated wafers. One of the most remarkable stories of this kind, is said to have happened at Brussels in 1369. Some Jews having stolen several consecrated hosts out of a church, in contempt of the god supposed to be present under the form of bread, ran their knives into them, and instantly there streamed out great quantities of blood. Three of these wafers, no doubt the identical ones pierced by the Jews, are still preserved in St. Gudule's church at Brussels, where I have seen them, They being exposed with great pomp to public view, during the octave of an annual festival. For an account of this miracle, see *Deliees de Pais Bas*, v. 1. p. 121, 122, 123; see also *Description de Bruxelles*, p. 74, and 75. – A miracle, similar to this, is related in the *Memoirs of Brandenburgh* at the year 1279, where blood is said to have boiled up through the ground, from a consecrated host buried at Belitz. "Les Vierges miraculeuses, les images secourables, & les reliques des saints avoient alors une vertu toute singuliere. Le Sang de Belitz entr'autres étoit fort renommé. Voici ce qui c'étoit. Une cabaretiere de cette ville vola une hostie consacrée & l'enterra sous un tonneau dan sa cave, pour avoir meilleur debit de sa bierre: Elle en eut des remords elle denonca son crime au curé, qui vint en procession avec tout son attirail pontifical pour deterrer l'hostie. En ensoncant la pelle en terre

particular instances would in a great measure be unnecessary, because the account which I here give of these pretended miracles is, on all hands, agreed to be the true one. The few particulars mentioned at the bottom of the page, may serve, by way of illustration.

Such then being the nature and genius of the pretended miracles of the church of *Rome*, facts coinciding with the favourite opinions, and superstitious prejudices, of those to whom they were proposed; that the reports and accounts of them should undergo any strict examination, at the time of their being published, will appear highly improbable, when we consider, what certainly has always been the case, that the persons with whom such reports have gained any credit, had been trained up from their infancy in a persuasion that miraculous powers are continued in their church. A previous disposition of this kind, to admit miracles in general, a credulity and superstition thus ready to embrace every strange story, will naturally incline persons of this character to believe, without scrutiny, those particular miracles proposed to them, which are so framed as to be agreeable to their favourite sentiments. Nothing will be too wonderful to pass current, if it be connected with their religious opinions. This circumstance alone will reconcile all difficulties, remove all doubts, and secure, from being formally detected, stories which seem industriously to have been made up of the wildest inconsistencies, and strangest improbabilities, as experiments how far the credulity of the multitude may be wrought upon with success.

And this leads me naturally to observe that, as the *Popish* miracles have always been proposed to those whose superstition and prejudices previously disposed them to believe without examination, the credibility of these boasted wonders will become still more suspicious, if we add another circumstance – That they have always been set on foot, at least have always been encouraged and supported, by those who, by their influence and power, could prevent any examination which might tend to undeceive the world. – They have been the arts of the powerful *few*, to keep in awe the ignorant *many*, the forgeries of the rulers of the church, to countenance the corruptions with which they have disgraced the church; to add a sanction to doctrines and practices visibly calculated to extend their own

---

on vit bouillonner du sang, & tout le monde cria au miracle. L'imposture étoit trop grossiere, & l'on scait que c'étoit du sang de bœuf, que la cabaretiere avoit versé. Ces mircles ne laissoient pas que de faire impression sur l'esprit des peuples." M. de Brandenburgh, p. 265. The observation of the *Royal Memoir Writer* that such miracles, though they bore visible marks of imposture, failed not to make impressions on the minds of the people, is founded on this truth, that where there is a previous disposition to believe, no imposture will be too gross to be admitted, especially when the impostures are of such a kind as to be countenanced by those whose empire over the understandings of the people is boundless.

influence, to add to their own riches, and to give themselves an unlimited command over their fellow-Christians, though at the expense of their common Christianity.

This then being the case, it would have been next to impossible to have set about an examination of these pretences to miracles. For were we even to allow, that those to whom they were proposed, had the best inclination in the world not to believe but upon proper evidence, the danger which must attend their giving any signs of this inclination, would deter every one in his senses from attempting a detection. He who would set himself up to oppose a fraud supported by the authority and influence of the rulers of the church in a country where, in matters of religion, the civil magistrate is guided by the priest, would soon find reason to repent of his temerity.

Can there therefore, be any hesitation in refusing to admit the truth of miraculous facts backed and supported by those who alone had the means of detecting the fraud, if there was any; and who having the sword in their own hands, would never point it against themselves, to punish their own impostures?[150]

---

[150] The author of the *Essay on Miracles*, p. 193, has thought proper to expatiate on the story related by the *cardinal de Retz*, of a door-keeper of the cathedral at Saragossa who recovered a lost leg, by rubbing the stump of it with the holy oil. He sets off the evidence of this miracle to the greatest advantage, as attested by a contemporary writer, a person of eminence, and of a libertine and unbelieving character; and the fact of such a nature that there could be no ambiguity about it, and so public as to be known to all the inhabitants of Saragossa. But it is obvious that the evidence of this miracle labours under both the defects just mentioned. There was here, on the one hand, the power and influence of the clergy, particularly the canons of the church (who are the persons quoted by the Cardinal as his witnesses) asserting and supporting a story the belief of which, by increasing the veneration for the miraculous image of the Virgin which is in their church (to which image the holy oil no doubt, owed its efficacy) would be a sure means of increasing the wealth of their community. And on the other hand, there was the blind credulity of the superstitious inhabitants of *Saragossa*, bred up from their infancy with a persuasion that miracles were performed by the church, zealously devoted to the worship of the Blessed Virgin, and eager to embrace without examination, whatever might do honour to the image of her, which is thought the glory of their city. – There is a story in *Carte's Life of the Duke of Ormonde*, which I shall here quote, as it shews us how little regard ought to be paid to miracles published amongst those who are previously disposed to believe such stories, and where there is power and influence acting upon superstition and credulity. "Whilst he (the Marquis of Ormonde) was there (at Lyons) he called at a shop to have his peruke mended. The master was a cripple, both hands and feet, but said he would direct his sister to mend it as it ought to be. The Marquis taking another peruke from him, went to gaze about the streets, and stepping accidentally into the next church, he saw a chapel in it, which was hung with the presents of several votaries who had received cures from our lady. Among the rest he observed an inscription as well as offering, made by the very man he had left. When he came back to the peruke-maker, he asked him about it, wondering he should do so, being still decrepid. The man answered, that he thought that he was rather better than he had been, and hoped that by doing honour to the lady before hand, he might the sooner

Having employed more attention than perhaps was necessary, on the extraordinary works, which gentlemen of your way of thinking have usually put upon the same footing of credibility with the Gospel miracles, though the manifest fabrications of imposture, I now proceed to take into consideration another class of them – Works, really performed, but which required no miraculous interposition, being brought about by the operation of causes merely natural.

Many instances of this kind might be assigned, but I shall, in a great measure, confine myself to one single instance, as most to my purpose of all others, because most insisted upon by my antagonists, – an instance which has been a favourite topic in all the late debates concerning miracles, and which has furnished you and your friends with matter of triumph, as if the objections drawn from it were unanswerable. – I scarcely need inform you that I am now speaking of the miracles ascribed to the *Abbé Paris*, and said to be performed at his tomb, in the metropolis of a neighbouring kingdom, within these thirty years.

The author of the *Free Inquiry into the miraculous Powers of the primitive Church* is at great pains to place these works in a distinguished point of view. For after filling three or four pages with an account of them set off to the greatest advantage, he concludes with the following reflection.

"Let our declaimers then on the authority of the fathers, produce, if they can, any evidence of the primitive miracles half so strong, as what is alleged for the miracles of the *Abbé Paris*: or, if they cannot do it, let them give us a reason why we must receive the one and reject the other: or, if they fail likewise in this, let them be so ingenuous at last as to confess, that we have no other part left but either to admit them all, or reject them all, for otherwise they can never be thought to act consistently."[151]

The above quotation aims only at the credibility of the miracles attested by the fathers; but a late celebrated author on the side of infidelity, and whose opinions I have already[152] examined, has urged the miracles ascribed to the *Abbé Paris*, as what affect the credibility of all miracles in general.

---

enjoy the rest of her benefit." *Carte*, vol. 2d. p. 180, ad. An. 1658. Is it to be imagined that this fellow would have ventured to assert this glaring falsehood, in so awful a manner, had he not known that any thing would pass unnoticed, and unexamined, that might do *honour to our lady?*

[151] See Middleton's Free Inquiry, p. 226.

[152] See above from page 8, to page 35.

"There surely (says he) never was so great a number of miracles ascribed to one person, as those which were lately said to have been wrought in France upon the tomb of the *Abbé Paris* the famous *Jansenist*, with whose sanctity the people were so long deluded. The curing of the sick, giving hearing to the deaf, and sight to the blind, were every where talked of as the effects of the holy sepulchre. But what is more extraordinary, many of the miracles were immediately proved upon the spot, before judges of unquestioned credit and distinction, in a learned age, and on the most eminent theatre that is now in the world. Nor is this all; a relation of them was published and dispersed every where; nor were the *Jesuits*, though a learned body, supported by the civil magistrate, and determined enemies to those opinions in whose favour the miracles were said to have been wrought, ever able distinctly to refute and detect them. Where shall we find such a number of circumstances agreeing to the corroboration of one fact? And what have we to oppose to such a cloud of witnesses, but the absolute impossibility or miraculous nature of the events which they relate? And this, surely, in the eyes of all reasonable people, will alone be regarded as a sufficient refutation."[153]

What he has thus confidently asserted to the public, has been often insisted on by yourself in our private debates. You used to talk of it as a point not to be disputed, that the marks of genuine miracles laid down by *Mr. Leslie,*[154] in his *Short Method with the Deists*, are applicable to the miracles ascribed to the *Abbé Paris*: that these facts had an indisputable

---

[153] Philosophical Essays, p. 195.

[154] Mr. Leslie's four rules of judging of the credibility of miracles, are first, That the matter of facts be such, as that men's outward senses, their eyes, and ears, may be judges of it. Secondly, That it be done publicly in the face of the world. Thirdly, That not only public monuments be kept up in memory of it, but some outward actions be performed. Fourthly, That such monuments, and such actions or observances be instituted, and do commence from the time that the matter of fact was done.

The *Short Method with the Deists*, has always been looked upon as Mr. Leslie master-piece. It may seem strange, therefore, that the French should claim this treatise as theirs. And yet they do; for I find it inserted, with some inconsiderable variations from the English copy, in the last edition of the works of *Abbé de St. Real*. But that Mr *Leslie* was the author of this excellent book, is obvious from the following reasons. First, this piece never had a place amongst St. *Real's* works, till long after his death, and after the publication of it by *Leslie*, so that we have no authority for its being St. *Real's* besides that of booksellers and publishers. Secondly, the learned *Le Clerc*, when he attacked the *Short Method*, which was above ten years after St. *Real's* death, attributed it to the *Englishman*. Thirdly, the allusion to *Stone-henge*, and what is mentioned about *Charles Blount* speak strongly for an *English* author. And, Fourthly, the *French* appears to be a translation from this circumstance, that whenever it differs from the *English* copy it is patched up from other parts of Mr. *Leslie's* works. – His Defence of the Short Method, &c.

right to his two first marks; being such as that men's senses could judge of their certainty, and, also, being performed openly in the heart of a great city, and in the presence of crouds of spectators; that with regard to his two later marks, they were only intended as tests by which to try miracles said to be performed in a distant age; whereas the miracles ascribed to the *Abbé Paris*, had this peculiar advantage of being performed within our own memory: in a word, that you saw no way how a Christian could extricate himself out of this labyrinth, and reject the miracles of the *Jansenist* saint,[155] without having equal reason to reject those of the founder of Christianity.

[155] A short account of the Jansenists and Jansenism, will be proper in this place. The Jansenists are so denominated from Jansenius Bishop of *Ipres*, who died 1638. His opinions gaining ground in France were complained of by the Jesuits, to Rome, and condemned by Innocent the Xth in 1653, and by Alexander the VIIth in 1657. In the bulls of these two popes, five propositions, said to be extracted from Jansenius's book, called Augustinus, were condemned, and as they contain the distinguishing tenets ascribed to the Jansenists, by their antagonists, I shall insert them here. *First,* some of God's commands are impossible to be fulfilled by righteous men even though they endeavour with all their power to obey them, because the grace by which they should be enabled to fulfil them is wanting. *Secondly,* in our present state of corrupt nature, man never resists inward grace. *Thirdly,* In our present, corrupt state, it is not requisite in order to a man's having merit or demerit, that he should have such a freedom of will as excludes necessity; that which excludes compulsion is sufficient. *Fourthly,* The Semi-Pelagians admitted the necessity of inward preventing grace not only to the beginning of faith, but also to every future act of it; but they were heretics because they asserted that this grace might be resisted. *Fifthly,* The Semi-Pelagians are heretics, for saying that Christ died for all men in general. – The condemnation of these five propositions gave rise to vast animosities and controversies in France, till, at last, in 1668, the Pope was prevailed upon to require no more from the Jansenists, than that they should subscribe to the condemnation of the five propositions in general, without mentioning their being contained in the book of Jansenius. This they agreed to; and this transaction is usually called the Peace of Jansenism. But the calm was of short duration. For so early in 1679, we find Mr. Arnaud, the famous Champion of Jansenism, retiring out of France, not thinking himself safe, any longer there. He was followed in his retreat by Pasquier Quesnel, a priest of the Oratory, whose *Moral Reflections on the New Testament,* published at Brussels in 1698, occasioned the revival of the disputes with greater violence than ever. An approbation, prefixed to this book, by the Bishop of Chalons (afterwards Cardinal de Noailles and Archbishop of Paris) occasioned the condemnation of it. For the Jesuits bearing this prelate a grudge, immediately began their intrigues, and after several unsuccessful applications at length in 1713, got Clement the XIth to publish the famous bull or constitution, usually called *Unigenitus,* because it begins with these words, Unigenitus Filius Dei, &c. &c. By this bull *one hundred and one propositions,* said to be extracted from Father Quesnel's book, were condemned as false, captious, blasphemous, ill sounding, scandalous, impious, rash, bordering upon heresy, heretical, &c. &c. without giving any particular proposition its proper qualification. Lewis the XIVth now in his dotage, and under the direction of the Jesuits, favoured this bull so much, that Cardinal de Noailles and seven or eight bishops refusing to accept it, *Letters de Cachet* were prepared against them, when the king's death opened a new scene. The government having now changed hands a change of

Such, then, being the use made of the pretended miracles of the *Abbé Paris,*[156] an examination of them becomes very necessary, and shall now be entered upon. And I am not without hope that I have it in my power to give you such a view of these boasted facts as will satisfy you how unfair a representation of them we have had in the above quotations from Dr. *Middleton,* and the author of the *Essay on Miracles,* and consequently with how little reason they have been set up in opposition to the miracles of the New Testament.

measures also ensued, and the duke of *Orleans,* the regent, not willing to hazard the peace of the kingdom, by a persecution of the opposers of the bull, by an edict enjoined silence concerning it, as the best method of deciding the controversy. This injunction of silence, as it was all the Jansenists could desire, greatly displeased the court of Rome. But though the Pope threatened excommunication to those who received not the constitution, Cardinal de Noailles and his party, disregarded the thunder of the conclave, and appealed to a general council: hence they were called *appellants.* Thus far all went well with them. But Noailles, now doating, being prevailed upon to submit, the Duke of Orleans dying, and the Jesuits once more getting footing at court, from that period down to the present time, the Jansenists have been under a cloud, and the reception of the bull so strenuously insisted on, as to produce the late proceedings which have ended in the banishment of the parliament of Paris.

[156] It may not be unentertaining to give some account of this person, to whose intercession so many wonders have been ascribed – The *Abbé Paris* was a gentleman of very good family of the robe, and eldest son of a counsellor of the parliament of Paris. From his earliest youth he discovered a remarkable turn for the extravagancies of devotion. As he grew up, this got so far the better of his reason, that he relinquished all pretensions of succeeding to his father's post, to a younger brother, and dedicated himself to the church, mortifying himself with continual fastings, and scarcely ever stirring from before his crucifix. Not thinking this enough to insure his salvation, he quitted every advantage his birth had given him, and having sold his estate, buried himself in an obscure retreat, known only to the sick an needy whom he administered unto, and relieved. With all this sanctity he was, in his own opinion, the greatest of sinners. This diffidence was the grand principles of his conduct; it made him punish himself with the most severe penances, tear his flesh with most cruel flagellations, in short, practise all the extravagancies of the wildest fanatic; a name, which, if a weak judgement and a warm fancy be characteristics of fanaticism, belonged to the blessed Deacon, an appellation which our Abbé was honoured with, who thought himself unworthy of the higher order of priesthood. Having acquired a vast reputation of sanctity among the Jansenists, he died on the first of May, 1727, (not 1725 as Dr. Middleton says) and was buried in the church-yard of St. Medard at Paris, near the South wall of the church, a tomb-stone being put up that covered the extent of his grave, which, from the time of his death, was frequented by his admirers. The number of worshippers increasing daily, an opinion of the efficacy of worshipping there gained ground also. By degrees it was rumoured about, that the sick had by their prayers at the tomb been restored to health; and cures of an astonishing nature had been wrought by the intercession of the blessed Deacon; till, at length, in the year 1731 these reports having put the whole city of Paris in a ferment, and St. Medard's Church-yard being crouded from morning to night with sick praying for relief, the civil magistrate, unable by any other means to stem the torrents and close the list of miracles, fell upon the expedient of debarring all approach to the scene of wonders,

An infinite number of treatises concerning them were published in *France*: but the pompous book of Mr. *de Montgeron* for, and the Pastoral Letters of the Archbishop of *Sens*, against them, contain all that can be offered on either side, and all that is necessary to enable us to form our judgement of the affair. These I have perused with care, and shall quote with fidelity, and upon the whole, satisfy you that all the extraordinary facts ascribed to the *Abbé Paris* may be included under these two heads; First, that in many instances, fraud and imposture were fairly proved and detected, and Secondly, that the cures *really* performed at the tomb, can be accounted for by natural causes which I shall assign.

First, then, that fraud and imposture were detected in many instances, was notorious to all the world, at the very time, and is confirmed to us by all the vouchers which the nature of the thing allows. Suffer me to mention two or three, from the Archbishop of *Sens*; from which it will appear how little reason the author of the *Essay on Miracles* had for asserting – *that the Jesuits, a learned body, supported by the civil magistrates, and determined enemies to those opinions in whose favour the miracles were said to have been wrought, were never able distinctly to refute or detect them.*

Six of these cures had been corroborated by a verbal process taken by order of *Cardinal de Noailles*, in 1728, before a commissary appointed by him. Three or four years after, above twenty of the curés of *Paris*, presented a petition to *Noailles*'s successor in the see of that city, requesting that four of these cures might be solemnly published to the people as miracles. Whence, then, their silence as to the other two? It arose from the notorious

by walling up the sepulchre. It was on this occasion, that the following frequently repeated distich was made, and put upon the wall.

De par le Roi – defence à Dieu
De faire miracles en ce lieu.

Our saint's miracles, after this, became less frequent, though some were attributed still to him, as in the case of Gautier related by Montgeron; and even to this day, he performs wonderful feats among the *Convulsionaries*, whose extravagancies have done so much discredit to the cause of Jansenism, that the sober part of that sect have not only disclaimed all connexion with them, but have also employed some of their ablest writers to expose their frantic absurdities. These convulsionists well deserve this appellation; for they have amongst them adepts who can, with pleasure, work themselves up to the strangest agitations and convulsions, practising feats which would entertain a Bartholomew fair audience. Mr. Powel the fire-eater may have learnt his art among them, for they have some who are invulnerable by fire; others, again, like another set of jugglers, are impenetrable by the point of a sharp sword. In the year 1749 being at Paris, I was invited to go to one of their meetings, where I was told I should be entertained with the exploits of one of their famous heroes, who could not only bring on convulsions when he pleased, but when he was in that state, would lie on the floor and allow his breast to be beat with a stone or hammer. Though my curiosity was not so great as to make me a witness of this myself, the person whom I had my information from, had seen the operation.

detection of imposture in the cases of *Jacques Laurent Menedrieus*, and *Jean Nivet*, which last person in particular, was, in consequence of a fresh examination, made in 1732, produced and found to be as lame and blind as ever, though eleven witnesses had attested his cure, in 1728, before the commissary, who chose to be content with their evidence, without requiring them to produce *Nivet* himself.

In a subsequent petition to their archbishop, the same zealous friends of the *Abbé Paris* requested the publication of a great many other cures of a later date than the four already presented by them. But fraud and imposture could be proved now, as well as before. One of the cases was of the *Sieur le Doulx*, who was said to have been cured of a fever by having some reliques of the *Abbé Paris* put under his head, when he was given over, and had received the sacraments. Now the imposture, here, was detected by the sick person himself, who in a letter written by him to the Bishop of *Laon* declares, that the whole was a trick of the *Jansenist* community of *St. Hilaire,* who had pressed upon him a confessor, and administered the sacraments to him, which might be looked upon as marks of his being dangerously ill, but was far from being the case. *Laleu* a laceman, and *Anne Coulon,* said to be born deaf and dumb, and represented as having received their cure at the sepulchre of the Abbé were afterwards proved to have always enjoyed their faculties of speech and hearing, though in an imperfect degree. – *Anne le France* was said to be cured of a complication of distempers, and amongst others of a disorder in her eyes. On an examination made by the archbishop of *Paris*, it appeared from the testimony of all her relations, that she had never been in the dangerous way represented, particularly that she had never had any disorder in her eyes. – As ingenious a piece a fraud as any, was detected in the case of the widow *de Lorme,* who pretended to be struck with the palsy, for going to the tomb with an intention to ridicule. Her own confession of the contrivance, and other authentic documents, brought this to light.

It would be needless to multiply instances (which I could easily do) because those already mentioned, are sufficient to prove that some of the pretended miraculous cures were detected to be the offspring of fraud. But if this be certain, it is equally so, that, in many of the cases alleged, no fraud was detected. If the certainty of some of the cures could have been disputed, the Archbishop of *Sens,*[157] and other prelates would not have laboured so much, as we know they did, to prove, from the circumstances of them, that they were operations of the devil.

---

[157] The title of the Archbishop's performance is – *Instruction Pastorale de Monseigneur J. Joseph Languet, Archeveque des Sens; – ci-devant Eveque de Soïssons, au Sujet des pretendus Miracles du Diacre de St. Madard, & des Convulsions arrivees à son Tombeau.* There are three parts, published at three different times. In the first, the

An examination, therefore, of those cures performed at the tomb of the *Abbé Paris*, the evidence of which stands unimpeached of fraud, becomes necessary, and I flatter myself that I shall be able to divert them of that miraculous garb with which ignorance and credulity have dressed them up, and which infidelity and scepticism affect to cloath them in, that they serve their purposes in their attacks against the credibility of all miracles whatever.

...

Archbishop endeavours to shew that the pretended miracles have neither certainty nor evidence; in the second, that the circumstances of them prove they are rather the operations of the devil than of God; in the third, he would establish this point, that no regard is to be paid to miracles in opposition to the body of chief pastors united to their head. – Had the prelate been satisfied, that he made good his first head, the other two would have been quite superfluous.

11
OWEN MANNING

[Owen Manning], *An inquiry into the grounds and nature of the several species of ratiocination. In which the argument made use of in the philosophical essays of D. Hume, Esq; is occasionally taken notice of. By A. G. O. T. V. O. C.* London: printed for C. and W. Marsh, [1754], [2], 9–66 p.
Selections from Sections 2 and 7; from 1754 edition.

Owen Manning (1721–1801) was an Anglican cleric, author of a variety of theological works, and noted historian of Surrey. His first work, *An Inquiry into the Grounds and Nature of the Several Species of Ratiocination* lacks a publication date, but was probably published in 1754 in view of the *Monthly Review* article on it that appeared in December of that year. The work is an analysis of three different kinds of reasoning: demonstration, moral evidence, and presumption. In Section 2 he argues that the first principles of moral evidence – that is, moral obligations – are not demonstrable, but are instead beliefs due to involuntary persuasions. Drawing on Hume's account of necessary connection, Manning argues that a first cause of the world cannot be strictly demonstrated, but must be involuntarily believed. Manning parallels his demonstration/moral evidence distinction with Hume's knowledge/belief distinction. On Manning's interpretation of Hume, then, Hume contends that miracles are unreasonable because they lack strict demonstration. Thus, the miracle of Christianity noted at the close of "Of Miracles" is that "we believe [only] in consequence of an immediate impulse". For Manning, Hume could be "either an infidel or an enthusiast". In Section 7 he criticises Hume for making experience the exclusive test of natural events. Writing for the *Monthly Review*, William Rose offers a mixed evaluation of Manning's work:

> In the course of his enquiry he advances several things concerning experience, testimony, and the credibility of facts; but without that clearness, that accuracy, and precision, which are necessary, in order to a satisfactory discussion of such subjects. [*Monthly Review*, December 1754, Vol. 11, pp. 469–470]

The following is from the 1754 and only edition of Manning's *Inquiry*.

SECT. II.

...

It is farther observable, that the assent produced in the mind, by *this* sort of argument, is what we call *belief*, in opposition to what is the natural effect of *demonstrative* proof, which is *knowledge*. "Belief," (says Mr. Locke)[158]

"is the admitting or receiving any proposition for true, upon arguments or proofs, that are found to *persuade* us to receive it as true, without certain *knowledge* that it is so. In all the parts of *knowledge*, each step has its *visible* and *certain* connection; in *belief*, not so. That which makes me *believe*, is something *extraneous* to the thing I believe: Something *not evidently* joined on both sides to, and not so manifestly shewing the agreement or disagreement of, those ideas that are under consideration."

And this natural distinction between *belief* and *knowledge*, which are indeed not only different *degrees*, but different *kinds* of assurance, may serve to throw light on an argument made use of by Mr. *David Hume*; in which, I believe, he has been generally misunderstood, and, as I conceive, for want of the proper attention, in many of his readers, to the different *kinds* of evidence, and the different effects of them. That gentleman seems to contend, that the existence of a *first* cause cannot be *conclusively* argued from the phænomena of the visible world, because the validity of the proof depends upon the supposition of a *necessary connection* in nature, which we cannot explane, and which we cannot justify our admission or assumption of, as a *principle*, from any other consideration, than a *persuasion* of mind equally involuntary and unaccountable. Now, if this be the case; and if Mr. *Locke*'s account of the matter also be true; that, in an argument productive of *knowledge* there must needs be a *visible* and certain connection throughout; or otherwise, that the operation of it must terminate in that different kind of assurance only, which we call *belief*; I do not see how Mr. *Hume*'s allegation can reasonably be controverted, unless the proposition in dispute can be made out to a demonstration, in some *other* manner. He does not deny the existence of the supposed relation of cause and effect; nor does he any where dispute the *proper* force and efficacy of the argument grounded thereupon: he may therefore, for ought that appears to the contrary, *believe* also the conclusion usually

---

[158] Essay on human Understanding, B. IV. C. xv. §. 3.

established upon that argument. He only affirms that the *first* principle is not a *necessary* truth; that the *proof* struck out from it, is therefore not of the *demonstrative* kind; and that the *conclusion*, of consequence, does not amount to that sort of assurance which alone can, properly and philosophically speaking, be entitled to the character of *knowledge*. And hence it is, as I take it, that he speaks of *this* method of conviction, and the assent it produces, and also of the assurance we have of *any other* truth deducible *from this*, as not the proper exercise or effect of *reason*. Because, though *every* species of deduction by the use of that faculty be, in a loose and popular sense, distinguished by that name; yet *reasoning* truly and philosophically speaking, always procedes upon *necessary principles*, through *steps* also *necessarily* connected, to *conclusions* therefore which also *cannot but* take place, *i.e.* which are *absolutely* and *infallibly* certain.

Thus, when he applies his argument to the discussion of the important point concerning the general credibility of *miracles*, he declares himself of opinion, that the notion of their credibility is not warrantable upon any principles of *reasoning*. His meaning, I presume, is, that no matter of *fact* contrary to universal experience, being credible, but upon the previous assurance of a *power* in nature adequate to the production of it, that is, upon the supposed *necessary* connection of *cause* and *effect*; if such necessary connection cannot be *shewn* to exist in nature, we cannot arrive at *knowledge*, properly so called, with respect to the existence of such *power*. It will therefore only be matter of *belief*, upon arguments or proofs, (as Mr. *Locke* says) "that are indeed found to *persuade* us to receive it as true, though without *certain knowledge* that it is so." – And hence also, *miracles* will only be matter of *belief*; because not having any *knowledge* of the requisite *power* that amounts to more than this, the issue is to be tried by the appeal to *experience*; which holding *universally against* the existence of them, and but *partially* confirming the evidence *in favour* of them, will determine (according to Mr. *H.*) *against* the credibility of them.

And hence we may account for his resolving the general reception christianity has met with, into the principle of *faith*: By which he means, I suppose, that it is not credible on the grounds of what, according to the *strictly* philosophical sense of the word, we understand by *reasoning*; *viz.* not on the principles of mathematical *demonstration*. Not that we *believe* in consequence of an *immediate* impulse; nor that *deductions* are not made use of, e'er the mind is wrought up to the assent it yields: but, that the *first* principles of our deductions being *involuntary* persuasions, of which we can give no account, the *argument* constructed upon them does not proceed by *necessarily* connected proofs; and so, the whole process, however it be an act of *nature*, is not an exercise of *reason*, in the philosophical acceptation of the term. – This gentleman indeed, for ought I know, may be as great an *unbeliever* as his adversaries have endeavoured to represent him: But it is to God and himself only, for any thing that can be inferred from the argument he has hitherto made public. His own reasonings must have operated upon his mind in a very extraordinary manner indeed, if, in *mere* consequence of *them*, he is either an *infidel* or an *enthusiast*. But this by the way.

...

SECT. VII.

...

Mr. *David Hume*, who has handled the subject of the credibility of facts in general, with great perspicuity and precision, has concluded that such as are totally contrary to human Experience are not capable of being ascertained by human Testimony. But this can only hold good on a supposition which that Gentleman seems to have adopted without sufficient grounds, *viz.* that Experience is an *exclusive* test of what is credible or incredible in the order of natural events. As far indeed as that test *alone* is considered, the conclusion *will* hold good; because whatever be the value of the general argument from Experience, a *greater* degree will necessarily prevail upon the comparison with a *less*. But to consider that *alone* as a test, in the present case, is, as I apprehend, to consider the grounds of credibility too partially. An Event will be credible which is *contrary* to our past Experience, to any person that is persuaded of the Existence of a Power equal to the production of it: And every man's *persuasion* in *this* point stands exactly on the *same* foundation with the *persuasion*, on the *other* hand, that an Event of any kind will *therefore* come to pass, in certain circumstances, because it has always taken place in the same circumstances *heretofore*. The inference, in the *latter* case, can only be accounted for from an impulse of *nature*; and, on the same principle, every thing is defensible in like manner that is affirmed in the *former*. In a word, the *supposed* conjunction of any two events, in time *to come*, has no more relation to their *actual* conjunction in time *past*, than the *supposed* existence of a first cause has to the *actual* existence of the several finite natures of the Universe. *Neither* indeed can be inferred, as *absolute certainties*; and, as *natural probabilities*, they rest exactly on the same foundation.

12
JOHN LELAND

John Leland, *A view of the principal deistical writers of the last and present century.* London: B. Dod, 1755–1756, 2 vol. and Supplement. Letters 17–21; from 1757 edition.

John Leland (1691–1766) was an English Presbyterian minister who settled in Ireland. Beginning in 1733, he authored several books attacking deists and defending traditional notions of Christianity and revelation. Leland's greatest work is his multi-volume *View of the Principal Deistical Writers*, published in a series of volumes in 1755 and 1756. The finished work consists of 36 letters to his friend Dr. Thomas Wilson. Six of these letters pertain to Hume, five of which are included below.[159] In letter 17, Leland disputes Hume's argument in "Of a Particular Providence" that our knowledge of God as creator is restricted to the effects that we see in his creation. According to Leland, Hume fails to distinguish between a *necessary cause*, and a *free cause*. A necessary cause "acts up to the utmost of its power, and therefore the effect must be exactly proportioned to it". Free causes, by contrast, "have a power of producing effects, which they do not actually produce". Since God is a free cause, we can ascribe attributes to him beyond what we see in the effects. In Letter 18 he discusses Part 1 of Hume's "Of Miracles". After laying out Hume's argument, Leland contends that "we learn from it what is conformable to the ordinary course and order of things, but we cannot learn or pronounce from experience that it is impossible [that] things, or events, should happen in any particular instance contrary to that course".

In Letter 19 Leland turns to Part 2. In response to Hume's four points against the veracity of miracle testimonies, Leland argues that these do not pertain to the New Testament miracles. In response to Hume's discussion of the miracles at the Abbé De Pâris's tomb, Leland notes five ways in which those reports of miracles are inferior to the reports in the New Testament. First, the miracles at the Abbé's tomb were reported in support of the Jansenist religious sect; the New Testament miracles were not

---

[159] Letters 16–19 were originally published in as letters 1–4 in the 1755 edition of Volume 2; letters 20–21 were originally published as letters 3 and 4 in the 1756 Supplement. Letter 16 is included in *Early Responses to Hume's Metaphysical and Epistemological Writings* (2000); portions of Letter 21 are included in *Early Responses to Hume's Moral, Literary and Political Writings* (1999).

reported in support of any leading religious sect. Second, unlike New Testament miracles, the alleged miracles at the Abbé's tomb were not truly miraculous, and could easily be explained through natural causes. Third, unlike the New Testament miracles, the alleged miracles at the Abbé's tomb carry the marks of superstition. Fourth, unlike the New Testament miracles, fraud was detected in many of the alleged miracles at the Abbé's tomb. Finally, the New Testament miracles were performed for "an end worthy of the divine wisdom and goodness".

At the outset of Letter 20 Leland inserts a brief critique of Hume that he received from a recently deceased young gentleman. The unnamed author attacks Hume's central contention that it is most reasonable to believe the view that is backed by the strongest evidence. According to the author, there are many instances in life in which we pursue a course of action that has a lesser amount of support. Leland then discusses the anonymous critique. He argues that there is no real opposition of evidence between reports of miracles and the unnatural status of miracle events themselves. He believes that Hume wrongly pits these two against each other by referring to miracles as absurdities. In point of fact, according to Leland, the only evidence that counts against reports of miracles would involve the veracity of the eyewitnesses. And, in the case of the New Testament miracles, the testimonies have a high degree of credibility, with nothing that counts against their veracity. In Letter 21, Leland gives a biographical sketch of the Abbé De Pâris, and argues that his excessively ascetic and fanatical lifestyle discredits allegations that God performed miracles at his tomb. In a brief Postscript, he favourably discusses Douglas's *Criterion* (1752).

For reviews of Leland's *View*, see *Early Responses to Hume*, Volume 1, which also includes Leland's discussion of Hume's moral theory in Letter 21.

LETTER XVII.

Observations on Mr. Hume's *essay concerning a particular providence and a future state. His attempt to shew that we cannot justly argue from the course of nature to a particular intelligent cause, because the subject lies entirely beyond the reach of human experience, and because God is a singular cause, and the universe a singular effect, and therefore we cannot argue by a comparison with any other cause, or any other effect. His argument examined, whereby he pretends to prove, that since we know God only by the effects in the works of nature, we can judge of his proceedings no farther than we now see of them, and therefore cannot infer any rewards or punishments beyond what is already known by experience and observation. The usefulness of believing future retributions acknowledged by Mr.* Hume, *and that the contrary doctrine is inconsistent with good policy.*

SIR,

It appears from what was observed in my former letter, that few writers have carried scepticism in philosophy to a greater height than Mr. *Hume.* I now proceed to consider those things in his writings that seem to be more directly and immediately designed against religion. Some part of what he calls his *Philosophical Essays concerning Human Understanding,* manifestly tends to subvert the very foundations of natural religion, or its most important principles. Another part of them is particularly levelled against the proofs and evidences of the Christian revelation.

The former is what I shall first consider, and shall therefore examine the eleventh of those essays, the title of which is, *concerning a particular providence and a future state.* Mr. *Hume* introduces what he offers in this essay as sceptical paradoxes advanced by a friend, and pretends by no means to approve of them. He proposes some objections as from himself, to his friend's way of arguing; but takes care to do it in such a manner, as to give his friend a superiority in the argument. And some of the worst parts of this essay are directly proposed in his own person. The essay may be considered as consisting of two parts. The one seems to be designed against the existence of God, or of one supreme intelligent cause of the universe: The other, which appears to be the main intention of the essay, is particularly levelled against the doctrine of a future state of rewards and punishments.

I shall begin with the former, because it comes first in order to be considered, though it is not particularly mentioned till towards the conclusion of the essay. He observes in the person of his Epicurean friend, that

"while we argue from the course of nature, and infer a particular intelligent cause, which at first bestowed, and still preserves order in the universe, we embrace a principle which is both uncertain and useless. The reason he gives why it is uncertain is, because the subject lies entirely beyond the reach of human experience."[160]

This is a specimen of the use our author would make of the principles he had laid down in the preceding essays. He had represented Experience as the only foundation of our knowledge with respect to matters of fact, and the existence of objects: that it is by experience alone that we know the

---

[160] Hume's Philosophical Essays, p. 224.

relation of cause and effect; and he had also asserted, that not so much a probable argument can be drawn from experience to lay a foundation for our reasoning from cause to effect, or from effect to cause. I shall not add any thing here to what was offered in my former letter to shew the absurdity, the confusion, and inconsistency of these principles. I shall only observe, that this very writer, who had represented all arguments drawn from experience, with relation to cause and effect, as absolutely uncertain, yet makes it an objection against the argument from the course of nature to an intelligent cause, that *the subject lies entirely beyond the reach of human experience.* What is the meaning of this is not easy to apprehend. It will be readily allowed, that we do not know by experience the whole course of nature; yet enough of it falls within the reach even of human observation and experience, to lay a reasonable foundation for inferring from it a supreme intelligent cause. In that part of the universe which cometh under our notice and observation, we may behold such illustrious characters of wisdom, power, and goodness, as determine us by the most natural way of reasoning in the world, to acknowledge a most wise, and powerful, and benign author and cause of the universe. The inference is not beyond the reach of our faculties, but is one of the most obvious that offereth to the human mind. But perhaps what the author intends by observing that *this subject lies entirely beyond the reach of human experience,* is this, That notwithstanding the admirable marks of wisdom and design which we behold in the course of nature, and order of things, we cannot argue from thence to prove a wise and intelligent cause of the universe, or that there was any wisdom employed in the formation of it, because neither we, nor any of the human race, were present at the making of it, or saw how it was made. This must be owned to be a very extraordinary way of reasoning, and I believe you will easily excuse me if I do not attempt a confutation of it.

Mr. *Hume,* after having argued thus in the person of his *Epicurean* friend, comes in the conclusion of this essay to propose another argument as from himself.

"I much doubt, saith he, whether it be possible for a cause to be known only by its effect, or to be of so singular and particular a nature as to have no parallel, and no similarity with any other cause or object, that has ever fallen under our observation. 'Tis only when two species of objects are found to be constantly conjoined, that we can infer the one from the other. And were an effect presented which was entirely singular, and could not be comprehended under any known species, I do not see that we could form any conjecture or inference at all concerning its cause. If experience, and observation, and analogy be, indeed, the only guides we can reasonably follow in inferences of this nature; both the effect and cause must bear a similarity and resemblance to other effects and causes which we know, and which we have found in many instances to be conjoined with each other."[161]

Mr. *Hume* leaves it to his friend's reflections to *prosecute the consequences of this Principle,* which he had hinted before, might lead *into Reasonings of too nice and delicate a nature* to be insisted on. The argument, as he hath managed it, is indeed sufficiently obscure and perplexed. But the general intention of it seems to be this, that all our arguings from cause to effect, or from effect to cause proceed upon analogy, or the comparing similar causes with similar effects. Where therefore there is supposed to be a singular cause to which there is no parallel (though he much doubts whether there can be cause of so singular a nature) and a singular effect, there can be no arguing from the one to the other: Because in that case we cannot argue by a comparison with any other cause, or any other effect. Except therefore we can find another world to compare this with, and an intelligent cause of that world, we cannot argue from the effects in this present world to an intelligent cause: *i.e.* We cannot be sure there is one God, except we can prove there is one other God at least; or that this world was formed and produced by a wise intelligent cause, unless we know of another world like this, which was also formed by a wise intelligent cause, and perhaps not then neither: For he seems to insist upon it, that there should be *many instances* of such causes and effects being *conjoined with each other,* in order to lay a proper foundation for *observation, experience,* and *analogy, the only guides we can reasonably follow in inferences of this nature.* He immediately after observes, that "according to the antagonists of *Epicurus,* the universe, an effect quite singular and unparalleled, is always supposed to be the proof of a Deity, a cause no less singular and unparalleled." If by calling the universe a singular and unparalleled effect, he intends to signify that no other universe has come under our observation, it is very true: But it by no means follows, that we cannot argue from the evident marks of wisdom and design which we may observe in this universe that we do know, because we do not know any thing of any other universe. This grand universal system, and even that small part of it that we are more particularly acquainted with, comprehendeth such an amazing variety of phenomena, all which exhibit the most incontestable proofs of admirable wisdom, power, and diffusive goodness, that one would think it scarce possible for a reasonable mind to resist the evidence. But such is this subtil metaphysical gentleman's way of arguing in a matter of the highest consequence, the absurdity of which is obvious to any man of plain understanding. It is of a piece with what he had advanced before,

---

[161] Hume's Philosophical Essays, p. 232, 233.

that there is no such thing as cause or effect at all, nor can any probable inference be drawn from the one to the other, than which, as hath been already shewn, nothing can be more inconsistent with common sense, and the reason of all mankind.

The other thing observable in this essay, and which seems to be the principal intention of it, relateth to the proof of a Providence and a Future State. He introduces his friend as putting himself in the place of *Epicurus*, and making an harangue to the people of *Athens*, to prove that the principles of his philosophy were as innocent and salutary as those of any other philosophers. The course of his reasoning or declamation is this: That

> "the chief or sole argument brought by philosophers for a divine Existence is derived from the order of nature; where there appear such marks of intelligence and design, that they think it extravagant to assign for its cause, either chance, or the blind unguided force of matter. That this is an argument drawn from effects to causes; and that when we infer any particular cause from an effect, we must proportion the one to the other, and can never be allowed to ascribe to the cause any qualities, but what are exactly sufficient to produce the effect. And if we ascribe to it farther qualities, or affirm it capable of producing any other effect, we only indulge the licence of conjecture without reason or authority."[162]

That therefore

> "allowing God to be the author of the existence or order of the Universe, it follows, that he possesses that precise degree of power, intelligence, and benevolence, which appears in his workmanship, but nothing farther can ever be proved.[163] Those therefore are vain reasoners, and reverse the order of nature, who instead of regarding this present life, and the present scene of things as the sole object of their contemplation, render it a passage to something farther. The Divinity may indeed possibly possess attributes, which we have never seen exerted, and may be governed by principles of action, which we cannot discover to be satisfied: But we can never have reason to infer any attributes, or any principles of action in him, but so far as we know them to be exerted or satisfied."

He asks, "are there any marks of distributive Justice in the world?" And if it be said, that the "justice of God exerts itself in part, but not in its full

[162] Hume's Philosophical Essays, p. 215.

[163] Ibid. p. 220.

extent," he answers, "that we have no reason to give it any particular extent, but only so far as we see it at present exert itself."[164] That

"indeed, when we find that any work has proceeded from the skill and industry of man, who is a being whom we know by experience, and whose nature we are acquainted with, we can draw a hundred inferences concerning what may be expected from him, and these inferences will all be founded on experience and observation. But since the Deity is known to us only by his productions, and is a single being in the Universe, not comprehended under any species or genus, from whose experienced attributes or qualities we can by analogy infer any attribute or quality in him, we can only infer such attributes or perfections, and such a degree of those attributes, as is precisely adapted to the effect we examine. But farther attributes or farther degrees of those attributes, we can never be authorized to infer or suppose by any rules of just reasoning."

He adds, that

"the great source of our mistakes on this subject is this. We tacitly consider ourselves as in the place of the Supreme Being, and conclude, that he will on every occasion observe the same conduct, which we ourselves in his situation would have embraced as reasonable and eligible. Whereas it must evidently appear contrary to all rules of analogy to reason from the intentions and projects of men to those of a Being so different, and so much superior – so remote and incomprehensible, who bears less analogy to any other being in the universe, than the sun to a waxen taper."

He concludes therefore, "that no new fact can ever be inferred from the religious Hypothesis: no reward or punishment expected or dreaded beyond what is already known by practice and observation."[165] This is a faithful extract of the argument in this essay, drawn together as closely as I could, without the repetitions with which it aboundeth.

I shall now make a few remarks upon it.

The whole of his reasoning depends upon this maxim, that when once we have traced an effect up to its cause, we can never ascribe any thing to the cause but what is precisely proportioned to the effect, and what we ourselves discern to be so: nor can we infer any thing farther concerning the cause, than what the effect, or the present appearance of it, necessarily leads to. He had to the same purpose observed in a former essay; that "it

---

[164] Ibid. p. 203.

[165] Hume's *Philosophical Essays*, p. 230, 231.

is allowed by all philosophers, that the effect is the measure of the power."[166] But this is far from being universally true. For we in many instances clearly perceive, that a cause can produce an effect which it doth not actually produce, or a greater effect than it hath actually produced. This gentleman's whole reasoning proceeds upon confounding necessary and free causes, and indeed he seems not willing to allow any distinction between them, or that there are any other but necessary and material causes.[167] A necessary cause acts up to the utmost of its power, and therefore the effect must be exactly proportioned to it. But the case is manifestly different as to free and voluntary causes. They may have a power of producing effects, which they do not actually produce. And as they act from discernment and choice, we may, in many cases, reasonably ascribe to them farther views than we discern or discover in their present course of action. This author himself owns, that this may be reasonably done with respect to man whom we know by experience, and whose nature and conduct we are acquainted with; but denies that the same way of arguing will hold with respect to the Deity. But surely when once we come from the consideration of his works to the knowledge of a self-existent and absolutely perfect Being, we may from the nature of that self-existent and absolutely perfect cause reasonably conclude, that He is able to produce certain effects beyond what actually come under our present notice and observation, and indeed that He can do whatsoever doth not imply a contradiction. This Universe is a vast, a glorious, and amazing system, comprehending an infinite variety of parts. And it is but a small part of it that comes under our own more immediate notice. But we know enough to be convinced, that it demonstrateth a wisdom as well as power beyond all imagination great and wonderful. And we may justly conclude the same concerning those parts of the Universe that we are not acquainted with. And for any man to say, that we cannot reasonably ascribe any degree of wisdom or power to God but what is exactly proportioned to that part of the universal frame which comes under our own particular observation, is a very strange way of arguing. The proofs of the wisdom and power of God, as appearing in our part of the system, are so striking, that it is hard to conceive, how any man that is not under the influence of the most obstinate prejudice, can refuse to submit to their force. And yet there are many phænomena, the reasons and ends of which we are not at present able to assign. The proper conduct in such a case, is to believe there are most wise reasons for these things, though we do not now discern those reasons, and to argue from the uncontested characters of wisdom in things that we do know, that this most wise and powerful agent, the author of

[166] Ibid. p. 125.

[167] Ibid. p. 131, 132, 141, 151.

nature, hath also acted with admirable wisdom in those things, the designs and ends of which we do not know. It would be wrong therefore to confine the measures of his wisdom precisely to what appeareth to our narrow apprehensions in that part of his works, which falleth under our immediate inspection. This was the great fault of the *Epicureans,* and other atheistical philosophers, who judging by their own narrow views, urged several things as proofs of the want of wisdom and contrivance, which upon a fuller knowledge of the works of nature, furnish farther convincing proofs of the wisdom of the great Former of all things.

In like manner with respect to his goodness, there are numberless things in this present constitution, which lead us to regard him as a most benign and benevolent Being. And therefore it is highly reasonable, that when we meet with any phænomena, which we cannot reconcile with our ideas of the divine goodness, we should conclude, that it is only for want of having the whole of things before us, and considering them in their connexion and harmony, that they appear to us with a disorderly aspect. And it is very just in such a case to make use of any reasonable hypothesis, which tendeth to set the goodness of God in a fair and consistent light.

The same way of reasoning holds with regard to the justice and right-eousness of God as the great Governor of the world. We may reasonably conclude from the intimate sense we have of the excellency of such a character, and the great evil and deformity of injustice and unrighteousness, which sense is implanted in us by the author of our beings, and from the natural rewards of virtue, and punishment of vice even in the present constitution of things; that he is a lover of righteousness and virtue, and an enemy to vice and wickedness. Our author himself makes his *Epicurean friend* acknowledge, that in the present order of things, virtue is attended with more peace of mind, and with many other advantages above vice.[168] And yet it cannot be denied, that there are many instances obvious to common observation, in which vice seemeth to flourish and prosper, and virtue to be exposed to great evils and calamities. What is to be concluded from this? Is it that because the Justice of God here sheweth itself only *in part,* and not *in its full extent* (to use our author's expression) therefore righteousness as in God is imperfect in its degree, and that he doth not possess it in the full extent of that perfection, nor will ever exert it any farther than we see him exert it in this present state? This were an unrea-sonable conclusion concerning a being of such admirable perfection, whose righteousness as well as wisdom must be supposed to be infinitely superior to ours. It is natural therefore to think that this present life is only a part of the divine scheme, which shall be compleated in a future state.

But he urgeth, that the great source of our mistakes on this subject is, that

---

[168] Hume's *Philosophical Essays,* p. 221.

"we tacitly consider ourselves as in the place of the supreme Being, and conclude that he will on every occasion observe the same conduct, which we ourselves in his situation would have embraced as reasonable and eligible. Whereas it must evidently appear contrary to all rules of analogy, to reason from the intentions and purposes of men to those of a Being so different and so much superior, so remote and incomprehensible."[169]

But though it were the highest absurdity to pretend to tie down the infinite incomprehensible Being to our scanty model, and measures of acting, and to assume that he will *on every occasion,* for so our author is pleased to put the case, observe the same conduct that we should judge eligible: since there may be innumerable things concerning which we are unable to form any proper judgment, for want of having the same comprehensive view of things that he hath: yet on the other hand, there are some cases so manifest that we may safely pronounce concerning them, as worthy or unworthy of the divine perfections. And as our own natures are the work of God, we may reasonably argue from the traces of excellencies in ourselves to the infinitely superior perfections in the great Author of the Universe, still taking care to remove all those limitations and defects with which those qualities are attended in us. This is what Mr. *Hume* himself elsewhere allows in his *Essay on the Origin of our Ideas.*

"The idea of God, saith he, as meaning an infinitely intelligent, wise, and good Being arises from reflecting on the operations of our own minds, and augmenting those qualities of goodness and wisdom without bound or limit." See his *Philosophical Essays*, p. 24, 25.

Since therefore we cannot possibly help regarding goodness and benevolence, justice and righteousness, as necessary ingredients in a worthy and excellent character, and as among the noblest excellencies of an intellectual Being, we are unavoidably led to conclude, that they are to be found in the highest possible degree of eminency in the absolutely perfect Being, the Author and Governor of the world. These are not mere arbitrary suppositions, but are evidently founded in nature and reason. And though in many particular instances we through the narrowness of our views cannot be proper judges of the grounds and reasons of the divine administrations, yet in general we have reason to conclude, that if there be such a thing as goodness and righteousness in God, or any perfection in him correspondent to what is called goodness and righteousness in us, he will order it so that in the final issue of things a remarkable difference shall be made between the righteous and the wicked: that at one time or other, and

---

[169] Hume's Philosophical Essays, p. 230.

taking in the whole of existence, virtue, though now for a time it may be greatly afflicted and oppressed, shall meet with its due reward; and vice and wickedness, though now it may seem to prosper and triumph, shall receive its proper punishment. Since therefore, by the observation of all ages, it hath often happened, that in the present course of human affairs, good and excellent persons have been unhappy, and exposed to many evils and sufferings; and bad and vicious men have been in very prosperous circumstances, and have had a large affluence of all worldly enjoyments even to the end of their lives; and that, as this gentleman himself elsewhere expresseth it, "such is the confusion and disorder of human affairs, that no perfect oeconomy or regular distribution of happiness or misery, is in this life ever to be expected."[170] It seems reasonable to conclude, that there shall be a future state of existence, in which these apparent irregularities shall be set right, and there shall be a more perfect distribution of rewards and punishments to men according to their moral conduct. There is nothing in this way of arguing but what is conformable to the soundest principles of reason, and to the natural feelings of the human heart. But though a future state of retributions in general be probable, yet as many doubts might still be apt to arise in our minds concerning it, an express revelation from God assuring us of it in his name, and more distinctly pointing out the nature and certainty of those retributions, would be of the most signal advantage.

I shall have occasion to resume this subject, when I come to consider what lord *Bolingbroke* hath more largely offered in relation to it. At present it is proper to observe that though Mr. *Hume* seems to allow his *Epicurean* friend's reasoning to be just, yet he owns, that

> "in fact men do not reason after that manner; and that they draw many consequences from the belief of a divine existence, and suppose that the Deity will inflict punishments on vice, and bestow rewards on virtue, beyond what appears in the ordinary course of nature. Whether this reasoning of theirs (adds he) be just or not, is no matter; its influence on their life and conduct must still be the same. And those who attempt to disabuse them of such prejudices, may for aught I know be good reasoners, but I cannot allow them to be good citizens and politicians: since they free men from one restraint upon their passions; and make the infringement of the laws of equity and society in one respect more easy and secure."[171]

I think it follows from this by his own account, that he did not act a wise or good part, the part of a friend to the public or to mankind, in publishing

---

[170] Hume's Moral Political Essays, p. 244, 245.

[171] Hume's Philosophical Essays, p. 231.

this Essay, the manifest design of which is to persuade men, that there is no just foundation in reason for expecting a future state of rewards and punishments at all. Nor is the concession he here makes very favourable to what he addeth in the next page, concerning the universal liberty to be allowed by the state to all kinds of philosophy. According to his own way of representing it, *Epicurus* must have been cast, if he had pleaded his cause before the people; and the principal design of this Essay, which seems to be to shew not only the reasonableness, but harmlessness of that philosophy, is lost. For if the spreading of those principles and reasonings is contrary to the rules of good policy; and the character of good citizens, if they have a tendency to free them from a strong *restraint upon their passions,* and to make the *infringement of the laws of equity and society more easy and secure;* then such principles and reasonings, according to his way of representing the matter, ought in good policy to be restrained, as having a bad influence on the community.

There is one passage more in this essay, which may deserve some notice. It is in page 230, where he observes that

"God discovers himself by some faint traces or out-lines, beyond which we have no authority to ascribe to him any attribute or perfection. What we imagine to be a superior perfection may really be a defect. Or, were it ever so much a perfection, the ascribing it to the supreme Being, where it appears not to have been really exerted to the full in his works, favours more of flattery and panegyric, than of just reasoning and sound philosophy."

The course of his arguing seems to be this. That it would favour of *flattery,* not of *sound reasoning,* to ascribe any attribute or perfection to God, which *appears not to have been exerted to the full in his works.* And he had observed before, That "it is impossible for us to know any thing of the cause, but what we have antecedently, not inferred, but *discovered to the full* in the effect."[172] It is plain therefore, that according to him we ought not to ascribe any perfection to God, but what is not merely *inferred,* but *discovered to the full* in his works. It is also manifest, that according to him there is no attribute or perfection of the Deity exerted or discovered to the full in his works. For he had said just before, that he *discovers himself only by some faint traces or outlines.* The natural conclusion from these premises taken together is plainly this. That it would be flattery and presumption in us to ascribe any attribute or perfection to God at all. And now I leave it to you to judge of the obligations the world is under to this writer. In one part of this Essay he makes an attempt to subvert the proof of the existence

[172] Ibid. p. 222.

of God, or a supreme intelligent cause of the universe. And here he insin-
uateth, that it would be wrong to ascribe any perfection or attribute to him
at all. And the main design of the whole Essay is to shew, that no argument
can be drawn from any of his perfections, to make it probable that there
shall be rewards and punishments in a future state, though he acknowledgeth that it is of great advantage to mankind to believe them.

You will not wonder after this, that this gentleman, who hath endeavoured to shake the foundations of natural religion, should use his utmost
efforts to subvert the evidences of the Christian revelation. What he hath
offered this way will be the subject of some future letters.

LETTER XVIII.

An examination of Mr. Hume's *Essay on Miracles. A summary of the first
part of that Essay; which is designed to shew, that miracles are incapable
of being proved by any testimony or evidence whatsoever. His main
principle examined, that experience is our only guide in reasoning
concerning matters of fact; and that miracles, being contrary to the
established laws of nature, there is an uniform experience against the
existence of any miracle. It is shewn, that no argument can be drawn
from experience, to prove that miracles are impossible, or that they
have not been actually wrought. Miracles not above the power of God,
nor unworthy of his wisdom. Valuable ends may be assigned for
miracles. They are capable of being proved by proper testimony. This
applied to the resurrection of Christ. And it is shewn, that the evidence
set before us in Scripture is every way sufficient to satisfy us of the truth
of it, supposing that evidence to have been really given there represented.*

SIR,

I now proceed to consider Mr. *Hume*'s celebrated Essay on Miracles,
which is the tenth of his *Philosophical Essays*, and has been mightily
admired and extolled, as a masterly and unanswerable piece. I think no
impartial man will say so, that has read the ingenious and judicious answer
made to it by the Reverend Mr. *Adams*, now Rector of *Shrewsbury*. It is
intitled, "An Essay in answer to Mr. *Hume*'s Essay on Miracles, by *William
Adams*, M. A." That which I have by me is the second edition, with
additions, *London*, 1754. Besides this, I have seen a short, but excellent
discourse, by the Reverend Dr. *Rutherforth*, intitled, "The Credibility of
Miracles defended against the author of the Philosophical Essays. In a
discourse delivered at the primary visitation of the Right Reverend *Thomas*
Lord Bishop of Ely, – *Cambridge*, 1751." These in my opinion are sufficient. But since you desire that I would also take a particular notice of Mr.

Hume's Essay, I shall obey your commands, and enter a distinct consideration of this boasted performance.

Mr. *Hume* introduceth his Essay on Miracles in a very pompous manner, as might be expected from one who sets up in his Philosophical Essays, for teaching men better methods of reasoning, than any Philosopher had done before him. He had taken care at every turn to let his readers know how much they are obliged to him for throwing new light on the most *curious* and *sublime subjects*, with regard to which the most celebrated philosophers had been *extremely defective* in their researches. And now he begins his Essay on Miracles with declaring, that "he flatters himself that he has discovered an argument, which, if just, will, with the wise and learned, be an everlasting check to all kinds of superstitious delusion; and consequently, will be useful as long as the world endures. For so long, he presumes, will the account of miracles and prodigies be found in all profane history."[173]

This Essay consisteth of two parts. The first, which reacheth from p. 173 to p. 186, is designed to shew, that no evidence which can be given, however seemingly full and strong, can be a sufficient ground for believing the truth and existence of miracles: Or, in other words, that miracles are in the nature of things incapable of being proved by any evidence or testimony whatsoever. The second part is intended to shew, that supposing a miracle capable of being proved by full and sufficient evidence or testimony, yet in fact there never was a *miraculous event in any history* established upon such evidence. The first is what he seems principally to rely upon. And indeed, if this can be proved, it will make any particular enquiry into the testimony produced for miracles, needless.

The method he makes use of in the first part of his Essay, to shew, that no evidence or testimony that can be given is a sufficient ground for a reasonable assent to the truth and existence of miracles, is this. He lays it down as an undoubted principle; that experience is our only guide in reasoning concerning matters of fact, and at the same time insinuates, that this guide is far from being infallible, and is apt to lead us into error and mistakes. He observes, That the validity and credibility of human testimony is wholly founded upon experience: That in judging how far a testimony is to be depended upon, we balance the opposite circumstances, which may create any doubt or uncertainty: That the evidence arising from testimony may be destroyed, either by the contrariety and opposition of the testimony, or by the consideration of the nature of the facts themselves: That when the facts partake of the *marvellous* and *extraordinary*, there are two opposite experiences with regard to them; and that which is the most credible is to be preferred, though still with a diminution of its credibility

---

[173] Hume's Philosophical Essays, p. 174.

in proportion to the force of the other which is opposed to it: That this holdeth still more strongly in the case of miracles, which are supposed to be contrary to the laws of nature. For experience being our only guide; and an uniform experience having established those laws, there must be an uniform experience against the existence of any miracle: And an uniform experience amounts to a full and entire proof. To suppose therefore any testimony to be a proof of a miracle, is to suppose one full proof for a miracle, opposed to another full proof in the nature of the thing against it, in which case those proofs destroy one another. Finally, that we are not to believe any testimony concerning a miracle, except the falshood of that testimony should be more miraculous than the miracle itself which it is designed to establish. He also gives a hint, that as it is impossible for us to know the attributes or actions of God, otherwise than from the experience which we have of his productions, we cannot be sure that he can effect miracles, which are contrary to all our experience, and the established course of nature: And therefore miracles are impossible to be proved by any evidence.

Having given this general idea of this first part of Mr. *Hume's* Essay on Miracles, I shall now proceed to a more particular examination of it.

It is manifest that the main principle, which lieth at the foundation of his whole scheme, is this: That experience is our only "guide in reasoning concerning matters of fact."[174] You will have observed, from what hath been remarked in my former letters, that this author brings up the word *experience* upon all occasions. It is, as he hath managed it, a kind of cant term, proposed in a loose indeterminate way, so that it is not easy to form a clear idea of it, or of what this writer precisely intends by it. He had declared, that it is only by experience that we come to know the existence of objects: That it is only by experience that we know the relation between cause and effect: And at the same time had endeavoured to shew, that experience cannot furnish so much as even a probable argument concerning any connection betwixt cause and effect, or by which we can draw any conclusion from the one to the other. He had afterwards applied the same term experience, to shew that no argument can be brought to prove the existence of one supreme intelligent cause of the Universe; because this is *a subject that lies intirely beyond the reach of human experience*; and that we can have no proof of a future state of retributions, because we know no more concerning providence, than what we learn from experience in this present state. And now he comes to try the force of this formidable word against the existence of miracles, and to raise an argument against them from experience.

---

[174] Hume's Philosophical Essays, p. 174.

But that we may not lose ourselves in the ambiguity of the term as he employs it, let us distinctly examine what sense it bears as applied to the present question. In judging of the truth of the maxim he hath laid down, *viz.* that experience is our only guide in reasoning concerning matters of fact; it is to be considered, that the question we are now upon properly relates not to future *events*, as the author seems sometimes to put it,[175] but to past matter of fact. What are we therefore to understand by that experience, which he makes to be our only guide in reasoning concerning them? Is it our own particular personal experience, or is it the experience of others as well as our own? And if of others, is it the experience of some others only, or of all mankind? If it be understood thus, that every man's own personal observation and experience is to be his only guide in reasoning concerning matters of fact; so that no man is to believe any thing with relation to any facts whatsoever, but what is agreeable to what he hath himself observed or known in the course of his own particular experience; this would be very absurd, and would reduce each man's knowledge of facts into a very narrow compass; it would destroy the use and credit of history, and of a great part of experimental philosophy, and bring us into a state of general ignorance and barbarism. Or, is the word Experience to be taken in a larger and more extensive sense, as comprehending not merely any particular man's experience, but that of others too? In this case we have no way of knowing experience, but by testimony. And here the questions recurs; Is it to be understood of the experience of all mankind, or of some persons only? If the experience referred to be the experience or observation of some persons only, or of a part of mankind, how can this be depended on as a certain guide? For why should their experience be the guide, exclusively of that of others? And how do we know, but that many facts may be agreeable to the experience of others, which are not to theirs? But if the experience referred to be the experience of all mankind in general, that must take in the experience both of all men in the present age, and of those in past times and ages; and it must be acknowledged, that this rule and criterion is not easily applicable. For will any man say, that we are to believe no facts but what are agreeable to the experience of mankind in all ages? Are we in order to this, to take in whatsoever any man or men in any age or country have had experience of? And to judge by this, how far it is reasonable to believe any past facts, or facts of which we ourselves have not had sensible evidence? Even on this view of the case, it might probably take in many facts of a very extraordinary nature, and which have happened out of the common course of things; of which there have been instances in the experience and observation of different nations and ages. And at this rate experience will not be inconsistent with the belief even of

---

[175] Hume's Philosophical Essays, p. 175.

miracles themselves, of which there have been several instances recorded in the history of mankind.

But farther, in reasoning from experience, either our own or that of others, concerning matters of fact, it is to be considered, what it is that we propose to judge or determine by experience in relation to them. Is it whether these facts are possible, or whether they are probable, or whether they have been actually done? As to the possibility of facts, experience indeed, or the observation of similar events known to ourselves or others, may assure us that facts or events are possible, but not that the contrary is impossible. Concerning this, experience cannot decide any thing at all. We cannot conclude any event to be impossible, merely because we have had no experience of the like, or because it is contrary to our own observation and experience, or to the experience of others. For as this gentleman observes in another part of his Essays, "The contrary of every matter of fact is still possible; because it can never imply a contradiction."[176] And again he says, speaking of matter of fact, "there are no demonstrative arguments in the case, since it implies no contradiction, that the course of nature may change."[177] No argument therefore can be brought to demonstrate any thing or fact to be impossible, merely because it is contrary to the course of our own observation and experience, or that of mankind, provided it doth not imply a contradiction, or provided there be a power capable of effecting it. Another thing to be considered, with regard to facts, is whether they are probable: And here experience, or the observation of similar events, made by ourselves or others, may be of great use to assist us in forming a judgement concerning the probability of past facts, or in forming conjectures concerning future ones. But if the question be, Whether an event has actually happened, or a fact has been done, concerning this, experience taken from an observation of similar events, or the ordinary course of causes and effects, cannot give us any assurance or certainty to proceed upon. We cannot certainly conclude, that any fact or event has been done, merely because we or others have had experience or observation of a fact or event of a like nature. Nor on the other hand can we conclude, that such a certain event hath not happened, or that such a fact hath not been actually done, because we have not had experience of a like action or event being done, or have had experience of the contrary being done. The rule therefore which he lays down of judging which side is supported by the greater number of experiments, and of balancing the opposite experiments, and deducing the lesser number from the greater, in order to know the exact force of the superior evidence,[178] is very uncertain and fallacious,

[176] Hume's Philosophical Essays, p. 48.

[177] Hume's Philosophical Essays, p. 62.

[178] Ibid. p. 176.

if employed in judging whether matters of fact have really been done. For the fact referred to, and the evidence attending it, may be so circumstanced, that though it be a fact of a singular nature, and to which many instances of a different kind may be opposed, we may yet have such an assurance of its having been actually done, as may reasonably produce a sufficient conviction in the mind. The proper way of judging whether a fact or event, of which we ourselves have not had sensible evidence, hath been actually done, is by competent testimony. And this in common language is distinguished from experience, though this writer artfully confounds them.

This therefore is what we are next to consider; *viz.* the force of human testimony, and how far it is to be depended upon.

And with regard to the validity of the evidence arising from human testimony, he observes, That "there is no species of reasoning more common, more useful, and even necessary to human life, than that derived from the testimony of men, and the reports of eye-witnesses and spectators." The whole certainty or assurance arising from testimony he resolveth into what he calls *past experience*. That "it is derived from no other principle than our observation of the veracity of human testimony, and of the usual conformity of facts to the report of witnesses." And he mentions as grounds of the belief of human testimony, that "men have commonly an inclination to truth, and a sentiment of probity; that they are sensible to shame when detected in a falshood; and that these are qualities discovered by experience to be inherent in human nature."[179] But he might have put the case much more strongly by observing, that human testimony, by the acknowledgement of all mankind, may be so circumstanced, as to produce an infallible assurance, or an evidence so strong, that, as our author expresseth it in another case, none *but a fool or a madman* would doubt of it. It is a little too loose to say in general, that it is *founded only on past experience*. It hath its foundation in the very nature of things, in the constitution of the world and of mankind, and in the appointment of the Author of our beings, who it is manifest hath formed and designed us to be in numberless instances determined by this evidence, which often comes with such force, that we cannot refuse our assent to it without the greatest absurdity, and putting a manifest constraint upon our nature.[180] Mr. *Hume* himself, in his Essay on Liberty and Necessity, hath run a parallel between moral and physical evidence, and hath endeavoured to shew that the one is as much to be depended on as the other. He expressly saith that "when we consider how aptly natural and moral evidence link

[179] Hume's Philosophical Essays, p. 176, 177.

[180] See concerning this, Ditton on the Resurrection, part. 2.

together, and form only one chain of argument, we shall make no scruple to allow, that they are of the same nature, and derived from the same principles."[181]

It will be easily granted, what our author here observes, That

"there are a number of circumstances to be taken into consideration in all judgements of this kind: And that we must balance the opposite circumstances that create any doubt or uncertainty, and when we discover a superiority on any side, we incline to it, but still with a diminution of assurance in proportion to the force of its antagonist."[182]

Among the particulars, which may diminish or destroy the force of any argument drawn from human testimony, he mentions the contrariety of the evidence, contradictions of witnesses, their suspicious character, &c. And then proceeds to take notice of "what may be drawn from the nature of the fact attested, supposing it to partake of the extraordinary and the marvellous." He argueth, that

"in that case the evidence resulting from the testimony receives a diminution greater or less in proportion as the fact is more or less unusual. When the fact attested is such a one as has seldom fallen under our observation, here is a contest of two opposite experiences, of which the one destroys the other as far its force goes; and the superior can only operate upon the mind by the force which remains."

This is a plausible, but a very fallacious way of reasoning. A thing may be very unusual, and yet, if confirmed by proper testimony, its being unusual may not diminish its credit, or produce in the mind of a thinking person a doubt or suspicion concerning it. Indeed vulgar minds, who judge of every thing by their own narrow notions, and by what they themselves have seen, are often apt to reject and disbelieve a thing, that is not conformable to their own particular customs or experience. But wiser men, and those of more enlarged minds judge otherwise: and provided a thing comes to them sufficiently attested and confirmed by good evidence, make its being unusual no objection at all to is credibility. Many uncommon facts, and unusual phenomena of nature, are believed by the most sagacious philosophers, and received as true without hesitation upon the testimony of persons who are worthy of credit, without following the author's rules; or making their own want of experience or observation an objection against

---

[181] Hume's Philosophical Essays, p. 144.

[182] Hume's Philosophical Essays, p. 177.

those accounts. And upon this dependeth no small part of our knowledge. Mr. *Adams* hath very well illustrated this by several instances, and hath justly observed, That the most uniform experience is sometimes outweighed by a single testimony; because experience in this case is only a negative evidence, and the slightest positive testimony is for the most part an over-balance to the strongest negative evidence that can be produced.[183]

Our author here very improperly talks of a *contest between two opposite experiences*, the one of which destroys the other. For when I believe a thing unusual, I do not believe a thing opposite to mine own experience, but different from it, or a thing of which I have had no experience; though if it were a thing contrary to my own experience, provided it were confirmed by sufficient testimony, this is not a valid argument against its truth, nor a sufficient reason for disbelieving it. This gentleman himself hath mentioned a remarkable instance of this kind in the Indian prince, who refused to believe the *first relations concerning the effects of frost*. This instance, though he laboureth the point here, and in an additional note at the end of his book, is not at all favourable to his scheme. He acknowledgeth, that in this case of freezing, the event follows *contrary to the rules of analogy, and is* SUCH AS A RATIONAL INDIAN *would not look for.* The constant experience in those countries, according to which the waters are always fluid, and never in a state of hardness and solidity, is against freezing. This, according to his way of reasoning, might be regarded as a proof drawn from the constant experience, and the uniform course of nature, as far as they knew it. Here then is an instance, in which it is reasonable for men to believe upon good evidence an event no way conformable to their experience, and contrary to the rule of analogy, which yet he seems to make the only rule by which we are to judge of the credibility and truth of facts.

From the consideration of facts that are unusual, he proceeds to those that are miraculous, which is what he hath principally in view. And with regard to these he endeavoureth to shew that no testimony at all is to be admitted.

"Let us suppose, saith he, that the fact which they affirm, instead of being only marvellous, is really miraculous; and suppose also that the testimony considered apart, and in itself, amounts to an entire proof; in that case there is proof against proof, of which the strongest must prevail, but still with a diminution of its force in proportion to that of its antagonist."[184]

[183] Adams's Essay, in answer to Hume on Miracles, p. 19, 20.

[184] Hume's Philosophical Essays, p. 108.

It may be proper to remark here, that this writer had in a former Essay defined a proof to be *such an argument drawn from experience as leaves no room for doubt or opposition.*[185] Admitting this definition, it is improper and absurd for him to talk of *proof against proof.* For since a proof, according to his own account of it, leaves no room for doubt or opposition; where there is a proper proof of a fact, there cannot be a proper proof at the same time against it: For one truth cannot contradict another truth. And no doubt his intention is to signify that there can be no proof given of a miracle at all, and that the proof is only of the other side. For as he there adds, "A miracle is a violation of the laws of nature, and as a firm and unalterable experience hath established those laws" [he should have said, hath discovered to us that these are the established laws, i.e. that this is the ordinary course of nature] "the proof against a miracle from the very nature of the fact is as entire as any argument from experience can possibly be imagined." He repeats this again afterward, and observes, that

"there must be an uniform experience against every miraculous event, otherwise the event would not merit the appellation; and as an uniform experience amounts to a proof, there is here a direct and full proof from the nature of the fact, against the existence of any miracle."[186]

He seems to have a very high opinion of the force of this way of reasoning, and therefore takes care to put his reader again in mind of it in the latter part of his Essay.

"'Tis experience alone, saith he, which gives authority to human testimony; and 'tis the same experience that assures us of the laws of nature. When therefore these two kinds of experience are contrary, we have nothing to do, but to subtract the one from the other – And this subtraction with regard to all popular religions amounts to an entire annihilation."[187]

And it is chiefly upon this that he foundeth the arrogant censure, which, with an unparalleled assurance, he passeth upon all that believe the Christian religion; *viz.* That "whosoever is moved by faith to assent to it, is conscious of a continued miracle in his own person, which subverts all the principles of his understanding, and gives him a determination to

---

[185] Ibid. p. 93.

[186] Hume's Philosophical Essays, p. 181.

[187] Ibid. p. 202.

believe whatever is most contrary to custom and experience." It is thus that he concludes his Essay, as if he had for ever silenced all the advocates for Christianity, and they must henceforth either renounce their faith, or submit to pass with men of his superior understanding for persons miraculously stupid, and utterly lost to all reason and common sense.

Let us therefore examine what there is in this argument, that can support such a peculiar strain of confidence; and I believe it will appear, that never was there weaker reasoning set off with so much pomp and parade.

There is one general observation that may be sufficiently obvious to any man, who brings with him common sense and attention, and which is alone sufficient to shew the fallacy of this boasted argument. And it is this. That the proof arising from experience, on which he layeth so mighty a stress, amounteth to no more than this, that we learn from it what is conformable to the ordinary course and order of things, but we cannot learn or pronounce from experience that it is impossible things, or events, should happen in any particular instance contrary to that course. We cannot therefore pronounce such an event, though it be contrary to the usual course of things, to be impossible, in which case no testimony whatsoever could prove it. And if it be possible, there is place for testimony. And this testimony may be so strong, and so circumstanced, as to make it reasonable for us to believe it. And if we have sufficient evidence to convince us that such an event hath actually happened, however extraordinary or miraculous, no argument drawn from experience can prove that it hath not happened. I would observe by the way, that when this gentleman talks of an *uniform experience*, and *a firm and unalterable experience* against the existence of all miracles, if he means by it, such an universal experience of all mankind, as hath never been counteracted in any single instance, this is plainly supposing the very thing in question; and which he hath no right to suppose, because, by his own acknowledgement, mankind have believed in all ages that miracles have been really wrought. By uniform experience therefore in this argument must be understood the general or ordinary experience of mankind in the usual course of things. And it is so far from being true, as he confidently affirms that such an uniform experience amounts to a *full* and direct *proof* from the nature of the fact against the existence of any miracle, that it is no proof against it at all. Let us judge of this by his own definition of a miracle. "A miracle, saith he, may be accurately defined, a transgression of a law of nature by a particular volition of the Deity, or by the interposal of some invisible agent." Now our uniform experience affordeth a full and direct proof, that such or such an event is agreeable to the established laws of nature, or to the usual course of things, but it yieldeth no proof at all, that there cannot in any particular instance happen any event contrary to that usual course of things, or to what we have hitherto experienced; or that such an event may not be brought about by a particular volition of the Deity, as our author expresseth it, for valuable ends worthy of his wisdom and goodness.

He cannot therefore make his argument properly bear, except he can prove, that miracles are absolutely impossible. And this is what he sometimes seems willing to attempt. Thus, speaking of some miracles pretended to have been fully attested, he asks, "What have we to oppose to such a cloud of witnesses, but the absolute impossibility, or *miraculous nature* of the event?"[188] Where he seems to make the *miraculous nature* of an event, and the absolute impossibility of it, to be the same thing. And he elsewhere makes an attempt to prove, that we have no reason to think, that God himself can effect a miracle. He urges, that "though the Being, to whom the miracle is ascribed, be in this case Almighty, it does not, upon that account, become a whit more probable: since 'tis impossible for us to know the attributes or actions of such a Being, otherwise than from the experience we have of his productions, in the usual course of nature."[189] But when once we conclude from the effects in the works of nature, that he is Almighty, as this gentleman seems here to grant, we may from his being Almighty, reasonably infer, that he can do many things, which we do not know that he hath actually done, and can produce many effects, which he hath not actually produced. For an Almighty Being can do any thing that doth not imply a contradiction. And it can never be proved, that a miracle, or an event contrary to the usual course of nature, implieth a contradiction. This writer himself expressly acknowledgeth, in a passage I cited before, that "it implies no contradiction, that the course of nature may change."[190] And he repeats it again afterwards, that "the course of nature may change."[191] And as to the extraordinariness of any fact, he saith, that "even in the most familiar events, the energy of the cause is as unintelligible, as in the most extraordinary and unusual."[192] What we call the course of nature is the appointment of God, and the continuance of it dependeth upon his power and will. It is no more difficult to him, to act contrary to it in any particular instance than to act according to it. The one is in itself as easy to Almighty Power as the other. The true question then is concerning the divine will, whether it can be supposed, that God, having established the course of nature, will ever permit or order a deviation from the regular course, which his own wisdom hath established. And with regard to this, it will be readily granted, that it is highly proper and wisely

[188] Hume's Philosophical Essays, p. 195.

[189] Ibid. p. 95.

[190] Ibid. p. 62.

[191] Ibid. p. 66.

[192] Ibid. p. 114.

appointed, that in the ordinary state of things, what are commonly called the laws of nature should be maintained, and that things should generally go on in a fixed stated course and order; without which there could be no regular study or knowledge of nature, no use or advantage of experience, either for the acquisition of science, or the conduct of life. But though it is manifestly proper, that these laws, or this course of things, should generally take place, it would be an inexcusable presumption to affirm, that God, having established these laws, and this course of nature in the beginning, hath bound himself never to act otherwise than according to those laws. There may be very good reasons worthy of his great wisdom for his acting sometimes contrary to the usual order of things. Nor can it in that case be justly pretended, that this would be contrary to the immutability of God, which is *Spinosa*'s great argument against miracles: For those very variations, which appear so extraordinary to us, are comprehended within the general plan of his providence, and make a part of his original design. The same infinite wisdom, which appointed or established those natural laws, did also appoint the deviations from them, or that they should be over-ruled on some particular occasions; which occasions were also perfectly foreseen from the beginning by his all-comprehending mind. If things were always to go on without the least variation in the stated course, men might be apt to overlook or question a most wise governing providence, and to ascribe things (as some have done) to a fixed immutable fate or blind necessity, which they call nature. It may therefore be becoming the wisdom of God, to appoint that there should be, on particular occasions, deviations from the usual established course of things. Such extraordinary operations and appearances may tend to awaken in mankind a sense of a Supreme Disposer and Governor of the world, who is a most wise and free as well as powerful Agent, and hath an absolute dominion over nature; and may also answer important ends and purposes of moral government, for displaying God's justice and mercy, but especially for giving attestation to the divine mission of persons, whom he seeth fit to send on extraordinary errands for instructing and reforming mankind, and for bringing discoveries of the highest importance to direct men to true religion and happiness.

It appeareth then that no argument can be brought from experience to prove, either that miracles are impossible to the power of God, or that they can never be agreeable to his will. And therefore it is far from yielding a direct and full proof against the existence of miracles. It may illustrate this to consider some of the instances he himself mentions. "Lead cannot of itself remain suspended in the air: Fire consumes wood, and is extinguished by water." Our uniform experience proves, that this is the usual and ordinary course of things, and agreeable to the known laws of nature: It proves, that lead cannot naturally and ordinarily, or by its own force, be suspended in the air; but it affordeth no proof at all, that it cannot be

thus suspended in a particular instance by the will of God, or by a supernatural force or power. In like manner our experience proves, that fire
consumes wood in the natural course of things, but it yieldeth no proof that
in a particular instance the force of the fire may not be suspended or over-
ruled, and the wood preserved from being consumed by the interposal of
an invisible agent. Another instance he mentions is, that "it is a miracle that
a dead man should come to life: Because that has never been observed in
any age or country."[193] But its never having been observed, if that had been
the case, would have furnished no proof at all that a dead man cannot be
raised to life by the power and will of God, when a most valuable and
important end is to be answered by it. And if we have good evidence to
convince us, that a man had been really dead, and that man was afterwards
really restored to life (and this is a matter of fact of which our senses can
judge, as well as of any other fact whatsoever) no argument can be drawn
from experience to prove, that it could not be so. Our experience would
indeed afford a proof, that no merely natural human power could effect
it; or that it is a thing really miraculous, and contrary to the usual course
of nature: But it would not amount to a full and direct proof, or indeed to
any proof at all, that it could not be effected by the divine power.

And now we may judge of the propriety of the inference he draws from
the argument as he had managed it.

"The plain consequence is," saith he, "and 'tis a general maxim worthy
of our attention, that no testimony is sufficient to establish a miracle,
unless the testimony be of such a kind, that its falshood would be more
miraculous than the fact which it endeavours to establish. And even in
that case, there is a mutual destruction of arguments, and the superiority
only gives us an assurance suitable to that degree of force, which remains
after deducing the inferior. When any one tells me, that he saw a dead
man restored to life, I immediately consult with myself whether it would
be more probable, that this person should either deceive or be deceived,
or that the fact he relates should really have happened: I weigh the one
miracle against the other, and according to the superiority which I
discover, I pronounce my decision, and always reject the greater
miracle."[194]

You cannot but observe here, this writer's jingle upon the word miracle.
As he had talked of proof against proof, so he here talks as if in the case
he is supposing there were miracle against miracle; or as if the question
were concerning two extraordinary miraculous facts, the one of which is

---

[193] Hume's Philosophical Essays, p. 181.

[194] Hume's Philosophical Essays, p. 182.

opposed to the other. But whereas in that case one should think the greater miracle ought to take place against the lesser, this gentleman, with whom miracle and absurdity is the same thing, declares that he always *rejects the greater miracle.* But to quit this poor jingle, it is allowed that the raising a dead man to life must, if ever it happened, have been a very signal miracle; *i.e.* as he defines it, a volition of a law of nature by a particular volition of the Deity. The question therefore is, Whether any evidence is given, which may be depended on, to assure us, that however strange or extraordinary this event may be, yet it hath actually happened. That the thing itself is possible to the Deity, however it be contrary to the usual course of nature, cannot be reasonably contested: Because it cannot be proved to involve a contradiction, or any thing beyond the reach of Almighty Power. For it would be to the last degree absurd to say, that he who formed this stupendous system, or who contrived and fabricated the wonderful frame of the human body, and originally gave it a principle of life, could not raise a dead man to life. It would be a contradiction, that the same man should be living and dead at the same time, but not that he that was dead should afterwards be restored to life. And therefore if it be the will of God, and his wisdom and goodness seeth it proper for answering any very important purposes, he is able to effect it. But then whether he hath actually effected it, is another question. And here it will be readily owned, that in a case of so extraordinary a nature, the evidence or testimony upon which we receive it, ought to be very strong and cogent.

Mr. *Hume* is pleased here to put the case in a very loose and general way. "When any one tells me (saith he) that he saw a dead man restored to life, I immediately consider with myself, whether it be more probable, that this person should either deceive or be deceived, or that the fact he relates should really have happened." He puts it, as if there was nothing to depend upon but the testimony of a single person, without any assignable reason for so extraordinary an event. And when thus proposed, naked of all circumstances, no wonder that it hath an odd appearance. But that we may bring the question to a fair issue, let us apply it to what our author without doubt had principally in his view, the resurrection of our Lord Jesus Christ. Taking the case therefore according to the representation given of it in the holy Scriptures, let us examine whether, supposing all those circumstances to concur which are there exhibited, they do not amount to a full and satisfactory evidence, sufficient to lay a just foundation for a reasonable assent to it. Let us then suppose, that in a series of writings, published by different persons in different ages, and all of them uncontestably written long before the event happened, a glorious and wonderful Person was foretold, and described by the most extraordinary characters, who should be sent from heaven to teach and instruct mankind, to guide them in the way of salvation, and to introduce an excellent dispensation of truth and righteousness: That not only the nation and family from which he was to spring, the place of his birth, and time of his appearing, was distinctly pointed out, but it was foretold that he should endure the most grievous sufferings and death, and that afterwards he should be exalted to a divine dominion and glory, and that the *Gentiles* should be enlightened by his doctrine, and receive his law: That accordingly, at the time which had been signified in those predictions, that admirable Person appeared: That he taught a most pure and heavenly doctrine, prescribed the most holy and excellent laws, and brought the most perfect scheme of religion which had ever been published to the world; and at the same time exhibited in his own sacred life and practice an example of the most consummate holiness and goodness: That in proof of his divine mission he performed the most wonderful works, manifestly transcending the utmost efforts of all human power or skill, and this in a vast number of instances, and in the most open and public manner, for a course of years together: That he most clearly and expressly foretold, that he was to undergo the most grievous sufferings, and a cruel and ignominious death, and should afterwards rise again from the dead on the third day: And to this he appealed as the most convincing proof of his divine mission: That accordingly he suffered the death of the cross in the face of a vast multitude of spectators: And notwithstanding the chief men of the *Jewish* nation, by whose instigation he was crucified, took the most prudent and effectual precautions to prevent an imposition in this matter, he rose again from the dead at the time appointed with circumstances of great glory, in a manner which struck terror into the guards, who were set to watch the sepulchre: That afterwards he shewed himself alive to many of those who were most intimately acquainted with him, and who, far from discovering a too forward credulity, could not be brought to believe it, till they found themselves constrained to do so by the testimony of all their senses: That as a farther proof of his resurrection and exaltation, they who witnessed it were themselves enabled to perform the most wonderful miracles in his name, and by power derived from him, and were endued with the most extraordinary gifts and powers, that they might spread his religion through the world, amidst the greatest oppositions and discouragements: That accordingly this religion, though propagated by the seemingly meanest and most unlikely instruments, and not only destitute of all worldly advantages, but directly opposite to the prevailing superstitions, prejudices and vices both of *Jews* and *Gentiles*, and though it exposed its publishers and followers to all manner of reproaches, persecutions and sufferings, yet in that very age made the most surprising progress, in consequence of which the religion of Jesus was established in a considerable part of the world, and so continueth unto this day. Such is the view of the evidence of the resurrection of Jesus. And taking it altogether, it forms such a concatenation of proofs, as is every way suitable to the importance of the fact, and which was never equaled in any other case. And to suppose all this evidence, to have been given in attestation to a falshood, involveth in it the most palpable absurdities. It is to suppose, either that God would employ his own prescience and power to give testimony to an impostor, by a series of the most illustrious prophecies and numerous uncontrolled miracles: Or that good beings superior to man would extraordinarily interpose for the same purpose, to countenance and derive credit to a person falsely pretending to be sent from God, and feigning to act in his name: Or, that evil spirits would use all their arts and power to attest and confirm a religion, the manifest tendency of which was to destroy idolatry, superstition and vice, where-ever it was sincerely believed and embraced, and to recover mankind to holiness and happiness; which is a contradiction to their very nature and character: It is to suppose that a number of persons would combine in attesting falshoods in favour of a person who they knew had deceived them, and of a religion contrary to their most inveterate and favourite prejudices, and by which they had a prospect of gaining nothing but misery, reproach, sufferings, and death; which is absolutely contrary to all the principles and passions of the human nature: It is to suppose that persons of the greatest simplicity and plainness would act the part of the vilest impostors: Or, that men who were so bad, so false, and impious, as to be capable of carrying on a series of the most solemn impositions in the name of God himself, would at the hazard of all that is dear to men, and in manifest opposition to all their worldly interests, endeavour to bring over the nations to embrace a holy and self-denying institution: Or, that if they were enthusiasts, who were carried away by the heat of their own distempered brains to imagine, that for a series of years together the most extraordinary facts were done before their eyes, though no such things were done at all, and that they were themselves enabled actually to perform the most wonderful works in the most open and public manner, though they performed no such works; it is to suppose that such mad enthusiasts, who were also mean and contemptible in their condition, and for the most part ignorant and illiterate, were not only capable of forming the noblest scheme of religion which was ever published to mankind, but were able to overcome all the learning, wealth, power, eloquence of the world, all the bigotry and superstition of the nations, all the influence and artifices of the priests, all the power and authority of the magistrates: That they did this by only alleging that they had a commission in the name of a person who had been crucified, whom they affirmed, but without giving any proof of it, to have been risen from the dead, and to be exalted as the Saviour and Lord of mankind. All this is such a complication of absurdities, as cannot be admitted but upon principles that are absolutely abhorrent to the common sense and reason of men. It were easy to enlarge farther on this subject, but this may suffice at present; especially considering that Mr. *Adams* hath urged many things to this purpose with great clearness and force, in his answer to Mr. *Hume*'s Essay, p. 31–36. And what is there to oppose to all this? Nothing but the single difficulty of restoring a dead man to life, which is indeed a very extraordinary and miraculous event, but is not above the power of God to effect, and supposing a good and valid reason can be assigned for it worthy of the divine wisdom and goodness, involveth in it no absurdity at all. And such a reason it certainly was to give an illustrious attestation to the divine mission of the Holy Jesus, and to the divine original of the most excellent dispensation of religion that was ever published among men. To talk, as this author does, of the diminution of the evidence in proportion to the difficulty of the case is trifling. For the evidence is here supposed to be fully proportioned to the difficulty and importance of the case: Since there is both a power assigned every way able to effect it, and a valuable end which makes it reasonable to think it was becoming the divine wisdom and goodness to interpose for effecting it.

You will perhaps think this may be sufficient with regard to the first part of Mr. *Hume*'s Essay on Miracles. In my next I shall endeavour to make it appear, that we have the highest reason to think that the evidence, which hath been argued to be sufficient if given, was really and actually given: And shall answer the several considerations he hath offered to shew that supposing miracles capable of being proved by evidence or testimony, yet no evidence was ever actually given for miracles, which can be reasonably depended upon.

LETTER XIX.

Reflections on the second part of Mr. Hume's *Essay on Miracles, which is design to shew, that in fact there never was a miraculous event established upon such evidence as can be depended on. What he offers concerning the necessary conditions and qualifications of witnesses in the case of miracles considered. It is shewn that the witnesses to the miracles in proof of Christianity had all the conditions and qualifications, that can be required to render any testimony good and valid. Concerning the proneness of mankind in all ages to believe wonders, especially in matters of religion. This no reason for rejecting all miracles without farther examination. The miracles wrought in proof of Christianity not done in an ignorant and barbarous age. His pretence that different miracles wrought in favour of different religions destroy one another, and shew that none of them are true. The absurdity of this way of reasoning shewn. Instances produced by him of miracles well attested, and which yet ought to be rejected as false and incredible. A particular exami-*

nation of what he hath offered concerning the miracles attributed to the Abbé de Paris, and which he pretends much surpass those of our Saviour in credit and authority.

SIR,

I now proceed to consider the second part of Mr. *Hume*'s Essay on Miracles. The first was designed to shew, that miracles are incapable of being proved by any evidence whatsoever, and that no evidence or testimony that could be given, let us suppose it never so full and strong, would be a sufficient ground for believing the truth and existence of miracles. And now in his second part he proceeds to shew, that supposing a miracle capable of being proved by full and sufficient evidence or testimony, yet in fact there never was a *miraculous* event in any history established upon such evidence as can reasonably be depended upon. To this purpose he offereth several considerations. The first is designed to prove, that no witnesses have ever been produced for any miracle, which have all the necessary conditions and qualifications, to render their testimony credible. The second consideration is drawn from the proneness there has been in mankind in all ages to believe wonders; and the more for their being absurd and incredible; especially in matters of religion; and that therefore in this case all men of sense should reject them without farther examination. His third observation is, that they are always found to abound most among ignorant and barbarous nations. His fourth observation is drawn from the opposite miracles wrought in different religions, which destroy one another; so that there is no miracle wrought, but what is opposed by an infinite number of others. He then goes on to give an account of some miraculous facts which seem to be well attested, and yet are to be rejected as false and incredible. This is the substance of this part of his Essay, which he concludes with an insolent boast as if he thought he had so clearly demonstrated what he undertook, that no man who had not his *understanding* miraculously *subverted* could opposite. But I apprehend, it will appear upon a distinct examination of what he hath offered, that there is little ground for such confident boasting.

The principal consideration is that which he hath mentioned in the first place, drawn from the want of competent testimony to ascertain the truth of miraculous facts. He affirms,

"That there is not to be found in all history any miracle attested by a sufficient number of men, of such unquestionable good sense, education, and learning, as to secure us against all delusion in themselves; of such undoubted integrity, as to place them beyond all suspicion of any design to deceive others; of such credit and reputation in the eyes of mankind, as to have a great deal to lose in case of being detected in any falshood;

and at the same time attesting facts performed in such a public manner, and in so celebrated a part of the world, as to render the detection unavoidable: All which circumstances are requisite to give us a full assurance in the testimony of men."[195]

Here he supposes, that where these circumstances concur, we may have *full assurance in the testimony of men* concerning the facts they relate, however extraordinary and unusual. Let us therefore examine the conditions and qualifications he insists upon as necessary to render a testimony good and valid, and apply them to the testimony of the witnesses of Christianity, and the extraordinary miraculous facts whereby it was confirmed, especially that of our Saviour's Resurrection.

The first thing he insisteth upon is, that the Miracle should be *attested by a sufficient number of men*. He hath not told us, what number of witnesses he takes to be sufficient in such a case. In some cases very few may be sufficient. Yea, a single evidence may be so circumstanced as to produce a sufficient assurance and conviction in the mind, even concerning a Fact of an extraordinary nature: though where there is a concurrence of many good witnesses, it is undoubtedly an advantage, and tendeth to give farther force to the evidence. And as to this, Christianity hath all the advantages that can reasonably be desired. All the Apostles were the authorised witnesses of the principal facts by which Christianity is attested. So were the seventy Disciples, and the hundred and twenty mentioned *Acts* i. 15, 21, 22. who had been with Jesus from the commencement of his personal ministry to his ascension into heaven: to which might be added many others who had seen his illustrious miracles, as well as heard his excellent instructions. The accounts of these things were published in that very age, and the Facts were represented as having been done, and the discourses as having been delivered, in the presence of multitudes; so that in effect they appealed to thousands in *Judea, Jerusalem,* and *Galilee.* It is true, that as to the Resurrection of Christ, this was not a Fact done before all the people;[196] but there was a number of witnesses to it, sufficient to attest any fact. Christ shewed himself alive after his passion to several persons at different times; whose testimony gave mutual support and force to one another. He shewed himself also to all the Apostles in a body, to several other disciples, and at last to five hundred at once.[197] To which it may be added, that all the extraordinary facts and wonderful works wrought by the Apostles and first publishers of Christianity, many of

---

[195] Hume's Philosophical Essays, p. 183.

[196] See this accounted for vol. i. p. 183, 184.

[197] Ibid. p. 175, 176.

which were of a very public nature, and done in the view of multitudes, came in aid of their testimony.

As to the qualifications of the witnesses, the first thing he requireth is, that "they should be of such unquestioned good sense, education, and learning, as to secure us against all delusion in themselves." The reason why this gentleman here mentioneth *learning* and *education*, as necessary qualifications in witnesses, is evident. It is undoubtedly with a view to exclude the Apostles, who, except St. *Paul*, appear not to have been persons of education and learning. But no court of judicature, in enquiring into facts, looks upon it to be necessary that the persons giving testimony to the truth of those facts should be persons who had a learned education: It is sufficient, if they appear to be persons of sound sense and honest characters, and that the facts were such as they had an opportunity of being well acquainted with. And thus it was with regard to the first witnesses of Christianity. They were not indeed persons eminent for their learning, knowledge, and experience in the world. If they had been so, this might probably have been regarded as a suspicious circumstance, as if they had themselves laid the scheme, and it was the effect of their own art and contrivance. But they were persons of plain sense, and sound understanding, and perfectly acquainted with the facts they relate. This sufficiently appeareth from their writings, and the accounts they have left us. Their narrations are plain and consistent, delivered in a simple unaffected stile, without any pomp of words, or ostentation of eloquence or literature on the one hand, and on the other without any of the rants of enthusiasm. All is calm, cool, and sedate, the argument of a composed spirit. There is nothing that betrayeth an overheated imagination: nor do they ever fly out into passionate exclamations, even where the subject might seem to warrant it. The facts they relate were of such a nature, and so circumstanced, that they could not themselves be deceived in them, supposing they had their senses, or be made to believe they were done before their eyes, when they were not done. This must be acknowledged as to the facts done during Christ's personal Ministry. For they were constantly with him in his going out and coming in, and had an opportunity of observing those facts in all their circumstances for a course of years together; and therefore could be as perfectly assured of them, as any man can be of any facts whatsoever, which he himself hears and sees. And as to his resurrection, they were not forward rashly to give credit to it by an enthusiastic heat. They examined it scrupulously, and would not receive it, till compelled by irresistible evidence, and by the testimony of all their senses.

The next thing he insisteth upon is, that "the witnesses should be of such undoubted integrity, as to place them beyond all suspicion of any design to deceive others." Apply this to the witnesses of the miraculous Facts whereby Christianity was attested, and it will appear that never were there persons, who were more remote from all reasonable suspicion of fraud, or a design to impose falshood upon mankind. They appeared by their whole temper and conduct to be persons of great probity, and unaffected simplicity, strangers to artful cunning, and the refinements of human policy. It mightily strengthens this, when it is considered, that as the case was circumstanced, they could have no temptation to endeavour to impose these things upon the world if they had not been true, but had the strongest inducements to the contrary. They could have no prospect of serving their worldly interest, or answering the ends of ambition, by preaching up a religion contrary to all the prevailing passions and prejudices of *Jews* and *Gentiles*, a principal article of which was salvation through a crucified Jesus. They could scarce have had a reasonable expectation of gaining so much as a single proselyte, to so absurd and foolish a scheme, as it must have been, supposing they had known that all was false, and that Jesus had never risen at all. How could it have been expected in such a case, that they should be able to persuade the *Jews* to receive for their messiah, one that had been put to an ignominious death by the Heads of their nation, as an impostor and deceiver? Or, that they should persuade the *Gentiles* to acknowledge and worship a crucified *Jew* for their Lord, in preference to their long-adored Deities, and to abandon all their darling superstitions for a strict and self-denying discipline? The only thing that can be pretended as a possible inducement to them, to endeavour to impose upon mankind, is what this writer afterwards mentions.

"What greater temptation, saith he, than to appear a Missionary, a Prophet, and Ambassador from heaven? Who would not encounter many dangers and difficulties, to attain so sublime a character? or, if persuaded of it himself, would scruple a pious fraud in prospect of so holy an end."[198]

But there is no room for such a suspicion in the case we are now considering. If they had pretended a revelation in favour of a Messiah, suited to the *Jewish* carnal notions and prejudices, who was to erect a mighty worldly dominion, arrayed with all the pomp of secular glory and grandeur, they might have expected honour and applause in being looked upon as his ministers. But what honour could they propose from being regarded as the disciples and apostles of one that had been condemned, and put to a shameful death by public authority? To set up his Ambassadors, and pretend to be inspired by his spirit and to be commissioned by him to go through the world, preaching up Jesus Christ, and him crucified: This was in all appearance the readiest way they could take to expose themselves

---

[198] Hume's Philosophical Essays, p. 200.

to general scorn, derision, and reproach: And they must have been absolutely out of their senses, to have expected that any veneration should be paid to them under this character, supposing they had no other proof to bring of their crucified Master's being risen, and exalted in glory as the universal Lord and Saviour, but their own word. Thus it appears that they could have no inducements or temptations, according to all the principles or motives that usually work upon the human mind, to attempt to impose this Scheme of Religion, and the facts by which it was supported, if they had known them to be false: and if they had been false, they must have known them to be so. But this is not all. They had the strongest possible inducements to the contrary. The Scheme of religion they preached, and which these facts were designed to attest, was directly opposite to their own most rooted prejudices. On the supposition of Christ's not having risen, they must have been sensible that he had deceived them; that the promises and predictions with which he had amused them were false; and that consequently they could have no hopes from him either in this world or in the next. At the same time they could not but foresee, that by pretending he was risen from the dead, and setting him up for the Messiah after he had been crucified, they should incur the indignation of the body of their own nation, and the hatred and contempt of those in chief authority among them. They could not possibly expect any thing but what they met with, persecutions, reproaches, shame and sufferings both from *Jews* and *Gentiles*. Their exposing themselves to these things may be accounted for, if they were persuaded that what they witnessed was really true; though even in that case it required great virtue and constancy, and divine supports. But that they should in manifest opposition to their own religious prejudices and worldly interests, without the least prospect of any thing to be gained by it here or here after, persist to the very death in attesting a falshood known by themselves to be so; and that they should, for the sake of one who they knew had deceived them, expose themselves to the greatest evils and sufferings to which all men have naturally the strongest aversion, is a supposition that cannot be admitted with the least appearance of reason, as being absolutely subversive of all the principles and passions of human nature. Our author ought to acknowledge the force of this reasoning, since he taketh pains throughout his whole Essay on Liberty and Necessity, to shew that we may in many cases argue as surely and strongly from the power and influence of motives on the human mind, as from the influence of physical causes; and that there is as great a certainty, and as necessary a connexion in what are called moral causes as in physical. This author undoubtedly in that Essay carrieth it too far, when, in order to subvert human liberty, he would have it thought, that in all cases the power of motives worketh with as necessary a force upon the mind, as any physical cause doth upon the effect. But that in many particular cases things may be so circumstanced with regard to moral causes, as to afford a certainty equal to what arises from physical, cannot reasonably be denied. And such is the case here put. And he expressly declareth, that

"we cannot make use of amore convincing argument than to prove, that the actions ascribed to any person are contrary to the course of nature, and that no human motives in such circumstances, could ever induce them to such a conduct."[199]

This writer farther requireth, that "the witnesses should be of such Credit and Reputation in the eyes of Mankind as to have a great deal to lose in case of being detected in any falshood." If the meaning be, that they must be persons distinguished by their rank and situation in the world, and of great reputation for knowledge, and for the eminency of their station and figure in life; this in the case here referred to would instead of strengthening have greatly weakened the force of their testimony. It might have been said with some shew of plausibility, that such persons by their knowledge and abilities, their reputation and interest, might have it in their power to countenance and propagate an imposture among the people, and give it some credit in the world. If the facts recorded in the gospel, the miracles and resurrection of Jesus Christ, had been patronized and attested by the Chief Priests and Rulers of the *Jewish* Nation, it would undoubtedly have been pretended that they had political designs in view, and that considering their authority and influence they might more easily impose those things upon the multitude. On this view of things the evidence for those important facts would have been far less convincing than now it is. And therefore the Divine wisdom hath ordered it far better, in appointing that the first witnesses of the Gospel were not the worldly *wise*, *mighty*, or *noble*, but persons of mean condition, and yet of honest characters, without power, authority, or interest. And whereas this writer urgeth, that the witnesses ought to be of *such reputation as to have a great deal to lose in case of being detected in a falshood,* it ought to be considered, that a man of true probity, though in a low condition, may be as unwilling to be branded as a cheat and an impostor, and as desirous to preserve his good name, which may be almost all he has to value himself upon, as persons of greater figure and eminence in the world, who may more easily find means to support themselves, and to evade detection and punishment. The Apostles indeed rejoiced that they were counted *worthy to suffer shame for the name of Christ*, Acts v. 41. But this was not owing to their being insen-

---

[199] Hume's philosophical Essays, p. 135.

sible to shame, but to the testimony of a good conscience, and to the full persuasion they had of Christ's divine Mission, and the divinity of the Religion they preached in his name. This particularly was the principle upon which St. *Paul* acted, who was a man of reputation among the *Jews*, and would never have made a sacrifice of this, and of all his worldly interests and expectations, to join himself to a despised persecuted party, and against whom he himself had conceived the strongest prejudices, if he had not been brought over by an evidence which he was not able to resist, to the acknowledgement of the Christian faith, and of the extraordinary facts on which it was established.

The last thing insisteth upon is, that the facts attested by the witnesses should be "performed in such a public manner, and in so celebrated apart of the world, as to render the Detection unavoidable." This may be applied with the greatest propriety to the extraordinary and miraculous Facts by which Christianity was attested. Justly doth St. *Paul* appeal to king *Agrippa* in the admirable apology he made before him and the *Roman* Governor *Festus*, and which was delivered before a numerous and august assembly of *Jews* and *Romans*, that *none of these things were hidden from him: for, saith he, this thing was not done in a corner.* Acts xxvi. 26. Christ's whole personal Ministry, and the wonderful works he wrought, were transacted not in private and secret, but in the most open and public manner possible, in places of the greatest concourse, and before multitudes of people assembled from all parts. The same may be said of many of the miracles wrought by the apostles in the name and by the power of a risen Jesus. And particularly never was there any event of a more public nature than the extraordinary effusion of the Holy Ghost on the day of Pentecost. The first publishers of Christianity preached the religion of Jesus, and performed miracles in confirmation of it, not merely in small villages, or obscure parts of the country, but in populous cities, in those parts of the world that were most celebrated for the liberal arts, learning, and politeness. They published that religion, and the wonderful Facts by which it was supported, throughout the *Lesser Asia*, *Greece*, *Italy*; in the cities of *Jerusalem*, *Antioch*, *Ephesus*, *Cornith*, *Thessalonica*, *Philippi*, *Athens*, and *Rome* itself. If therefore their pretences had been false, they could scarce have possibly escaped a detection. Especially considering that they were everywhere under the eye of watchful Adversaries, unbelieving *Jews* as well as Heathens, who would not have failed to detect and expose the imposture, if there had been any. As to what the author afterwards allegeth, that

"in the infancy of new religions the wise and learned commonly esteem the matter too inconsiderable to deserve their attention and regard. And when afterwards they would willingly detect the cheat, in order to undeceive the deluded multitude, the season is now gone, and the

Records and Witnesses, who might clear up the matter, are perished beyond recovery."[200]

This pretence hath no place in the case we are now considering with regard to Christianity. That religion met with the greatest opposition even in its infancy. Persons of principal authority in the nation where it first arose, bent their attention and employed their power to suppress it. And in all the places where it was afterwards propagated, there were unbelieving *Jews,* who used their utmost efforts to stir up the Heathens against it, who of themselves were strongly inclined by their own prejudices to oppose it: and this at the very time when if the facts had been false, it would have been the easiest thing in the world, to have detected the falshood; which in that case must have been known to thousands; since many of the facts appealed to were of a very public nature.

Thus I have considered the conditions and qualifications he insisteth upon as necessary to give us a *full assurance in the testimony of men* with regard to miracles; and have shewn, that all the conditions that can be reasonably desired concur with the highest degree of evidence in the Testimony given by the apostles and first witnesses of Christianity, to the extraordinary facts whereby its divine authority was established. Their Testimony had some advantages which no other Testimony ever had. St. *Luke* observes, that *with great power gave the apostles witness of the Resurrection of the Lord Jesus,* Acts iv. 33. The Testimony they gave was accompanied with a Divine power. The force of their Testimony did not depend merely on their own veracity, but may be said to have been confirmed by the attestation of God himself. It is with the utmost propriety therefore that the sacred writer of the epistle to the *Hebrews* representeth *God as bearing them witness, both with signs and wonders, and with divers miracles and gifts of the Holy Ghost, according to his own will,* Hebr. ii. 4. and it is incontestably true in fact, that so strong and convincing was the evidence, that great numbers of both *Jews* and *Gentiles* were brought over in that very age to the faith of a crucified and risen Saviour. Nor was this the effect of a too forward credulity, since it was in direct opposition to their prejudices, passions, and worldly interests. The Principles and Inducements, which usually lead men to form wrong and partial judgments, lay wholly on the other side, and instead of being favourable to Christianity tended rather to determine men to disbelieve and reject it. So that it may be justly said, that the Propagation of that Scheme of religion which is held forth in the Gospel had something in it so wonderful, taking in all the circumstances of the case, that it affordeth a manifest and most convincing proof of the truth of the extraordinary Facts upon which it was founded.

---

[200] Hume's philosophical Essays, p. 202.

I now proceed to make some observations upon the other Considerations this Gentleman offers in this second Part of his Essay; and which indeed can at best pass, for no more than Presumptions; and only shew, that the Testimony given to Miracles is not rashly to be admitted, and that great care and caution is necessary in judging of them, which will be easily allowed

The second Consideration, and upon which he seemeth to lay a great stress is this: That "we may observe in human nature a Principle, which, if strictly examined, will be found to diminish extremely the assurance we might have from human Testimony, in any kind of Prodigy." He says,

> "That though for the most part we readily reject any Fact that is unusual and incredible in an ordinary degree, yet when any thing is affirmed utterly absurd and miraculous, the mind rather more readily admits such a Fact, upon account of that very circumstance, which ought to destroy all its authority. The passion of *Surprize* and *Wonder* arising from Miracles, being an agreeable Emotion, gives a sensible tendency towards the belief of those Events from which it is derived. – But if the Spirit of Religion join itself to the love of wonder, there is an end of common Sense; and human Testimony in these circumstances loses all pretensions to authority."[201]

And again he observes, that

> "should a miracle be ascribed to any new system of religion, men in all ages have been so much imposed on by the ridiculous stories of this kind, that this very circumstance will be a full proof of a cheat, and sufficient with all men of sense, not only to make them reject the fact, but even reject it without farther examination."

And he repeats it again, that it "should make us form a general resolution never to lend any attention to it, with whatever specious pretext it may be covered."[202] He here undertaketh, to answer for all *men of sense*, that they will reject all miracles produced in proof of religion without farther examination: because men in all ages have been much imposed on by ridiculous stories of this kind. But this certainly is the language, not of reason and good sense, which will dispose a man fairly to examine, but of the most obstinate prepossession and prejudice. No kinds of historical facts, whether of an ordinary or extraordinary nature, can be mentioned, in which men have not been frequently imposed upon. But this is no just reason for

---

[201] Hume's Philosophical Essays, p. 184, 185.

[202] Ibid. p. 204, 205.

rejecting such facts at once without examination: and the man that would do so, instead of proving his superior good sense, would only render himself ridiculous. That there have been many false miracles will be readily acknowleged; but this doth not prove that there never have been any true ones. It ought indeed to make us very cautious, and to examine miracles carefully before we receive them; but is no reason at all, or a very absurd one, for rejecting them all at once without examination and inquiry. Thus to reject them can only be justified upon this principle, that it is not possible there should be a true miracle wrought in favour of any system of religion. But by what medium will he undertake to prove this? He seems expresly to admit, that in other cases, "there may possibly be miracles, or violations of the usual course of nature, of such a kind as to admit of proof from human Testimony."[203] This concession is not very consistent with what he had laboured in the first part of his essay to shew, with regard to all miracles in general, *viz.* that they are incapable of being proved by any testimony. But now, provided miracles be not produced in proof of religion, he seems willing to allow, that they may *possibly admit of proof from human testimony.* The only case therefore in which they are never to be believed, is when they are pretended to be wrought in favour of religion. But in this he seems to have both the reason of the thing, and the general sense of mankind against him. It is certainly more reasonable to believe a miracle, when a valuable end can be assigned for it, than to believe it when we cannot discern any important end to be answered by it at all. And one of the most valuable ends for which a miracle can be supposed to be wrought seems to be this, to give an attestation to the divine mission of persons sent to instruct mankind in religious truths of great importance, and to lead them in the way of salvation. Our author seems sometimes to lay a mighty stress on the general opinion and common *sentiments* of mankind.[204] And there are few notions, which, by his own acknowledgement, have more generally obtained in all nations and ages, than this, that there have been miracles actually wrought on some occasions, especially in matters of religion, and that they are to be regarded as proofs of a divine interposition. This is a principle which seems to be conformable to the natural sense of the human mind.

The observation he makes concerning the *agreeable Emotion* produced by the *passion of wonder and surprize*, and the strong propensity *there is in mankind to the extraordinary and the marvellous,* proves nothing against this principle. The passion of wonder and surprize was certainly not given us in vain, but for very wise purposes, and it may be presumed, that this passion, as well as others, may be rightly exercised upon proper

---

[203] Ibid. p. 203.

[204] Hume's Essays, moral and political, p. 307.

objects. But I cannot agree with this gentleman, that men are naturally disposed and inclined to believe a thing the rather for its being *utterly absurd and miraculous,* especially in matters of religion. They may indeed, and often do believe absurdities; but they never believe a thing merely because it is absurd, but because, taking all considerations together, they do not look upon it to be absurd. It may be observed by the way, that this writer here makes *absurd* and *miraculous* to be terms of the same signification, whereas they are vary different ideas. A miracle, when supposed to be wrought by a power adequate to the effect, and for excellent ends, is indeed wonderful, but has no absurdity in it at all. It is true, there have often been very absurd things recommended to popular belief under the notion of miracles. And such pretended miracles have been received without much examination, when wrought in favour of the established superstition. But even miracles are received with difficulty, when they are wrought in opposition to it; and where the influence of the priesthood, the prejudices of the vulgar, and the authority of the magistrate, are on the other side: Which was the case of Christianity at its first appearance. Considering the nature of that religion, how contrary it was to the prevailing notions and prejudices both of the *Jews* and *Gentiles,* the strictness of the morals it prescribed, the scheme of salvation through a crucified Saviour which it proposed, the meanness of the instruments by which it was propagated, and the numberless difficulties it had to encounter with; the miracles wrought in attestation to it could not have met with a favourable reception in the world, if there had not been the most convincing evidence of their being really wrought. The strangeness of the facts, instead of producing belief, would rather have turned to its disadvantage, and could scarce have failed being detected in such circumstances, if they had been false.

His third observation is, that it "forms a very strong presumption against all supernatural relations, that they are always found chiefly to abound among ignorant and barbarous nations; or if a civilised people have ever given admission to any of them, they have received them from ignorant and barbarous ancestors."[205] But no presumption can be drawn from this to the prejudice of Christianity, which did not make its appearance in an ignorant and barbarous age, but at a time when the world was greatly civilized, and in nations where arts and learning had made a very great progress. And it must be considered, that it had not only their inveterate prejudices, their darling passions, and inclinations, but their pretended miracles to encounter with; extraordinary facts received from their ancestors, who *transmitted them,* as he expresseth it, *with that inviolable Sanction and Authority, which always attends antient and received opinions.* How strong and

[205] Hume's philosophical Essays, p. 186, 187.

cogent therefore must the force of the evidence in behalf of the Christian religion, and the extraordinary miraculous facts designed to support it, have been, which in the hands of such mean instruments, could make so great a progress in a civilized and enlightened age, and proved too hard for the religion of the empire; which besides its being interwoven with the civil establishment, had the prescription of many ages to plead, and was supported by pretended miracles, prodigies and oracles? Mr. Hume is pleased to take notice on this occasion of the management of that cunning impostor *Alexander*.[206] But though the better to carry on the cheat, he had laid the scene among the barbarous *Paphlagonians*, who were reckoned among the most stupid and ignorant of the human race; and not only put in practice all the arts of imposture (though it doth not appear that he pretended to work miracles among the people, or put the proof of his authority upon them) but had procured a powerful interest among the great to support him, he and his impostures soon sunk into oblivion, and so undoubtedly would Christianity too have done, if its extraordinary facts had no better foundation in truth and fact than his pretensions had.

"I may add (saith he) as a fourth reason, which diminishes the authority of prodigies, that there is no testimony for any, even those which have not been expresly detected, that is not opposed by an infinite number of witnesses; so that not only the miracle destroys the credit of the testimony, but even the Testimony destroys itself." He goes on to observe, that

"in matters of religion whatever is different is contrary: That it is impossible that all these different religions should be established on a solid foundation: That every miracle pretended to have been wrought in any of these religions, as it is designed to establish that particular system, has the same force to overthrow every other system; and consequently to destroy the credit of those miracles on which that system was established. So that all the prodigies of different religions are to be regarded as contrary facts, and the evidences of those prodigies as opposite to one another."[207]

This writer is here pleased to confound *prodigies* and *miracles*, which ought to be distinguished. Many things that have passed under the notion of prodigies, are very far from being miracles in the strict and proper sense, in which we are now considering them. And if we speak of miracles properly so called, the supposition he here goes upon, *viz.* that all religions have been founded upon miracles, and have put the proof of their authority upon them, is manifestly false. It is well known, that *Mahomet* did not

---

[206] Hume's Philosophical Essays, p. 188, 189.

[207] Ibid. p. 190, 191.

pretend to establish his religion by miracles, nor indeed can it be proved that any systems of religion had any tolerable pretensions of being originally founded upon miracles, but the *Jewish* and *Christian*; and these, tho' in some respects *different*, are not *contrary*, but mutually support each other; the former being introductive and preparatory to the latter. But if his supposition should be admitted, that all religions in the world have been founded upon the credit of miracles, it is hard to comprehend the force of his reasoning. By what logic doth it follow, that because miracles have been believed by mankind in all ages and nations to have been wrought in proof of religion, therefore miracles were never really wrought at all in proof of religion, nor are they ever to be believed in any single instance? With the same force it may be argued that because there have been and are many opposite schemes of religion in the world, therefore their being opposite to one another proves that they are all false, and that there is no such thing as true religion in the world at all. But let us suppose never so great a number of falshoods opposed to truth, that opposition of falshood to truth, doth not make truth to be less true, or destroy the certainty and evidence of it. Supposing the religions to be opposite, and that miracles are said to be wrought in attestation to those opposite religions, it may indeed be fairly concluded that they cannot be all true, but not, that none of them is so. Our author himself seems to be apprehensive that this might be looked upon as a fallacious way of reasoning.

"This argument (saith he) may appear very subtle and refined; but is not in reality different from the reasoning of a Judge, who supposes that the credit of two witnesses, maintaining a crime against any one, is destroyed by the testimony of two others, who affirm him to have been two hundred leagues distant at the same instant when the crime is said to have been committed."[208]

This gentleman has here given us a most extraordinary specimen, how well qualified he would be to determine causes, if he sat in a court of Judicature. If there came several witnesses before him, and their testimony was opposite to one another, he would without farther examination reject them all at once, and make their opposition to one another to be alone a proof that they were all false, and none of them to be depended upon. But it hath been hitherto thought reasonable, when testimonies are opposite, to weigh and compare those testimonies, in order to form a proper judgment concerning them. In the case of *Alibi's*, which is the case the author here puts, the testimonies do not always destroy one another. A just and impartial Judge will not immediately reject the testimonies on both

---

[208] Hume's Philosophical Essays, p. 192.

sides without examination, because they contradict one another, which is the method our author seems here to recommend as reasonable, but will carefully compare them, that he may find out on which side the truth lies, and which of the testimonies is most to be credited, and will give his judgment accordingly. This certainly is the course which right reason prescribeth in all cases where there is an opposition of testimony, and which it is to be presumed this gentleman himself would recommend in every case, but where the cause of religion is concerned. For here, notwithstanding all his pretensions to freedom of thinking, his prejudices are so strong, that he is for proceeding by different weights and measures from what he and all mankind would judge reasonable in every other instance. He hath shewed himself so little qualified to judge impartially in matters of this nature, that I believe *men of sense*, to use his own phrase, will lay very little stress on any judgment he shall think fit to pronounce in this cause.

The only part of Mr. *Hume*'s Essay on miracles, which now remaineth to be considered, is that which relateth to some particular accounts of miraculous facts, which he would have us believe are as well or better attested, than those recorded in the Gospels, and yet are to be rejected as false and incredible. The first instance he mentioneth is that of the Emperor *Vespasian*'s curing a blind and a lame man at *Alexandria*, and which he affirms is one of the best attested miracles in all profane History. This has been urged by almost every Deistical writer who hath treated of Miracles: And how little it is to the purpose in the present controversy hath been often shewn. Not to repeat what Mr. *Adams* hath well urged concerning it, it may be sufficient to observe, that it appeareth from the accounts given us by the historians who mention it,[209] that the design of these miracles was to give weight to the authority of *Vespasian;* newly made Emperor by the great men and the army, and to make it believed that his elevation to the imperial throne was approved by the gods. I believe every reasonable man will be of opinion, that in any case of this kind there is great ground to suspect artifice and management. And who would be so presumptuous to make too narrow a scrutiny into the truth of miracles, in which the interests of the Great, and the authority of a mighty Emperor, were so nearly concerned? And if, as this writer observes from *Tacitus*, some who were present continued to relate these facts, even after *Vespasian* and his family were no longer in possession of the empire; it doth not appear, that the persons referred to were such as had been the secret of the management, which probably lay in few hands; or if they were, it is not to be wondered at that they should afterwards be unwilling to own the part they had in this

---

[209] Tacit. Hist. lib. 4. versus finen. Sueton, in Vespas. cap. 8.

affair; especially since no methods were made use of to oblige them to discover the fraud.

The next instance he produceth is the miracle pretended to have been wrought at *Saragossa*, and mentioned by Cardinal *De Retz*, who by Mr. *Hume*'s own account did not believe it. But certainly a man must have his head very oddly turned to attempt to draw a parallel between the miracles of our Saviour and his Apostles, and miracles pretended to have been wrought in a country where the inquisition is established, where the influence and interests of the Priests, the superstitions and prejudices of the People, and the authority of the civil Magistrate, are all combined to support the credit of those miracles, and where it would be extremely dangerous to make a strict enquiry into the truth of them: and even the expressing the least doubt concerning them might expose a man to the most terrible of all evils and sufferings.

But that which Mr. *Hume* seems to lay the greatest stress upon, and on which he enlarges for some pages together, is, the miracles reported to have been wrought at the tomb of the Abbé *de Paris*. Having observed that in the *Recueil des Miracles de l'Abbé de Paris*, there is a parallel run between the miracles of our Saviour, and those of the Abbé, he pronounces, that

"if the inspired writers were to be considered merely as human testimony, the *French* author is very moderate in his comparison, since he might with some appearance of reason pretend, that the *Jansenist* miracles must surpass the others in credit and authority."[210]

This has been of late a favourite topic with the Deists. Great triumphs have been raised upon it, as if it were alone sufficient to destroy the credit of the miraculous facts recorded in the New Testament. I shall therefore make some observations upon it, though in doing so I shall be obliged to take notice of several things which Mr. *Adams* hath already observed in his judicious reflections upon this subject, in his answer to Mr. Hume's Essay on Miracles, from page 65 to 78.

The account Mr. *Hume* pretends to give of the whole affair is very unfair and disingenuous, and is absolutely unworthy of any man that makes pretensions to a free and impartial enquiry.

He positively asserts, that the miraculous facts were so strongly proved, that the Molinists or Jesuits were never able distinctly to refute or detect them: And that they could not deny the truth of the facts, but ascribed them to witchcraft and the devil. And yet certain it is, that the Jesuits or Molinists did deny many of the facts to be true as the Jansenists related them; that they asserted them to be false, and plainly proved several of them to be so.

[210] Hume's Philosophical Essays, p. 196.

Particularly the Archbishop of *Sens* distinctly insisted upon twenty-two of those pretended miraculous facts, all which he charged as owing to falshood and imposture.

He farther observes, that twenty-two of the Curez or Rectors of *Paris* pressed the Archbishop of *Paris* to examine those miracles, and asserted them to be known to the whole world. But he knew, or might have known, that some of those very miracles which those gentlemen desired might be particularly enquired into, and which they represented as undeniably true and certain, were afterwards examined, and the perjury of the principal witnesses plainly detected.[211] And the Archbishop, who, he tells us, wisely forbore an enquiry, caused a public judicial inquest to be made, as Mr. *Adams* observes, and in an ordonnance of *November* 8, 1735, published the most convincing proofs, that the miracles so strongly vouched by the Curez, were forged and counterfeited.[212]

Mr. *Hume* is pleased to observe, that "the Molinist party tried to discredit those miracles in one instance, that of Mademoiselle *la Franc*, but were not able to do it." Where he speaks, as if this were the single instance in which they tried to discredit those miracles, which is far from being true. This indeed was taken particular notice of, because it was the first history of a miraculous Fact which the *Jansenists* thought fit to publish, with a pompous dissertation prefixed. It was cried up as of such unquestionable truth, that it could not be denied without doubting of the most certain facts. And yet the story was proved to be false in the most material circumstances by forty witnesses judicially examined upon oath. It was plainly proved, that she was considerably better of her maladies before she went to the tomb at all: That she was no stronger when she returned from the tomb, than she was when she went to it; and that she still stood in need of remedies afterwards. Mr. *Hume* indeed takes upon him to declare, that the proceedings were the most irregular in the world, particularly in citing but few of the *Jansenist* witnesses, whom they tampered with. And then he adds, 'Besides they were soon overwhelmed with a cloud of new witnesses, an hundred and twenty in number, who gave oath for the miracles." He doth not say, they all gave oath for this particular miracle, but for the miracles. And indeed most of those testimonies were very little to the purpose, and seemed to be designed rather for parade and show than for proof. And nothing turned more to the disadvantage of the *Jansenists*, than their endeavouring still to maintain the credit of this miracle, after the falshood of it had been so evidently detected. The more witnesses they endeavoured to produce for this, the more they rendered themselves

---

[211] See Mr. Des Voeux's Critique General, page 242, 243.

[212] Adams's Essay, p. 71.

suspected in all the rest. They alleged some want of formality in the proceedings, but were never able to disprove the principal circumstances of the facts alleged on the other side, and which were absolutely inconsistent with the truth and reality of the miracle.[213]

Mr. *Hume* refers his reader to the *Recueil des Miracles de l' Abbé Paris* in three volumes: but especially to the famous book of Mr. *de Montgeron*, a counsellor or judge of the parliament of *Paris*, and which was dedicated to the *French* King. But if he had read on both-sides, or had thought fit to lay the matter fairly before his reader, he might have informed him that these books have been solidly answered by Mr. *Des Voeux*, a very ingenious and judicious author, who had himself been bred up among the *Jansenists*, and was at *Paris* part of the time that this scene was carrying on. See his *Lettres sur les Miracles*, published in 1735, and his *Critique Generale du livre de Mr. de Montgeron*, 1741. See also what relates to this subject in the 19th and 20th Tomes of the *Bibliotheque Raisonnée*.

There never was perhaps a book written with a greater air of assurance and confidence, than that of Mr. *de Montgeron*. He intitles it, *The Truth of the Miracles wrought by the intercession of Mr. de Paris and other Appellants, demonstrated against M. the Archbishop of Sens*. It was natural therefore to expect, that he would have attempted to justify all those miracles which that prelate had attacked. But of twenty-two which are distinctly insisted upon by the Archbishop, there are seventeen which Mr. *de Montgeron* does not meddle with. He hath passed by those of them against which the strongest charges of falshood and imposture lay. Five of the miracles attacked by the Archbishop, he takes pains to justify, to which he has added four more which that Prelate had not distinctly considered. Mr. *Des Voeux*, who has examined this work of Mr. *de Montgeron* with great care and judgment, hath plainly shewn that there are every-where to be discovered in it marks of strong prepossession.[214] Carried away by the power of his prejudices, and by his affection to the *Jansenist* cause, to which he was greatly attached, he has in several instances disguised and misrepresented facts in a manner which cannot be excused or vindicated. The last-mentioned author has charged him with faults not merely of inadvertency, but with direct falsifications designed to impose upon the public. See the sixth letter of his *Critique Generale*, page 208, *et. seq*. Mr. *Hume* has taken care not to give his reader the least hint of any thing of this nature.

---

[213] This whole matter is set in a clear light in Mr. Des Voeux's Dissertat. sur les miracles, &c. p. 46. 49. and in his Critique General, p. 204, 231, 232.

[214] The character of Mr. de Montgeron is well represented by Mr. Adams in his answer to Hume, p. 74, 75.

The remarks which have been now made may help us to judge of Mr. *Hume*'s conduct in his management of this subject.

I shall now proceed to make some observations upon the remarkable differences there are between the miracles recorded in the Gospels, and those ascribed to the Abbé *de Paris*, by considering which it will appear, that no argument can be justly drawn from the latter to discredit the former, or to invalidate the proof produced for them.

I. One observation of no small weight is this. At the time when the miracles of the Abbé *de Paris* first appeared, there was a strong and numerous party in *France*, and which was under the conduct of very able and learned men, who were strongly prepossessed in favour of that cause which those miracles seemed to be intended to support. And it might naturally be expected, that these would use all their interests and influence for maintaining and spreading the credit of them among the people. And so it actually happened. The first rumours of these miracles were eagerly laid hold on; and they were cried up as real and certain miracles, and as giving a clear decision of Heaven on the side of the appellants, even before there was any regular proof so much as pretended to be given them.[215] To which it may be added, that the beginning of this whole affair was at a very promising conjuncture, viz. when the Cardinal *de Noailles* was archbishop of *Paris*; who, whatever may be said of his capacity and integrity, which Mr. *Hume* highly extols, was well known to be greatly inclined to favour the cause of the appellants. It was therefore a situation of things very favourable to the credit of those miracles, that they first appeared under his administration, and were tried before his officials. And though the succeeding archbishop was no friend to the *Jansenists*, yet when once the credit of those miracles was in some measure established, and they had got the popular vogue on their side, the affair was more easily carried on. But at the first appearance of Christianity, the circumstances of things were entirely different. There were indeed parties among the *Jews*, the most powerful of which were the *Pharisees* and the *Saducees*, besides the priests and rulers of the *Jews*, and the Sanhedrim or great council of the nation. But not one of these afforded the least countenance to the first witnesses and publishers of the Christian religion. Our Lord, far from addicting himself to any party, freely declared against what was amiss in every one of them. He opposed the distinguishing tenets of the *Saducees*, the traditions, superstitions, and hypocrisy of the *Pharisees*, and the prejudices of the vulgar. Christianity proceeded upon a principle directly contrary to that in which all parties among the *Jews* were agreed, *viz.* upon the doctrine of

---

[215] See Critique General, Lettre vi.

a spiritual kingdom, and a suffering Messiah. And accordingly all the different sects and parties, all the powers civil and ecclesiastical, united their interests and endeavours to oppose and suppress it. Whatever suspicion therefore might be entertained with regard to the miracles said to have been wrought at the tomb of the Abbé *de Paris*, which had a strong party from the beginning prepared to receive and support them; no such suspicion can reasonably be admitted as to the truth and reality of the extraordinary facts whereby Christianity was attested, which, as the case was circumstanced, could scarce possibly have made their way in the manner they did, or have escaped detection, if they had not been true.

II. Another consideration, which shews a remarkable difference between the miracles recorded to have been wrought by our Saviour and his apostles, and those ascribed to the Abbé *de Paris*, is this: That the former carry plain characters of a divine interposition, and a supernatural power, and the latter, even taking their own account of them, do not appear to be evidently miraculous, they may be accounted for without supposing any thing properly supernatural in the case. Our Lord Jesus Christ not only healed all manner of diseases, but raised the dead. He commanded the winds and the seas, and they obeyed him: He searched the hearts, and knew the thoughts of men: He gave many express and circumstantial predictions of future contingencies, both relating to his own sufferings and death, and to his consequent resurrection and exaltation, and relating to the calamities that should come upon the Jews, the destruction of *Jerusalem* and the temple, and the wonderful propagation and establishment of his church and kingdom in the world, which it was impossible for any man, judging by the rules of human probability, to foresee. He not only performed the most wonderful works himself, but he imparted the same miraculous powers to his disciples, and poured forth upon them the extraordinary gifts of the Holy Ghost, as he had promised and foretold; gifts of the most admirable nature, which were never paralleled before nor since, and which were peculiarly fitted for spreading and propagating the Christian religion. With regard to these and other things which might be mentioned, no man has ever pretended to draw a comparison between the miracles ascribed to the Abbé *de Paris* and those of our Saviour. And accordingly one of the most zealous and able advocates for the former, M. *Le Gros* expresly acknowlegeth, that there is *an infinite difference between them*, and declares that he *will never forget that difference*. The only instance in which a parallel is pretended to be drawn, is with regard to miraculous cures, which alone considered are the most uncertain and equivocal of all miracles. Diseases have often been suprisingly cured without any thing that can be properly called miraculous in the case. Wonderful has been the effect of medicines administered in certain circumstances: and some maladies, after having long resisted all the art and power of remedies, have gone themselves by the force of nature, or by some surprising and unexpected turn, in a manner that cannot be distinctly explained; yet it may be observed, that there were several circumstances attending the miraculous cures wrought by our Saviour and his apostles, which plainly shewed them to be divine. The cures were wrought in an instant by a commanding word. The blind, the lame, those that laboured under the most obstinate and inveterate diseases found themselves immediately restored at once with an Almighty facility. If there had been only a few instances of this kind, it might possibly have been attributed to some odd accident, or hidden cause, which could not be accounted for. But the instances of such complete and instantaneous cures wrought by our Saviour were very numerous. They extended to all manner of diseases, and to all persons without exception who applied to him. Yea, he cured some that did not apply to him, who did not know him, or who were his enemies, and had no expectation of a cure, in which cases it could not be pretended that imagination had any share. In all these respects there was a remarkable difference between the miraculous cures wrought by our Saviour, and those pretended to have been wrought at the tomb of the Abbé *de Paris*. Several of the most boasted cures, and which were pretended to have been sudden and perfected at once, appear from their own accounts to have been carried on by slow degrees, and therefore might have been brought about in a natural way. Some of these cures were days, weeks, and even months before they were perfected. One nine days devotion followed another, and they were suffered to languish and continue praying and supplication for a considerable time together; and if the cure happened, and the distemper came to a crisis during the course of their long attendance, and whilst they were continuing their devotions, this passed for a miraculous cure, though it might well be done without any miracle at all. Especially as several of those persons continued to be taking remedies, even whilst they were attending at the tomb. It is manifest from the relations published by themselves, that with regard to several of those who were pretended to be miraculously cured, their maladies had already begun to abate, and they had found considerable ease and relief in a natural way before they came to the tomb at all. And some of them seem by the force of their imagination to have believed themselves cured, when they were not so, or to have taken a temporary relief for an absolute cure. Several of the cures, the accounts of which were published with great pomp, could not with any propriety be said to have been perfected at all; since the persons said to have been cured still continued infirm, and had returns of their former disorders. This can scarce be supposed, if the cures had been really miraculous, and owing to an extraordinary exertion of the power of God, who would not have left his own work imperfect. See all these things fully proved by many instances in M. *des Voeux's* letters *sur les Miracles*; particularly in the fifth of those letters.

To all which it may be added, that of the vast numbers who came to the tomb to be cured, and who had recourse to the Abbé's intercession, there were but few on whom the cures were wrought, in comparison of those who found no benefit at all, though they applied to him with the utmost devotion, and continued to do so for a long time together. And indeed considering how many there were that applied for help and cure, and how much they were prepossessed with the notions countenanced in the *Romish* church, of the power of departed Saints, of the prevalency of their intercession, and the efficacy of their relics, and to what a height their imagination was raised by their prejudices in favour of the appellants, by the high opinion they had of the Abbé's extraordinary sanctity, by the rumours of miracles daily spread and propagated, and by the vast crouds which attended at the tomb, it would have been really a wonder, if amongst the multitude that came for cure, there had not been several who found themselves greatly relieved. The advocates for the miracles mightily extol the extraordinary faith and confidence the sick persons had in the intercession of the blessed Deacon, as they call him. And the force of their imagination, when carried to so extraordinary a pitch, might in some particular cases produce great effects. Many wonderful instances to this purpose have been observed and recorded by the ablest physicians, by which it appears what a mighty influence imagination, accompanied with strong passions, hath often had upon human bodies, especially in the cure of diseases. It hath often done more in a short time this way, than a long course of medicines have been able to accomplish. It is not therefore to be much wondered at, that as the case was circumstanced, amidst such a multitude of persons some surprizing cures were wrought. But it could not be expected that the effect would be constant and uniform. If it answered in some instances, it would fail in many more. And accordingly so it was with regard to these pretended miraculous cures. And if this had been the case in the extraordinary cures wrought by our Saviour, there would have been ground of suspicion, that what some have alleged might possibly have been true, that his miracles owed their force, not to any supernatural energy, but to the power of imagination. But taking these miracles as they are recorded in the Gospels, it is manifest that there can be no just ground for such a pretence. They exhibit evident proofs of a divine interposition, which cannot be said of these reported to have been wrought at the Abbé's tomb. M. *de Montgeron*, in his book dedicated to the King, published an account of eight or nine cures. And it is to be supposed, that he fixed upon those which, he thought, had the appearance of being most signally miraculous. And yet the very first of these miracles; *viz.* that affirmed to have been wrought upon *Don Alphonso de Palacio,* appeareth plainly by taking the whole of the relation, as M. *Montgeron* himself hath given it, to have had nothing in it properly miraculous, as Mr.

Adams hath clearly shewn.[216] And with regard both to that and the other miracles so pompously displayed by M. *de Montgeron*, M. *Des Voeux* has very ingeniously and judiciously, after a distinct examination of each of them, made it appear that they might have been wrought without supposing any miraculous or supernatural interposition at all. See the last letter of his *Critique Generale*.

III. Another consideration, which shews the great difference there is between the miracles wrought at the first establishment of Christianity, and those said to have been wrought at the tomb of the Abbé *de Paris*, and that no argument can reasonably be brought from the latter to the prejudice of the former, is taken from the many suspicious circumstances attending the latter, from which the former were entirely free. Christ's miracles were wrought, in a grave and decent, in a great but simple manner, becoming one sent of God, without any absurd or ridiculous ceremonies, or superstitious observances. But the miracles of the Abbé *de Paris* were attended with circumstances that had all the marks of superstition, and which seemed designed and fitted to strike the imagination. The earth of his tomb was often made use of, or the waters of the well of his house. The nine days devotion was constantly used, and frequently repeated again and again by the same persons; a ceremony derived originally from the Pagans, and which hath been condemned as superstitious by some eminent divines of the *Romish* church.[217] Another circumstance to be observed with relation to Christ's miracles, is that, as hath been already hinted, they were not only perfected at once, but the persons found themselves healed and restored without trouble or difficulty. But in the case of the cures affirmed to have been wrought at the Abbé's tomb, it appeareth from their own accounts, not only that they were gradual and slow, but that the person on whom these cures were wrought, frequently suffered the most grievous and excessive pains and torments, and which they themselves represent to have been greater than ever they had felt before, or were able to express; and these pains often continued for several days together in the utmost extremity.[218] To which may be added the violent agitations and convulsions, which became so usual on these occasions, that they came at length to be regarded as symptoms of the miraculous cures; though they could not be properly regarded in this view, since many of those who had those convulsions found no relief in their maladies, and even grew worse than before. They were frequently attended with strange contortions, sometimes

---

[216] Adams's Essay, in answer to Hume, p. 75, 77.

[217] Lettres sur les Miracles, p. 258, 259, 336, 337.

[218] Ibid. p. 339. & *seq.*

frightful, sometimes ridiculous, and sometimes inconsistent with the rules of modesty and decency.[219] And accordingly they have been condemned by some of the most eminent *Jansenist* divines. In 1735 there was published at *Paris* a remarkable piece, intitled, *Consultation sur les Convulsions*, sign by thirty appellant doctors, men of great reputation among the *Jansenists* for learning, judgment, and probity; the greater part of whom had at first entertained favourable thoughts of those convulsions; and some of them had publickly declared them to be the work of God. But now they pronounced them to be unworthy of God, of his infinite majesty, wisdom, and goodness: They declared that it was folly, a fanaticism, a scandal, and in one word, a blasphemy against God, to attribute to him these operations; and did not scruple to intimate, that they rendered the miraculous cures, to which they were pretended to be annexed, suspected. These doctors, who were called the *Consultants*, condemned all the convulsions in general. Others of the *Jansenist* divines, whom M. *de Montgeron* has distinguished by the title of the *Antisecouristes*, and whom he acknowledges to be among the most zealous appellants, and to be persons of great merit and eminence, though they did not condemn all the convulsions, yet passed a very severe censure upon those of them which that gentleman looks upon to be the most extraordinary and miraculous of all. And with regard to these convulsions in general it may be observed, that, by the acknowledgement of the most skilful physicians, nervous affections have frequently produced strange symptoms; that they are often of a catching contagious nature, and easily communicated; and that they may be counterfeited by art. Many of those that were seized by Mr. *Heraut*, the Lieutenant de Police, acknowledged to him that they had counterfeited convulsions. In consequence of which there was an ordonnance published by the King, *January* 27, 1732, for searching out and apprehending those impostors. And yet Mr. *Hume* has thought proper to represent it, as if Monsieur *Heraut*, though he had full power to seize and examine the *witnesses* and *subjects* of these miracles, *could never reach any thing satisfactory against them.*

---

[219] Some of those that were seized with these convulsions, or pretended to be so, were guilty of the most extravagant follies. They pretended to prophecy, and uttered several predictions, which the event soon proved to be false. One of them went so far as to foretel that the church-yard of St. *Medard*, which had been shut up by the King's order, should be opened, and that M. *de Paris* should appear in the church in the presence of great numbers of people on the first of *May* following. See this and other remarkable things relating to these convulsions in M. *Vernet's* Traité del la Verité del la Religion Chretienne, Sect. 7. chap. 22, 23. And there cannot be a greater proof of the power of M. *de Montgeron's* prejudices, than that, in the last edition of his book in three volumes 4to, he has particularly applied himself to support and justify these convulsions.

There must be owned to be circumstances, which administer just grounds of suspicion, and which make a wide difference between the miracles pretended to have been wrought at the tomb of the Abbé *de Paris,* and those that were performed by our Saviour, and by the Apostles in his name.

IV. The next observation I shall make is this, that several of the miracles ascribed to the Abbé, and which were pretended to be proved by many witnesses, were afterwards clearly convicted of falshood and imposture; which bringeth a great discredit upon all the rest. Whereas nothing of this kind can be alleged against the miracles by which Christianity was attested. The affair of *Anne le Franc,* of which some account was given above, shews, as M. *Des Voeux* justly observes, how little dependence is to be had upon informations in this cause directed by *Jansenists.* But this is not the only instance of this kind. They had published, that *La Dalmaix* had been miraculously cured by the Abbé's intercession; and this was proved by a letter pretended to have been written by herself. And yet this pretended miraculous cure was afterwards denied by the person herself, by her mother, and all her sisters: And by a sentence of court of judicature of *May* 17, 1737, a person was declared to be convicted of having forged that, and some other letters under the name of *Dalmaix.*[220] The Sieur *le Doux* openly retracted the relation of miracle said to have been wrought upon himself. M. *Des Voeux* gives several other instances of false miracles, published by the *Jansenists,* and afterwards acknowledged to be so.[221] *Jean Nivet* was represented, by decisive informations, as cured of his deafness, and yet it is certain that he was deaf after, as well as before. The record of the informations made by Mr. *Thomassin* is full of contradictions, which discover the falshood and perjury of the principal actress, and of the only witness of the miracle, as the archbishop of *Sens* has well proved. Many of which proofs are passed over in silence by M. *le Gros,* who undertook to answer him.[222] Some of the witnesses and persons concerned withdrew, to escape the search that was made for them, and to shun the examination and inquiry which the king had ordered; and others, who had attested that they were cured by the intercession of the Abbé *de Paris*, afterwards retracted it. The certificates themselves, on which so great a stress is laid, tend in many instances to increase the suspicion against those facts, which they were designed to confirm. The very number of those certificates, many of which are nothing at all to the purpose, and serve only for shew, are plain proofs of art and design. The manner of

---

[220] Vernet ubi supra, Chap. XXI.

[221] Lettres sur les Miracles, p. 171, *et seq.* Critique Generale, p. 204, &c. 233, 234.

[222] Lettres sur les Miracles, p. 242, 243.

drawing up those certificates, and the relations of the miracles, and the style and form of expression, shew that the persons in whose names they are drawn, had the assistance of persons of a capacity much superior to their own. Long pieces in a correct style, and in perfect good order, were published under the name of mean and illiterate persons. M. *le Gros* owns, that the relation of *Genevieve Colin* was reformed as to the style by a person whom she desired to do it. Thus they had it in their power, under pretence of reforming, to alter it, and got the simple person to sign the whole. Five witnesses in the case of *Anne le Franc* depose, that their certificates left with the notary were altered, falsified, and embellished with divers circumstances. Many of the relations which were at first published, and were not thought full enough, were afterwards suppressed, and do not appear in M. *de Montgeron's* collection, and others more ample were substituted in their stead, and embellished with many striking circumstances, which were omitted in the first relation. Many of the witnesses in their depositions carry it farther, than according to their own account they could have any certain knowledge. Some of them appear to have been surprized into their testimonies by false or imperfect representations; and artifices were employed to procure certificates from physicians, without bringing the case fully before them, or suffering them fairly to examine it.

To all which it may be added, that there is great reason to suspect, that many poor people feigned maladies, and pretended to be cured, on purpose to procure the gifts, and benefactions of others; which many of them did to good advantage. It is well known, and has been often proved, that in the *Romish* church there have been instances of persons, who made a trade of feigning maladies, and pretending to be miraculously cured. Such a one was *Catharine des Pres*, who was afterwards convicted by her own confession; of which Father *Le Brun* hath given a particular account, *Hist. Crit. des Prat. Superstit.* liv. ii. cap. 4. who hath also detected several other false miracles which had been believed by numbers of that church. And may we not reasonably suspect the same of many poor people, who came to the tomb of the Abbé *de Paris*? See all these things shewn in M. *Des Voeux's Lettres sur les Miracles, Lettre* V. VI. and especially in the VIIth and VIIIth Letters of his *Critique Generale*; where he particularly examineth every one of the miracles produced by M. *de Montgeron.* It is his observation, that the more carefully we consider those relations, and compare them with the pieces that are designed to justify them, the more plainly the falshood of them appeareth. And accordingly he hath found out not merely a single contradiction, but numerous contradictions in the relations of the several miracles, compared with the certificates, and the pieces produced in justification of them. And therefore he asketh with good reason, what becomes of demonstrations, built on such relations, and such certificates? He very properly observes, that the falsity even of a small number of facts, which are pretended to be proved by certificates, that were collected by those who took pains to verify the miracles, are sufficient to discredit all others founded on such certificates.

If the same things could have been justly objected against the miracles recorded in the New Testament, Christianity, considering the other disadvantages it laboured under, could never have been established. But the case with regard to these miracles was very different. They were not indeed proved by certificates, which may be procured by art and management. The first publishers of the Christian religion did not go about to collect evidences and testimonies. Nor was there any need of their doing so in facts that were publicly known, and the reality of which their enemies themselves were not able to deny. They acted with greater simplicity, and with an open confidence of truth. Their narrations are plain and artless; nor do they take pains to prepossess or influence the reader, either by artful insinuations, or too *violent assertions*; which our author mentions as a suspicious circumstance. Never were any of their enemies able to convict them of falshood. Far from ever denying the facts they had witnessed, or withdrawing for fear of having those facts inquired into, as several did in the other case, they openly avowed those facts before the public tribunals, and before persons of the highest authority; they never varied in their testimony, but persisted in it with an unfainting constancy, and sealed it with their blood. And it gives no small weight to their testimony, that they witnessed for facts which were designed to confirm a scheme of religion contrary to their own most rooted prejudices. Nor can it be alleged, that they were themselves divided about the reality and divinity of the miracles wrought by Christ and his apostles, much less that they rejected and condemned many of them as foolish, scandalous, and injurious to the Divine Majesty; which was the censure passed upon some of the extraordinary facts relating to the Abbé *de Paris*, by the most eminent *Jansenist* divines.

Finally, the last observation I shall make is this: That the miracles of our Saviour and his apostles appear to have been wrought for an end worthy of the divine wisdom and goodness. The declared design of them was to give an attestation to the divine mission of the most excellent person that ever appeared in the world, and to confirm the best scheme of religion that was ever published, the most manifestly conducive to the glory of God, and to the salvation of mankind. Here was an end worthy of God, and for which it was fit for him to interpose in the most extraordinary manner. And accordingly this religion thus attested and confirmed was established in the world, and soon triumphed over all opposition. All the power of the adversary, civil or sacerdotal, could not put a stop to its progress, or to the wonderful works done in confirmation of it. The effects which followed, considering the amazing difficulties it had to struggle with, and the seeming weakness and meanness of the instruments made use of to propagate it, proved the reality of those miracles, and that the whole was carried on by a divine power. But if we turn our views on the other hand to the miracles pretended to have been wrought at the tomb of the Abbé *de Paris*, it doth not appear that they answered any valuable end. There has indeed been an end found out for them; *viz.* to give a testimony from heaven to the cause of the appellants. But we may justly conclude from the wisdom of God, that in that case it would have been so ordered as to make it evident that this was the intention of them, and that he would have taken care that no opposition from men should prevail to defeat the design for which he interposed in so extraordinary a manner. But this was far from being the case. Mr. *Hume* indeed tells us, that

"no *Jansenist* was ever at a loss to account for the cessation of the miracles, when the churchyard was shut up by the king's edict. 'Twas the touch of the tomb which operated those extraordinary effects, and when no one could approach the tomb, no effect could be expected."[223]

But supposing that the design of those extraordinary divine interpositions was to give a testimony from heaven to the cause of the appellants, it is absurd to imagine that it would have been in the power of an earthly prince, by shutting up the tomb to put a stop to the course of the miraculous operations, and to render the design of God of none effect.[224] It strengthens this, when it is farther considered, that the whole affair of these pretended miracles turned in the issue rather to the disadvantage of the cause it was designed to confirm. It hath been already observed, that some of the most eminent among the appellant doctors, and who were most zealously attached to that cause, were greatly scandalised at several of those miracles, and especially at the extraordinary convulsions which generally attended them. The censures they passed upon them gave occasion to bitter contentions, and mutual severe reproaches and accusations. Some of the *Jansenist* writers themselves complain, that whereas before there was an entire and perfect union and harmony among them, as if they had been all of one heart and soul, there have been since that time cruel divisions and animosities, so that those who were friends before became irreconcilable enemies.[225] And can it be imagined, that God would execute his designs in so imperfect a manner? That he would exert his own divine power to give

---

[223] Hume's Philosophical Essays p. 208.

[224] M. de Montgeron indeed will not allow that the miraculous operations ceased at the shutting up of the tomb; but by the miraculous operations, he principally understands the convulsions, which continued still to be carried on; but which many of the principal Jansenists were far from looking upon as tokens of a divine interposition.

[225] Crit. Gener. lettre v. p. 159, & seq.

testimony to that cause, and yet do it in such away as to weaken that cause instead of supporting it, to raise prejudices against it in the minds of enemies instead of gaining them, and to divide and offend the friends of it instead of confirming and uniting them? Upon the whole, with regard to the attestations given to Christianity, all was wise, consistent, worthy of God, and suited to the end for which it was designed. But the other is a broken, incoherent scheme, which cannot be reconciled to itself, nor made to consist with the wisdom and harmony of the divine proceedings. The former therefore is highly credible, though the latter is not so.

The several considerations which have been mentioned do each of them singly, much more all of them together, shew such signal differences between the miracles recorded in the Gospels, and those ascribed to the Abbé *de Paris*, that it must argue a peculiar degree of confidence to pretend to run a parallel between the one and the other, much more to affirm, as Mr. *Hume* has done, that the latter *much surpass* the former in *credit and authority*. This only shews how gladly these gentlemen would lay hold on any pretence to invalidate the evidences of Christianity. Thus Mr. *Chubb*, in a discourse he published on miracles, in which he pretends impartially to represent the reasonings on both sides, produced with great pomp, a pretended miracle wrought in the *Cevennes* in 1703, and represented it as of equal credit with those of the Gospel. M. *le Moyne*, in his answer to him, hath evinced the falshood of that story in a manner that admits of no reply.[226] And yet it is not improbable, that some future Deist may see fit some time or other to revive that story, and oppose it to the miracles recorded in the New Testament.

Mr. *Hume* concludes his Essay with applauding his own performance, and is the better pleased with the *way of reasoning* he has made of, as he thinks, "it may serve to confound those dangerous friends, or disguised enemies to the Christian religion, who have undertaken to defend it by the principles of human reason. Our most holy religion (saith he) is founded on faith, not on reason:[227]And 'tis a sure method of exposing it to put such

---

[226] Le Moyne on Miracles, p. 422, &c.

[227] This author who takes care to make the principles of his philosophy subservient to his designs against religion, in the fifth of his *Philosophical Essays*, where he undertakes to treat of the nature of belief, gives such an account of it as seems to exclude reason from any share in it at all. He makes the difference between *faith* and *fiction* to consist wholly in some sentiment of feeling, which is annexed to the former, not to the latter: That the sentiment of belief is nothing but the conception of an object more lively and forcible, more intense and steady than what attends the mere fiction of the imagination: And that this manner of conception arises from the customary conjunction of the object with something present to the memory or senses. See his *Philosophical Essays*, p. 80–84. This gentleman is here, as in many other places, sufficiently obscure, nor is it easy to form a distinct notion of what he intends. But his design seems to be to exclude reason or the understanding from having any thing to

a trial, as it is by no means fitted to endure." And he calls those, who undertake to defend religion by reason, *pretended Christians.*[228] Such a mean and ungenerous sneer is below animadversion. All that can be gathered from it is, that these gentlemen are very uneasy at the attempts which have been made to defend Christianity in a way of reason and argument. They it seems are mightily concerned for *the preservation* of our holy faith, and in their great friendship for that cause would give it up as indefensible. And if the best way of befriending the Christian religion be to endeavour to subvert the evidences by which it is established, our author hath taken effectual care to convince the world of his friendly intentions towards it. As to the brief hints he hath given towards the end of his Essay against the *Mosaic* history, and the miracles recorded there, I shall not here take any notice of them, both because Mr. *Adams* hath clearly and succinctly obviated them in his answer to the Essay, p. 88–94, and because I shall have occasion to resume this subject, when I come to make observations on Lord *Bolingbroke's* Posthumous Works, who hath with great virulence and bitterness, used his utmost efforts to expose the *Mosaic* writings.

LETTER XX.

Additional observations relating to Mr. Hume. *A transcript of an ingenious paper containing an examination of Mr.* Hume's *arguments in his* Essay *on Miracles.* Observations upon it. *The evidence of matters of fact may be so circumstanced as to produce a full assurance. Mr.* Hume *artfully confounds the evidence of past facts with the probability of the future. We may be certain of a matter of fact after it hath happened, though it might beforehand seem very improbable that it would happen. Where full evidence is given of a fact, there must not always be a deduction made on the account of its being unusual and extraordinary. There is strong and positive evidence of the miracles wrought in attestation to Christianity, and no evidence against them. The miraculous nature of the facts no proof that the facts were not done. A summary of Mr.* Hume's

do with belief, as if reason never had any influence in producing, directing, or regulating it; which is to open a wide door to enthusiasm. But this is contrary to what we may all observe, and frequently experience. We in several cases clearly perceive, that we have reason to regard some things as fictitious, and others as true and real. And the reasons which shew the difference between a fiction and a reality shew that we ought in reason to believe the one and not the other: And so reason may go before the sentiment of belief, and lay a just foundation for it, and be instrumental to produce it. And in this case the belief may be said to be strictly rational.

[228] Hume's Philosophical Essays. p. 204, 205.

argument against the evidence of miracles. The weakness of it shewn. Considering the vast importance of religion to our happiness, the bare possibility of its being true should be sufficient to engage our compliance.

SIR,

The four preceding letters comprehend all the observations that were made upon Mr. *Hume* in the second volume of the *View of the Deistical writers*, 8*vo* edit. But soon after that volume was published I received a letter from a gentleman of sense and learning, which particularly relates to that part of it which was designed in answer to Mr. *Hume*. He was pleased to say it gave him *uncommon satisfaction*, and at the same time sent me a paper which he seemed to be very well pleased with, that had been drawn up by a young gentleman then lately dead. It was designed as a confutation of Mr. *Hume* upon his own principles, which he thought had not been sufficiently attended to in the answers that had been made to that writer; and he allowed me, if I should be of opinion that any thing in it might be serviceable to a farther confutation of Mr. *Hume*, to make use of his sentiments either by way of note or appendix, as I should judge most convenient. I returned an answer in a letter which I shall here insert, as it containeth some reflections that may be of advantage in relation to the controversy with Mr. *Hume*. But first it will be proper to lay before the reader the paper itself here referred to, which is concisely drawn, and runs thus:

An EXAMINATION *of Mr.* HUME's *Arguments in his* ESSAY ON MIRACLES.

The objects of human understanding may be distinguished either into propositions asserting the relation between general ideas, or matters of fact.

In the former kind, we can arrive at certainty by means of a faculty in our souls, which perceives this relation either instantly or intimately, which is called Intuition, or else by intermediate ideas, which is called Demonstration.

But we can only form a judgement of the latter by experience. No reasoning *a priori* will discover to us, that water will suffocate, or the fire consume us, or that the loadstone will attract steel: and therefore no judgement can be made concerning the truth or falshood of matters of fact, but what is constantly regulated by custom and experience; and can therefore never go higher than probability.

When we have frequently observed a particular event to happen in certain circumstances, the mind naturally makes an induction, that it will happen again in the same circumstances. When this observation has been long, constant, and uninterrupted, there our belief that it will happen again approaches infinitely near to certainty. Thus no man has the least doubt of the sun's rising to-morrow, or that the tide will ebb and flow at its accustomed periods. But where our observations are broke in upon by frequent interruptions and exceptions to the contrary; then we expect such an event with the least degree of assurance: and in all intermediate cases, our expectations are always in proportion to the constancy and regularity of the experience.

This method of reasoning is not connected by any medium or chain of steps; but is plainly to be observed in all animate beings; brutes as well as men.[229] And it would be as absurd to ask a reason, why we expect to happen again, that which is regularly come to pass a great many times before, as it is to enquire, why the mind perceives a relation between certain ideas?

They are both distinct faculties of the soul. And as it has been authorised by some writers of distinction, to give the denomination of sense to the internal as well as external perceptions; the one may be called the *speculative*, and the other the *probable sense*.

From this last-mentioned principle Mr. *Hume* has deduced an argument to shew, that there is great improbability against the belief of any miraculous fact, how well soever attested: and as religion may seem to be greatly affected by this conclusion (supposing it to be true), before we come directly to consider the argument, it may not be amiss to enquire how far religion, as a practical institution, may be concerned therein?

And for this purpose it is to be observed, that probable evidence for the truth or falshood of any matter of fact differs essentially from demonstration, in that the former admits of degrees, in the greatest variety, from the highest moral certainty, down to the lowest presumptions; which the latter does not.

Let it also be further observed, that probable evidence is in its nature but an imperfect kind of information, the highest degree of which can never reach absolute certainty, or full proof: and yet to mankind with regard to their practice, it is in many cases the very guide of their lives.

Most of our actions are determined by the highest degrees of probability. As for instance, what we do in consequence of the sun's rising to-morrow: of the seasons regularly succeeding one another: and that certain kinds of meat and drink will nourish. Others are determined by lesser degrees. Thus Rhubarb does not always purge, nor is Opium a soporific to every person that takes it: and yet for all that they are of constant use for these purposes in medicine. In all cases of moment, when to act or forbear may

---

[229] May not the so long sought after distinction between brutes and men consist in this? That whereas the human understanding comprehends both classes; the brutal sagacity is confined only to matters of fact.

be attended with considerable damage, no wise man makes the least scruple of doing what he apprehends may be of advantage to him, even though the thing was doubtful, and one side of the question as supportable as the other. But in matters of the utmost consequence, a prudent man will think himself obliged to take notice even of the lowest probability; and will act accordingly. A great many instances might be given in the common pursuits of life, where a man would be considered as out of his senses, who would not act, and with great diligence and application too, not only upon an over-chance, but even where the probability might be greatly against his success.

Suppose a criminal under sentence of death was promised a pardon, if he threw twelve with a pair of dice at one throw: here the probability is thirty-six to one against him; and yet he would be looked upon as mad, if he did not try. Nothing in such a case would hinder a man from trying, but the absolute impossibility of the event.

Let us now apply this method of reasoning to the practice of religion. And supposing the arguments against miracles were far more probable than the evidence for them, yet the vast importance of religion to our happiness in every respect would still be very sufficient to recommend it to the practice of every prudent man; and the bare possibility that it might prove true, were there nothing else to support it, would engage his assent and compliance: or else he must be supposed to act differently in this respect to what he generally does in all the other concerns of his life. So that whether Mr. *Hume's* reasonings be true or false, religion has still sufficient evidence to influence the practice of every wise and considerate man.

This being premised; let us now proceed to consider Mr. *Hume's* arguments.

His reasoning may be briefly expressed in this manner:

We have had a long universal and uninterrupted experience, that no events have happened contrary to the course of nature, from constant and unvaried observations. We have therefore a full proof, that the uniform course has not been broke in upon, nor will be, by any particular exceptions.

But the observation of truth depending upon, and constantly following human testimony, is by no means universal and uninterrupted, and therefore it does not amount to a full proof that it either has, or will follow it in any particular instance.

And therefore the proof arising from any human testimony, can never equal the proof that is deduced against a miracle from the very nature of the fact.

This I take to be a full and fair state of this gentleman's reasoning.

But the answer is very plain. If by human testimony, he would mean the evidence of any one single man indifferently taken, then indeed his second proposition would be true. But then the conclusion will by no means follow from it. But if by human testimony he would understand the evidence of any collection of men, then the second proposition is false; and consequently the conclusion must be so too.

That twelve honest persons should combine to assert a falshood, at the hazard of their lives, without any view to private interest, and with the certain prospect of losing every thing that is and ought to be dear to mankind in this world, is according to his own way of reasoning, as great a miracle to all intents and purposes, as any interruption in the common course of nature: because no history has ever mentioned any such thing; nor has any man in any age ever had experience of such a fact.

But here it may be objected, that though it be allowed to be as great a miracle for twelve honest men to attest a falshood contrary to their plain interest in every respect, as that any alteration should happen in the common course of nature, yet these evidences being equal, they only destroy one another, and still leave the mind in suspence.

This objection draws all its force from Mr. *Hume*'s assertion, that an uniform and uninterrupted experience amounts to a full proof, which when examined will not be found true; and indeed I wonder that a writer of his accuracy should venture on such an expression, since it is confessed on all hands, that all our reasonings concerning matters of fact, ever fall short of certainty, or full proof.

And besides, the very same objection which he makes against the veracity of human testimony, to weaken its authenticity, may be retorted with equal force against his unvaried certainty of the course of nature: for doubtless the number of approved histories we have relating to miracles, will as much lessen the probability of what he calls a full proof on his side of the question, as all the forgeries and falshoods that are brought to discredit human testimony, will weaken it on the other.

But the best way to be assured of the falshood of this objection is to examine it by what we find in our own minds; for that must not be admitted as an universal principle, which is not true in every particular instance.

According to Mr. *Hume*, we have a full proof of any fact attested by twelve honest disinterested persons. But would not the probability be increased, and our belief of such a fact be the stronger, if the number of witnesses was doubled? I own my mind immediately assents to it. But if this be true, it will then evidently follow, that the proof against a miracle, arising from the nature of the fact, may, and has been exceeded by contrary human testimony.

Suppose, as before, that the testimony of twelve persons is just equal to it, and we have the evidence of twenty, for any particular miracle recorded in the Gospel; then subtracting the weaker evidence from the stronger, we

shall have the positive evidence of eight persons, for the truth of a common matter of fact.
Q.E.D.

The answer I returned to the letter in which this paper was inclosed was in substance as follows:

SIR,
I am very much obliged to you for the kind manner in which you have expressed yourself with regard to me. And it is a pleasure to me to find that my reply to Mr. *Hume* is approved by a gentleman of so much good sense, and of such eminency in his profession, as I am well informed you are accounted to be.

I agree with you that Mr. *Hume* is an elegant and subtle writer, and one of the most dangerous enemies to Christianity that have appeared among us. He has a very specious way of managing an argument. But his subtlety seems to have qualified him not so much for clearing an obscure cause, as for puzzling a clear one. Many things in his *Philosophical Essays* have a very plausible appearance, as well as an uncommon turn, which he visibly affects; but upon a close examination of them I think one may venture to pronounce, that few authors can be mentioned who have fallen into greater absurdities and inconsistencies. And it were to be wished there was not a sufficient ground for the severe censure you pass upon him, when you say, that

"with all his art he has plainly discovered a bad heart, by throwing out some bitter sneers against the Christian revelation, which are absolutely inconsistent with a serious belief, or indeed with any regard for it, though in some parts of his writings he affects a different way of speaking."

You observe, that "we seem to be greatly deficient in the logick of probability, a point which Mr. *Hume* had studied with great accuracy." And I readily own, that there is a great appearance of accuracy in what Mr. *Hume* hath advanced concerning the grounds and degrees of probability, and the different degrees of assent due to it. But though what he hath offered this way seems plausible in general, he hath been far from being fair or exact in his application of it.

The paper you have sent inclosed to me, and which you tell me was drawn up by the young gentleman you mention, contains a sketch of an attempt to shew how Mr. *Hume* might be confuted on his own principles, and is executed in such a manner, that one cannot but regret that a gentleman of so promising a genius, and who might have proved signally useful, was snatched away by a fever about the twentieth year of is age. You allow me to make what use of it I judge proper, and seem to expect that I should tell you my sentiments of it with the utmost frankness and candour. And this obligeth me to acquaint you, that though I look upon the confutation of Mr. *Hume* in the way this gentleman hath managed it to be subtil and ingenious, yet in some things it doth not seem to me to be quite so clear and satisfactory, as were to be wished in a matter of so great consequence. He has, I think, from a desire of confuting Mr. *Hume* upon his own principles, been led to make too large concessions to that gentleman, and hath proceeded upon some of his principles as true and valid, which I think may be justly contested.

Mr. *Hume* frequently intimates, that there neither is nor can be any certainty in the evidence given concerning matters of fact, or in human testimony, which can be securely depended on; and that at best, it can be only probable. And the ingenious author of the paper having observed after Mr. *Hume*, that we can form no judgment concerning the truth or falshood of matter of fact, but what is constantly regulated by custom or experience, adds, that "it can never go higher than probability." And again he saith, that "probable evidence is in its nature but an imperfect kind of information; the highest degree of which cannot reach absolute certainty or full proof." Where he seems not to allow that the evidence concerning matters of fact can ever arrive at such a certainty as to make up a *full proof.* And he repeats it again, that "it is confessed on all hands, that all our reasonings concerning matters of fact ever fall short of certainty or full proof." And yet if we allow Mr. *Hume*'s definition of a full proof, that it is *such arguments from experience as leave no room for doubt or opposition*, the evidence for a matter of fact may be so circumstanced as to amount to a full proof, and even to a certainty. For I can see no reason for confining certainty to the evidence we have by intuition or by demonstration. In treating of certainty as distinguished from probability, a two fold certainty may very properly be allowed. The one is the certainty by intuition or by demonstration. The other is a certainty relating to matter of fact. This is indeed of a different kind from the former: But I think it may no less justly be called certainty, when it so fully satisfieth the mind as to leave not the least room for doubt concerning it, and produceth a full assurance. And that this is often the case with relation to matters of fact cannot reasonably be denied. The words *sure* and *certain* are frequently applied in common language to things of this kind, and for aught I see very properly. And in the best and exactest writers it is often described under the term of *moral certainty*, an expression which this gentleman himself makes use of.[230] And

---

[230] The ingenious gentleman seems to grant what may be sufficient, when he saith, that probability *in some cases approaches infinitely near to certainty*. If it be allowed, that

it is a great mistake to imagine, that the word *moral* in that case is always used as a term of diminution, as if it were not to be intirely depended on. It is only designed to shew that this certainty is of a different kind, and proceedeth upon different grounds from that which ariseth from demonstration; but yet it may produce as strong an assurance in the mind, and which may undoubtedly be depended upon. That there was a war carried on in *England* in the last century between King and Parliament, I only know by human testimony. But will any man say, that for that reason I cannot be sure of it? Many cases might be mentioned with regard to matters of fact which we know by human testimony, the evidence of which is so strong and convincing, that we can no more reasonably doubt of it, than of the truth of any proposition which comes to us demonstrated by the strictest reasoning. Mr. *Hume* himself seems sensible, that it would be wrong to say that every thing which is not matter of demonstration comes only under the notion of probability. And therefore though he frequently seems to class all matters of fact under the head of probabilities, yet in the beginning of his Essay on Probability, he seems to find fault with Mr. *Locke* for dividing all arguments into *demonstrative* and *probable*, and observes, that to conform our language more to common use, we should divide arguments into *demonstrations, proofs*, and *probabilities*: where he seems to place what he calls *proofs*, which he explains to be such arguments from experience as leave no room for doubt or opposition, in a higher class than probabilities. And Mr. *Locke* himself, though he seems to confine certainty to demonstration, yet allows concerning some probabilities arising from human testimony, that

> "they rise to certainty, that they govern our thoughts as absolutely, and influence our actions as fully as the most evident demonstration; and in what concerns us we make little or no difference between them and certain knowledge. Our belief thus grounded rises to assurance."[231]

And in that case I think probability is too low a word, and not sufficiently expressive, or properly applicable to things of this kind. For according to Mr. *Locke*'s account of it, and the common usage of the word, that is said

matter of fact may be so certain, that the mind may be fully assured of it, and so as to leave no room for a reasonable doubt, this is all that is really necessary in the present controversy, And this is what Mr. *Hume* himself seems sometimes to allow. But at other times he gives such an account of human testimony as tends to render it in all cases uncertain. And the design of his representing it as never rising higher than probability, seems to be to convey an idea of uncertainty and doubt as inseparably attending all human testimony. And to guard against the wrong use that may be made of this is the design of what I have here observed.

[231] Essay on Human Understanding, book iv. chap. xv. sect. 6.

to be probable which is *likely to be true*, and of which we have *no certainty*, but only *some inducements*, as Mr. *Locke* speaks, to believe and receive them as true.

Another thing observable in Mr. *Hume*'s reasoning on this subject is, that in treating of probability or the evidence of facts, which he foundeth wholly upon experience, he confoundeth the evidence of past facts with that of the future. And the young gentleman himself seems not sufficiently to distinguish them. The instances he produceth to shew, that the judgments which the mind forms concerning the probability of events *will always be in proportion to the constancy and regularity of the experience*, all relate to the probability of future events from the experience of the past. But the question about the probability of any future fact hath properly nothing to do in the present controversy between Mr. *Hume* and his adversaries, which relateth wholly to the evidence of past facts. And it is only an instance of this writer's art, that by confounding these different questions he may perplex the debate, and throw dust in the eyes of his readers. It will be granted that with relation to future facts or events, the utmost evidence we can attain to from past observation or experience is a high degree of probability; but with relation to past matters of fact, we may in many cases arrive at a certainty, or what Mr. *Hume* calls full proof, yea, it often happens, that the evidence of past facts may be so circumstanced, that we may be certain that such an event really came to pass, though if the question had been put before the event, the probability from past experience would have been greatly against it. Nothing therefore can be more weak and fallacious than Mr. *Hume*'s reasoning, when from this principle of forming conclusions concerning future events from past experience, he endeavoureth to deduce an argument against the belief of any miraculous fact, how well soever attested. For though, if the question were concerning a future miracle in any particular instance, if we should judge merely from past experience, the probability might seem to lie against it; yet if the question be concerning a past miraculous fact, there may be such proof of it, as may not leave room for a reasonable doubt that the miracle was really done, though before it was done it might seem highly improbable that it would be done.

Another fallacy Mr. *Hume* is guilty of, is his supposing that in all cases where the fact in itself considered is unusual, and out of the way of common experience, whatever be the evidence given for it, there must still be a deduction made, and the assent given to it is always weakened in proportion to the usualness of the fact. Now this doth not always hold. A fact of an extraordinary nature may come to us confirmed by an evidence so strong, as to produce a full and undoubted assurance of its having been done: And in such a case there is no deduction to be made; nor is the assent we give to the truth of the fact at all weakened on the account of its being unusual and extraordinary. Thus, *e.g.* that a great king should be openly put to death by his own subjects upon a pretended formal trial before a court of judicature, is very unusual, and before it came to pass would have appeared highly improbable; but after it happened, there is such evidence of the fact as to produce a full assurance that it was really done, and the man who should go about seriously to make a doubt of it, and make a formal deduction from the credit of the evidence, on the account of the strangeness of the fact, and should pretend that we must believe it with an assent only proportioned to the evidence which remaineth after that deduction, would under pretence of extraordinary accuracy only render himself ridiculous. It will indeed be readily owned, that more and greater evidence may be justly required with regard to a thing that is unusual and out of the common course, than is required for a common fact; but when there is evidence given sufficient to satisfy the mind, its being unusual and extraordinary ought not to be urged as a reason for not giving a full credit to it, or for pretending that the testimony concerning it is not to be depended upon. For the evidence for a fact out of the course of common observation and experience, may be so circumstanced as to leave no room for the least reasonable doubt. And the assent to it may be as strong and firm as to any the most common and ordinary event. Nor is any thing in the case to be deducted from the credit of the evidence, under pretence of the fact's being unusual or even miraculous.

You will allow me on this occasion to take notice of a passage in your letter, in which, after having observed that Mr. *Hume* had studied the point about probability, and treated upon it with great accuracy, you give it as your opinion, that "the best way of answering him would be in the way himself has chalked out by comparing the degrees of probability in the evidence on both sides, and deducting the inferior." Here you seem to suppose that there is evidence on both sides in the case of miracles, and that upon balancing the evidence, that which hath the higher degrees of probability ought to be preferred, at the same time making a deduction from it in proportion to the weight of the contrary evidence. But the supposition you here proceed upon appears to me to be a wrong one; *viz.* That in the case in question there is evidence on both sides, and consequently an opposition of evidence; *i.e.* evidence against the miracles wrought in proof of Christianity, as well as evidence for them. There is indeed positive strong evidence on one side, to shew that those facts were really done, an evidence drawn from testimony so circumstantiated, that it hath all the qualifications which could be reasonably desired to render it full and satisfactory.[232] But what evidence is there on the other side? No counter-evidence or testimony to shew the falshood of this is pretended by Mr.

---

[232] See this fully shewn in answer to Mr. *Hume*, p. 254, & seq.

Hume to be produced. Nor are there any circumstances mentioned attending the evidence itself, which may justly tend to render it suspicious. Nothing is opposed to it but the miraculous nature of the facts, or their being contrary to the usual course of nature. And this cannot properly be said to be any evidence to prove that the facts were not done, or that the testimony given to them was false. Nor needs there any deduction to be made in the assent we give to such a full and sufficient testimony as is here supposed, on that account: because as the case was circumstanced, it was proper that those facts should be beyond and out of the common course of nature and experience: and it was agreeable to the wisdom of God, and to the excellent ends for which those facts were designed, that they should be so: since otherwise they would not have answered the intention, which was to give a divine attestation to an important revelation of the highest use and benefit to mankind.

It is an observation of the ingenious author of the paper you sent me,

"That twelve honest persons should combine to assert a falshood at the hazard of their lives without any view to private interest, and with the certain prospects of losing every thing that is and ought to be dear to mankind in this world, is, according to Mr. *Hume's* own way of reasoning, as great a miracle to all intents and purposes, as any interruption in the common course of nature."

But then he observes, that the thing these witnesses are supposed to attest being also a miracle, contrary to the usual course of nature, it may be objected, that these evidences being equal, they only destroy one another, and still leave the mind in suspense. The answer he gives to this does not seem to me to be sufficiently clear. He first observes, That

"this objection draws all its force from Mr. *Hume's* assertion, that an uniform and uninterrupted experience is a full proof, which when examined will not be found true, because it is confessed on all hands, that all our reasonings concerning matters of fact ever fall short of certainty, or full proof."

But besides that this doth not always hold, since it hath been shewn, that our reasonings concerning matters of fact may in some cases amount to such a certainty as may be justly called a full proof: it may still be urged, that an uniform uninterrupted experience, though not strictly a full proof, yet is such a proof against a miracle as is able to counter-balance the evidence for it: in which case the objection still holds, and the mind is kept in suspense. And the gentleman himself seems afterwards to grant, that a fact's being contrary to the usual course of nature affordeth such a proof against it from the nature of the thing, as is sufficient to counterpoise the evidence of twelve such witnesses as are supposed, though he thinks it would not do so, if the number of witnesses were doubled; and that this shews that the proof against a miracle arising from the nature of the fact may be exceeded by contrary human testimony, which is what Mr. *Hume* denies. And he argues, that if we suppose the testimony of twelve persons for a miracle to be just equal to the evidence arising from the nature of the thing against it, and that we have the evidence of twenty for any particular miracle recorded in the Gospel, then subtracting the weaker evidence from the stronger, we shall have a surplus of the positive testimony of eight persons, without any thing to oppose to it.

I am persuaded, that the design of the ingenious gentleman inputting the case after this manner, was not to signify it as his real opinion, that the testimony of twelve such witnesses as are here supposed in proof of a miracle's having been really wrought, did not more than countervail the argument against it arising from the strangeness of the fact: But he had a mind to put the case as strongly as he could in favour of Mr. *Hume,* and yet to shew that there might still be and excess of proof, according to his own principles, on the side of miracles: which destroys his main hypothesis, that the evidence for a miracle can never exceed the evidence against it. It appears to me however, that this is making too large a concession, and that it is not the properest way of putting the case. It proceedeth upon the supposition which hath been already shewn to be a wrong one, that a thing's being miraculous, or contrary to the usual course of nature, is alone in all circumstance a proper *proof* or *evidence* against the truth of the fact; whereas the case may be so circumstanced, that the miraculousness of the fact is in reality no *proof* or *evidence* against it at all. It will indeed be acknowledged, as was before hinted, that greater evidence is required with regard to a fact which is miraculous, than for any fact in the common and ordinary course. But when such evidence is given to prove that a miraculous fact was really done, as is suitable to the importance of the fact, and which cannot be rejected without admitting suppositions which are manifestly absurd; in such a case, a thing's being miraculous is no just reason for not giving a full assent to the testimony concerning it. For its being miraculous, in the case that hath been put, hath nothing in it absurd or incredible; whereas that twelve men of sound minds, and honest characters should combine to attest a falshood in opposition to all their worldly interests and prejudices, and to every principle that can be supposed to influence human nature, without any assignable cause for such a conduct (which has been shewn to be the case with regard to the witnesses for Christianity) is absolutely absurd, nor can in any way be accounted for. As to the pretence, that in this case there is a miracle on both sides, and that the one is to be opposed to the other, and destroys its evidence; this sophism which has imposed upon many, and in which the chief strength of Mr. *Hume's Essay* lies, deriveth its whole force from an abuse of the word miracle, and a confounding, as this writer hath artfully done, a miracle and an absurdity, as if it were the same thing. That twelve men should in the circumstances supposed combine to attest a falshood, at the hazard of their lives and of every thing dear to men, cannot properly be called a miracle according to any definition that can be reasonably given of a miracle, or even according to Mr. *Hume's* own definition of a miracle, that "it is a transgression of a law of nature by a particular volition of the Deity, or by the interposal of some invisible agent;" but is a manifest absurdity. But in the case of an extraordinary event contrary to the usual course of natural causes, and wrought for a very valuable purpose, and by a power adequate to the effect, there is indeed a proper miracle, but no absurdity at all. It is true, that its being unusual and out of the ordinary course of observation and experience, is a good reason for not believing it without a strong and convincing evidence, a much stronger evidence than would be necessary, in common and ordinary facts. But when there is an evidence of its having been actually done, which hath all the requisites that can be justly demanded in such a case, and at the same time sufficient reasons are assigned worthy of the divine wisdom and goodness to shew that it was proper it should be done, its being unusual and extraordinary is no proof at all that it hath not been done, nor can in any propriety of speech be called an *evidence* against it: and therefore no subtraction is to be made from the credit given to such a supposed full and sufficient evidence merely on this account. Perhaps my meaning will be better understood by applying it to a particular instance. And I chuse to mention that which is the principal miracle in proof of Christianity, our Lord's resurrection. The fact itself was evidently miraculous, and required a divine power to accomplish it. It was therefore necessary, in order to lay a just foundation for believing it, that there should be such an evidence given as was proportioned to the importance and extraordinariness of the fact. And that the evidence which was given of it was really such an evidence, appears, I think, plainly from what I have elsewhere observed concerning it.[233] But if we should put the case thus, that not only was the fact extraordinary in itself, and out of the common course of nature, but the evidence given of it was insufficient, and not to be depended upon, and had circumstances attending it which brought it under a just suspicion: or, if contrary evidence was produced to invalidate it: *e.g.* If the soldiers that watched the sepulchre, instead of pretending that the body of Jesus was stolen away while they were asleep, which was no evidence at all, and was a plain acknowledgement that they knew nothing at all of the matter, had declared

---

[233] See above, p. 249, & seq.

that the disciples came with a powerful band of armed men, and overpowered the guard, and carried away the body: or, if any of the *Jews* had averred, that they were present and awake when the soldiers slept, and that they saw the disciples carry away the body: or, if any of the disciples to whom Jesus appeared, and who professed to have seen and conversed with him after his resurrection, had afterwards declared, that they were among the disciples at those times when he was pretended to have appeared, and that they saw no such appearances, nor heard any such conversations as were pretended. On this supposition it might be properly said that there was evidence given on both sides; *viz.* for and against Christ's resurrection, and consequently that there was a real opposition of evidence; in which case it would be necessary carefully to examine the evidences, and compare them one with another, in order to judge which of them deserved the greater credit, and how far one of them weakened or impaired the force of the other. But as the case was circumstanced, since there was a very strong positive evidence given that Christ really rose from the dead, and shewed himself alive after his resurrection by many infallible proofs, and no contrary evidence produced against it, nor any thing alleged to render the evidence that was given of it justly suspected; and since there are also very good reasons assigned worthy of the divine wisdom and goodness, which rendered it highly proper that Christ should be raised from the dead: on this view of the case, the extraordinariness of the fact, alone considered, cannot with any propriety be called an *evidence* against the truth of it, nor be justly urged as a reason for not yielding a full assent to the evidence concerning it. For it was necessary to the ends proposed by the divine wisdom, that the fact should be of an extraordinary and miraculous nature, and if it had not been so, it would not have answered those ends. I think therefore it may justly be affirmed, that taking the case in all its circumstances, considering the great strength and force of the evidence that is given for the fact, and the many concurring proofs and attestations by which it was confirmed, together with the excellent and important ends for which it was designed, there is as just ground to believe that Christ really rose again from the dead, as that he was crucified; though the latter be a fact not out of the ordinary course of nature, and the former was evidently so. And here it may not be improper to mention a remarkable observation of Mr. *Locke*, he had in giving an account of the grounds of probability supposed one ground of it to be the conformity of a thing with our *own knowledge, observation, and experience.* And after taking notice of several things to this purpose, he observes, That

"though common experience and the ordinary course of things have justly a mighty influence on the minds of men, to make them give or refuse credit to any thing proposed to their belief, yet there is one case wherein the strangeness of the fact lessens not the assent to a fair testimony given of it. For where such supernatural events are suitable to ends aimed at by him who has the power to change the course of nature; there under such circumstances they may be the fitter to procure belief, by how much the more they are beyond or contrary to common observation. This is the proper case of miracles, which, well attested, do not only find credit themselves, but give it also to other truths which need such a confirmation."[234]

Thus this great master of reason is so far from thinking with Mr. *Hume,* that a thing's being miraculous, or beyond the common course of observation and experience, absolutely destroys all evidence of testimony that can be given concerning the truth of the fact; that in his opinion it doth not so much as lessen the assent given to it upon a fair testimony; provided the supernatural facts thus attested were suitable to the ends of the divine wisdom and goodness, *i.e.* wrought in attestation to a revelation of the highest importance, and of the most excellent tendency; and that in that case the more evidently miraculous the fact is, the fitter it is to answer the end proposed by it.

The ingenious author of the paper you sent me has very properly summed up Mr. *Hume*'s argument against the evidence of miracles, thus:

We have had a long universal and uninterrupted experience, that no events have happened contrary to the course of nature, from constant and unvaried observations. We have therefore a full proof that this uniform course has not been broken in upon, nor will be by any particular exceptions.

But the observation of truth depending upon, and constantly following human testimony is by no means universal and uninterrupted. And therefore it does not amount to a full proof, that it either has or will follow in any particular instance.

And therefore the proof arising from any human testimony, can never equal the proof that is deduced against a miracle from the very nature of the fact.

This he takes to be a full and fair state of Mr. *Hume*'s reasoning: and it appears to me to be so. And he says,

"The answer is plain. If by human testimony he would mean of any one single man indifferently taken, then his second proposition would be true; but then the conclusion would by no means follow from it. But if by

---

[234] Locke's Essay on Human Understanding, book iv. chap. xvi. sect. 13.

human testimony he would understand the evidence of any collection of men, then the second proposition is false, and consequently the conclusion is so too."

This answer relateth only to the second proposition.[235] But it might have been said, that neither of the propositions are to be depended upon, and that they are utterly insufficient to support the conclusion he would draw from them. For as to the first proposition, it assumes the very point in question. It affirms that no events have ever happened contrary to the course of nature; and that this we know by a long, universal, and uninterrupted experience. If this be meant of the universal and uninterrupted experience of all mankind in all ages, which alone can be of any force in the present argument, how doth it appear that we know by universal and uninterrupted experience, that no such events have ever happened? Are there not several events of this kind recorded by credible testimonies to have happened? The whole argument then is upon a wrong foundation. It proceedeth upon an universal and uninterrupted experience, not broken in upon in several instances. And there is good testimony to prove that it hath been broken in upon in several instances. And if it hath been broken in upon in any instances, no argument can be brought from experience to prove that it hath not, or may not be broken in upon: and so the whole reasoning falls. If it be alledged, that these testimonies, or indeed any testimonies at all, ought not to be admitted in this case; the question returns. For what reason ought they not to be admitted? If the reason be, as it must be according to Mr. *Hume,* because there is an universal uninterrupted experience against them, this is to take it for granted, that no such events have ever happened. For if there have been any instances of such events, the experience is not universal and uninterrupted. So then we see what the boasted argument against miracles from uniform experience comes to. It in effect comes to this, that no such events have ever happened, because no such events have ever happened.

As to the second proposition, though if we speak of human testimony in general, it will be easily allowed, that it is not to be absolutely and universally depended upon; yet, as hath been already hinted, it may in particular instances be so circumstanced as to yield a satisfying assurance, or what

---

[235] Though the ingenious gentleman hath not directly and formally answered the first proposition, yet he has plainly shewn that he doth not admit it, when he saith, That "the very same objection Mr. *Hume* makes against the veracity of human testimony to weaken its authenticity, may be retorted with equal force against his unvaried certainty of the course of nature. And that doubtless the many approved histories we have relating to miracles, will as much lessen the probability of what he calls a full proof on his side of the question, as all the forgeries and falshoods that are brought to discredit human testimony will weaken it on the other.

may not improperly be called a full proof. Even the testimony of a particular person may in some cases be so circumstanced, as to leave no room for reasonable suspicion or doubt. But especially if we speak of what this gentleman calls *a collection of men*, this may in some cases be so strong, as to produce a full and intire conviction, however improbable the attested fact might otherwise appear to be. And therefore if we meet with any testimonies relating to particular events of an extraordinary nature, they are not immediately to be rejected under pretence of their being contrary to past experience; but we must carefully examine the evidence brought for them, whether it be of such a kind as to make it reasonable for us to believe them. And that the evidence brought for the miraculous facts recorded in the Gospel are of this kind hath been often clearly shewn.

The only farther reflection I shall make on this gentleman's paper is, that it contains good and proper observations concerning our being determined in matters of practice by probabilities. – That in all cases of moment, where to act or forbear may be attended with considerable damage, no wise man makes the least scruple of doing what he apprehends may be of advantage to him, even though the thing were doubtful. But in matters of the utmost consequence, a prudent man will think himself obliged to take notice of the lowest probability, and will act accordingly. – This he applies to the practice of religion, and observes, that considering the vast importance of religion to our happiness in every respect, – the bare possibility that it might prove true, were there nothing else to support it, would engage his assent and compliance: or else he must be supposed to act differently in this respect to what he generally does in all the other concerns of his life.

This observation is not intirely new, but it is handsomely illustrated by this gentleman, and seems very proper to shew, that those who neglect and despise religion, do in this, notwithstanding their boasted pretences, act contrary to the plain dictates of reason and good sense. But we need not have recourse to this supposition. The evidence on the side of religion is vastly superior. And if this be the case, no words can sufficiently express the folly and unreasonableness of their conduct, who take up with slight prejudices and presumptions in opposition to it; and by choosing *darkness rather than light*, and rejecting *the great salvation* offered in the Gospel, run the utmost hazard of exposing themselves to a heavy condemnation and punishment.

Thus I have taken the liberty you allowed me of giving my thoughts upon the paper you sent me. I cannot but look upon the young gentleman's attempt to be a laudable and ingenious one, though there are some things in his way of managing the argument, which seem not to have been thoroughly considered, and which, I am satisfied, he would have altered, if he had lived to take an accurate review of the subject.

This, with a few additions since made to it, is the substance of the answer I returned to the worthy gentleman who had wrote to me, and which I have here inserted, because there are some things in it that may tend to the farther illustration of what I had offered in my remarks on Mr. *Hume's Essay on* Miracles. My next will contain some additional observations relating to the Abbé *de Paris*, and the miracles attributed to him; together with reflections on some passages in Mr. *Hume's Enquiry concerning the Principles of Morals*, which seem to be intended to expose Christianity.

LETTER XXI.

Some reflections on the extraordinary sanctity ascribed to the Abbé de Paris. He carried superstition to a strange excess, and by his extraordinary austerities voluntarily hastened his own death. His character and course of life of a different kind from that rational and solid piety and virtue which is recommended in the Gospel. Observations on some passages in Mr. Hume's Enquiry concerning the Principles of Morals. *He reckons self-denial, mortification, and humility among the Monkish virtues, and represents them as not only useless, but as having a bad influence on the temper and conduct. The nature of self-denial explained, and its great usefulness and excellency shewn. What is to be understood by the mortification required in the Gospel. This also is a reasonable and necessary part of our duty. Virtue, according to Mr. Hume, hath nothing to do with sufferance. But by the acknowledgement of the wisest moralists one important office of it is to support and bear us up under adversity. The nature of humility explained. It is an excellent and amiable virtue.*

SIR,

The miracles of the Abbé *de Paris* have made so great a noise in the world, and so much advantage hath been taken of them by the enemies of Christianity, and particularly by Mr. *Hume*, that I thought it necessary to consider them pretty largely above in the nineteenth Letter. Some things have occurred since, which have some relation to that matter, and which I shall here take notice of.

In that Letter, p. 321. mention is made of the high opinion the people had conceived of the Abbé's extraordinary sanctity, as what tended very much to raise their expectations of miracles to be wrought at his tomb, and by his intercession. If we inquire whence this opinion of his extraordinary sanctity arose, and upon what it was founded, we shall find it to have been principally owing to the excessive austerities in which he exercised himself for several years, of which therefore, and of some remarkable things in his life and character, it may not be improper to give some account. The particulars I shall mention are set forth at large by the learned Mr. *Mosheim* in a dissertation on the miracles of the Abbé *de Paris*, and which I did not meet with till after the publication of the second volume of the *View of the Deistical Writers*. It is intitled *Inquisitio in veritatem miraculorum Francisci de Paris sæculi nostri thaumaturgi*.[236] What he there tells us concerning Mons. *de Paris* is faithfully taken from those who hold him in the highest admiration, the *Jansenistical* writers. And from their accounts it sufficiently appears, that his whole life, and especially the latter part of it, was one continued scene of the most absurd superstition, and which he carried on an excess that may be thought to border upon madness.

He was the eldest son of an ancient, rich, and honourable family, and therefore born to an opulent fortune: though his father, when he saw his turn of mind, very prudently left him but a part of it, and that in the hands, and under the care of his younger brother. But though he still had an ample provision made for him, he voluntarily deprived himself of all the conveniencies, and even the necessaries of life. He chose one obscure hole or cottage after another to live in, and often mixed with beggars, whom he resembled so much in his customs, sordid and tattered garb, and whole manner of his life, that he was sometimes taken for one, and was never better pleased, than when this exposed him in the streets and ways to derision and contempt. Poverty was what he so much affected, that though he applied to his brother for what his father had left him, yet that he might not have the appearance of being rich, he chose not to take it as what was legally due to him, but to supplicate for it in the humblest terms, as for an alms freely bestowed upon a miserable object that had nothing of his own. And yet afterwards in his last will, he disposed of it as his own to various uses as he thought fit, especially for the benefit of those who had been sufferers for the Jansenist cause. For several of the last years of his life he seemed to make it his business to contrive ways to weaken, or harass, and torment his body, and thereby hasten his own death. Whilst he gave away his income to the poor, he himself voluntarily endured all the evils and hardships which attended the extremity of want and poverty. Mean and wretched was his garb, black bread, water and herbs, but without oil, salt, or vinegar, or any thing to give them favour, was his only sustenance, and that but once a day. He lay upon the ground, and was worn away with continual watching. After his death were found his hair shirt, an iron cross, a girdle, stomacher, and bracelets of the same metal, all bestuck with sharp points. These were the instruments of penitence, with which he was wont to chastise himself, the plain marks of which he bore

---

[236] Vide Jo. Laur. Moshemii Dissertationum ad Historiam Ecclesiasticam pertinentium Volumen secundum.

in his body. By such a course he brought himself not only into great weakness of body, but into disorders of mind: And this, which was the natural effect of his manner of living, he attributed to the influence of the devil, whom God had in just judgment permitted to punish him for his sins. And in inquiring into the causes of the divine displeasure, he fixed upon this, that he had still too great a love for human learning an knowledge, and therefore from thenceforth did all he could to divest himself of it, and would have sold his well furnished library, if he had not been prevented by some of his friends, whose interest it was to preserve it. For two years together he refused to come to the holy supper, under pretence that it was not lawful for him to come, God having required him to abstain from it: And it was with great difficulty that he was brought to it at last, by the threatenings and even reproaches of his confessor. Finally, that no kind of misery might be wanting to him, he chose for his companion to dwell with him in his cottage, a man that was looked upon to be crazy, and who treated him in the most injurious manner. He did all he could to hide himself from his friends in one sorry cottage after another, and about a month before his death fixed himself in a little lodge in the corner of a garden, exposed to the sun and wind. When by such severities he had brought himself into an universal bad habit of body, and it was visible to his friends, that if he continued in that course he could not long support under it, a physician was called in, who only desired him to remove to a more commodious habitation, to allow himself more sleep, and a better diet, and especially to take nourishing broths for restoring his enfeebled constitution. But all the persuasions of his physician, confessor, and of his friends, and the tears of an only brother, could not prevail with him to follow an advice so reasonable and practicable; though he was assured that if he used that method there was great hope of his recovery, and that his life could not be preserved without it. And when at last to satisfy their importunity, he seemed so far to comply, as to be willing to take some broth, it was only an appearance of complying, for he took care to give such orders to the person who was to prepare it for him, that it really yielded little or no nourishment. Thus it was manifest, that he had determined to hasten, as much as in him lay, his own death. And accordingly he told his confessor, that this life had nothing in it to make it worth a Christian's care to preserve it. His friends acknowlege that his death was the effect "of the almost incredible austerities that he exercised during the last four years of his life." His great admirer of the Abbé *de Asfeld* testifies, that he heard him declare it as his purpose to yield himself a slow sacrifice to divine justice. And this his extraordinary course of austerities, together with the zeal he expressed to the very last for the *Jansenist* cause, which he shewed also by the dispositions he made in his will, as well as by his appealing, as with dying breath, to a future general council against the constitution *Unigenitus*, procured him so extraordinary a reputation, that he has passed for one of the greatest saints that ever appeared in the Christian church. No sooner was he dead, but an innumerable multitude of people ran to his corpse, some of whom kissed his feet, others cut off part of his hair as a remedy against all manner of evil; others brought books or bits of cloth to touch his body, as believing it filled with a divine virtue. Thus were they prepared to believe and expect the most wonderful things.

Whosoever impartially considers the several things that have been mentioned, and which are amply verified in the places referred to in the margin;[237] will not think the learned *Mosheim* in the wrong, when he pronounceth that it cannot in consistency with reason be supposed, that God should extraordinarily interpose by his own divine power, to do honour to the bones and ashes of a man weak and superstitious to a degree of folly, and who was knowingly and wilfully accessory to his own death. In vain do his admirers, as he himself had done, extol his thus destroying himself as an offering up himself a voluntary sacrifice to divine justice. If a man should under the same pretence dispatch himself at once with a pistol or poniard, would this be thought a proper justification of his conduct? And yet I see not why the pretence might not as well hold in the one case as in the other; since it makes no great difference, whether the death was swifter or slower, provided it was brought on with a deliberate intention and design.

How different is this from the beautiful and noble idea of piety and virtue which the Gospel furnisheth us with, and from the perfect pattern of moral excellence which is set us by our blessed Saviour himself in his own holy life and practice! That the great apostle St. Paul was far from encouraging such austerities as tended to hurt and destroy the bodily health, sufficiently appeareth from the advice he gave to *Timothy, Drink no longer water, but use a little wine, for thy stomach's sake, and thine often infirmities.* I Tim. v. 23. He condemneth those that under pretence of extraordinary purity, were for observing the *ordinances* and *traditions* of men, *Touch not, taste not, handle not*; and brands their practice under the name of will *worship*, a *voluntary humility*, and *neglecting*, or as the word might be rendered, *not sparing the body*, Col. ii. 20, 21, 22, 23. That which in the case of Abbé *de Paris* is cried up by his admirers as a carrying religion to the highest degree of perfection, *viz.* his abstaining from flesh and confining himself to herbs, is represented by the apostle *Paul* as a sign of weakness in the faith. *Rom.* xiv. 2.

It hath always appeared to me to be the glory of the Christian religion, as prescribed in the New Testament, that the piety it teacheth us is solid and rational, remote from all superstitious extremes, worthy of a God of

---

[237] See *Mosheim*, ut supra, from p. 364. to p. 395.

infinite wisdom and goodness to require, and becoming the true dignity of the reasonable nature. It comprehendeth not only immediate acts of devotion towards God, but a diligent performance of all relative duties, and the faithful discharge of the various offices incumbent upon us in the civil and social life. It requireth us indeed to bear with a noble fortitude the greatest evils, when we are regularly called to suffer for the cause of God, but not rashly to expose ourselves to those evils, or to bring them upon ourselves.

The wise and beneficent author of nature hath stored the whole world about us with a variety of benefits: And can it be thought to be agreeable to his will, that instead of tasting his goodness in the blessings he vouchsafeth us, we should make a merit of never allowing ourselves to enjoy them? How much more rational is it to receive those blessings with thankfulness, and enjoy them with temperance, according to that of St. *Paul*, *Every creature of God is good, and nothing to be refused, if it be received with thanksgiving: For it is sanctified by the word of God and prayer.* I Tim. iv. 4, 5. Can it be pleasing to our merciful heavenly father, that we should not merely humble and chasten ourselves on special occasions, but make it our constant business to torment ourselves, and to impair and destroy the bodies he hath given us, and there by unfit ourselves for the proper offices of life? Is it reasonable to imagine, that under the mild dispensation of the Gospel; which breathes an ingenuous cheerful spirit, and raiseth us to the noble liberty of the children of God, the best way of recommending ourselves to his favour should be to deny ourselves all the comforts he affordeth us, and to pass our lives in perpetual sadness and abstinence? Could it be said in that case, that *Godliness is profitable unto all things, having promise of the life that now is, and of that which is to come?* I *Tim.* iv. 8. It is true, that mortification and self-denial are important Gospel-duties, but how different from the extremes of superstitious rigour will appear, when I come to vindicate the evangelical morality against the objections of Mr. *Hume*. It was not indeed till Christians began to degenerate from that lovely form of rational, solid piety and virtue, of which Christ himself exhibited the most perfect example, that they laid so mighty a stress on those severe and rigorous austerities, which neither our Saviour nor his apostles had commanded. And in this respect some of those who were antiently deemed heretical sects carried it to a greater degree of strictness than the orthodox themselves. And many zealots there have been in false religions, and particularly some of the heathen devotees in the *East-Indies*, who in severe penances, and rigid austerities, and in voluntary torments inflicted on their own bodies, have far exceeded the Abbé *de Paris* himself.

...

POSTSCRIPT.

After great part of this Work was finished, and sent to the press, I met with a book which I have read with great pleasure, intitled, *The Criterion; or Miracles examined, with a view to expose the pretensions of Pagans and Papists; to compare the miraculous Powers recorded in the* New Testament, *with those said to subsist in latter times, and to shew the great and material difference between them in point of evidence: from whence it will appear, that the former must be true, and the latter may be false.* The subject is evidently both curious and important, and is treated by the author, who, I hear, is the Rev. Mr. *Douglass*, in a judicious and masterly way. It was published at *London* in 1754, and therefore before the publication of the second volume of the *View of the Deistical Writers.* And if I had then seen it, I should certainly have thought myself obliged to take particular notice of it. The worthy author has made judicious observations upon Mr. *Hume's Essay on Miracles*, especially that part of it which relateth to the miracles ascribed to the Abbé *de Paris*, which he has insisted on for an hundred pages together. And it is no small satisfaction to me, that there is a perfect harmony between what this learned author has written on this subject, and what I have published in the preceding part of this work, though neither of us knew of the other's work. He shews, as I have endeavoured to do, that fraud and imposture were plainly detected in several instances: and that where the facts were true, natural causes sufficient to produce the effect may be assigned, without supposing any thing miraculous in the case. This he has particularly shewn, with regard to each of the miracles insisted on by Mr. *de Montgeron*, which he accounts for much in the same way that Mr. *des Voeux* hath more largely done, though he had not seen that gentleman's valuable writings, to which I have frequently referred for a fuller account of those things which I could do little more than hint at. The reader will find in Mr. *Douglas's* work a full proof of the wonderful force of the imagination, and the mighty influence that strong impressions made upon the mind, and vehement passions raised there, may have in producing surprising changes on the body, and particularly in removing diseases: of which he hath produced several well attested instances, no less extraordinary than those attributed to the Abbé *de Paris*, and which yet cannot reasonably be pretended to be properly miraculous.

As I have thought myself obliged to take notice of that part of this gentleman's book, which hath so near a connection with the work in which I have been engaged; so it is but just to observe, that it is also, with regard to every other part of it, a learned and accurate performance.

What he proposes to shew is, that the evidence for the Gospel facts is as extraordinary as the facts themselves; and that no just suspicion of fraud or falshood appeareth in the accounts; while every thing is the reverse, with regard to the evidence brought for the Pagan or Popish miracles.

What he proposes to shew is, that the evidence for the Gospel facts is as extraordinary as the facts themselves; and that no just suspicion of fraud or falshood appeareth in the accounts; while every thing is the reverse, with regard to the evidence brought for the Pagan or Popish miracles.

He observes, That the extraordinary facts ascribed to a miraculous inter-position among the Pagans of old, or the Christians of latter times, are all reducible to these two classes. The accounts are either such as, from the circumstances thereof, appear to be false; or, the facts are such as, by the nature thereof, they do not appear to be miraculous. – As to the first, the general rules he lays down, by which we may try the pretended miracles amongst Pagans and Papists, and which may set forth the grounds on which we suppose them to be false, are these three: – That either they were not published to the world till long after the time when they were said to be performed: – Or, they were not published in the places, where it is pretended the facts were wrought, but were propagated only at a great distance from the scene of action: – Or, they were suffered to pass without due examination, because they coincided with the favourite opinions and prejudices of those to whom they were reported; or, because the accounts were encouraged and supported by those who alone had the power of detecting the fraud, and could prevent any examination, which might tend to undeceive the world. These observations he applies to the Pagan and Popish miracles; some of the most remarkable of which he distinctly mentions, and shews, that there are none of them that do not labour under one or other of these defects.

After considering those pretended miracles, which, from the circum-stances of the accounts given of them, appear to be false, he next proceedeth to those works, which, though they may be true, and ascribed by ignorance, art, or credulity, to supernatural causes, yet are really natural, and may be accounted for, without supposing any miraculous interposition. And here he enters on a large and particular discussion of the miracles attributed to the Abbé *de Paris*, and some other miracles that have been much boasted of in the Romish church.

Having fully examined and exposed the Pagan and Popish miracles, he next proceeds to shew, That the objections made against them, and which administer just grounds of suspicion, cannot be urged against the Gospel miracles. And here he distinctly shews, *First*, That the facts were such that, from the nature of them, they must needs be miraculous, and cannot be accounted for in a natural way, or by any power of imagination, or strong impressions made upon the mind. And, *Secondly*, That those facts are such as, from the circumstances of them, they cannot be false. And to this purpose, he makes it appear, that they were published and appealed to at the time when they were performed; and were coeval with the preaching of Christianity, which was manifestly founded upon them. – They were also published and attested at the places where the scene of them was laid, and on the spot on which they were wrought. – And the circumstances, under which they were first published, give us an assurance, that they underwent a strict examination, and consequently, that they could not have escaped detection, had they been impostures.

Mr. *Douglass* thinks it not sufficient barely to prove, that the testimony for the Gospel-miracles is stronger than that which supporteth any other pretended miracles; he farther shews, by a variety of considerations, that it is the strongest that can be supposed, or that, from the nature of the thing, could be had. And then he proceeds to observe, that besides the unexceptionable proof from testimony, the credibility of the Gospel-miracles is confirmed to us, by collateral evidences of the most striking nature, and which no spurious miracles can boast of: – Such as – the great change that was thereby introduced into the state of religion. – The proofs that God was with the first publishers of Christianity, in other instances besides those of miracles, particularly in assisting them supernaturally in the knowlege of the scheme of religion which they taught, and of which they were not capable of being the authors or inventors, and enabling them to give clear predictions of future events. – And particularly he insisteth upon that most express and circumstantial prediction of the destruction of the city and temple of *Jerusalem*, and the dispersion of the *Jewish* nation, as a demonstration that *Jesus* acted under a supernatural influence. – The last thing he urgeth as a collateral evidence is, That the miracles recorded in Scripture were performed by those who assumed the character of prophets, or teachers sent from God, and their miracles were intended as credentials to establish their claim, to add authority to the messages they delivered, and the laws they taught. – A character which, he shews, both the Pagan and Popish miracles are entirely destitute of.

This is a brief account of the plan of Mr. *Douglass*'s work, which fully answereth the title: and it is with great pleasure I take this opportunity to acknowlege the merit of the learned author, and the service he hath done to the Christian and Protestant cause.

I am, Sir, &c.

13
WILLIAM ROSE

[William Rose], review of *Four Dissertations*, in *The Monthly Review*, February 1757, Vol. 16, pp. 122–139.
Complete review.

When Hume's *Four Dissertations* appeared in 1757, three British journals reviewed the work. The reviews in both the *Monthly Review* and the *Critical Review* appeared in February. The *Monthly Review* – the older of the two journals – was founded in 1749 by Ralph Griffiths (1720–1803), who was a regular reviewer for earlier review journals. The articles in the *Monthly Review* appeared anonymously. However, each month Griffiths penned abbreviations of the names of the reviewers into his personal copy of the *Monthly* (a microfilm of his annotated copy is available in the *English Literary Periodicals* microfilm series). Griffiths's abbreviations have been identified and catalogued by Benjamin Christie Nangle in *The Monthly Review First Series: 1749–1789* (1934), and *The Monthly Review Second Series: 1790–1815* (1955). According to Nangle's catalogue, the reviewer of the *Monthly Review* article was William Rose (1719–1786). A Scotsman and proprietor of a school in Chelsea, Rose regularly reviewed philosophy books for the journal and is responsible for reviewing seven of Hume's works in the *Monthly*. Like most of his other reviews of Hume, Rose gives a sympathetic evaluation of this work. He begins with a general assessment of Hume's writings, first praising their originality and elegance, but regretting that he uses his abilities to covertly attack the religion of his country. Rose focuses mainly on the "Natural History of Religion", presenting excerpts and summaries. He states that the essay "abounds with shrewd reflections, and just observations, upon human nature: mixed with a considerable portion of that sceptical spirit, which is so apparent in all his works; and with some insinuations, artfully couched, against the Christian religion". Regarding the "Of the Passions", Rose comments that "What he says upon the subject, is extremely ingenious, and deserves the philosophical reader's attentive perusal". Rose concludes with brief summaries of "Of Tragedy", and "Of the Standard of Taste".

Four Dissertations. 1. *The Natural History of Religion*. 2. *Of the Passions*.
   3. *Of Tragedy*. 4. *Of the Standard of Taste*. By David Hume, *Esq*;
   12mo. 3s. Millar.

There are but few of our modern Writers, whose works are so generally
read, as those of Mr. Hume. And, indeed, if we consider them in one view,
as sprightly and ingenious compositions, this is not at all to be wondered
at: there is a delicacy of sentiment, an original turn of thought, a
perspicuity, and often an elegance, of language, that cannot but recommend
his writings to every Reader of taste. It is to be regretted, however, that such
a genius should employ his abilities in the manner he frequently does. In
his attacks upon the religion of his country, he acts not the part of an open
and generous enemy, but endeavours to weaken its authority by oblique
hints, and artful insinuations. In this view his works merit little, if any,
regard; and few Readers, of just discernment, we apprehend, will envy him
any honours his acuteness, or elegance, can possibly obtain, when they are
only employed in filling the mind with the uncomfortable fluctuations of
scepticism, and the gloom of infidelity. But leaving general reflections, let
us proceed to give an account of the Dissertations now before us; the first
of which is entitled, *The Natural History of Religion*.

   This Dissertation Mr. Hume introduces with observing, that there are
two questions in regard to religion, which challenge our principal attention,
viz. that concerning its foundation in reason, and that concerning its origin
in human nature. The first question, which is the most important, admits,
he says, of the clearest solution. The whole frame of nature bespeaks an
intelligent Author; and no rational enquirer can, after serious reflection,
suspend his belief a moment with regard to the primary principles of
genuine theism and religion. But the other question, concerning the origin
of religion in human nature, admits of some more difficulty. The belief of
invisible intelligent power, has been very generally diffused over the human
race, in all places, and in all ages; but it has neither, perhaps, been so
universally, we are told, as to admit of no exceptions, nor has it been, in
any degree, uniform in the ideas which it has suggested. Some nations have
been discovered, who entertained no sentiments of religion, if travellers and
historians may be credited; and no two nations, and scarce any two men,
have ever agreed precisely in the same sentiments.

   'It would appear, therefore,' continues Mr. Hume,

'that this pre-conception springs not from an original instinct, or primary
impression of nature, such as gives rise to self-love, affection betwixt the
sexes, love of progeny, gratitude, resentment; since every instinct of this
kind has been found absolutely universal in all nations and ages, and has
always a precise, determinate object, which it inflexibly pursues. The first

religious principles must be secondary; such as may easily be perverted by various accidents and causes, and whose operation too, in some cases, may, by an extra-ordinary concurrence of circumstances, be altogether prevented. What those principles are, which give rise to the original belief, and what those accidents and causes are, which direct its operation, is the subject of our present enquiry?'

Mr. Hume is of opinion, that if we consider the improvement of human society, from rude beginnings to a state of greater perfection, it will appear, that Polytheism or Idolatry, was, and necessarily must have been, the first and most antient religion of mankind. In order to support this opinion, he observes, that the farther we mount up into antiquity, the more we find mankind plunged into Idolatry. The North, the South, the East, the West, give their unanimous testimony to this fact: As to the doubtful and sceptical principles of a few Philosophers, or the Theism, and that too not entirely pure, of one or two nations, these form no objection worth regarding. According to the natural progress of human thought too, he says, the ignorant multitude must first entertain some groveling and familiar notion of superior powers, before they stretch their conception to that perfect Being, who bestowed order on the whole frame of nature: and we may as reasonably imagine, that men inhabited palaces before huts and cottages, or studied geometry before agriculture, as assert, that the Deity appeared to them a pure spirit, omniscient, omnipotent, and omnipresent, before he was apprehended to be a powerful, though limited Being, with Human passions and appetites, limbs, and organs. In a word, our Author thinks it impossible, that theism could, from reasoning, have been the primary religion of the human race, and have afterwards, by its corruption, given birth to Idolatry, and to all the various superstitions of the Heathen world.

If we would therefore indulge our curiosity, he says, in enquiring concerning the origin of religion, we must turn our thoughts towards Idolatry or Polytheism, the primitive religion of uninstructed mankind. And here he observes, that if men were led into the apprehension of invisible, intelligent power, by a contemplation of the works of nature, they could never possibly entertain any conception but of one single Being, who bestowed existence and order on this vast machine, and adjusted all its parts, according to one regular plan, or connected system. On the other hand, if, leaving the works of nature, we trace the footsteps of invisible power, in the various and contrary events of human life, we are necessarily led into Polytheism, and to the acknowledgement of several limited and imperfect Deities. Storms and tempests ruin what is nourished by the sun; the sun destroys what is fostered by the moisture of dews and rains. War may be favourable to a nation, whom the inclemency of the seasons afflicts with famine: sickness and pestilence may depopulate a kingdom, amidst the most profuse plenty. In short, the conduct of events, or what we call the plan of a particular Providence, is so full of variety and uncertainty, that if we suppose it immediately ordered by any intelligent Being, we must acknowledge a contrariety in their designs and intentions, a constant combat of opposite powers, and a repentance, or change of intention in the same power, from impotence or levity.

It may be concluded therefore, Mr. Hume imagines, that in all nations which have embraced Polytheism, or Idolatry, the first ideas of religion arose not from a contemplation of the works of nature; but from a concern with respect to the events of life, and from the incessant hopes and fears which actuate the human mind. Accordingly we find, it is said, that all Idolaters, having separated the provinces of their Deities, have recourse to that invisible agent, to whose authority they are immediately subjected, and whose province it is to superintend that course of actions, in which they are at any time engaged. Juno is invoked at marriages; Lucina at births; Neptune receives the prayers of seamen; and Mars of warriors. Each natural event is supposed to be governed by some intelligent agent; and nothing prosperous, or adverse can happen in life, which may not be the subject of peculiar prayers or thanksgivings.

In further treating of this subject, Mr. Hume observes, that we are placed in this world as in a great theatre, where the true springs and causes of every event, are entirely unknown to us; nor have we either sufficient wisdom to foresee, or power to prevent, those ills with which we are continually threatened. We hang in perpetual suspence betwixt life and death, health and sickness, plenty and want; which are distributed amongst the human species by secret and unknown causes, whose operation is oft unexpected, and always unaccountable. These *unknown causes* then, we are told, become the constant object of our hope and fear; and while the passions are kept in perpetual alarm by an anxious expectation of the events, the imagination is equally employed in forming ideas of those powers, on which we have so entire a dependence. No wonder then, Mr. Hume says, that mankind being placed in such an absolute ignorance of causes, and being at the same time so anxious concerning their future fortunes, should immediately acknowledge a dependance on invisible powers, possessed of sentiment, and intelligence. The *unknown causes*, which continually employ their thought, appearing always in the same aspect, are all apprehended to be of the same kind of species. Nor is it long before we ascribe to them thought, and reason, and passion, and sometimes even the limbs and figures of men, in order to bring them nearer to a resemblance with ourselves.

Our Author goes on to consider the gross Polytheism and Idolatry of the vulgar, and to trace all its various appearances in the principles of human nature, whence they are derived. Whoever learns by argument, he observes, the existence of invisible, intelligent power, must reason from the admirable contrivance of natural objects, and must suppose the world to be the workmanship of that Divine Being, the original cause of all things. But the vulgar polytheist, so far from admitting that idea, deifies every part of the universe, and conceives all the conspicuous productions of nature to be themselves so many real Divinities. The sun, moon, and stars, are all Gods, according to his system: fountains are inhabited by nymphs, and trees by hamadryads: even monkies, dogs, cats, and other animals, often become sacred in his eyes, and strike him with a religious veneration. And thus, however strong men's propensity to believe invisible, intelligent power, in nature, their propensity is equally strong to rest their attention on sensible, visible objects; and in order to reconcile these opposite inclinations, they are led to unite the invisible power with some visible object.

Mr. Hume observes further, that the Deities of the vulgar are so little superior to human creatures, that where men are affected with strong sentiments of veneration or gratitude, for any hero, or public benefactor, nothing can be more natural than to convert him into a God, and fill the Heavens after this manner, with continual recruits from amongst mankind. Most of the Divinities of the antient world are supposed to have once been men, and to have been beholden for their *apotheosis* to the admiration and affection of the people. And the real history of their adventures, corrupted by tradition, and elevated by the marvellous, became a plentiful source of fable; especially in passing through the hands of Poets, Allegorists, and Priests, who successfully improved upon the wonder and astonishment of the ignorant multitude.

Polytheism, or idolatrous worship, he says, being founded entirely in vulgar traditions, is liable to this great inconvenience, that any practice, or opinion, however barbarous or corrupted, may be authorized by it; and full scope is left for knavery to impose on credulity, till morals and humanity be expelled from the religious systems of mankind. At the same time he observes, Idolatry is attended with this evident advantage, that, by limiting the powers and functions of its Deities, it naturally admits the Gods of other sects and nations to a share of divinity, and renders all the various Deities, as well as rites, ceremonies, or traditions, compatible with each other.

Theism is opposite, both in its advantages and disadvantages, as it supposes one sole Deity, the perfection of reason and goodness, it should, our Author says, if justly prosecuted, banish every thing frivolous, unreasonable, or inhuman, from religious worship, and set before men the most illustrious example, as well as the most commanding motives of justice and benevolence. These mighty advantages are not, indeed, over balanced, (for that is not possible) but somewhat diminished, we are told, by inconveniences, which arise from the vices and prejudices of mankind. While one sole object of devotion is acknowledged, the worship of other Deities is regarded as absurd and impious. Nay, this unity of object seems naturally to require the unity of faith and ceremonies, and furnishes designing men with a pretext for representing their adversaries as prophane, and the objects of divine, as well as human, vengeance. For as each sect is positive, that its own faith and worship are entirely acceptable to the Deity; and as no one can conceive, that the same Being should be pleased with different and opposite rites and principles; the several sects fall naturally into animosity, and mutually discharge on each other, that sacred zeal and rancour, the most furious and implacable of all human passions.

The tolerating spirit of Idolaters, both in antient and modern times, Mr. Hume says, is very obvious to any one, who is the least conversant in the writings of historians, or travellers; and the intolerance of almost all religions, which have maintained the unity of God, is as remarkable as the contrary principle in Polytheists. The implacable narrow spirit of the Jews, we are told, is well known. Mahommedism set out with still more bloody principles, and even to this day deals out damnation, though not fire and faggot, to all other sects. And if, amongst Christians, the English and Dutch have embraced the principles of toleration, this singularity has proceeded from the steady resolution of the civil magistrate, in opposition to the continued efforts of priests and bigots.

'I may venture to affirm,' continues our Author,

'that few corruptions of Idolatry and Polytheism are more pernicious to political society, than this corruption of Theism, when carried to the utmost height. The human sacrifices of the Carthaginians, Mexicans, and many barbarous nations, scarce exceed the Inquisition, and persecutions of Rome and Madrid. For besides, that the effusion of blood may not be so great in the former case, as in the latter; besides this, I say, the human victims, being chosen by lot, or by some exterior signs, affect not in so considerable a degree, the rest of the society. Whereas virtue, knowledge, love of liberty, are the qualities which call down the fatal vengeance of Inquisitors; and when expelled, have the society in the most shameful ignorance, corruption, and bondage. The illegal murder of one man by a tyrant, is more pernicious than the death of a thousand by pestilence, famine, or any undistinguishing calamity.'

From the comparison of Theism and Idolatry, our Author proceeds to form some other observations, in order to confirm the vulgar saying, that the corruption of the best things gives rise to the worst. He tells us, that where the Deity is represented as infinitely superior to mankind, this belief, though altogether just, is apt, when joined with superstitious terrors, to sink the human mind into the lowest submission and abasement, and to represent the monkish virtues of mortification, pennance, humility, and passive suffering, as the only qualities which are acceptable to him. But where the Gods are conceived to be only a little superior to mankind, and to have been many of them advanced from that inferior rank, we are more at our ease in our addresses to them; and may even, without profaneness, aspire sometimes to a rivalship, and emulation of them. Hence activity, spirit, courage, magnanimity, love of liberty, and all the virtues which aggrandize a people.

He observes further, to the same purpose, that if we examine, without prejudice, the antient Heathen Mythology as, contained in the Poets, we shall not discover in it any such monstrous absurdity, as we may be apt at first to apprehend. Nay, so natural does Mr. Hume think the whole mythological system, that in the vast variety of planets and worlds contained in the universe, he thinks it more than probable, that, somewhere or other, it is really carried into execution.

'The chief objection to it,' says he,

'with regard to this planet, is, that it is not ascertained by any just reason or authority. The antient tradition insisted on by the Heathen Priests and Theologers, is but a weak foundation, and transmitted also such a number of contradictory reports, supported, all of them, by equal authority, that it became absolutely impossible to fix a preference among them. A few volumes therefore must contain all the Polemical writings of Pagan Priests, and their whole theology must consist more of traditional stories, and superstitious practices, than of philosophical argument and controversy.

But where Theism forms the fundamental principle of any popular religion, that tenet is so conformable to sound reason, that philosophy is apt to incorporate itself with such a system of theology. And if the other dogmas of that system be contained in a sacred book, such as *the Alcoran*;[238] or be determined by any visible authority, like that of the Roman Pontiff; speculative reasoners naturally carry on their assent, and embrace a theory which has been instilled into them by their earliest education, and which also possesses some degree of consistence and uniformity. But as these appearances do often, all of them, prove deceitful, philosophy will soon find herself very unequally yoked with her new associate; and instead of regulating each principle as they advance together, she is at every turn perverted to serve the purposes of superstition: for, besides the unavoidable incoherencies which must be reconciled and adjusted, one may safely affirm, that all popular theology, especially the scholastic, has a kind of appetite for absurdity and contra-

---

[238] *The Koran*, Mr. Hume should have said.

diction. If that theology went not beyond reason and common sense, her doctrines would appear too easy and familiar. Amazement must of necessity be raised. Mystery affected, darkness and obscurity sought after; and a foundation of merit afforded the devout votaries who desire an opportunity of subduing their rebellious reason, by the belief of the most unintelligible sophisms.

Ecclesiastical history sufficiently confirms these reflections. When a controversy is started, some people pretend always with certainty, to conjecture the issue. Which ever opinion, says they, is more contrary to plain sense, is sure to prevail; even where the general interest of the system requires not that decision. Though the reproach of heresy may for some time be bandied about amongst the disputants, it always rests on the side of reason. Any one, it is pretended, that has but learning enough to know the definition of *Arian, Pelagian, Erastian, Socinian, Sabellian, Eutychian, Nestorian, Monothelite, &c.* not to mention *Protestant*, whose fate is yet uncertain, will be convinced of the truth of this observation. And thus a system becomes more absurd in the end, merely from its being reasonable and philosophical in the beginning.

To oppose the torrent of scholastic religion, by such feeble maxims as these, that *it is impossible for the same thing to be and not to be*, that *the whole is greater than a part*; that *two and three make five*; is pretending to stop the ocean with a bull-rush. Will you set up profane reason against sacred mystery? No punishment is great enough for your impiety. And the same fires which were kindled for heretics, will serve also for the destruction of philosophers.'

After several other reflections on this subject, Mr. Hume goes on to observe, that notwithstanding the dogmatical imperial style of all superstition, the conviction of the religionists, in all ages, is more affected than real, and scarce approaches, in any degree, to that solid belief and persuasion which governs us in the common affairs of life. Men dare not avow, even to their own hearts, the doubts, which they entertain on such subjects; they make a merit of implicit faith, and disguise to themselves their real infidelity, by the strongest asseverations, and most positive bigotry. But nature is too hard for all their endeavours, and suffers not the obscure, glimmering light, afforded in those shadowy regions, to equal the strong impressions made by common sense, and by experience. The usual course of men's conduct belies their words, and shews, that the assent in these matters is some unaccountable operation of the mind, betwixt disbelief and conviction, but approaching much nearer to the former than the latter.

'Since therefore,' continues Mr. Hume,

'the mind of man appears of so loose and unsteady a contexture, that even at present, when so many persons find an interest in continually employing on it the chissel and the hammer, yet are they not able to engrave theological tenets with any lasting impression; how much more must this have been the case in antient times, when the retainers to the holy function were so much fewer in comparison? No wonder that the appearances, were then very inconsistent, and that men, on some occasions, might seem determined infidels, and enemies to the established religion, without being so in reality; or at least without knowing their minds in that particular.'

In the further prosecution of this subject, our Author observes, that in every religion, however sublime the verbal definition which it gives of its divinity, many of the votaries, perhaps the greatest number, will still seek the divine favour, not by virtue and good morals, which alone can be acceptable to a perfect Being, but either by frivolous observances, by intemperate zeal, by rapturous extasies, or by the belief of mysterious and absurd opinions. Nay, if we should suppose, he says, what seldom happens, that a popular religion were found, in which it was expressly declared, that nothing but morality could gain the Divine favour; if an order of Priests were instituted to inculcate this opinion, in daily sermons, and with all the arts of persuasion; yet so inveterate are the people's prejudices, that for want of some other superstition, they would make the very attendance on these sermons the essentials of religion, rather than place them in virtue and good morals. The manner in which he accounts for this, is as follows:

The duties, he says, which a man performs as a friend or parent, seem merely owing to his benefactor, or children; nor can he be wanting these duties, without breaking through all the ties of nature and morality. A strong inclination may prompt him to the performance: a sentiment of order and moral beauty joins its force to these natural ties; and the whole man, if truly virtuous, is drawn to his duty without any effort or endeavour. Even with regard to the virtues which are more austere, and more founded on reflection, such as public spirit, filial duty, temperance, or integrity; the moral obligation, in our apprehension, removes all pretence to religious merit; and the virtuous conduct is esteemed no more than what we owe to society, and to ourselves. In all this a superstitious man finds nothing which he has properly performed for the sake of his Deity, or which can peculiarly recommend him to the divine favour and protection. He considers not, that the most genuine method of serving the Divinity, is by promoting the happiness of his creatures. He still looks out for some more immediate service of the Supreme Being, in order to allay those terrors with which he is haunted. And any practice recommended to him, which either serves to no purpose in life, or offers the strongest violence to his natural inclinations; that practice he will more readily embrace, on account of those very circumstances, which should make him absolutely reject it. It seems the more purely religious, that it proceeds from no mixture of any other motive or consideration. And if, for its sake, he sacrifices much of his ease and quiet, his claim of merit appears still to rise upon him, in proportion to the zeal and devotion which he discovers. In restoring a loan, of paying a debt, his Divinity is no way beholden to him; because these acts of justice are what he was bound to perform, and what many would have performed, were there not God in the universe. But if he fast a day, or give himself a sound whipping, this has a direct reference, in his opinion, to the service of God. No other motive could engage him to such austerities. By these distinguished marks of devotion, he has now acquired the Divine favour; and may expect, in recompence, protection and safety in this world, and eternal happiness in the next.

Mr. Hume concludes this long Dissertation, which takes up near half the volume, in the following manner. 'Though the stupidity of men, barbarous and uninstructed, be so great,' says he,

'that they may not see a sovereign Author in the more obvious works of nature, to which they are so much familiarized; yet it scarce seems possible, that any one of good understanding should reject that idea, when once it is suggested to him. A purpose, an intention, a design, is evident in every thing; and when our comprehension is so far enlarged, as to contemplate the first rise of this visible system, we must adopt, with the strongest conviction, the idea of some intelligent cause or author. The uniform maxims too, which prevail through the whole frame of the universe, naturally, if not necessarily, lead us to conceive this intelligence as single and undivided, where the prejudices of education oppose not so reasonable a theory. Even the contrarities of nature, by discovering themselves every where, become proofs of some consistent plan, and establish one single purpose or intention, however inexplicable and incomprehensible.

Good and ill are universally intermingled and confounded; happiness and misery, wisdom and folly, virtue and vice. Nothing is pure, and entirely of a piece. All advantages are attended with disadvantages. an universal compensation prevails in all conditions of Being and Existence. And it is scarce possible for us, by our most chimerical wishes, to form the idea of a station or situation altogether desirable. The draughts of life, according to the Poet's fiction, are always mixed from the vessels on each hand of Jupiter. Or if any cup be presented altogether pure, it is drawn only, as the same Poet tells us, from the left-hand vessel.

The more exquisite any good is, of which a small specimen is afforded us, the sharper is the evil allied to it; and few exceptions are found to this uniform law of nature. The most sprightly wit borders on madness; the highest effusions of joy produce the deepest melancholy; the most ravishing pleasures are attended with the most cruel lassitude and disgust; the most flattering hopes make way for the severest disappointments. And, in general, no course of life has such safety (for happiness is not to be dreamed of) as the temperate and moderate, which maintains, as far as possible, a mediocrity, and a kind of insensibility, in every thing.

As the good, the great, the sublime, the ravishing, are found eminently in the genuine principles of Theism, it may be expected, from the analogy of nature, that the base, the absurd, the mean, the terrifying, will be discovered equally in religious fictions and chimeras.

The universal propensity to believe in invisible, intelligent power, if not an original instinct, being at least a general attendant of human nature, it may be considered as a kind of mark or stamp, which the Divine Workman has set upon his work; and nothing, surely, can more dignify mankind, than to be thus selected from all the other parts of the creation, and to bear the image or impression of the universal Creator. But consult this image, as it commonly appears in the popular religions of the world, how is the Deity disfigured in our representations of him! What caprice, absurdity, and immorality are attributed to him! How much is he degraded, even below the character which we should naturally, in common life, ascribe to a man of sense and virtue!

What a noble privilege is it of human reason, to attain the knowledge of the Supreme Being; and, from the visible works of nature, be enabled to infer so sublime a principle as its supreme Creator? But turn the reverse of the medal, survey most nations and most ages. Examine the religious principles, which have in fact prevailed in the world; you will scarcely be persuaded, that they are other than sick mens dreams: or perhaps will regard them more as the playsome whimsies of monkeys in human shape, than the serious, positive, dogmatical observations of a Being, who dignifies himself with the name of rational.

Here the verbal protestations of all men: nothing they are so certain of as their religious tenets. Examine their lives, you will scarcely think they repose the smallest confidence in them.

The greatest and truest zeal gives us no security against hypocrisy: the most open impiety is attended with a secret dread and compunction.

No theological absurdities so glaring, as have not, sometimes, been embraced by men of the greatest and most cultivated understanding. No religious precept, so rigorous, as have not been adopted by the most voluptuous and most abandoned of men.

Ignorance is *the mother of devotion.* A maxim that is proverbial, and confirmed by general experience. Look out for a people entirely devoid of religion: if you find them at all, be assured that they are but a few degrees removed from brutes.

What so pure as some of the morals included in some theological systems? What so corrupted, as some of the practices to which these systems give rise?

The comfortable views exhibited by the belief of a futurity, are ravishing and delightful: but how quickly vanish on the appearance of its terrors, which keep a more firm and durable possession of the human mind?

The whole is a riddle, an ænigma, an inexplicable mystery. Doubt, uncertainty, suspence of judgment, appear the only result of our most accurate scrutiny, concerning this subject. But such is the frailty of human reason, and such the irresistable contagion of opinion, that even this deliberate doubt could scarce be upheld, did we not enlarge our view, and opposing one species of superstition to another, set them a quarrelling, while we ourselves, during their fury and contention, happily make our escape into the calm, though obscure, regions of philosophy.'

Thus have we given a pretty full view of what is contained in Mr. Hume's first Dissertation; which abounds with shrewd reflections, and just observations, upon human nature: mixed with a considerable portion of that sceptical spirit, which is so apparent in all his works; and some insinuations, artfully couched, against the Christian religion. We shall content ourselves with a general view of the other three Dissertations, that we may not stretch this article beyond its just bounds.

Mr. Hume's design in the second Dissertation is to shew, that, in the production and conduct of the passions, there is a certain regular mechanism, which is susceptible of as accurate a disquisition, as the laws of motion, optics, hydrostatics, or any part of natural philosophy. His theory of the passions depends entirely on the double relations of sentiments and ideas, and the mutual assistance which these relations lend to each other. What he says upon the subject, is extremely ingenious, and deserves the philosophical reader's attentive perusal.

The third Dissertation is a very short one, consisting only of sixteen pages. The design of it is to account for the pleasure which the spectators of a well-wrote tragedy receive, from sorrow, terror, anxiety, and other passions, which are in themselves disagreeable and uneasy. Fontenelle's account of this phænomenon, (*Reflections sur la Poetique*, sect. 36) Mr. Hume thinks just and convincing; though it still wants, he imagines, some new addition, in order to make it answer fully. He observes, that the force of imagination, the energy of expression, the power of numbers, the charms of imitation, are all naturally, of themselves, delightful to the mind; and that when the object presented lays also hold of some affection, the pleasure still rises upon us, by the conversion of this subordinate movement, into that which is predominant. The passion, though, perhaps, naturally, and when excited by the simple appearance of a real object, it may be painful; is yet so smoothed, and softened, and mollified, when raised by the finer arts, that it affords the highest entertainment. To confirm this reasoning, our Author observes, that if the movements of the imagination be not predominant above those of the passion, a contrary effect follows; and the former, being now subordinate, is converted into the latter, and still farther increases the pain and affliction of the sufferer.

'An action,' says he,

'represented in tragedy, may be too bloody, and attrocious. It may excite such movements of horror, as will not soften into pleasure; and the greatest energy of expression bestowed on descriptions of that nature, serves only to augment our uneasiness. Such is that action represented in *The Ambitious Step-mother*, where a venerable old man, raised to the heighth of fury and despair, rushes against a pillar, and striking his head upon it, besmears it all over with mingled brains and gore. The *English* theatre abounds too much with such images.'

In the fourth Dissertation, Mr. Hume endeavours to fix *a standard of Taste*; a rule by which the various sentiments of men may be reconciled; or, at least, a decision afforded, confirming one sentiment, and condemning another. In treating this curious and much controverted subject, he observes, that none of the rules of composition are fixed by reasonings *à priori*, or can be esteemed abstract conclusions of the understanding, from comparing those habitudes and relations of ideas, which are eternal and immutable. Their foundation, he says, is the same with that of all the practical sciences, experience; nor are they any thing, but general observations, concerning what has been universally found to please, in all countries, and in all ages. But though all the general rules of art are founded only on experience, and on the observation of the common sentiments of human nature, the feelings of men, we are told, will not, on every occasion, be conformable to these rules. Those finer emotions of the mind are of a very tender and delicate nature, and require the concurrence of many favourable circumstances, to make them play with facility and exactness, according to their general and established principles. The least exterior hindrance to such small springs, or the least internal disorder, disturbs their motion, and confounds the operation of the whole machine. When we would make an experiment of this nature, and would try the force of any beauty or deformity, we must chuse with care a proper time and place, and bring the fancy to a suitable situation and disposition. A perfect serenity of mind, a recollection of thought, a due attention to the object; if any of these circumstances be wanting, our experiment will be fallacious, and we shall be unable to judge of the catholic and universal beauty. The relation which nature has placed betwixt the form and the sentiment, will at least be more obscure; and it will require greater accuracy to trace or discern it. We shall be able to ascertain its influence not so much from the operation of each particular beauty, as from the durable admiration which attends those works, that hath survived all the caprices of mode and fashion, all the mistakes of ignorance and envy.

Amidst all the variety and caprices of taste, Mr. Hume observes, that there are certain general principles of approbation or blame, whose influence a careful eye may trace in all operations of the mind. Some particular forms or qualities, from the original structure of the internal fabric, are calculated to please, and others to displease; and if they fail of their effect in any particular instance, it is from some apparent defect or imperfection in the organ. A man in a fever would not insist on his palate as able to decide concerning flavours; nor would one affected with the jaundice, pretend to give a verdict with regard to colours. In each creature, we are told, there is a sound and a defective state; and the former alone can be supposed to afford us a true standard of taste and sentiment. If in the sound state of the organs, there be an entire, or a considerable uniformity of sentiment among men, we may thence derive an idea of the perfect and universal beauty; in like manner as the appearance of the objects in day-light to the eye of a man in health, is denominated their true and real colour, even while colour is allowed to be merely a phantasm of the senses.

There are many and frequent defects, our Author tells us, in the internal organs, which prevent, or weaken the influence of those general principles, on which depends our sentiment of beauty or deformity. And one obvious cause, why many feel not the proper sentiment of beauty, is the want of that *delicacy* of imagination, which every one talks of, and every one pretends to. Now as Mr. Hume's design in this dissertation, is to mingle some light of the understanding with the feelings of sentiment, he endeavours to give a more accurate definition of delicacy, than has hitherto been attempted.

'Though it be certain,' says he,

'that beauty and deformity, no more than sweet and bitter, are not qualities in objects, but belong entirely to the sentiment, internal or external; it must be allowed, that there are certain qualities in objects, which are fitted by nature to produce those particular feelings. Now as these qualities may be found in a small degree, or may be mixed and confounded with each other, it often happens, that the taste is not affected with such minute qualities, or is not able to distinguish all the particular flavours, amidst the disorder in which they are presented. Where the organs are so fine, as to allow nothing to escape them; and at the same time so exact as to perceive every ingredient in the composition: this we call delicacy of taste, whether we employ these terms in the natural or metaphorical sense. Here then the general rules of beauty are of use; being drawn from established models, and from the observation of what pleases or displeases, when presented singly and in a high degree: and if the same qualities, in a continued composition, and a smaller degree, affect not the organs with a sensible delight or uneasiness, we exclude the person from all pretensions to this delicacy.

It is acknowledged to be the perfection of every sense or faculty, to perceive with exactness its most minute objects, and allow nothing to escape its notice and observation. The smaller the objects are which become sensible to the eye, the finer is that organ, and the more elaborate its make and composition. A good palate is not tired by strong flavours; but by a mixture of small ingredients, where we are still sensible of each part, notwithstanding its minuteness and its confusion with the rest. In like manner, a quick and acute perception of beauty and deformity must be the perfection of our mental taste, nor can a man be satisfied with himself while he suspects, that any excellence, or blemish, in a discourse, has passed him unobserved. In this case, the perfection of the man, and the perfection of the sense, or feeling, are found to be united. A very delicate palate, on many occasions, may be a great inconvenience, both to a man himself, and to his friends; but a delicate taste of wit or beauty, must always be a desirable quality, because it is the source of all the finest and most innocent enjoyments, of which human nature is susceptible. In this decision, the sentiments of all mankind are agreed. Wherever you can fix or ascertain a delicacy of taste, it is sure to be approved of; and the best way of fixing it, is to appeal to those models and principles which have been established by the uniform approbation and experience of nations and ages.'

Mr. Hume goes on to observe, that nothing tends further to increase and improve this delicacy of taste, than practice in a particular art, and the frequent survey or contemplation of a particular species of beauty. When objects of any kind, are first presented to the eye, or imagination, the sentiment, he says, which attends them, is obscured and Confused: and the mind is, in a great measure, incapable of pronouncing concerning their merits or defects. The taste cannot perceive the several excellencies of the performance, much less distinguish the particular character of each excellency, and ascertain its quality and degree. If it pronounce the whole in general to be beautiful or deformed, it is the utmost which can be expected; and even this judgment, a person so unpractised will be apt to deliver with great hesitation and reserve. But allow him to acquire experience in those objects, his feeling becomes more exact and nice: he not only perceives the beauties and defects of each part, but marks the distinguishing species of each quality, and assigns it suitable praise or blame. A clear and distinct sentiment attends him through the whole survey of the objects, and he discerns that very degree and kind of approbation, or displeasure, which each part is naturally fitted to produce.

It is impossible, Mr. Hume observes, further, to continue in the practice of contemplating any order of beauty, without being frequently obliged to form *comparisons* between the several species and degrees of excellency, and estimating their proportion to each other. A man, he says, who has had no opportunity of comparing the different kinds of beauty, is totally unqualified to pronounce an opinion, with regard to any object presented to him; and he alone who has had opportunities of seeing, and examining and weighing the several performances, admired in different ages and nations, is capable of rating the merits of a work exhibited to his view, and assigning its proper rank among the productions of genius. But to enable him the better to perform this, he must preserve his mind free, we are told, from all prejudice, and allow nothing to enter into his consideration, but the very object which is submitted to his examination.

'When any work is addressed to the Public,' says Mr. Hume,

'though I should have a friendship or enmity with the Author, I must depart from this particular situation; and considering myself as a man in general, forget, if possible, any individual Being, and my peculiar circumstances. A person influenced by prejudice, complies not with this condition; but obstinately maintains his natural position, without entering into that required by the performance. If the work be addressed to persons of a different age or nation, he makes no allowance for their peculiar views and prejudices; but, full of the manners of his own times, rashly condemns what seemed admirable in the eyes of those for whom alone the discourse was calculated. If the work be executed for the Public, he never sufficiently enlarges his comprehension, or forgets his interests as a friend or enemy, as a rival or commentator. By this means his sentiments are perverted; nor have the same beauties and blemishes the same influence upon him, as if he had imposed a proper violence on his imagination, and had forgot himself for a moment. So far his taste evidently departs from the true standard, and of consequence loses all credit and authority.'

As in all questions submitted to the understanding, prejudice is destructive of sound judgment, and perverts all operations of the intellectual faculties, it is no less contrary, Mr. Hume observes, to good taste; nor has it less influence to corrupt our sentiments of beauty. It belongs to *good sense*, he says, to check its influence in both cases; and in this respect, as well as in many others, reason, if not an essential part of taste, is at least requisite to the operations of it.

Thus, we are told, though the principles of taste be universal, and nearly, if not entirely, the same in all men; yet few are qualified to give judgment on any work of art, or establish their own sentiment as the standard of beauty. When the critic has no delicacy, he judges without any distinction, and is only affected by the grosser and more palbable qualities of the object: the finer touches pass unnoticed and disregarded. Where he is not aided by practice, his verdict is attended with confusion and hesitation. Where no comparison has been employed, the most frivolous beauties, such as rather merit the name of defects, are the objects of his admiration. Where he lies under the influence of prejudice, all his natural sentiments are perverted. Where good sense is wanting, he is not qualified to discern the beauties of design and reasoning, which are the highest and most excellent. Under some or other of these imperfections, the generality of men labour; and hence a true judge in the finer arts is observed, even during the most polished ages, to be so rare a character: strong sense united to delicate sentiment, improved by practice, perfected by comparison, and cleared of all prejudice, can alone entitle critics to this valuable character; and the joint verdict of such, wherever they are to be found, is the true standard of taste and beauty.

But notwithstanding our Author's endeavours to fix a standard of taste, and reconcile the various apprehensions of men, there still remain two sources of variation; which, though they be not sufficient to confound all the boundaries of beauty and deformity, will often serve, he says, to vary the degrees of our approbation or blame. The one is the different humours of particular men; the other, the particular manners and opinions of our age and country. The general principles of taste are uniform in human nature: where men vary in their judgments, some defect or perverseness in the faculties may commonly be remarked; proceeding either from prejudice, from want of practice, or want of delicacy; and there is just reason for approving one taste, and condemning another. But where there is such a diversity in the internal frame, or external situation, as is entirely blameless on both sides, and leaves no room to give one the preference above the other, in that case, a certain diversity of judgment is unavoidable, and we seek in vain for a standard, by which we can reconcile the contrary sentiments.

There are many other pertinent reflections, and pretty illustrations, in this ingenious Dissertation, besides those we have mentioned; but we must refer the curious Reader, who is desirous of further satisfaction, to the work itself.

14
THE CRITICAL REVIEW

Review of *Four Dissertations*, in *The Critical Review*, February 1757, Vol. 3, pp. 97–107, March, pp. 209–216.
Complete review.

The review of *Four Dissertations* in the *Critical Review* was generally unfavourable and consists largely of quotations. The first instalment of the two-part review covers the "Natural History of Religion". The reviewer warns the reader to view this work cautiously and "separate the truth of what is advanced from the manner of delivering it". He concludes noting that the "Natural History" lacks the novelty and force of argument that one would expect from Hume. The author also criticises the logical flow of the dissertation: "A deficiency in our author's arrangement of his notions, and a want of method and connection is also visible throughout the whole, occasioned perhaps by some castration of the original." It is noteworthy that shortly after this review Hume wrote to his publisher addressing the issue of the arrangement of the "Natural History":

I find it has been often objected to My natural History of Religion, that it wants order. That I may obviate that Objection, I am resolv'd to prefix the enclosd Contents to it, if the Volume be not yet finish'd, which I hope it is not. These are the Titles of the several Sections. I shoud likewise desire, that the Title of each Section be prefixd to the Section. This will help the Reader to see the Scope of the Discourse. If you make a whole Leaf of a Title Page to the Natural History, the Summary of the Contents may be printed on it: If you do not, it may be printed at the End of the natural History. [Hume to William Strahan, May 25, 1757]

Regarding "Of the Passions", the reviewer questions the originality of Hume's theory: "there need [be] no Mr. *Hume*, the great philosopher, to acquaint us with discoveries made so long ago, and so often repeated. This whole dissertation, to say the truth, appears to us very trite and superficial; and unworthy of so eminent a writer. But no authors are always equal to themselves." Regarding "Of Tragedy", the reviewer expresses disappointment: "Instead of an essay on the construction of several parts of the drama which we expected, we meet only with a cold philosophical enquiry." The reviewer is also disappointed with "Of the Standard of

Taste": "instead of fixing and ascertaining the standard of taste as we expected, our author only leaves us in the same uncertainty as he found us." Nevertheless, the reviewer concludes, that the final essay is the best of the four.

ARTICLE I.

Four Dissertations. 1. *The Natural History of Religion.* 2. *Of the Passions.* 3. *Of Tragedy.* 4. *Of the Standard of Taste.* By David Hume; *Esq;* 12*mo. Pr.* 3*s.* Millar.

The ingenious Mr. *Hume*, already so well known to the learned world by his four volumes of essays, and the history of *Great Britain*, hath once more excited the attention of the public by the dissertations now before us, which are addressed in a short but spirited and well-written dedication to his friend the Rev. Mr. *Hume*, author of[239] *Douglas* a tragedy.

The first dissertation seems, like an elder brother, to have swallowed up the patrimony of all the rest, it being at least as long as the other three; which may, perhaps, be easily accounted for from our author's partiality to his favourite topic. It contains the natural history of religion, and though apparently written with a greater degree of cautious circumspection than we expected, sufficiently discovers that sceptical dissent from received opinions; and paradoxical singularity for which this gentleman hath been so highly blamed by some, and so much admired by others. Concerning this, however, we shall leave our readers to judge, after premising, that authors of such acknowledged and distinguished abilities as Mr. *Hume*, are always to be read with care and caution, more especially on subjects of this nature, because wherever there is a power to please and to persuade, there is also a power to mislead and to betray: it will become us, therefore to be upon our guard, to separate the truth of what is advanced from the manner of delivering it, and not so far to stretch our complaisance to any writer, as from an admiration of his stile, to adopt his principles, and imbibe his sentiments on every occasion.

Mr. *Hume* observes in his introduction, that the belief of invisible, intelligent power has been very generally diffused over the human race, in all places and in all ages; but it has neither perhaps been so universal as to

---

[239] This tragedy has lately been acted at *Edinburgh* to crouded audiences with universal applause: Our author, Mr. *David Hume*, calls it in his dedication one of the most interesting and pathetic pieces that was ever exhibited on any theatre; gives it the preference to the *Merope* of *Maffei* and *Voltaire*, and is of opinion, that the writer of it possesses the true theatric genius of *Shakespear* and *Otway*, refined from the unhappy barbarism of the one, and licentiousness of the other.

admit of no exceptions, nor has it been, in any degree, uniform in the ideas, which it has suggested. Some nations have been discovered, who entertained no sentiments of religion, if travellers and historians may be credited; and no two nations, and scarce any two men, have ever agreed precisely in the same sentiments. It would appear, therefore, that this preconception springs not from an original instinct or primary impression of nature, such as gives rise to self-love, affection betwixt the sexes, love of progeny, gratitude, resentment; since every instinct of this kind has been found absolutely universal in all nations and ages, and has always a precise, determinate object, which it inflexibly pursues. The first religious principles must be secondary; such as may easily be perverted by various accidents and causes, and whose operation too, in some cases, may, by an extraordinary concurrence of circumstances, be altogether prevented.

He then proceeds to enquire what those principles are which give rise to the original belief, and what those accidents and causes are which direct its operation.

Polytheism or idolatry (*says he*) was and necessarily must have been the first and most ancient religion of mankind, which appears from the clear testimony of history, which represents polytheism as the popular and established system; and to suppose that in more ancient time, that is to say, farther back than history can reach, men entertained the principles of pure theism, is highly absurd; because it is to assert, that while they were ignorant and barbarous they discovered truth, but fell into error as soon as they acquired learning and politeness. We may as reasonably imagine, that men inhabited palaces before huts and cottages, or studied geometry before agriculture; as assert that the deity appeared to them a pure spirit, omniscient, omnipotent, and omnipresent, before he was apprehended to be a powerful, though limited being, with human passions and appetites, limbs and organs. The mind rises gradually, from inferior to superior: By abstracting from what is imperfect, it forms an idea of perfection: And slowly distinguishing the nobler parts of its frame from the grosser, it learns to transfer only the former, much elevated and refined, to its divinity.

Besides that, if men were at first led into the belief of one supreme being, by reasoning from the frame of nature, they could never possibly leave that belief, in order to embrace idolatry; but the same principles of reasoning, which at first produced, and diffused over mankind, so magnificent an opinion; must be able, with greater facility, to preserve it.

It is impossible then that theism could, from reasoning, have been the primary religion of human race, and have afterwards, by its corruption, given birth to idolatry and to all the various superstitions of the heathen world. Reason, when very obvious, prevents these corruptions: When abstruse, it keeps the principles entirely from the knowledge of the vulgar, who are alone liable to corrupt any principles, or opinions.

If we would, therefore, indulge our curiosity, in enquiring concerning the origin of religion, we must turn our thoughts towards idolatry or polytheism, the primitive religion of uninstructed mankind.

Now in all nations which have embraced polytheism or idolatry, the first ideas of religion arose not from a contemplation of the works of nature, but from a concern with regard to the events[240] of life, and from the incessant hopes and fears, which actuate the human mind. Accordingly, we find, that all idolaters, having separated the provinces of their deities, have recourse to that invisible agent, to whose authority they are immediately subjected, and whose province it is to superintend that course of actions, in which they are, at any time, engaged. *Juno* is invoked at marriages; *Lucina* at births. Agitated by hopes and fears of this nature, especially the latter, men scrutinize, with a trembling curiosity, the course of future causes, and examine the various and contrary events of human life. And in this disordered scene, with eyes still more disordered and astonished, they see the first obscure traces of divinity. All[241] human life, especially before the institution of order and good government, being subject to fortuitous accidents; it is natural, that superstition should prevail every where in barbarous ages, and put men on the most earnest enquiry concerning those invisible powers, who dispose of their happiness or misery.

Hence every place was stored with a croud of local deities, and thus idolatry has prevailed, and still prevails among the greatest part of uninstructed mankind.

---

[240] The conduct of events (*says* Mr. Hume p. 12.) or what we call the plan of a particular providence, is so full of variety and uncertainty, that, if we suppose it immediately ordered by any intelligent beings, we must acknowledge a contrariety in their designs and intentions, a constant combat of opposite powers, and a repentance or change of intention in the same power, from impotence or levity.

This assertion of Mr. *Hume's* it will become our divines to take into their consideration.

[241] The following observations (p. 21. of the dissertations) is founded on truth and experience:

'If we examine our own hearts or observe what passes around us, (*says* Mr. Hume) we shall find, that men are much oftener thrown on their knees by the melancholy than by the agreeable passions. Prosperity is easily received as our due, and few questions are asked concerning its cause or author. It engenders cheerfulness and activity and alacrity and a lively enjoyment of every social and sensual pleasure: And during this state of mind, men have little leisure or inclination to think of the unknown, invisible regions. On the other hand, every disastrous accident alarms us, and sets us on enquiries concerning the principles whence it arose: Apprehensions spring up with regard to futurity: And the mind, sunk into diffidence, terror, and melancholy, has recourse to every method of appeasing those secret, intelligent powers, on whom our fortune is supposed entirely to depend.

The only point of theology, in which we shall find a consent of mankind almost universal, is, that there is invisible, intelligent power in the world: but whether this power be supreme or subordinate, whether confined to one being or distributed amongst several, what attributes, qualities, connexions or principles of action ought to be ascribed to those beings; concerning all these points, there is the widest difference in the popular systems of theology.

Our author then ridicules what but to mention is indeed sufficiently to expose, the ancient mythology, so full of absurdity and contradiction; and observes, in regard to the heathen deities, that to ascribe the origin and fabric of the universe to these imperfect beings never enter'd into the imagination of the polytheists and idolaters of former ages, who seem throughout to have rather embraced the idea of generation than that of creation or formation, and to have thence accounted for the origin of the universe. So far was it indeed from being esteemed profane in those days to account for the origin of things without a deity, that *Thales, Anaximenes, Heraclitus*, and others, who embraced that system of cosmogony, past unquestioned; while *Anaxagoras*, the first and undoubted theist among the philosophers, was perhaps the first that ever was accused of atheism.

The common people were never likely to derive from reasoning their systems of religion; when philologers and mythologists, we see, scarce ever discovered so much penetration. And even the philosophers, who discoursed of such topics, readily assented to the grossest theory, and admitted the joint origin of gods and men from night and chaos; from fire, water, air, or whatever they established to be the ruling elements.

Our author then endeavours to trace the various appearances of the polytheism and idolatry of the vulgar in the principles of human nature, whence they are derived. He observes on this head, that the polytheist never learns by argument the existence of invisible intelligent power, or from the contrivance of nature's objects deduces a divine being, but without ever admitting any such idea deifies every part of the universe, his attention rests on visible and sensible objects; hence arose allegories physical and moral. The same principles did also naturally deify mortals, superior in power, courage, or understanding, and produce hero-worship; along with fabulous history and mythological tradition, in all its wild and unaccountable forms.

The doctrine, notwithstanding, of one supreme deity, the author of nature, is very ancient, has spread itself over great and populous nations, and among them has been embraced by all ranks and conditions of persons: But whoever thinks that it has owed its success to the prevalent force of those invincible reasons, on which it is undoubtedly founded, would show himself little acquainted with the ignorance and stupidity of the people, and their incurable prejudices in favour of their particular superstitions.

We may conclude, therefore, that since the vulgar, in nations, which have embraced the doctrine of theism, still build it upon irrational and superstitious opinions, they are never led into that opinion by any process of argument, but by a certain train of thinking, more suitable to their genius and capacity.

It appears certain, that, though the original notions of the vulgar represent the Divinity as a very limited being, and consider him only as the particular cause of health or sickness; plenty or want; prosperity or adversity; yet when more magnificent ideas are urged upon them, they esteem it dangerous to refuse their assent. But the assent of the vulgar is, in this case, merely verbal, and that they are incapable of conceiving those sublime qualities, which they seemingly attribute to the deity. Their real idea of him, notwithstanding their pompous language, is still as poor and frivolous as ever.

Who can express the perfections of the Almighty, say the *Mahometans?* Even the noblest of his works, if compared to him, are but dust and rubbish. How much more must human conception fall short of his infinite perfections? His smile and favour renders men for ever happy; and to obtain it for your children, the best method is to cut off from them, while infants, a little bit of skin, about half the breadth of a farthing. Take two bits of cloath, say the *Roman catholics*, about an inch or an inch and a half square, join them by the corners with two strings or pieces of tape about sixteen inches long, throw this over your head, and make one of the bits of cloth lie upon your breast, and the other upon your back, keeping them next your skin: There is not a better secret for recommending yourself to that infinite Being who exists from eternity to eternity.

It is remarkable, that the principles of religion have a kind of flux and reflux in the human mind, and that men have a natural tendency to rise from idolatry to theism, and to sink again from theism into idolatry.

The feeble apprehensions of men cannot be satisfied with conceiving their deity as a pure spirit and perfect intelligence; and yet their natural terrors keep them from imputing to him the least shadow of limitation and imperfection. They fluctuate betwixt these opposite sentiments. The same infirmity still drags them downwards, from an omnipotent and spiritual deity to a limited and corporeal one, and from a corporeal and limited deity to a statue or visible representation. The same endeavour at elevation still pushes them upwards, from the statue or material image to the invisible power, and from an invisible power to an infinitely perfect deity, the creator and sovereign of the universe.

Polytheism is liable to this inconvenience, that any practice or opinion, however barbarous or corrupted, may be authorised by it. But then it has its peculiar advantages also, that by limiting the powers and functions of its duties, it admits the gods of other sects and nations to a share of divinity, and renders the various deities, rites, ceremonies and traditions compatible with each other. Whilst on the other hand, theism is attended with this disadvantage, viz. that whilst one sole object of devotion is acknowledged, the worship of other deities is regarded as absurd and impious. Nay, this unity of object seems naturally to require the unity of faith and ceremonies, and furnishes designing men with a pretext for representing their adversaries as prophane, and the subjects of divine as well as human vengeance. For as each sect is positive, that its own faith and worship are entirely acceptable to the deity, and as no one can conceive, that the same being should be pleased with different and opposite rites and principles; the several sects fall naturally into animosity, and mutually discharge on each other that sacred zeal and rancour, the most furious and implacable of all human passions.

The intolerance of almost all religions, which have maintained the unity of God, is as remarkable as the contrary principle in polytheists. The implacable, narrow spirit of the *Jews* is well known. Mahometanism set out with still more bloody principles; and even to this day, deals out damnation, tho' not fire and faggot to all other sects. And if, amongst christians, the *English* and *Dutch* have embraced the principles of toleration, this singularity has proceeded from the steddy resolution of the civil magistrate, in opposition to the continued efforts of priests and bigots.

I may venture to affirm, that few corruptions of idolatry and polytheism are more pernicious to political society than this corruption of theism, when carried to the utmost height. The human sacrifices of the *Carthaginians*, *Mexicans*, and many barbarous nations, scarce exceed the inquisition and persecutions of *Rome* and *Madrid*. For besides, that the effusion of blood may not be so great in the former case as in the latter; besides this, I say, the human victims, being chosen by lot or by some exterior signs, affect not, in so considerable a degree, the rest of the society. Whereas virtue, knowledge, love of liberty, are the qualities, which call down the fatal vengeance of inquisitors; and when expelled, leave the society in the most shameful ignorance, corruption, and bondage. The illegal murder of one man by a tyrant is more pernicious than the death of a thousand by pestilence, famine, or any undistinguishing calamity.

Where the deity is represented as infinitely superior to mankind, this belief, tho' altogether just, is apt, when joined with superstitious terrors, to sink the human mind into the lowest submission and abasement, and to represent the monkish virtues of mortification, pentance, humility and passive suffering, as the only qualities, which are acceptable to him. But where the gods are conceived to be only a little superior to mankind, and to have been, many of them, advanced from that inferior rank, we are more at our ease in our addresses to them, and may even, without profaneness, aspire sometimes to a rivalship and emulation of them. Hence activity, spirit, courage, magnanimity, love of liberty, and all the virtues, which aggrandize a people. But the corruption of the[242] best things always beget the worst.

Mr. *Hume's* remark (p. 83) bears perhaps a little too hard on the orthodox, and devotee.

'We may observe (*says he*) that notwithstanding the dogmatical imperious style of all superstition, the conviction of the religionists, in all ages, is more affected than real, and scarce ever approaches, in any degree, to that solid belief and persuasion, which governs us in the common affairs of life. Men dare not avow, even to their own hearts, the doubts, which they entertain on such subjects: they make a merit of implicite faith; and disguise to themselves their real infidelity, by the strongest asseverations and most positive bigotry. But nature is too hard for all their endeavours, and suffers not the obscure, glimmering light, afforded in those shadowy regions, to equal the strong impressions, made by common sense and by experience. The usual course of mens conduct belies their words, and shows, that the assent in these matters is some unaccountable operation of the mind betwixt disbelief and conviction, but approaching much nearer the former than the latter.'

Mr. *Hume* in this place, after some severe strokes of ridicule on antient and modern superstition, proceeds to assert, that the primary religion of mankind must have arisen from an anxious fear of future events; but at the same time observes, that whilst our natural terrors present the notion of a devilish and malicious deity, our propensity to praise leads us to acknowledge an excellent and divine. And the influence of these opposite principles is various, according to the different situation of the human

---

[242] Mr. *Hume* in expatiating on the absurdity of some doctrines of our brethren the *catholics*, among other anecdotes, gives us the following:

'A famous general, at that time in the *Muscovite* service, having come to *Paris* for the recovery of his wounds, brought along with him a young *Turk*, whom he had taken prisoner. Some of the doctors of the *Sorbonne* (who are altogether as positive as the dervises of *Constantinople*) thinking it a pity, that the poor *Turk* should be damned for want of instruction, solicited *Mustapha* very hard to turn christian, and promised him; for his encouragement, plenty of good wine in this world, and paradise in the next. These allurements were too powerful to be resisted; and therefore, having been well instructed and catechized, he at last agreed to receive the sacraments of baptism and the Lord's supper. The priest, however, to make every thing sure and solid, still continued his instructions; and began his catechism next day with the usual question, *How many Gods are there? None at all*, replies *Benedict*; for that was his new name. *How! None at all!* cries the priest. *To be sure* said the honest proselyte. *You have told me all along that there is but one God: and yesterday I eat him.*'

understanding. Hence therefore is a kind of contradiction betwixt the different principles of human nature which enter into religion.

Lucian observes, that a young man, who reads the history of the gods in *Homer* or *Hesiod*, and finds their factions, wars, injustice, incest, adultery, and other immoralities so highly celebrated, is much surprised afterwards, when he comes into the world, to observe, that punishments are by law inflicted on the same actions, which he had been taught to ascribe to superior beings. The contradiction is still perhaps stronger betwixt the representations given us by some latter religions and our natural ideas of generosity, lenity, impartiality, and justice; and in proportion to the multiplied terrors of these religions, the barbarous conceptions of the divinity are multiplied upon us.

It is certain, that, in every religion, however sublime the verbal definition, which it gives of its divinity, many of the votaries, perhaps the greatest number, will still seek the divine favour, not by virtue and good morals, which alone can be acceptable to a perfect being, but either by frivolous observance, by intemperate zeal, by rapturous extasies, or by the belief of mysterious and absurd opinions.

Nay, if we should suppose, what seldom happens, that a popular religion were found, in which it was expressly declared, that nothing but morality could gain the divine favour; if an order of priests were instituted to inculcate this opinion, in daily sermons, and with all the arts of persuasion; yet so inveterate are the people's prejudices, that for want of some other superstition, they would make the very attendance on these sermons the essentials of religion, rather than place them in virtue and good morals.

This universal bias in human nature towards superstition and enthusiasm, in preference to plain morality, Mr. *Hume* endeavours to account for, by observing, that the duties, which a man performs as a friend or parent, seem merely owing to his benefactor or children; nor can he be wanting to these duties, without breaking thro all the ties of nature and morality. A strong inclination may prompt him to the performance: a sentiment of order and moral beauty joins its force to these natural tyes: and the whole man, if truly virtuous, is drawn to his duty, without any effort or endeavour. Even with regard to the virtues, which are more austere, and more founded on reflection, such as public spirit, filial duty, temperance, or integrity; the moral obligation, in our apprehension, removes all pretence to religious merit; and the virtuous conduct is esteemed no more than what we owe to society and to ourselves. In all this, a superstitious man finds nothing, which he has properly performed for the sake of his deity, or which can peculiarly recommend him to the divine favour and protection. He considers not, that the most genuine method of serving the divinity is by promoting the happiness of his creatures. He still looks out for some more immediate service of the supreme being, in order to ally those terrors, with which he is haunted. And any practice recommended to him, which either serves to no purpose in life, or offers the strongest violence to his natural inclinations; that practice he will the more readily embrace, on account of those very circumstances, which should make him absolutely reject it. It seems the more purely religious, that it proceeds from no mixture of any other motive or consideration. And if, for its sake, he sacrifices much of his ease and quiet, his claim of merit appears still to rise upon him, in proportion to the zeal and devotion, which he discovers. In restoring a loan, or paying a debt, his divinity, is no way beholden to him; because these acts of justice are what he was bound to perform, and what many would have performed, were there no god in the universe. But if he fast a day, or give himself a sound whipping; this has a direct reference, in his opinion, to the service of God. No other motive could engage him to such austerities. By these distinguished marks of devotion, he has now acquired the divine favour; and may expect, in recompence, protection and safety in this world, and eternal happiness in the next.

To which we may add, that, even after the commission of crimes, there arise remorses and secret horrors, which give no rest to the mind, but make it have recourse to religious rites and ceremonies, as expiations of its offences. Whatever weakens or disorders the internal frame promotes the interests of superstition.

And while we abandon ourselves to the natural, undisciplined suggestions of our timid and anxious hearts, every kind of barbarity is ascribed to the supreme being, from the terrors, with which we are agitated; and every kind of caprice, from the methods which we embrace, in order to appease him.

The truth of this observation is evident: it has indeed been made before, but perhaps never better express'd than by our author. What follows carries also with it an equal degree of conviction.

'The universal propensity (*says Mr. Hume*) to believe in invisible, intelligent power, if not an original instinct, being at least a general attendant of human nature, it may be considered as a kind of mark or stamp, which the divine workman has set upon his work; and nothing surely can more dignify mankind, than to be thus selected from all the other parts of the creation, and to bear the image or impression of the universal Creator. But consult this image, as it commonly appears in the popular religions of the world. How is the deity disfigured in the representation of him! What caprice, absurdity, and immorality are attributed to him! How much is he degraded even below the character which we should naturally, in common life, ascribe to a man of sense and virtue! What a noble privilege is it of human reason to attain the knowledge of the supreme being; and, from the visible works of nature, be enabled to infer so sublime a principle as its supreme Creator? But turn the reverse of the medal. Survey most nations and most ages. Examine the religious principles, which have, in fact, prevailed in the world. You will scarcely be persuaded, that they are other than sick mens dreams: or perhaps will regard them more as the playsome whimsies of monkeys in human shape, than the serious, positive, dogmatical asseverations of a being, who dignifies himself with the name of rational.'

The first dissertation concludes thus:

'The whole (*meaning, we are afraid, the whole of religion*) is a riddle, an ænigma, an inexplicable mystery. Doubt, uncertainty, suspense of judgment appear the only result of our most accurate scrutiny, concerning this subject. But such is the frailty of human reason, and such the irresistible contagion of opinion, that even this deliberate doubt could scarce be upheld; did we not enlarge our view, and opposing one species of superstition to another, set them a quarreling; while we ourselves, during their fury and contention, happily make our escape, into the calm, though obscure, regions of philosophy.'

Such are the sentiments of the ingenious Mr. *Hume*, as delivered to us in what he calls his *Natural History of Religion*, in which tho' the stile is animated, nervous, and correct throughout, and many of the remarks pertinent and just, we do not meet with that novelty, or force of argument which we expected from an author of such distinguished abilities: Nor can we indeed perceive *quo tendit*, to what use or purpose this dissertation was written. A deficiency in our author's arrangement of his notions, and a want of method and connection is also visible throughout the whole, occasioned perhaps by some castration of the original.

[To be continued.]

ART. II. *Mr.* Hume's *Dissertations continued.*

Mr. *Hume's* second dissertation treats of the passions, and was written, (as we are informed by himself at the conclusion of it,) with a design to prove, that 'in the production and conduct of the passions there is a certain regular mechanism, which is susceptible of as accurate a disquisition, as the laws of motion, optics, hydrostatics, or any part of natural philosophy;' an assertion which our readers will perhaps consider as rather paradoxical, and call upon Mr. *Hume* for much more convincing proofs than any he has produced in the essay before us, which in our opinion contains nothing new or entertaining on the occasion. The following, however, may serve as a specimen of our author's method of treating this subject.

'None of the passions (*says he*) seem to contain any thing curious or remarkable, except *Hope* and *Fear*, which, being derived from the probability of any good or evil, are mixed passions, that merit our attention.

Probability arises from an opposition of contrary chances or causes, by which the mind is not allowed to fix on either side; but is incessantly toss'd from one to another, and in one moment is determin'd to consider an object as existent, and in another moment as the contrary. The imagination or understanding, call it which you please, fluctuates betwixt the opposite views; and tho' perhaps it may be oftener turned to one side than the other, it is impossible for it, by reason of the opposition of causes or chances, to rest on either. The *pro* and *con* of the question alternately prevail; and the mind, surveying the objects in their opposite causes, finds such a contrariety as utterly destroys all certainty or established opinion.

Suppose, then, that the object, concerning which we are doubtful, produces either desire or aversion; it is evident, that, according as the mind turns itself to one side or the other, it must feel a momentary impression of joy or sorrow. An object, whose existence we desire, gives satisfaction, when we think of those causes which produce it; and for the same reason, excites grief or uneasiness from the opposite consideration. So that, as the understanding, in probable questions, is divided betwixt the contrary points of view, the heart must in the same manner be divided betwixt opposite emotions.

Now, if we consider the human mind, we shall observe, that, with regard to the passions, it is not like a wind-instrument of music, which in running over all the notes, immediately loses the sound when the breath ceases; but rather resembles a strong-instrument, where, after each stroke, the vibrations still retain some sound, which gradually and insensibly decays. The imagination is extremely quick and agile; but the passions, in comparison, are slow and restive: for which reason, when any object is presented, which affords a variety of views to the one and emotions to the other; tho' the fancy may change its views with great celerity; each stroke will not produce a clear and distinct note of passion, but the one passion will always be mixt and confounded with the other. According as the probability inclines to good or evil, the passion of grief or joy predominates in the composition; and these passions, being intermingled by means of the contrary views of the imagination, produce by the union the passions of hope or fear.

The passions of fear and hope may arise, when the chances are equal on both sides, and no superiority can be discovered in one above the other. Nay, in this situation the passions are rather the strongest, as the mind has then the least foundation to rest upon, and is tost with the greatest uncertainty. Throw in a superior degree of probability to the side of grief, you immediately see that passion diffuse itself over the composition, and tincture it into fear. Increase the probability, and by that means the grief; the fear prevails still more and more, till at last it runs insensibly, as the joy continually diminishes, into pure grief. After you have brought it to this situation, diminish the grief, by a contrary operation to that, which increased it, to wit, by diminishing the probability on the melancholy side; and you will see the passion clear every moment, till it changes insensibly into hope; which again runs, by slow degrees, into joy, as you increase that part of the composition, by the increase of the probability. Are not these as plain proofs, that the passions of fear and hope are mixtures of grief and joy, as in optics it is a proof, that a coloured ray of the sun, passing through a prism, is a composition of two others, when, as you diminish or increase the quantity of either, you find it prevail proportionably, more or less, in the composition?

In order to explain the causes of these passions, we must reflect on certain properties, which, tho' they have a mighty influence on every operation, both of the understanding and passions, are not commonly much insisted on by philosophers. The first of these is the association of ideas, or that principle, by which we make an easy transition from one idea to another.

The second property which I shall observe in the human mind, is a like association of impressions or emotions. All resembling impressions are connected together; and no sooner one arises than the rest naturally follow.

In the third place, it is observeable of these two kinds of association, that they very much assist and forward each other, and that the transition is more easily made, where they both concur in the same object.

Pain and pleasure, if not the sources of moral distinctions, are at least inseparable from them. A generous and noble character affords a satisfaction even in the survey; and when presented to us, tho' only in a poem or a fable, never fails to charm and delight us. On the other hand, cruelty and treachery displease from their very nature; nor is it possible ever to reconcile us to these qualities, either in ourselves or others. Virtue, therefore, produces always a pleasure distinct from the pride or self-satisfaction, which attends it: vice, an uneasiness separate from the humility and remorse.'

Mr. *Hume* then considers the nature and causes of pride and humility, and observes that the feeling or sentiment of pride is agreeable; of humility painful. An agreeable sensation is, therefore, related to the former; a painful, to the latter. And if we find, after examination, that every object, which produces pride, produces also a separate pleasure; and every object, that causes humility, excites in like manner a separate uneasiness; we must allow, in that case, that the present theory is fully proved and ascertained. The double relation of ideas and sentiments will be acknowledged incontestible.

Our author is pretty diffuse in his discussion of this point. What he says of the vain man has more of truth than novelty in it: "Every thing (*says he*) belonging to a vain man, is the best that is any where to be found. His houses, equipage, furniture, cloaths, horses, hounds, excel all others in his conceit; and it is easy to observe, that, from the least advantage in any of these, he draws a new subject of pride and vanity. His wine, if you will believe him, has a finer flavor than any other; his cookery is more exquisite; his table more orderly; his servants more expert; the air, in which he lives, more healthful; the soil, which he cultivates, more fertile; his fruits ripen earlier, and in greater perfection: such a thing is remarkable for its novelty; such another for its antiquity: this is the workmanship of a famous artist; that belonged once to such a prince or great man. All objects, in a word, which are useful, beautiful, or surprizing, or are related to such, may, by means of property, give rise to this passion. These all agree in giving pleasure. This alone is common to them; and therefore must be the quality that produces the passion, which is their common effect.

The following sentiments which seem to be laboriously drawn forth into corollaries, have nothing new or striking to recommend them, *viz.*

'When esteem is obtained after a long and intimate acquaintance, it gratifies our vanity in a peculiar manner.

The suffrage of those, who are shy and backward in giving praise, is attended with an additional relish and enjoyment, if we can obtain it in our favour.

Where a great man is nice in his choice of favourites, every one courts with greater earnestness his countenance and protection.

Praise never gives us much pleasure, unless it concur with our own opinion, and extol us for those qualities, in which we chiefly excel.

All objects appear great or little, merely by a comparison with those of the same species. A mountain neither magnifies nor diminishes a horse in our eyes: but when a *Flemish* and a *Welch* horse are seen together, the one appears greater and the other less, than when viewed apart.

What is distant, either in place or time, has not equal influence with what is near and contiguous.'

There need no ghost (*says* Shakespear) to tell us this: and surely there need no Mr. *Hume*, the great philosopher, to acquaint us with discoveries made so long ago, and so often repeated. This whole dissertation, to say the truth, appears to us very trite and superficial; and unworthy of so eminent a writer. But no authors are always equal to themselves;

> *Neque semper arcum*
> *Tendit Apollo.*

The title of Mr. *Hume's* third dissertation, *of Tragedy*, flatter'd us with the hopes of much pleasure and instruction, and when we had, as it were, prepared our appetites for one dish, we were a little disappointed at being obliged to sit down to another. Instead of an essay on the construction of several parts of the drama which we expected, we meet only with a cold philosophical enquiry into the cause of that 'unaccountable pleasure which the spectators of a well wrote tragedy receive from sorrow, terror, anxiety, and other passions which are in themselves disagreeable and uneasy.' For this Mr. *Hume* endeavours to account on the principles of the celebrated[243] *Fontenelle*, who observes, that in regard to tragedy, whatever dominion the senses and imagination may usurp over the reason, there still lurks at the bottom a certain idea of falshood in the whole of what we see. This idea, tho' weak and disguised, suffices to diminish the pain which we suffer from the misfortunes of those whom we love, and to reduce that affliction to such a pitch as converts it into a pleasure. We weep for the misfortune of a hero, to whom we are attached: in the same instant we comfort ourselves, by reflecting, that it is nothing but a fiction: and it is precisely that mixture of sentiments, which composes an agreeable sorrow and tears that delight us. To which Mr. *Hume* would add the force of eloquence, and remarks, that the impulse or vehemence, arising from sorrow, compassion, indignation, receives a new direction from the sentiments of beauty. The latter, being the predominant emotions, seize the whole mind, and convert the former into themselves, or at least tincture them so strongly as totally to alter their nature: and the soul, being at the same time roused by passion, and charmed by eloquence, feels on the whole a strong movement, which is altogether delightful.

Now the same principle (*says he*) takes place in tragedy, with this addition, that tragedy is imitation, which is always agreeable. The force of imagination, the energy of expression, the power of numbers, the charms of imitation; all these are naturally, of themselves, delightful to the mind; and when the object presented lays also hold of some affection, the pleasure still rises upon us, by the conversion of this subordinate movement, into

[243] In his reflections sur la Poetique.

that which is predominant. The passion, tho', perhaps, naturally, when excited by the simple appearance of a real object, it may be painful; yet is it smoothed, and softened, and mollified, when raised by the finer arts, that it affords the highest entertainment.

Mr. *Hume's* fourth dissertation *of the standard of Taste*, disappointed us almost as much as his third; for instead of fixing and ascertaining the standard of taste as we expected, our author only leaves us in the same uncertainty as he found us: and concludes with the philosopher of old, that all we know is, that we know nothing.

> 'Though the principles of taste (*says* Mr. Hume) be universal, and nearly, if not entirely the same in all men; yet few are qualified to give judgment on any work of art, or establish their own sentiment as the standard of beauty. The organs of internal sensation are seldom so perfect as to allow the general principles their full play, and produce a feeling correspondent to those principles. They either labour under some defect, or are vitiated by some disorder; and by that means excite a sentiment, which may be pronounced erroneous.
>
> Where then are true critics to be found? By what marks are they to be known? How distinguish them from pretenders? These questions are embarrassing; and seem to throw us back into the same uncertainty, from which, during the course of this dissertation, we have endeavoured to extricate ourselves.
>
> Where there is such a diversity in the internal frame or external situation as is entirely blameless on both sides, and leaves no room to give one the preference above the other; in that case a certain diversity of judgment is unavoidable, and we seek in vain for a standard, by which we can reconcile the contrary sentiments.'

Though Mr. *Hume* in this little essay hath not absolutely pointed out to us the true standard of taste, he has shewn not only that he knows what a delicate taste is, but that he is himself possessed of it. This short dissertation is indeed in our opinion much the best of the four, and contains some observations which we imagine will be agreeable to our readers, of which the following specimen may sufficiently convince them:

> 'One obvious cause (*says* Mr. Hume) why men feel not the proper sentiment of beauty, is the want of that delicacy of imagination, which is requisite to convey a sensibility of those finer emotions. This delicacy every one pretends to: every one talks of it; and would reduce every kind of taste or sentiment to its standard. But as our intention in this dissertation is to mingle some light of the understanding with the feelings of sentiment, it will be proper to give a more accurate definition of delicacy,

than has hitherto been attempted. And not to draw our philosophy from too profound a source, we shall have recourse to a noted story in *Don Quixote.*

'Tis with good reason, says *Sancho* to the squire with the great nose, that I pretend to have a judgment in wine: this is a quality hereditary in our family. Two of my kinsmen were once called to give their opinion of a hogshead, which was supposed to be excellent, being old and of a good vintage. One of them tastes it; considers it, and after mature reflection pronounces the wine to be good, were it not for a small taste of leather, which he perceived in it. The other, after using the same precautions, gives also his verdict in favour of the wine; but with the reserve of a taste of iron, which he could easily distinguish. You cannot imagine how much they were both ridiculed for their judgment. But who laugh'd in the end? On emptying the hogshead, there was found at the bottom an old key with a leather thong tied to it.

The great resemblance between mental and bodily taste will easily teach us to apply this story. Though it be certain, that beauty and deformity, no more than sweet and bitter, are not qualities in objects, but belong entirely to the sentiment, internal or external; it must be allowed, that there are certain qualities in objects, which are fitted by nature to produce those particular feelings. Now as these qualities may be found in a small degree or may be mixt and confounded with each other, it often happens, that the taste is not affected with such minute qualities, or is not able to distinguish all the particular flavours, amidst the disorder, in which they are presented. Where the organs are so fine, as to allow nothing to escape them; and at the same time so exact as to perceive every ingredient in the composition; this we call delicacy of taste, whether we employ these terms in the natural or metaphorical sense. Here then the general rules of beauty are of use; being drawn from established models, and from the observation of what pleases or displeases, when presented singly and in a high degree: and if the same qualities, in a continued composition and in a smaller degree, affect not the organs with a sensible delight or uneasiness, we exclude the person from all pretensions to this delicacy. To produce these general rules or avowed patterns of composition is like finding the key with the leathern thong; which justified the verdict of *Sancho's* kinsmen, and confounded those pretended judges, who had condemned them. Though the hogshead had never been emptied, the taste of the one was still equally delicate, and that of the other equally dull and languid: But it would have been more difficult to have proved the superiority of the former, to the conviction of every by-stander. In like manner, though the beauties of writing had never been methodized, or reduced to general principles; though no excellent models had ever been acknowledged; the different degrees of taste would still have subsisted, and the judgment of one man been preferable to that of another; but it would not have been so easy to silence the bad critic, who might always insist upon his particular sentiment, and refuse to submit to his antagonist. But when we shew him an avowed principle of art; when we illustrate this principle by examples, whose operation, from his own particular taste, he acknowledges to be conformable to the principle; when we prove, that the same principle may be applied to the present case, where he did not perceive nor feel its influence; he must conclude, upon the whole, that the fault lies in himself, and that he wants the delicacy, which is requisite to make him sensible of every beauty and every blemish, in any composition or discourse.'

A little further on he observes that practice is so advantageous to the discernment of beauty, that before we can pronounce judgment on any work of importance, it will even be requisite, that that very individual performance be more than once perused by us, and surveyed in different lights, with attention and deliberation. There is a flutter or hurry in thought, which attends the first perusal of any piece, and which confounds the genuine sentiment of beauty. The reference of the parts is not discerned: the true characters of style are little distinguished: the several perfections and defects seem wrapped up in a species of confusion, and present themselves indistinctly to the imagination. Not to mention, that there is a species of beauty, which, as it is florid and superficial, pleases at first; but being found incompatible with a just expression either of reason or passion, soon palls upon the taste, and is then rejected with disdain, at least rated at a much lower value.

What Mr. *Hume* has remark'd concerning prejudice and partiality, concerning the difference of taste at different periods of life, with several other occasional reflections adapted to his subject, contribute to make this dissertation entertaining and instructive.

We shall close this article with an extract from the latter part of our author's book which may be useful in examining the celebrated controversy concerning antient and modern learning;

'We often find (*says* Mr. Hume) one side excusing any seeming absurdity in the ancients from the manners of the age, and the others refusing to admit this excuse, or at least, admitting it only as an apology for the author, not for the performance. In my opinion, the proper bounds in this subject have seldom been fixed between the contending parties. Where any innocent peculiarities of manners are represented, such as those above mentioned, they ought certainly to be admitted; and a man who is shocked with them, gives an evident proof of false delicacy and refinement. The poet's *monument more durable than brass*, must fall to the ground like common brick or clay, were men to make no allowance for the continual revolutions of manners and customs, and would admit nothing but what was suitable to the prevailing fashion. Must we throw aside the pictures of our ancestors, because of their ruffs and fardingales? But where the ideas of morality and decency alter from one age to another, and where vicious manners are described, without being marked with the proper characters of blame and disapprobation; this must be allowed to disfigure the poem, and to be a real deformity. I cannot, nor is it proper I should, enter into such sentiments; and however I may excuse the poet, on account of the manners of his age, I never can relish the composition. The want of humanity and of decency, so conspicuous in the characters drawn by several of the ancient poets, even sometimes by *Homer* and the *Greek* tragedians, diminishes considerably the merit of their noble performances, and gives modern authors a great advantage over them. We are not interested in the fortune and sentiments of such rough heroes: we are displeased to find the limits of vice and virtue so confounded: and whatever indulgence we may give the writer on account of his prejudices, we cannot prevail on ourselves to enter into his sentiments, or bear an affection to characters, which we plainly discover to be blameable.'

15

THE LITERARY MAGAZINE: OR UNIVERSAL REVIEW

Review of *Four Dissertations*, in *The Literary Magazine: or Universal Review*, December 1757, Vol. 2, pp. 32–36.
Complete review.

The short-lived *Literary Magazine* was founded in 1756 by Samuel Johnson, and concluded publication in 1758. Although stating that "the literary world is greatly indebted to Mr. *Hume*" particularly for his originality, the reviewer is disappointed with the lack of novelty in both the "Natural History of Religion" and "Of the Passions". Regarding the former, he wishes that Hume used his talents to serve the cause of religion since, by exposing religion as a delusion, Hume risks introducing anarchy and confusion. Regarding "Of the Passions", the reviewer comments that "as in the former case, we do not perceive any thing new. This we should not mention if we were not talking of an author fond of novelty." Continuing with the fourth dissertation "Of the Standard of Taste", the reviewer notes "In one respect we were greatly disappointed: we expected that a writer of his philosophic turn and close way of thinking, would have endeavoured at settling some fixed and immutable standard, instead of subscribing to the proverb, that there is no disputing about tastes."

Four Dissertations by DAVID HUME, *Esq; printed for* A. Millar. *12 mo. 3s.*

The public curiosity will no doubt be greatly excited by these essays, from a gentleman who has before contributed both to their pleasure and instruction. The first of Mr. *Hume's* Dissertations is called, *The natural History of Religion*, in which he deduces the rise and progress of it. It must be observed that this Author, upon other occasions new and singular, and generally so with propriety, has in this discourse offer'd few or no positions, that are not to be found in other writers on this subject. That Polytheism was the natural religion of the unenlighted heathen world, it is very certain, and has often been advanced. Without attending to the connection between causes and their effects, and without considering that a superior all-intelligent mind might impress various laws of motion upon universal nature, untutored minds created deities to preside over the different modes of existence, nay, and their passions, their hopes and fears have further peopled the skies with visionary Gods, that had a supposed power of conferring the good or inflicting the evil, which they desired or wished to be averted from them. The history of these operations of the mind, Mr. *Hume* has exhibited in a very probable light. It was, however to be wished, that his talents had been employed on all occasions to serve the cause of religion, for two reasons; First, because if he were so much in the secret as to know us all to be under a delusion, it is *mentis gratissimus error*, and to undeceive us certainly would introduce anarchy and confusion. Secondly, because the Christian Religion inculcates such a scheme of Benevolence and Virtue, as cannot fail of being comfortable to us as individuals, and to render us more acceptable to each other as social beings.

The second essay is on the passions, in which, as in the former case, we do not perceive any thing new. This we should not mention if we were not talking of an author fond of novelty. He has, however, treated his subject in a clear and perspicuous manner; his stile is elegant, and, excepting that now and then the idiom of his country mixes insensibly with his language, it may for the most part boast of purity. As a specimen of his philosophy and stile, the reader is desired to take the following extract. After describing the single passions he adds:

'None of these passions seem to contain any thing curious or remarkable, except *hope* and *fear*, which being derived from the probability of doing good or evil, are mixt passions that merit our attention.

Probability arises from an opposition of contrary chances or causes, by which the mind is not allowed to fix on either side; but is incessantly tost from one to another, and in one moment is determined to consider an object as existent, and in another moment as the contrary. The imagination or understanding, call it as you please, fluctuates betwixt the opposite views; and tho' perhaps it may be oftener turned to one side than the other, it is impossible for it, by reason of the opposition of causes or chances to rest on either. The *pro* and *con* of the question alternately prevail; and the mind, surveying the objects in their opposite causes, finds such a contrariety as utterly destroys all certainty or established opinion.

Suppose, then, that the object, concerning which we are doubtful produces either desire or aversion; it is evident, that, according as the mind turns itself to one side or the other, it must feel a momentary impression of joy or sorrow. An object, whose existence we desire, gives satisfaction, when we think of those causes, which produce it; and for the same reason, excites grief or uneasiness, from the opposite consideration. So that, as the understanding, in probable questions, is divided betwixt the contrary points of view, the heart must in the same manner be divided betwixt opposite emotions.

Now, if we consider the human mind, we shall observe, that, with regard to the passions, it is not like a wind-instrument, of music, which, in running over all the notes, immediately loses the sound when the breath ceases; but rather resembles a string-instrument, where, after each stroke, the vibrations still retain some sound, which gradually and insensibly decays. The imagination is extremely quick and agile; but the passions, in comparison, are slow and restive: For which reason, when any object is presented, which affords a variety of views to the one, and emotions to the other; tho' the fancy may change its views with great celerity; each stroke will not produce a clear and distinct note of passion, but the one passion will always be mixt and confounded with the other. According as the probability inclines to good or evil, the passion of grief or joy predominates in the composition; and these passions, being intermingled by means of the contrary views of the imagination, produce by union the passions of hope or fear.'

Our author proceeds afterwards to the compound passions, which he accounts for in the following manner:

'In order to explain the causes of these passions, we must reflect on certain properties, which, tho' they have a mighty influence on every operation, both of the understanding and passions, are not commonly much insisted on by philosophers. The first of these is the *association* of ideas, or that principle, by which we make an easy transition from one idea to another. However uncertain and changable our thoughts may be, they are not entirely without rule and method in their changes. They usually pass with regularity from one object, to what resembles it, is contiguous to it, or produced by it.[244] When one idea is present to the imagination; any other, united by these relations, naturally follows it, and enters with more facility, by means of that introduction.

The *second* property, which I shall observe in the human mind, is a like association of impressions or emotions. All *resembling* impressions are connected together, and no sooner one arises, than the rest naturally follow. Grief and disappointment give rise to anger, anger to envy, envy to malice, and malice to grief again. In like manner our temper, when elevated with joy, naturally throws itself into love, generosity, courage, pride, and other resembling affections.

---

[244] See philosophical Essays. Essay iii.

In the *third* place, it is observable of these two kinds of association, that they very much assist and forward each other, and that the transition is more easily made, where they both concur in the same object. Thus, a man, who by any injury from another, is very much discomposed and ruffled in his temper, is apt to find a hundred subjects of hatred, discontent, impatience, fear, and other uneasy passions; especially, if he can discover these subjects in or near the person, who was the object of his first emotion. Those principles, which forward the transition of ideas, here occur with those, which operate on the passions; and both, uniting in one action, bestow on the mind a double impulse.'

In this Mr. *Hume* has agreeably reflected images with which we have been already conversant: there is one new position in this Dissertation, which appears somewhat surprising from one, who in general seems to think with precision.

'No one, says he, has ever been able to tell precisely, what *wit* is, and to shew why such a system of thought must be received under that denomination, and such another rejected. It is by taste alone we can decide concerning it; nor are we possest of any other standard, by which we can form a judgment of this nature. Now what is this *taste*, from which true and false wit in a manner receive their being, and without which no thought can have a title to either of these denominations? It is plainly nothing but a sensation of pleasure from true wit, and of disgust from false, without our being able to tell the reasons of that satisfaction or uneasiness. The power of exciting these opposite sensations is, therefore, the very essence of true or false wit; and consequently the cause of that vanity or mortification, which arises from one or the other.'

We thought Wit had been long since very justly defined, a similitude unexpectedly pointed out between two objects not apparently resembling each other, in such a manner as to give new lights to the subject, and excite the agreeable sensations of surprise. If this definition is just, as it certainly is, judgment and not taste is to decide it, tho' we allow that the gratifications of taste will greatly heighten it. As to the reasons of our satisfaction or uneasiness when wit is offer'd, we imagined *Bahours* had given us an excellent rule, which is, that no thought can be beautiful that is not true; and truth of the reverse of it, will always be agreeable or disgustful to the human mind. The rest of this Essay presents us different examples to enforce the above doctrine of the passions.

The third dissertation on Tragedy does not concern itself with rules for the mechanism of the drama, but enquires into the reasons why grief, terror, pity, and other sensations in themselves uneasy, should give us pleasure. This he accounts for upon principles that have been already subscribed to by many elegant *English* writers. His account of this matter stands as follows:

> 'It is certain, that the same object of distress which pleases in a tragedy, were it really set before us, would give the most unfeigned uneasiness, tho' it be the most effectual cure of languor and indolence. Monsieur *Fontenelle* seems to have been sensible to this difficulty; and accordingly attempts another solution of the phænomenon; at least, makes some addition to the theory abovementioned.
>
> "Pleasure and pain," says he, "which are two sentiments so different in themselves, differ not so much in their cause. From the instance of tickling, it appears, that the movement of pleasure pushed a little too far, becomes pain; and that the movement of pain, a little moderated, becomes pleasure. Hence it proceeds, that there is such a thing as a sorrow, soft and agreeable: it is a pain weakened and diminished. The heart likes naturally to be moved and affected. Melancholy objects suit it, and even disastrous and sorrowful, provided they are softened by some circumstance. It is certain, that on the theatre the representation has almost the effect of reality; but yet it has not altogether that effect. However we may be hurried away by the spectacle; whatever dominion the senses and imagination may usurp over the reason, there still lurks at the bottom a certain idea of falshood in the whole of what we see. This idea, tho' weak and disguised, suffices to diminish the pain which we suffer from the misfortunes of those whom we love, and to reduce that affliction to such a pitch as converts it into a pleasure. We weep for this misfortune of a hero, to whom we are attached: In the same instant we comfort ourselves, by reflecting, that it is nothing but a fiction: and it is precisely, that mixture of sentiments, which composes an agreeable sorrow, and produces tears that delight us. But as that affliction, which is caused by exterior and sensile objects, is stronger than the consolation, which arises from an internal reflection, they are the effects and symptoms of sorrow which ought to prevail in the composition." '

What the author adds from himself is very beautiful,

> 'All the passions, excited by eloquence, are agreeable in the highest degree, as well as those which are moved by painting and the theatre. The epilogues of *Cicero* are, on this account chiefly, the delight of every reader of taste; and it is difficult to read some of them without the deepest sympathy and sorrow. His merit, as an orator, no doubt, depends much on his success in this particular. When he had raised tears in his judges and audience, they were then the most highly delighted, and

expressed the greatest satisfaction with the pleader. The pathetic description of the butchery made by *Verres* of the *Sicilian* captains is a master-piece of this kind: but I believe none will affirm, that the being present at a melancholy scene of that nature would afford any entertainment. Neither is the sorrow here softened by fiction: for the audience were convinced of the reality of every circumstance. What is it then, which in this case raises a pleasure from the bosom of uneasiness, so to speak; and a pleasure, which still retains all the features and outward symptoms of distress and sorrow?

I answer: This extraordinary effect proceeds from that very eloquence, with which the melancholy scene is represented. The genius required to paint objects in a lively manner, the art employed in collecting all the pathetic circumstances, the judgment displayed in disposing them; the exercise, I say, of these noble talents, along with the force of expression, and beauty of oratorial numbers, diffuse the highest satisfaction on the audience, and excite the most delightful movements. By this means, the uneasiness of the melancholy passions is not only overpowered and effaced by something stronger of an opposite kind; but the whole movement of those passions is converted into pleasure, and swells the delight which the eloquence raises in us.'

Mr. *Hume's* fourth essay concerning the standard of taste, is very elegant and entertaining. In one respect we were greatly disappointed; we expected that a writer of his philosophic turn and close way of thinking, would have endeavoured at settling some fixed and immutable standard, instead of subscribing to the proverb, that there is no disputing about tastes. If by taste he meant the ideas of beauty or deformity excited in our own minds by external objects, there certainly is no disputing about them, because duller or finer faculties will always make a considerable alteration. Mr. *Hume*, however, allows this common saying to be true under many restrictions: if the dispute should be concerning the merit of *Ogleby* and *Milton*, *Bunyan* and *Addison*, they who should prefer the former, he allows, might be justly pronounced to have a bad taste. But where the comparison is between objects nearer to an equality, he leaves it undetermined. Surely a Criterion of beauty might be established to decide between objects that approximate as well as those that are widely distant: fixed principles of right and wrong, we should think, may be settled in literature as well as religion; as all poetry is imitation, the question should be whether the imitation is true, and if it is, he has a bad taste that does not feel it. Concerning the different degrees of fineness in our perceptions Mr. *Hume* has a very pleasing passage, which I shall here transcribe, the more especially as I think he reasons more closely here than in any other part of his Essay.

'One obvious cause, why many feel not the proper sentiment of beauty, is the want of that *delicacy* of imagination, which is requisite to convey a sensibility of those finer emotions. This delicacy every one pretends to: every one talks of it; and would reduce every kind of taste or sentiment to its standard. But as our intention in this dissertation is to mingle some light of the understanding with the feelings of sentiment, it will be proper to give a more accurate definition of delicacy, than has hitherto been attempted. And, not to draw our philosophy from too profound a source, we shall have recourse to a noted story in *Don Quixote.*

'Tis with good reason, says *Sancho* to the squire with a great nose, that pretend to have a judgment in wine: this is a quality hereditary in our family. Two of my kinsmen were once called to give their opinion of a hogshead, which was supposed to be excellent, being old and of a good vintage. One of them tastes it; considers it, and after mature reflection pronounces the wine to be good, were it not for a small taste of leather, which he perceived in it. The other, after using the same precautions, gives also his verdict in favour of the wine; but with the reserve of a taste of iron, which he could easily distinguish. You cannot imagine how much they were both ridiculed for their judgment. But who laughed in the end? On emptying the hogshead, there was found at the bottom, an old key with a leathern thong tied to it.

The great resemblance between mental and bodily taste will easily teach us to apply this story. Though it be certain that beauty and deformity, no more than sweet and bitter, are not qualities in objects, but belong entirely to the sentiment internal or external; it must be allowed, that there are certain qualities in objects, which are fitted by nature to produce those particular feelings. Now as these qualities may be found in a small degree, or may be mixt and confounded with each other, it often happens, that the taste is not affected with such minute qualities, or is not able to distinguish all the particular flavours, amidst the disorder, in which they are presented. Where the organs are so fine, as to allow nothing to escape them; and at the same time so exact as to perceive every ingredient in the composition: this we call delicacy of taste, whether we employ these terms in the natural or metaphorical sense. Here then the general rules of beauty are of use; being drawn from established models, and from the observation of what pleases or displeases, when presented singly and in a high degree: and if the same qualities, in a continued composition and in a smaller degree, affect not the organs with a sensible delight or uneasiness, we exclude the person from all pretensions to this delicacy. To produce these general rules, or avowed patterns of composition, is like finding the key with the leathern thong; which justified the verdict of *Sancho's* kinsmen, and confounded those pretended judges, who had condemned them. Though the hogshead had never been emptied, the taste of the one was still equally delicate, and that of the other equally dull and languid: But it would have been more difficult to have proved the superiority of the former, to the conviction of every by-stander. In like manner, though the beauties of writing had never been methodized, or reduced to general principles; though no excellent models had ever been acknowledged; the different degrees of taste would still have subsisted, and the judgment of one man been preferable to that of another; but it would not have been so easy to silence the bad critic, who might always insist upon his particular sentiment, and refuse to submit to his antagonist. But when we show him an avowed principle of art; when we illustrate this principle by examples, whose operation, from his own particular taste, he acknowledges to be conformable to the principle; when we prove that the same principle may be applied to the present case, where he did not perceive nor feel its influence: he must conclude, upon the whole, that the fault lies in himself, and that he wants the delicacy, which is requisite to make him sensible of every beauty and every blemish, in any composition or discourse.'

Upon the whole, the literary world is greatly indebted to Mr. *Hume*: he thinks more for himself than almost any of his contemporaries; and commonly with elegance and precision; insomuch that he bids very fair to be considered by posterity among the few classes of this age; notwithstanding his *Latitudinarian* sentiments in religious matters.
   – *Insanientis dum sapientiæ.*
   Consultus errat. –

16
CALEB FLEMING

[Caleb Fleming], *Three questions resolved. viz. what is religion? what is the Christian religion? what is the Christian catholic church? wherein popery is proved to have no claim, either as a religion, as the Christian religion, or as the Christian catholic-church. in three letters to — Esq. with a postscript on Mr. Hume's natural history of religion.* London, A Henderson, 1757, 3–56 p. Complete Postscript; from 1757 edition.

Caleb Fleming (1689–1779) was a dissenting minister whose views were anti-trinitarian and deistic. He was a prolific pamphleteer with over a hundred religious and political titles to his credit, most published anonymously. Fleming's *Three Questions Resolved* appeared anonymously in 1757. The complete title of the pamphlet, given above, summarizes its contents. In the Postcript, Fleming criticizes Hume's contention that religion is founded on principles of the imagination, as opposed to rational proofs for a single creator. He also criticizes Hume for identifying the history of superstition with that of true religion. Fleming concludes on a positive note, though, that, "Notwithstanding these sophisms, Mr. *Hume* has finely exposed superstition…and so far as he is a theist, he cannot be an enemy to genuine christianity". Writing for the *Monthly Review*, William Rose comments about the pamphlet that "We have here some just sentiments on religion in general, and on the Christian religion in particular, delivered with the utmost freedom" (*Monthly Review*, 1757, Vol. 16, pp. 470–472). The following is from the 1757 and only edition of *Three Questions Resolved*. The unusual punctuation and capitalization below are as appears in the original.

P.S. Mr. DAVID HUME, in *his natural history of religion*, allows its foundation in reason to be most obvious. "for no rational enquirer can, after serious reflexion, suspend his belief a moment with regard to the primary principles of genuine theism and religion." But then he thinks it more difficult to shew, "its origin in human nature."[245] on these principles he grounds his enquiry. But what can he mean by religion admitting the clearest solution, concerning the foundation it has in reason; yet, not so

[245] P. 1. [Pagination follows Hume's *Four Dissertations* (London, 1757).]

concerning its origin in human nature? may reason then be separated from human nature in the religion of mankind? is this possible? how shall it be done, when no rational enquirer can, after serious reflexion, suspend his belief one moment with regard to the primary principles of genuine theism and religion.

To secure his distinctions, "Polytheism or idolatry was, and necessarily must have been the first and most ancient religion of mankind. for, the most ancient records of the human race still present us with Polytheism as the popular and established system."[246] Does it not seem more natural to conclude, that from the creation mankind clearly saw the invisible things of God? but that when they knew God, they glorified him not as God, became wanton in their imaginations, and so corrupted the primary principles of pure theism. If the history of *Moses* be authentic, men degenerated from true theism to idolatry; and by their debaucheries brought on the destructive deluge. The primary religion of the new world, peopled by *Noah* and his family, surely could not be polytheism and idolatry. And certain we are, superstition, polytheism or idolatry could not be the primary profession of christians. especially since Mr. H. has said, "nothing indeed would prove more strongly the divine origin of any religion, than to find, (and happily this is the case with christianity) that it is free from a contradiction, so incident to human nature."[247] – Whatever was his design, this is the true character of genuine christianity, untouched by the over-officious fingers of men. and to which, this elegant writer seems much indebted for that charming description of theism, "a system which supposes one sole deity, the perfection of reason and goodness, which if justly prosecuted, will banish every thing frivolous, unreasonable, or inhuman from religious worship, and set before men the most illustrious example, as well as the most commanding motives of justice and benevolence."[248] It must be allowed a fine copy of the Gospel original; and could be taken from no other system.

This lively writer makes some very uncommon observations. "Men have a natural tendency to rise from idolatry to theism, and to sink again from theism into idolatry." and he concludes, "that religion and idolatry have one and the same origin." See his 8th section.

But in his 10th, "the corruption of the best things give rise to the worst."[249] – Of this we have some conception. not so of theism and polytheism having one origin. nor of the natural tendency in men to rise

---

[246] P. 3.

[247] P. 50.

[248] P. 59

[249] Also p. 63. *Corruptio optimi pessima.*

from idolatry to theism. and we should be inclined to ask some proof, how it comes to pass, that in this natural tendency to both extremes, we see not the mechanical vibrations of the pendulum equal, or nearly equal? how can we read over Mr. HUME'S *natural history of religion*, and give him credit, if this observation has any truth in it? why such an universal polytheism, if there be this natural tendency in man to rise from idolatry to theism?[250]

There is another discovery made by this Philosopher, and that is, "the origin of idolatry or polytheism, is, the active imagination of men, incessantly imployed, in cloathing the conception they have of objects, in shapes more suitable to its natural comprehensions."[251] which if conclusive, then religion and idolatry, theism and polytheism are equally natural to man; and have alike a very fanciful origination. –

But in truth, his idea of the religion of mankind, does not intend more, than the superstition which has arisen from depravity. for, sais he, "one may safely affirm, that all popular theology, especially the scholastic, has a kind of appetite for absurdity and contradiction. If that theology went not beyond reason and common sense, her doctrines would appear too easy and familiar. amazement must of necessity be raised: mystery affected: darkness and obscurity sought after: and a foundation of merit afforded the devout votaries, who desire an opportunity of subduing their rebellious reason, by the belief of the most unintelligible sophism."[252] Is not this *Sir*, a fair specimen of what he means by the religion of mankind? But could this be the first and most ancient religion of mankind? does he not explicitely own it could not?[253] "In short, all virtue, when men are reconciled to it by ever so little practice, is agreeable: all superstition is for ever odious and burthensome."[254] – and again, "after the commission of crimes, there arise remorses and secret horrors, which give no rest to the mind, but make it have recourse to religious rites and ceremonies, as expiations of its offences. Whatever weakens or disorders the internal frame, promotes the interests of superstition: and nothing is more destructive to them than a manly, steady virtue, which either preserves us from disastrous, melancholy accidents, or teaches us to bear them. During such calm sun-shine of the mind, these spectres of false divinity never make their appearance. On the other hand, while we *abandon our selves* to the undisciplined suggestions of our timid and anxious hearts, every kind of barbarity is ascribed to the supreme Being, from the terror with which we are agitated; and every kind

---

[250] Also p. 63. *Corruptio optimi pessima.*

[251] P. 55.

[252] P. 70.

[253] P. 55.

[254] P. 106.

of caprice, from the methods which we embrace, in order to appease him."[255]

I would not mistake this writer, and therefore produce another of his descriptions of the popular religions; in which he is very express in shewing, that these superstitions have not their origin in human nature. "And that it may safely be affirmed, many popular religions are really, in the conception of these more vulgar votaries, a spirit of Dæmonism; and the higher the deity is exalted in power and knowledge, the lower of course is he frequently depress'd in goodness and benevolence; whatever epithets of praise may be bestowed on him by his amazed adorers. Amongst idolaters, the words may be false, and belie the secret opinions: but amongst more exalted religionists, the opinion itself often contracts a kind of falsehood, and belies *the inward sentiment. The heart secretly detests such measures of cruel and implacable vengeance*; but the judgment dares not but pronounce them perfect and adorable. *And the additional misery of this inward struggle* aggravates all the other terrors, by which these unhappy victims to superstition are for ever bounded."[256]

From this citation, I would ask, whether Mr. *Hume* has not acknowledged, that idolatry and superstition are not natural to man? and that consequently, the principles of genuine theism and religion, must have their origin in human nature. – Superstition, the gloomy dread of deity, is no primary principle in the heart of man.[257] The opinion belies the inward sentiment: there is a secret detestation of it in the heart!

I presume to make the following conclusions.

Mr. *Hume*'s fundamental principles are manifestly wrong. he has called the superstition of the world, *a natural history of the religion of mankind*. he has affirmed, a natural tendency in man to rise out of idolatry into religion. he has strangely declared, that religion and superstition, theism and polytheism have one and the same origin; and this no better than the imagination. – Whereas, religion and reason in man, are inseparable. Religion could not arise out of superstition, theism out of polytheism. The universal spread of idolatry, by his own history, as universally confronts the proposition: and will not suppose it to have the least foundation in nature. for superstition has its origin in the disordered passions and imaginations of mankind; religion has its origin in a natural sovereignty which the reason of man exercises over these faculties. And from the nature of the thing, idolatry or polytheism could not be the primary profession of mankind; but must have been a corruption of pure theism and religion.

---

[255] P. 109.

[256] P. 98.

[257] Though it is affirmed to be so in the 13th Proposition.

Notwithstanding these sophisms, Mr. *Hume* has finely exposed superstition and popery: professeth himself an advocate of pure theism. and so far as he is a theist, he cannot be an enemy to genuine christianity.

17
WILLIAM WARBURTON

[William Warburton, Richard Hurd], *Remarks on Mr. David Hume's Essay on the natural history of religion: addressed to the Rev. Dr. Warburton.* London: printed for M. Cooper, 1757, [4], 76 p. Complete pamphlet; from 1757 edition.[258]

William Warburton (1698–1779) is the author of the brief critique of Hume's "Of Miracles" included earlier in this volume. Warburton's dislike for Hume continued over the years, and he occasionally made attacks on Hume in his various publications and correspondence. Similar to his tangential attack on Hume in *Julian*, Warburton criticises Hume in a footnote to his 1751 edition of Pope's *Dunciad* in *The Works of Alexander Pope*. Specifically, Warburton inserts the following footnote to Pope's verse, "But, 'Learn, ye DUNCES! not to scorn your God'" (*Dunciad*, 3.224):

> The hardest lesson a *Dunce* can learn. For being bred to *scorn* what he does not understand, that which he understands least he will be apt to *scorn* most. Of which, to the disgrace of all Government, and (in the Poet's opinion) even of that of DULLNESS herself, we have had a late example in a book entitled, *Philosophical Essays concerning Human Understanding.*

Such comments by Warburton caught the attention of Ralph Griffiths in his 1751 review of Pope's *Works* in the *Monthly Review*:

> the sarcasms and lashes which our annotator [i.e., Warburton] has so freely interspersed and bestowed upon some living writers of no mean rank, might as well have been spared, or have been rather introduced elsewhere, and not forced into the works of an Author, who at least that we have heard of, has no quarrel with Mr. *Edwards*, Mr. *Upton*, or Mr. *Hume*. [*Monthly Review*, January 1751, Vol. 5, pp. 97–102]

[258] Title Page: REMARKS | ON | Mr. DAVID HUME'S Essay | ON THE | Natural History of Religion: | ADDRESSED TO | The Rev. Dr. WARBURTON. | "To wash away a few slight stains be mine; | "Charge him with Heaven's artillery, bold DIVINE. [Alexander Pope, *Satires of Dr. John Donne*, IV, v. 280–285 – JF] | LONDON. | Printed for M. COOPER, in Pater-noster-row. | MDCCLVII. | [Price One Shilling.]

Aware of Warburton's scattered attacks, Hume wrote in a letter "When I am abus'd by such a Fellow as Warburton, whom I neither know nor care for, I can laugh at him" (Hume to John Stewart, February, 1754).

Prior to the publication of *Four Dissertations,* Warburton had seen a proof or advance copy of the ill-fated *Five Dissertations.* In early 1757 he penned the following to Andrew Millar – who was both Hume's and Warburton's bookseller – warning Millar of the irreligious nature of the "Natural History of Religion":

> I supposed you would be glad to know what sort of book it is which you are about to publish with Hume's name and yours to it. The design of the first essay [i.e., the "Natural History of Religion"] is the very same with all Lord Bolingbroke's, to establish naturalism, a species of atheism, instead of religion... . You have often told me of this man's moral virtues. He may have many, for aught I know; but let me observe to you, there are vices of the mind as well as of the body; and I think a wickeder mind, and more obstinately bent on public mischief, I never knew. [Warburton to Andrew Millar, February 7, 1757; quoted in Thomas Grose's "History of the Editions", in *The Philosophical Works of David Hume,* 1874, vol. 3, p. 61]

When Hume's *Four Dissertations* appeared, Warburton wrote critical comments in the margin of his copy of it. In his biography of Warburton,[259] long time friend Richard Hurd (1720–1808) describes the transformation of these marginal notes into the pamphlet, *Remarks on Mr. David Hume's Essay on the Natural History of Religion:*

> This book [i.e., *Four Dissertations*] came out early in 1757, and falling into the hands of Dr. Warburton, provoked him, by its uncommon licentiousness, to enter on the margin, as he went along, such remarks as occurred to him. And when that was too narrow to contain them all, he put down the rest on loose scraps of paper, which he stuck between the leaves. In this state the book was shewn to me (as I chanced at that time to be in London with the author) merely as a matter of curiosity, and to give me an idea of the contents, how mischievous and extravagant they were. He had then written remarks on about two thirds of the volume: And I liked them so well, that I advised him, by all means, to carry them on through the remaining parts of it, and then to fit them up, in what way he thought best, for public use, which I told him they very

---

[259] Richard Hurd (1720–1808), *A discourse, by way of general preface to the quarto edition of Bishop Warburton's works, containing some account of the life, ... of the author.* London: printed by John Nichols, 1794, vii, [1], 150 p.

well deserved. He put by this proposal slightly; but, when I pressed him again on this head, some time after, in a letter from Cambridge, he wrote me the following answer.

Warburton's letter of response to which Hurd refers is this:

> As to Hume, I had laid it aside ever since you were here. I will now, however, finish my skeleton. It will be hardly that. If then you think anything can be made of it, and will give yourself the trouble, we may perhaps between us do a little good, which I dare say we shall both think will be worth a little pains. If I have any force in the first rude beating out the mass, you are best able to give it the elegance of form and splendour of polish. This will answer my purpose, to labour together in a joint work to do a little good. I will tell you fairly, it is no more the thing it should be, than the Dantzick iron at the forge is the gilt and painted ware at Birmingham. It will make no more than a pamphlet; but you shall take your own time, and make it your summer's amusement, if you will. I propose it bear something like this title – 'Remarks on Mr. Hume's late Essay, called, *The Natural History of Religion*, by a Gentleman of Cambridge, in a Letter to the Rev. Dr. Warburton.' – I propose the address should be with the dryness and reserve of a stranger, who likes the method of the Letters on Bolingbroke's philosophy, and follows it here, against the same sort of writer, inculcating the same impiety, Naturalism, and employing the same kind of arguments. The address will remove it from me; the author, a gentleman of Cambridge, from you; and the secrecy of printing, from us both.

Hurd continues noting how he transcribed Warburton's marginal notes into publishable form, and added an introduction:

> I saw by this letter, he was not disposed to take much trouble about the thing. Accordingly his papers were soon after sent down to me at Cambridge, pretty much in the state I had seen them in at London, so far as they then went, only with additional entries in the latter part of the book. However, in this careless detached form, I thought his observations too good to be lost. And the hint of the *Address* suggested the means of preserving them, without any injury to his reputation, and indeed without much labour to myself. Having, therefore, transcribed the Remarks, with little alteration, I only wrote a short introduction and conclusion, merely to colour the proposed fiction; and in this form, sent them to the press. [*A discourse, by way of general preface to the quarto edition of Bishop Warburton's Works* (1794)]

Accordingly, the pamphlet appeared anonymously in 1757, six months after Hume's *Four Dissertations*, disguised as a letter *to* Warburton by an unnamed admirer.

The pamphlet is a page-by-page attack on Hume's "Natural History of Religion" in 21 remarks, as summarized here. (1) Hume's title is nonsense, for religion is a moral subject, not a natural one. Hume's distinction between "foundation in reason" and "foundation in human nature" is also nonsense since human nature is rational. He really means foundation in the fancy (or passions). (2) Hume argues in his *History* that an historian should not record religion. Yet, he records the unflattering aspects of religion, and should therefore take account of the good aspects. (3) Hume appeals to other ancient histories, but ignores Moses who, even if not divinely inspired, deserves historical consideration. (4) Hume inconsistently holds that the universe is designed, yet there is natural disharmony which leads to fear. (5) Against "Of Miracles", Warburton argues that laws of nature cannot discredit miracles since the idea of a law of nature is central to a miracle. (6) It makes no sense that the vulgar would discover a first cause, but philosophers would invent demigods. (7) Hume's hidden purpose seems to be to discredit revelation. (8) The disadvantages from polytheism arise from its nature and essence, whereas the disadvantages of monotheism arise from the abuse of it. (9) Hume argues that intolerance arises from a unity of faith and ceremony (caused by a unity of religious objects). But a unity of ceremony is not a necessary condition of a unity of religious objects. (10) In section 8 polytheism and monotheism are virtually alike; yet, in section 9, they are virtually dissimilar. (11) Hume quotes Machiavelli on how Catholicism encouraged passivity, which inclined people toward slavery. But Machiavelli meant the Gospel, not Catholicism, and the Gospel encourages no such thing. Hume also unfairly conceals his attack on Christianity by arguing that Islam's monotheism has contradictions, but Christianity's does not. According to Warburton, Hume "would have been much mortified" if we missed his hidden point. (12) Hume shows his partiality by citing Varro's suggestion that even children wouldn't believe Christianity. Hume distorts Rutilius who attacks the Jews, not Christians. (13) Hume unfairly represents Cicero by not reconciling his private belief with his public disbelief. (14) Hume inconsistently concedes that Newton, Locke, and Clarke were sincere in their belief, but also argues that religious belief is more affected than real. Hume argues that Christians doubt as much as pagans, though Christians are more guarded in their expressions. But expressions are all the data we have upon which to base such a judgment. (15) Hume claims that paganism is more reasonable than Christianity. But his criteria of "reasonable" ("noncontradictory" and "sitting lightly") also apply to nonsense. Hume claims that pagans were benevolent, but ignores many counterinstances.

Hume misrepresents Ramsay's point, who really argues how some philosophers portray God. (16) Fear and love have a different role in religious belief than the one Hume suggests. (17) Hume inconsistently claims that the vulgar give the highest attributes to the gods, yet the Athenian mob did not. (18) Human nature suggests that we amplify goodness. Hume says we do not (in the context of the propensity to adulate). (19) Hume says that morality has no place in religious rites, yet he gives an example of one. (20) Hume states that nothing is more destructive to superstition than a "manly steady virtue"; however, the kind of virtue that Hume has in mind is only a hardened roguery. (21) Warburton concludes sarcastically, "I have given a specimen of his philosophic virtues, his reasoning, his consistency, his knowledge, his truth, his candour, and his modesty...".

Writing for the *Monthly Review*, William Rose presents an objective summary of the *Remarks*, and concludes with the following:

Such is the account our Author gives of his Remarks, which are written in a smart lively manner, pretty much in the spirit of Dr. Warburton; and are intended to point out the contradictions and inconsistencies that are to be met with in Mr. Hume's Essay. The religion which Mr. Hume means to recommend in his Natural History, our Remarker says, is *Naturalism*, or the belief of a Creator and physical Preserver, but not moral Governor. Of the truth of this every Reader of the Essay must be left to judge for himself. [*Monthly Review*, August 1757, Vol. 17, pp. 189–191]

The *Critical Review* also offered a neutral review of the *Remarks*, which consisted mainly of excerpts. Their substantive comments, which appear in the opening paragraph, are as follows:

This little Pamphlet of seventy-six pages contains some short, but severe strictures on Mr. David Hume, addressed to the learned Dr. Warburton, with whose works our author seems to be intimately acquainted. He hath therefore professedly copied that ingenious writer's turn of thinking and expression, which he has done, as the Italians say, *con amore*. Whether the copy is exact, or, to use the painter's phrase, is done after the doctor's best manner or not, our readers will be able to determine by the following specimen: [*Critical Review*, May 1757, Vol. 3, pp. 398–401]

In his biography of Warburton, Hurd describes Warburton's reaction to the pamphlet after it appeared:

When Dr. Warburton saw the pamphlet, he said, I should have done much more, and worked up his hasty remarks in my own way. He doubted, also, whether the contrivance, as I had managed it, would not be seen through. But in this he was mistaken; for the disguise, as thin as it was, answered its purpose in keeping the real author out of sight.

Hume apparently learned of Hurd's and perhaps Warburton's authorship from his printer, William Strahan, who also printed the *Remarks*. In a letter to Strahan Hume promises to keep the secret:[260]

> I am positive not to reply a single Word to Dr Hurd; and I also beg of you not to think of it. His Artifices or Forgeries, call them which you please, are such common things in all Controversy that man woud be ridiculous who woud pretend to complain of them; and the Parsons in particular have got a License to practice them. I therefore beg of you again to let the Matter pass over in Silence. I have deliverd to Mr Becket a Volume of Essays. [Hume to William Strahan, June 1757]

Shortly after, in a letter to his bookseller Andrew Millar, Hume indicates his belief that Warburton himself authored the remarks:

> Apropos to Anger, I am positively assurd, that Dr Warburton wrote that Letter to himself which you sent me; and indeed the Style discovers him sufficiently. I shou'd answer him; but he attacks so small a Corner of my Building, that I can abandon it without drawing great Consequences after it. If he woud come into the Field, and dispute concerning the principal Topics of my Philosophy, I shou'd probably accept the Challenge. At present, nothing coud tempt me to take the Pen in hand, but Anger, of which I feel myself incapable, even upon this Provocation. [Hume to Andrew Millar, September 3, 1757]

In his private correspondences over the next few years, Hume made jokes about Warburton, the most colourful of which is this:

---

[260] The review from *London Review* of Hume's *Life* criticizes Strahan arguing that "It is a little remarkable that the gentleman, to whose care this manuscript [i.e. the "Natural History"] was entrusted, should have ever carried his hand so even between *religion* and *infidelity*, as to have been made the instrument of ushering into the world, with equal approbation, the doctrines of *divine grace*, and the dogmas of *human nature*", 1777, Vol. V, p. 202.

As to private News; there is little stirring; Only Dr Warburton turnd Mahometan, & was circumcis'd last Week. They say, he is to write a Book, in order to prove the Divine Legation of Mahomet; and it is not doubted but he will succeed as well as in proving that of Moses. I saw him yesterday in the Mall with his Turban; which really becomes him very well. [Hume to William Rouet, July 6, 1759]

In spite of Hume's belief that Warburton authored the *Remarks*, Hume nevertheless identifies Hurd as the author in *My Own Life*:

In this interval, I published at London my Natural History of Religion, along with some other small pieces: its public entry was rather obscure, except only that Dr. Hurd wrote a pamphlet against it, with all the illiberal petulance, arrogance, and scurrility which distinguish the Warburtonian school. This pamphlet gave me some consolation for the otherwise indifferent reception of my performance. [*My Own Life*]

In his biography of Warburton, Hurd put his own somewhat incorrect spin on Hume's reaction to the *Remarks*:

Mr. Hume in particular (understanding, I suppose, from his bookseller, who was also mine, that the manuscript came from me) was the first to fall into the trap. He was much hurt, and no wonder, by so lively an attack upon him, and could not help confessing it in what he calls his *own Life*; in which he has thought fit to honour me with greater marks of his resentment, than any other of the writers against him: nay the spiteful man goes so far as to upbraid me with being a *follower* (indeed, a closer, in this instance, than he apprehended) *of the Warburtonian school.*

In 1777, shortly after Hume's death, the *Remarks* were published again, with only minor changes in spelling and punctuation, probably introduced by the printer. The 1777 edition contains the following preface:

The bookseller to the reader: The following is supposed to be the Pamphlet referred to by the late Mr. David Hume, in Page 21, of his Life, *as being written by* Dr. Hurd. Upon my applying to the Bishop of Litchfield and Coventry for his permission to republish it, he very readily gave me his consent. His Lordship only added, he was sorry he could not take to himself the *whole* infamy of the charge brought against him; but that he should hereafter, if he thought it worth his while, explain himself more particularly on that subject. Strand, March, 1777. T. Cadell. [*Remarks... a new edition.* London: T. Cadell, 1777]

Warburton died in 1779, and in 1788 the first edition of his collected works appeared, which included the *Remarks* in Volume 7.[261] The 1788 edition retains the printer's alterations from the 1777 edition and introduces further changes, both major and minor. In 1794 Hurd published his belated biography *Discourse, by Way of General Preface* to this edition of Warburton's *Works* (quotations from which are presented above). There Hurd openly explains his own role in the *Remarks*,[262] and notes that the 1788 edition presents the *Remarks* "in their original form", presumably as appeared in Warburton's marginal comments. Comparison of the 1757 and 1788 editions indicates that Hurd's literary contribution to the piece was mainly in writing the opening address and conclusion. He also added to the body a few paragraphs and transitional sentences. The 1811 and 1848 editions of Warburton's *Works* follow the 1788 edition. In the text below I have followed the 1757 edition, which includes Hurd's contributions. Major changes that appear in the 1788 edition are given in footnotes.

---

[261] *The works of the Right Reverend William Warburton....* London: J. Nichols, 1788, 7 Vol. The *Analytical Review* comments on the collection in general that "it is plain from the publication itself, that the edition before us (which consists only of two hundred and fifty copies) was designed as a splendid monument to the memory of Warburton, rather than a work of public utility", Vol. 4, 1789, pp. 183–187.

[262] The *Analytical Review* comments on Hurd's account of the *Remarks* that "we learn nothing more from it, than what was before known, (excepting that Dr. Balguy does not appear to have had any hand in it)..." (1795, Vol. 21, p. 599). The *Critical Review* comments that "Those who are curious to see what share each writer had in this production, may satisfy themselves by comparing the pamphlet with the Remarks themselves, inserted in the sixth volume of Warburton's works" (August 1795, Vol. 14, p. 407).

REMARKS

O N

Mr. DAVID HUME's Eſſay

O N T H E

Natural Hiſtory of Religion:

ADDRESSED TO

The Rev. Dr. WARBURTON.

" To waſh away a few ſlight ſtains be mine;
" Charge him with Heaven's artillery, bold DIVINE.

L O N D O N.

Printed for M. COOPER, in Pater-noſter-row.

MDCCLVII.

[Price One Shilling.]

TO
The Rev. Dr. WARBURTON.[263]

REV. SIR,

I take leave to address myself to you as to the supposed Author of the FOUR LETTERS *on Lord Bolingbroke's Philosophy*.[264] Under this character, if indeed it belongs to you, you seem to have a right to the following Remarks; which are, in truth, little more than your own Remarks, only transferred from your Patrician, to this Plebeian Naturalist.

Permit me to say, that you have unmasked and for ever discredited the philosophical lucubrations of that unhappy Nobleman; who, in times that demanded the mere Politician to assist in impressing the belief of a moral Governor on the minds of men, was so forsaken of every patriot principle as to labour with all his might to exclude the Creator from his Works, and by the doctrine of an impious fatalism to emancipate an abandoned people from the FEAR OF GOD.

It became the eminence of your character to go forth against this bold invader of Heaven. Your conquest was complete. And what could one expect as the fruit of it, but that, this chieftain of Impiety being subdued, the rabble of the enemy would disperse and fly before you; at least that they would not rally again, till in future times some other Champion of their cause, as illustrious by his name and quality, should arise to reconduct them to the charge.

But, alas! the irreligious Spirit, tho' it may be disgraced, is not so easily suppressed. E'er the public had time to celebrate your triumphs, behold a puny Dialectician from the North, (for as Erasmus long since observed, *Scoti* DIALECTICIS ARGUTIIS *sibi blandiuntur*),[265] all over armed with doubts and disputation, steps forth into his place; and, with the same beggarly troop of routed sophisms, comes again to the attack.

---

[263] [In the 1788 edition the entire opening address is omitted, and begins directly with Remark I.]

[264] [Henry St. John Viscount Bolingbroke (1678–1751), controversial English Tory statesman whose philosophical writings appeared posthumously in five volumes from 1754 to 1777. In 1754–5 Warburton published in three installments *A View of Lord Bolingbroke's Philosophy* (London: J. and P. Knapton). Hume's philosophy was often associated with that of Bolingbroke. For example, an anthology titled *The Beauties of Hume and Bolingbroke* (London, 1782) presented in one volume selections from both authors, and opened with an essay comparing the two.]

[265] ["The Scots flatter (or delude) themselves with dialectical subtleties," *Praise of Folly*, LB IV 448B.]

But now, as the enemy is so contemptible, and the danger so little pressing, you may well enjoy your repose, and leave it to some inferior hand to chastise his insolence. And the very weakest may be equal to this attempt. For nothing remains but to employ against him the weapons which you have furnished; in a word, to draw again that sword of the spirit, which you had borrowed from the Sanctuary, and whose resistless splendour flashes, if not conviction, yet confusion in every face.

To this office I presume to devote myself. I have a portion at least of your zeal to animate my endeavours. And if my talents should be found as mean as those of my Adversary, this circumstance would not discourage me. The contest would only be more equal; and in such a quarrel the serious advocate for Religion would be sorry to owe his success to any thing but the goodness of his cause.

This, Sir, is all I had thought to say of myself. But being got on so seducing a subject, the importance, which every author is of to himself, makes me imagine that perhaps you may be tempted to push your inquiries concerning me somewhat farther. And if, haply, any such curiosity should be raised, tho' I have my reasons for being a little on the reserve with you, something at least I could be content to hazard for your satisfaction.

Of my *Person*, indeed, I must have leave to make no discovery. And to tell you the truth, I have taken such effectual precautions as to that particular, that I venture to say you will never know more of me than you do at present. You may believe, if you please, that my vanity has suffered something in resolving on this concealment.

But then in quality of *Author* of these Remarks, I have not the same scruples. It may be fitting, you should know something more of the WRITER's intention and character. And in this respect he is very ready to gratify you.

THE AUTHOR then of these Remarks on Mr. Hume's Essay is ONE who, as you would otherwise conclude from the Remarks themselves, hath made a diligent study of your works; is familiar and, in a manner, conscious to your turn of thinking upon all subjects; and interests himself, more particularly, in all your views and projects for the support and advancement of religious truth.

But notwithstanding this intimacy with you, which might be justly suspected of creating a bias in most minds, he arrogates to himself the merit of judging of you more freely, nay to be plain with you, more severely, than perhaps your enemies themselves. He is extremely apprehensive of being misled or imposed upon in matters of this high concern: he considers the difficulty of the subjects; the fascination of favourite principles; the errors to which the best and most watchful writers are liable: And is the last man in the world who, out of a fondness for your notions, would neglect or betray any useful truth. He is One therefore that weighs your arguments without considering your authority, or even the disgrace you might be thought to incur from the confutation of them. Reading and criticizing you with this spirit, you are not to wonder that he hath sometimes seen cause to censure, where others admire. He hath even considered your volumes with a diligence which might have profited your adversaries; for he hath detected, not inaccuracies only, but *weaknesses* in your writings, which the most malignant of them have overlooked. To make you amends for this mortification, he does you the justice to profess that those Adversaries, as far as he is acquainted with them, have universally done you wrong.

With all this suspicious and unrelenting criticism about him, he is ready to believe however that your views are honest: he acknowledges that the main of your System is strong and impregnable; he sees no reason for you to desert the great design you have undertaken; and admits that your talents for the execution of it, tho' not in his eyes what your fond admirers represent them, yet are such as may not unusefully, and, considering the times in which we live, may even creditably enough be employed by you in such a cause.

In a word, the AUTHOR of these Remarks is One who approves your Principles; or he would not have made use of them, even in this service. He thinks there is force and conviction in your Reasonings; or he would not have tried the strength of them upon others, and least of all upon so captious, versatile, and evasive a writer as Him, with whom he is here concerned. But what he takes upon himself to say he is most confident of, is your *zeal for the interests of truth and virtue*; without which, whatever your merit there might be in your writings, he could have no complacency in the writer.

In consequence of this last judgment, which he forms of you, he hath not scrupled to adopt your *manner* of composition, as well as Arguments. He knows what the gentle reader thinks of it. But he is not one of those cool opposers of Infidelity, who can reason without earnestness, and confute without warmth. He leaves it to others, to the soft Divine and courtly Controversialist, to combat the most flagitious tenets with serenity; or maintain the most awful of religious truths in a way, that misleads the unwary reader into an opinion of their making but little impression on the writer's own heart. For himself, he freely owns he is apt to *kindle* as he writes; and would even blush to repel an insult on sense and virtue with less vigour than every honest man is expected to shew in his own case.

At the same time he is not so blinded by his zeal, as to overlook a difference on OCCASIONS. He would not incur the ridicule of misapplying his strength; and is therefore content to soften his polemics a little, not in complaisance to such judges, but in conformity to his subject. Yet to put matters at the lowest, he remembers what the character of his piece should be, as delivered by a great Master – MULTÆ, ET CUM GRAVITATE, FACETIÆ:

QUODQUE DIFFICILE EST, IDEM ET PERORNATUS ET BREVIS.[266] And if he should not be thought to have catched the spirit of it so fully, as you have done on certain occasions, he pretends at least to have had this character in view, and to have copied it, as he was able; tho' at the hazard, he foresees, of passing with the too delicate critic, for a SERVILE IMITATOR.

This, Sir, is the whole of what he thinks fit to declare of himself. For the REMARKS themselves, which are here offered you, he pretends only, that they are such as occurred to him on a single reading of the Essay; that they were entered hastily on the margin, as he went along; and that he now transcribes them with little or no variation, for the public use. Nor let that Public take it amiss from the writer, that he treats them with this appearance of neglect. The various topics, he knows, which are touched upon in the Essay, might afford room for much useful and curious speculation. He knows too, what his Duty to the public requires from him on a proper occasion. But he never designed the following animadversions for an elaborate piece of instruction or entertainment to the learned reader. He would only employ a vacant hour in exposing to the laughter of every man, that can read, the futility, licence, and vanity of Mr. DAVID HUME.

REMARK I.

The writer, I have to do with, is a Veteran in the dark and deadly trade of Irreligion. But my concern at present is only with a volume of his, just now given to the public and entitled, FOUR DISSERTATIONS. And of these *Four*, I confine myself to the FIRST, which bears the portentous name of an Essay, *On the natural history of Religion.*[267]

The purpose of it is to establish NATURALISM on the ruins of RELIGION; of which, whether under Paganism and Polytheism, or under Revelation and the doctrine of the Unity, he professes to give the NATURAL HISTORY.[268]

And here let me observe it to his honour, that, tho' he be not yet got to THEISM, he is however on the advance and approaching to the borders of it;[269] having been in the dregs of Atheism when he wrote his Epicurean

---

[266] ["Many witticisms along with gravity: and what is difficult, the same person being flowery and brief."]

[267] [This paragraph is omitted in the 1788 edition.]

[268] [In the 1788 edition this paragraph reads, "The purpose of this ESSAY.... Mr. Hume professes to give...."]

[269] [George Horne writes, "In the *Natural History of Religion* Dr. Hurd thought our philosopher was approaching towards the *Borders* of Theism. But I never could find that he penetrated far into the *country*", *Letters on infidelity* (Oxford, 1784), p. 14].

arguments against the being of a God.[270] Sometime or other he may come to his senses. A few animadversions on the *Essay* before us may help him forwards. The thing is full of curiosities: And the very *title-page*, as I observed, demands our attention. It is called,

THE NATURAL HISTORY OF RELIGION.

You ask, why he chuses to give it this title. Would not the *Moral history of Meteors* be as full as sensible as the *Natural history of Religion*? Without doubt. Indeed had he given the history of what he himself would pass upon us for the only true Religion, namely, NATURALISM, or the belief of a God, the Creator and Physical Preserver, but not moral Governor of the world, the title of *Natural* would have fitted it well, because all *Morality* is excluded from the Idea.

But this great Philosopher is never without his Reasons. It is to insinuate, that what the world calls Religion, of which he undertakes to give the history, is not founded in the JUDGMENT, but in the PASSIONS only. However the expression labours miserably, as it does thro' all his profound Lucubrations. And where is the wonder that he who disdains to think in the mode of common sense, should be unable to express himself in the proprieties of common language?

As every Inquiry which regards Religion (says that respectable Personage) *is of the utmost importance, there are two questions in particular which challenge our principal attention, to wit, that concerning its foundation in reason, and that concerning its* ORIGIN IN HUMAN NATURE.[271]

Here we see, he aims at a distinction. And what he aims at is not hard to find. The question is, whether he has hit the mark. I am afraid, not. And then the discovery of his aim is only the detection of his ignorance. In a word, it is a distinction without a difference.

If man be rightly defined a *rational animal*, then his Nature, or what our Philosopher calls *human Nature*, must be a *rational* Nature. But if so, a FOUNDATION IN REASON and an ORIGIN IN HUMAN NATURE are not too different predicates, but one and the same only in different expressions. Do I say, therefore, that our Philosopher had no meaning, because he was unable to express any? Far be that from the Reverence due to this Rectifier of Prejudices. My objection at present is not to his Theology but his Logic. By *Origin in human Nature* he meant, Origin in the fancy or the Passions. For that Religion, which has the origin, here designed, is what the world calls RELIGION; and this he resolves into *fanaticism* or *superstition*: As that

---

[270] [In "Of a Particular Providence and of a Future State".]

[271] P. 1. *Nat. Hist. of Religion.* [Pagination follows Hume's *Four Dissertations* (London, 1757).]

Religion which has its *foundation in reason* is what the world calls NATURALISM, the Religion of Philosophers like himself, and which he endeavours in the Essay to establish.

But do not believe, I intend to meddle with this *Religion of Philosophers* any further than to expose it to the public contempt, as it deserves. Even I should be finely employed, not to say you, to enter into a formal confutation of Mr. David Hume's *Naturalism*. However I think it incumbent on me to prove, that this is indeed the Religion which this honest man means to recommend in his *Natural History*. For so heavy a charge ought never to be made without good evidence to support it.[272]

In his third Section, at the 16th page, he makes UNKNOWN CAUSES the origin of what men call *Religion*, that Religion which his History pretends to investigate.

"These UNKNOWN CAUSES, says He, become the constant object of our hope and fear; and while the passions are kept in perpetual alarm by an anxious expectation of the events, the imagination is equally employed in forming ideas of those powers, on which we have so entire a dependance."

He then goes on to acquaint us with the original of these UNKNOWN CAUSES.

"Could men anatomize Nature, according to the most probable, at least the most intelligible philosophy, they would find, that these *Causes* are nothing but the particular fabric and structure of the MINUTE PARTS OF THEIR OWN BODIES AND OF EXTERNAL OBJECTS; and that, by a regular and constant machinery, all the events are produced, about which they are so much concerned. But this Philosophy exceeds the comprehension of the ignorant multitude."[273]

Here we see, the original of these *unknown causes* is nothing but the result of MATTER and MOTION. And again,

"The Vulgar, that is, indeed, ALL MANKIND, a few excepted, being ignorant and uninstructed, never elevate their contemplation to the Heavens, or penetrate by their disquisitions into the SECRET STRUCTURE OF VEGETABLE OR ANIMAL BODIES; so as to discover a supreme mind or original providence, which bestowed order on every part of Nature.

[272] [This paragraph is omitted in the 1788 edition.]
[273] P. 17.

They consider these admirable works in a more confined and selfish view; and finding their own happiness and misery to depend on the secret influence and unforeseen concurrence of external objects, they regard, with perpetual attention, the UNKNOWN CAUSES, which govern all these natural events, and distribute pleasure and pain, good and ill, by their powerful, but silent, operation. The UNKNOWN CAUSES are still appealed to, at every emergence; and in this general appearance or confused image, are the perpetual objects of human hopes and fears, wishes and apprehensions. By degrees, the active imagination of men, uneasy in this abstract conception of objects, about which it is incessantly employed, begins to render them more particular, and to cloathe them in shapes more suitable to its natural comprehension. It represents them to be sensible, intelligent beings, like mankind; actuated by love and hatred, and flexible by gifts and entreaties, by prayers and sacrifices. HENCE THE ORIGIN OF RELIGION: *And hence the origin of idolatry or Polytheism.*"[274]

The *few excepted* out of the *whole race of mankind* are, we see, our Philosopher and his gang, with their Pedler's ware of *matter* and *motion, who penetrate by their disquisitions into the secret structure of vegetable and animal bodies*, to extract, like the Naturalist in Guliver, *Sunbeams out of Cucumbers*; just as wise a Project as this of raising Religion out of the intrigues of *matter and motion*.

All this shews how desirous our Essayist was of not being misunderstood: as meaning any thing else than Naturalism (or the belief of a Creator and Physical Preserver, but not Moral Governor) by the Religion he would recommend in the place of that Phantom, whose physical, or rather metaphysical, history he is writing. For this Phantom of a Religion, which acknowledges a *moral Governor*, arises, he tells us, from our ignorance of the result of *matter* and *motion*, caballing *in the minute parts of vegetable and animal bodies*.

The sum then of all he teaches is this; That that Religion, of which he professes himself a follower, and which has *its foundation in Reason*, is NATURALISM: and, That that Religion which *all mankind* follow, *a few excepted*, and of which he undertakes to give a *natural history*, is nothing but *Superstition* and *Fanaticism*, having *its origin in human Nature*; that is, in the imagination and the passions only.

REMARK II.

This fully justifies the censure, which has been passed upon him for his *History of Great Britain*; namely, that he owned no RELIGION but what

---

[274] Page 54–5.

might be resolved into SUPERSTITION or FANATICISM; having represented the established Episcopal Church, and the tolerated Presbyterian Form under the Names and the Ideas of Superstition and Fanaticism.[275] Indeed, (to do him justice,) tho' with much offence, yet without much malignity and contrary to his intention. For he ingenuously enough confessed, that he gave his History that attic seasoning for no other end than to fit it to the palate of a very polite people; whose virtues, having only reached him at a distance, had, as is usual, been much exaggerated. To make amends, however, for this false step, he thought proper to give an ample apology for his conduct towards the close of the second Volume of his History.[276] And this containing something more than an Insinuation that he believed, what his *Natural History of Religion* shews he does not believe, namely, the truth of Christianity, I shall take leave, without any suspicion of being thought to go out of my way, to consider it paragraph by paragraph.

This Sophism, says he, of arguing from the abuse of any thing, against the use of it, is one of the grossest, and at the same time the most common to which men are subject. The history of all ages, and none more than that of the Period which is our subject, offers us examples of the abuse of Religion: And we have not been sparing in this volume, more than in the former, to remark them. But whoever would from thence draw an inference to the disadvantage of Religion in general, would argue very rashly and erroneously.[277]

Thus he begins his Apology: And would not every Reader of him naturally believe that he was quoting the words of an animadverter upon him, in reproof of this very Sophistry; which he was going to answer? For who was it that had been *drawing this inference to the disadvantage of Religion*, but our wise Historian himself; who had acknowledged no Religion but one or other of these specieses, *Superstition* or *Fanaticism*; and had done his best to shew of what infinite mischief both of them were to

---

[275] [The first published volume of Hume's *History of Great Britain* (1754) contained two passages attacking Christianity. One passage argues that the first Protestant reformers were fanatical or "inflamed with the highest enthusiasm" in their opposition to Roman Catholic domination. The second passage labels Roman Catholicism a superstition which "like all other species of superstition... rouses the vain fears of unhappy mortals". These passages were dropped from subsequent editions of the *History*; they are reprinted in the Foreword to the Liberty Classics edition of Hume's *History of England* (1983), xiv–xvii.]

[276] [Volume II of Hume's *History* (published in 1757) contains a footnote which defends Volume I against charges of irreligion. His footnote was an abridged version of a preface he had drafted for Volume II, but never published. The complete draft of the preface is reprinted in E.C. Mossner's *The Life of David Hume* (1954), pp. 306–308. Ultimately, even the abridged footnote was dropped from later editions of the *History*.]

[277] *Hist. of Great Britain*, V. II. P. 449–50.

Society? The Reader may believe what he pleases; (and if he be a Reader of Mr. Hume, he will find exercise enough for his faith) but, this sage observation is our Historian's own. And the pleasantry of it, is, you are obliquely requested to consider it as a reproof, not of his own malice, but of the folly of his readers, who understood their Historian to be in *earnest* when he gave this picture of the religion of his country; whereas they had read him to little purpose, if they did not see him to be in the number of those who throw about them firebrands and death, and say, am I not in *jest*? However, to be fair, I am ready to excuse *his readers* in this (perhaps they can be excused in little else) for it is not to be disguised that their master does indeed make *the abuses of Religion* and *Religion itself* to be one and the same thing. All things considered therefore, I cannot but take this introduction to his apology, to be the pleading guilty with the insolent air of an Accuser, and, under the circumstances of a convict, talking the language of his judge.

However, tho' in his first Volume of History he neither spoke of, nor supposed any other Religion than what might be comprised either under superstition or fanaticism, yet here, in the second, he does indeed bring us acquainted with another, and defines it thus; *The proper office of Religion is to reform men's lives, to purify their hearts, to inforce all moral duties, and to secure obedience to the laws of the civil Magistrate.* Now, was Mr. David Hume only playing the Philosopher, I should take this to be no more than the Definition of a mere *moral mode*, known by the name of a *divine philosophy in the mind*; something fluctuating in the *brain* of these Virtuosi, and ennobled with the title of *Natural Religion*: But as he is writing History, and the History of Great Britain, where the *Religion of Jesus*, as he has since learnt, is yet professed, I can hardly persuade myself that he can mean any other, than a Religion whose abode is in the *heart*, and which expatiates into virtuous practice; and is therefore indeed capable of performing all these good things he speaks of. But why then, when he had heard so much of those bug-bear Counterfeits, *Superstition* and *Fanaticism*, was there not one Word slipt in, in recommendation of this *reforming Religion*? One word, in mere charity, for the honor of his dear country? That Strangers at least (for he writes at large and for all mankind) might not suspect, if ever indeed there was a true Religion amongst us, that these Impostors and Counterfeits had driven her quite away. Well; be not too hasty. To this he has an admirable Answer; and you shall have it in his own Words – *While it* [i.e. the true species of Religion, which he had just defined] *pursues these salutary purposes, its operations, tho' infinitely valuable, are secret and silent, and seldom come under the cognizance of history. The adulterate species of it alone, which inflames Faction, animates Sedition, and prompts Rebellion, distinguishes itself on the open theatre of the world, and is the great source of Revolutions and public Convulsions.*

The Historian therefore has scarce any occasion to mention any other kind of Religion, and he may maintain the highest regard for true piety, even while he exposes all the abuses of the false.

So it seems, that what *reforms men's lives, purifies their hearts, inforces moral duties, and secures obedience to the laws of the civil magistrate,* is not worth a wise Historian's Notice. If it were, he gives a very cogent reason why he should bring it to the Notice of his readers likewise, for he tells us that the effects of this are SECRET and SILENT. Should not the Historian therefore lend a tongue to this powerful but modest directress of human life, and bring her in all her lustre into our acquaintance? But *she seldom comes under the cognizance of History.* More shame for these false masters of the Ceremonies who so scandalously abuse their office.

Then it is, the Historian shines when he celebrates that *adulterate species of Religion, which inflames faction, animates sedition, and prompts rebellion*: For then it is that to these public Mischiefs he may add his own, and under the cover of the *adulterate species* inculcate to the people that all Religion is either *superstition* or *fanaticism.*

If this was not his purpose, and he had no other design than to write sober history, how could it ever enter into his head, that it was not at least equally his business to explain to us what that thing is which makes society happy, as what that is which makes it wretched and miserable? But from the honest man let us turn to the able writer, for in that light too he seems to have failed. It appears to me a matter of much greater importance that we should be brought acquainted with true religion and its blessings, than with the false and all its mischiefs: Because how shall we be able to avoid the latter, under our ignorance of the former, without running into the opposite extreme, and professing no religion at all? Now, tho' this perhaps is what our historian would be at, yet he has found by experience, his Readers are not so ready to follow as he is to lead.

Had our Historian only consulted the Dignity of his Subject, in this too he would have found a great difference; or if he could not, a great example at least was before his eyes, to have pointed out that difference; Lord BACON, in his history of Henry VII. This, which in many respects is a model for this kind of writing, is much larger and more precise in the account of those Laws by which Henry laid the foundation of a flourishing and happy Kingdom, than of the Insurrections and Rebellions which disturbed his own reign.[278] Had he taken our Author's route, and incurred the censure so justly due to it, I apprehend he had made a very foolish figure both amongst his contemporaries and posterity, by an apology of this kind. *The proper office of* LAWS *is to reform men's lives, to inforce all moral duties and to*

---

[278] [Francis Bacon, *The History of the Reign of King Henry the Seventh*, ed. J. Rawson Lumby (London, 1881), especially Ch. 4, "King Henry the Law-giver".]

secure obedience to the civil Magistrate; but while they pursue their salutary purposes, their operations, tho' infinitely valuable, are secret and silent, and seldom come under the cognizance of History. LAWLESS RAGE *alone, which inflames faction, animates Sedition, and prompts Rebellion, is what distinguishes itself on the open theatre of the world, and is the proper province of the Historian.* Suppose this great Historian, and He too was a *Philosopher,* had executed what he once projected, the history of his illustrious Mistress, are we to believe that because Walsingham's *Salutary operations* were done in *Secrecy* and in *Silence,* that there he would let them have lain, as *not coming under the cognizance of history,* and *only* buried[279] himself in a circumstantial detail of the rogueries and turbulencies of the sons of Loyola? Would he not have gained more honour to himself, and procured more benefit to his reader by revealing and explaining all the wheels and movements of that political machine, from which, as from the urn of a Demi-God, flowed abundance and felicity on his country, than by unravelling the intrigues of the Jesuits which spread sedition, rebellion and murders all around them?

But to see how differently men's heads are framed even amongst great Historians. TACITUS laments bitterly that his fortune had thrown him in an age, when there was nothing to write of but these horrors, *factions, seditions, public convulsions and Revolutions.*

"Opus aggredior opimum casibus, atrox præliis, discors seditionibus, ipsa etiam pace sævum: quatuor principes ferro interempti: tria bella civilia, plura externa, ac plerumque permixta."[280]

Our Christian Historian riots in these calamities; and thinks that *what inflames faction, animates sedition, prompts rebellion, and distinguishes itself on the open theatre of the world, is the only thing becoming the dignity of History.*

In a word, the offence he gave was for calling the Christian Religion, *Superstition* and *Fanaticism.* He says, it was *false* Religion, not the *true,* which he thus qualifies. He is asked then, how he came to say so much of the *false,* and nothing of the *true?* His answer is, That the true does everything in *secrecy and silence.* The greater occasion therefore was there for him to reveal this noble Mystery; for he tells us that both its aims and operations are *infinitely valuable.* If therefore he be for keeping it hid, like

---

[279] [In the 1777 and 1788 editions this word reads "busied".]

[280] ["I am setting about a work crowded with changes in fortune, cruel battles, discordant seditions, and even now the same horrors in peace; four rulers slain by the sword; three civil wars, many external wars, and frequently thoroughly mixed", Tacitus, *History*, Bk. I, Par. 2.]

a court-secret, or if, in his own words, *it comes not under his cognizance*, we must conclude, that either he knows little of the matter, or that he believes less.

In conclusion, his own Apology has reduced him to this Dilemma. If he says, he intends the definition of Religion here given, for the definition of the *Christian*, how came he to comprise all Religion, as he does in the first volume of his History, under the names of *Superstition* and *Fanaticism?* He there mentions no other species; and so great a Philosopher could not be guilty of an imperfect enumeration. If he says, he means *Natural Religion* by his definition; he only fixes the charge against him the more strongly, namely, Irreverence and contempt of Revelation.

Either way, you see, our Apologist comes off but lamely. But what then?

– To be of no Religion
Argues a *Subtle moral Understanding*
AND IT IS OFTEN CHERISH'D. –

Thus it has been said; and I observe it for our virtuous Author's consolation, notwithstanding the ill success of his History.[281]

REMARK III.

But from his *Civil* let us return to his *Natural History*; and see how he supports his Thesis. He does it by something between history and argument. He calls it both: And You[282] perhaps will think it neither.

The belief of one God, the physical preserver but not moral Governor of the Universe is, what we have shewn our Philosopher dignifies with the title of *the primary principles of genuin Theism and Religion.* Now, if the belief of one God, a moral Governor, was prior in time to Polytheism, it will follow, that NATURALISM or the belief of one God, a Physical preserver only, is not *genuin Theism and Religion.* Because in his endeavour to prove Polytheism the first in time, he has shewn the inability of mere uninstructed man to rise up to this knowledge, on the first Essay of his Reason; the consequence of which is, that if the infant world had this knowledge, it must have been taught them by Revelation, and whatsoever is so taught, must be *true.*

But it is become the general opinion (which, though it has been a long while growing, our philosopher hopes very speedily to eradicate) that a belief of one God, the moral Governor, was the first Religion; induced

---

[281] [This paragraph is omitted in the 1788 edition.]

[282] [In the 1788 edition this word is replaced with "some".]

thereto by the express assertion of an antient book confessedly of as good authority as any other record of very remote antiquity. Our Philosopher's business therefore is to disprove the Fact. And how do you think he sets about it? You see there are but two ways. Either to prove *a priori*, and from the nature of things that Polytheism must be before Theism; and then indeed he may reject history and record: Or else *a posteriori*, and from antient testimony; in which case, it will be incumbent on him to refute and set aside that celebrated record which expressly tells us, Theism was the first. Our honest Philosopher does neither. He insists chiefly on antient testimony, but is as silent concerning the Bible as if no such book had ever been written.

Lord Bolingbroke, you know, before him had employed this very medium of the priority of Polytheism to Theism, to inforce the same conclusion, namely, NATURALISM:[283] but knowing better how to reason, and being perhaps at that moment less disposed to insult common sense in so profligate a manner, he labours all he can to depreciate the authority of the Bible. But our North British Philosopher despises his reader too much to stand upon Punctilios with him: he roundly affirms that all antiquity is on his side; and, as if Moses had no human authority because he allows him no divine, he will not condescend so much as to do him the honour, he has done Sanconiathon,[284] of quoting him, tho' it was in order to confute him. But you shall hear his own words, because his egregious dishonesty has led him into as ridiculous an absurdity.

"As far as writing or history reaches, mankind, in antient times, appear universally to have been Polytheists. Shall we assert, that, in more antient times, before the knowledge of letters, or the discovery of any art or science, men entertained the principles of pure Theism? That is, while

---

[283] [In the 1788 edition this sentence reads "Lord Bolingbroke before him had employed...". Bolingbroke's position on original polytheism is this: "I do not believe mankind discerned the unity of God in the first dawnings of knowledge. But the impressions of the Creator are so strongly marked in the whole extent of the creation... that it must have been received into the minds of men as soon as they began to contemplate the face of nature, and to exercise their reason in such contemplations; and this was long before the commencement of any traditions that we find out of the books of Moses." *On the Rise and Progress of Monotheism*, in *The Philosophical Works* (London, 1754), Vol. II, p. 165.]

[284] [Sanchoniathon (or Sanchuniathon), legendary chronicler of ancient Phoenicia (now Lebanon) prior to the Trojan war, whose works Philo Herennius Byblius claimed to have translated. Contrary to the above claim, Hume neither quotes nor refers to Sanchoniathon. However, Bolingbroke does (*The Philosophical Works*, Vol. II, pp. 199–200).]

they were ignorant and barbarous, they discovered truth: But fell into error, as soon as they acquired learning and politeness."[285]

Shall we assert, says he. Why, no body ever asserted that Theism was before Polytheism but those who gave credit to their bible. And those who did so can easily evade his difficulty, *that it is not natural to think that before the knowledge of letters, or the discovery of any art or science men entertained the principles of pure Theism*; because this Bible tells us, that the first man did not gain the principles of pure Theism by *a knowledge of letters or the discovery of any art or science*, but by REVELATION. But this man, who had run into unlucky mistakes before concerning the state of Religion in South Britain, believed in good earnest that we had burnt our bibles, and that therefore it would be less generous to insult its ashes, than to bury them in silence. This, I think, can only account for that virtuous assurance where he says, that AS FAR AS WRITING OR HISTORY REACHES, MANKIND IN ANTIENT TIMES APPEAR UNIVERSALLY TO HAVE BEEN POLYTHEIST. And what system do you think it is, of the *origin of mankind*, which he espouses, instead of the Mosaic, to prove that Polytheism was the first Religion? No other, I will assure you, than the old Egyptian nonsense, which attempts to teach that men first started up like Mushrooms. In a word, the men on whose principles this wonderful Logician argues, never questioned the truth of his Thesis. To them therefore all this bustle of a discovery is ridiculous and impertinent. And those, who dispute the fact with him, the Religionists, he leaves in possession of all their arguments. So they laugh at it as an idle dream, raised on the absurdest of the Atheistic principles, the Epicurean.

To this ridicule the reader sees, our philosopher exposes himself, even if we believe him to be here speaking of *pure theism*, in the proper sense of the words; that is of the belief of a God, the *moral Governor of the World*. But *Ridicule* may not be all which this mighty *Theist* deserves. For what, if our Philosopher should mean by his *pure and geniun theism*, to which he denies a priority of being, his favourite NATURALISM? I should not be surprised, if he did: It is but running his *usual* philosophic course, from knavery to nonsense.

The reader, as he goes along, will see abundant reason for this charge. An Essay, then, so devoid of all manly sense, and even plausibility of reasoning, can afford a Remarker no other opportunity of entertaining the public with him, than that of drawing the picture of some of his characteristic features, some of the predominant qualities, of which he is made up. An admired Antient, I remember, has given us his opinion of this

---

[285] Page 4.

Godless Wisdom, which sets Heaven and Earth at defiance. It is according to him, ᾽ΑΜΑΘΙ´Α ΤΙ`Σ ΜΑ´ΛΑ ΧΑΛΕΠΗ`, ΔΟΚΥˆΣΑ ΕΙˆΝΑΙ ΜΕΓΙ´ΣΤΗ ΦΡΟ´ΝΗΣΙΣ.[286] The charge is severe; yet you have made it out, but too clearly, against this author's noble precursor in the waste spaces of Nature. I would now do as much by the disciple and follower; and to that end shall keep your example in view while I present the public with a few specimens of his philosophical virtues, his Reasoning, his Consistency, his Candour, and his Modesty; and all these promiscuously, as they rise in the natural disorder of his *Essay.*[287]

REMARK IV.

"Convulsions in Nature, says he, disorders, prodigies, MIRACLES, tho' the most opposite to the plan of a wise super-intendent, impress mankind with the strongest sentiments of religion; the causes of events seeming then the most unknown and unaccountable.[288]

Our philosopher forgets himself. He owns and admits *the plan of a wise superintendent*: this *plan* is essential to his NATURALISM. He owns and admits the actual existence of *convulsions in Nature, disorders and prodigies*: for these conform to his great principle of EXPERIENCE, his only rule of credit, and which therefore should be his rule of right. Yet these *convulsions, disorders, prodigies are*, he tells us, *most opposite to the plan of a wise superintendent*. Which in plain english is neither more nor less than, "That a wise superintendent crosses and defeats his own Plan."

You ask, how he fell into this absurdity? Very naturally. He was betrayed into it by his childish prejudice to MIRACLES: which happening to cross a hurt imagination, while he was in the neighbourhood of *Prodigies*, as Mountains and Giants always met together in the rencounters of Don Quixote, he would not let them pass without carrying with them some mark of his resentment. And having shewn, in a book written for that good purpose, that MIRACLES were *most opposite to the plan of a wise superintendent*, he was not content to brand miracles alone with this infamy, but (so dangerous it is to be found in ill company) he charges the same villany, on *Convulsions in nature, disorders and prodigies*, things in themselves very innocent, and by old experience known to have existed.

---

[286] ["Ignorance is very irksome, seeming to be the greatest thinking."]

[287] [In the 1788 edition this paragraph reads, "...of which he is made up. I shall therefore present the public...".]

[288] Page 44.

Thus a laudable zeal against his capital Enemy, MIRACLES, happening to be ill placed, this great philosophic detection of one of the prime master-wheels of superstition labours with immoveable nonsense.

REMARK V.

But now I have mentioned our Author's aversion to miracles, it may not be improper just to take notice, in passing, of that capital argument, which he and Lord Bolingbroke have borrowed from Spinoza against them.[289] "It is, that they are incredible, because contrary to all experience, and to the established course of Nature."

But is not this an admirable argument? A circumstance is urged against the reality of miracles, which must necessarily attend miracles, if there ever were any: their *essence* consisting in their being effects produced contrary to the common course of Nature; and their *end* in their being effects contrary to experience. For could they be esteemed the immediate work of the Lord of Nature, if they did not controll Nature? Or, could they be esteemed the extraordinary declaration of his will, if not contrary to our experience of the common course of Nature?

"But hold a little, he will say. It is indeed of the *essence* of a miracle, that it be contrary to common experience. But for this very reason I affirm, that no miracles at all can ever be proper objects of *Belief*. For why believe an event *against* all experience, upon a testimony the credibility of which is founded *in* Experience?"

Short and round, it must be owned. But, Good Sir, since you put the matter so home, one word in your ear about this same experience. To what *experience* is it that miracles are contrary? If you mean honestly and would answer to purpose, you must say, "To Experience in all SUCH CASES as those in which the existence of miracles is alledged." But what experience then do miracles contradict? Where do you find your *such cases*, in order to draw your argument from experience? In the moon, or in any other of the worlds which philosophers have found or fancied in the heavens? For in the world which we *men* inhabit I know not what *like cases* can be pretended. What then becomes of your *experience*? Or, rather how unhappy is your appeal to it, when *all* the experience, we have had, lies on the other side?

---

[289] [See Bolingbroke, *Philosophical Works*, Vol. V, pp. 99–102; Benedict de Spinoza, *Tractatus Theologico-Politicus*, Sect. VI.]

But this is only a brief hint to the wise. And our philosopher, in particular, is left to make his best of it. The reader sees, this is no time or place to pursue a consideration of such importance any further.[290]

REMARK VI.

There is a strange perversity in the arrangement of our Author's philosophical ideas, occasioned by the vain affectation of singularity.

Nothing hath been more uncontroverted, either in antient or modern times, than that the notion of the Unity, amongst the Pagans, arose from their *Philosophers*. No, says this penetrating Sage, it came from the *People*: and that by the most natural progress in the world.

"Men's exaggerated praises and compliments still swell their ideas upon them; and elevating their Deities to the utmost bounds of perfection, at last beget the attributes of UNITY and Infinity, Simplicity and Spirituality."[291]

"THE PEOPLE sure, the people are the sight."[292]

Turn this people to the South, and you see them fall down before Dogs and Cats and Monkeys. Place them to the North, and they worship stocks and stones. But give them once an Eastern aspect, and they shoot out into *praise* and *panegyric*, which presently produces a *first Cause*. It is pity but we could leave them here in quiet possession of their glory. It is not my fault that we cannot. Our Philosopher seems to be oppressed with his own discovery. Tho' the people might, in this manner, find out the *first cause*, yet he is sensible they knew not what to do with it, when they had it. They *would* not leave their false Gods for the true; they *could* not bring both to a good understanding; they had neither skill nor address to associate them together; and the true God was neither to be *praised* or *panegyrised* into an alliance with the false. What was to be done? Some philosophic fetch, much above the people, was, as he rightly observes, necessary to compleat the system of paganism. This the Philosophers performed, and finished all with a master-stroke.

"Such refined ideas, being somewhat disproportioned to VULGAR COMPREHENSION, remain not long in their original purity; but require to

---

[290] [The preceding four paragraphs are omitted in the 1788 edition (beginning with "But hold a little..."). The first of these paragraphs is a rhetorical representation of Hume's argument.]

[291] Page 55.

[292] [Alexander Pope, *The first epistle of the second book of Horace*, v. 323.]

be supported by the notion of inferior mediators or subordinate agents, which interpose betwixt mankind and their supreme deity. These demigods or middle beings, partaking more of human nature, and being more familiar to us, become the chief objects of devotion, and gradually recall that idolatry, which had been formerly banished by the ardent prayers and panegyrics of timorous indigent mortals."[293]

Thus the *vulgar*, you see, in their high flights of *praise and panegyric*, rose up to the discovery of a *first Cause*; while a set of *wiser men* are called in to restore the mob of middle deities to their pristine honours: And this, to suit the objects of worship to *vulgar comprehension*.

Now shallow men, like You or me, would say, why all this bustle and the bandying about of an unjointed System? Why did not one set of workmen undertake the whole? Or, if there was need of Coadjutors, how came the parties to act in so preposterous a manner, that the people assumed to themselves what belonged to the Philosophers, the *discovery of the first cause*; and the Philosophers undertook what belonged to the people, the *discovery of demi-gods and middle beings*? Or, will he say, that the *People* did both? discovered the Unity in their blind, *timorous and indigent* state, and, when they were so well informed, struck out, in a lucky moment, their gross system of Polytheism?

He may say what he will; but nobody shall persuade me but that an Author, who makes so great a figure himself in the various walks of Philosophy, would have given the honour of the whole to is own Profession; could it have been done without dimming and impairing, in so capital a matter, the illustrious character of an original thinker.

REMARK VII.

"The Getes (says our Historian) affirmed Zamolxis their Deity to be the only true God; and asserted the worship of all other nations to be addressed to fictions and Chimæras."[294]

This assertion contradicts all Antiquity, as well as the very nature and genius of Paganism itself. But what of that? It served an honest purpose: the purpose to which all his patriot endeavours tend, the discredit of Revelation. And on such an occasion a gratuitous assertion costs him nothing.

[293] Page 55–56.

[294] Page 53.

Now it hath been deemed one characteristic mark of favourable distinction in behalf of Revelation, that *the Jews affirmed the God of Israel to be the only true God; and asserted the worship of all other nations to be addressed to mere fictions and chimæras.* So far was well. But then he should have taken care not to contradict himself so very soon afterwards, where speaking of the universal genius of Paganism, he tells us,

"Idolatry is attended with this evident advantage, that by limiting the powers and functions of its deities, it naturally admits the Gods of other sects and nations to a share of divinity, and renders all the various deities, as well as rites, ceremonies or traditions, compatible with each other."[295]

But as this observation was not his own, being stolen from a late writer on the history of Paganism, it is no wonder he should so easily forget it.

REMARK VIII.

But the Paragraph (from which the last quotation is borrowed) will afford us further matter of speculation. It contains a detailed comparison between the advantages and disadvantages of IDOLATRY and THEISM; and thus the account is stated.

"POLYTHEISM or idolatrous worship, being founded entirely in vulgar traditions, is liable to this great inconvenience, that any practice or opinion, however barbarous or corrupted, may be authorized by it; and full scope is left for knavery to impose on credulity, till morals and humanity be expelled from the religious systems of mankind. At the same time, idolatry is attended with this evident ADVANTAGE, that, by limiting the powers and functions of its deities, it naturally admits the gods of other sects and nations to a share of divinity, and renders all the various deities, as well as rites, ceremonies, or traditions, compatible with each other. Theism is opposite both in its advantages and DISADVANTAGES."[296]

The advantages and disadvantages of *Polytheism* are, we see, such as arise from the *nature and essence* of idolatry. Would you not expect that the advantages and disadvantages of *theism* should have the same relation to their subject. Good logic seems to require it. But what of that, if his cause requires other management. He scruples not therefore to tell us in the same

[295] Page 58.

[296] Page 58–59.

page, that the *disadvantages* here mentioned as arising from Theism, come not from the *nature* but the abuse of it. "*They arise*," says he, "*from the vices and prejudices of mankind.*"

REMARK IX.

Still we are detained on the same spot; which is so fruitful of curiosities that there is no stirring from it. He is speaking of the absurdities or mischiefs, I cannot well say which, that arise from Revelation. And one, or perhaps both of these he intends to infer from the following observation.

"While one sole object of Devotion is acknowledged, the worship of other deities is regarded as absurd and IMPIOUS. Nay, this *unity of object seems naturally to require the* UNITY OF FAITH AND CEREMONIES, and furnishes designing men with a pretext for representing their adversaries as prophane, and the subjects of divine, as well as human vengeance."[297]

The calumnious insinuation, in this passage, about the origin of Persecution (the abuse, and not the reasonable consequence of a true principle) is below any body's notice. What I quote it for is a curious observation; tho' made, but on the by – *that the unity of object seems naturally to require the* UNITY OF FAITH AND CEREMONIES.

Unity of object, says he, *seems to require unity of faith*. I am apt to think it does. For if the object of belief be single, the belief can scarce be double: unless by a drunkenness of the Understanding, like that which doubles the objects of sense. But then, *that unity of object as naturally requires unity of ceremony*, is not so clear. *Unity of faith* is necessary, because *truth*, which is the general object of faith, is but *one*. But who ever affirmed, before our author, that *unity of ceremony* was necessary? *Ceremony* is only an expression of duty: And duty may be expressed a thousand different ways. *Unity of civil obedience*, under the same government, is necessary. But is *unity of civil obeisance* to the same Governor, equally necessary?

But in the brain of this paradoxical philosopher *Faith* and *Ceremonies* seem to have changed places. We see here how he has exalted *ceremonies*. You shall see next how he degrades *faith*.

He assures us, that "the *Egyptian Religion, tho' so absurd, yet bore so great a resemblance to the Jewish that the antient Writers, even of the greatest genius, were not able to observe any difference between them;*"[298] in proof of which he quotes Tacitus and Suetonius: And then adds, "*These wise Heathens, observing something in the* GENERAL AIR *and* GENIUS *and*

[297] Page 59.

[298] Page 76.

SPIRIT of the two Religions *to be the same*, ESTEEMED THE DIFFERENCES OF THEIR DOGMAS TOO FRIVOLOUS TO DESERVE ANY ATTENTION."[299] These *wise Heathens* were shrewd observers. But what then becomes of the wisdom of a much greater man, our Philosopher himself? who hath assured us, that *the general air and genius and spirit of the two Religions* were so far from being the *same* that they were totally different. For speaking of Revelation and Paganism, or of Theism and Polytheism, he found this remarkable difference in *the air and genius and spirit* of the two Religions, that

"Idolatry has this evident ADVANTAGE over Theism, that by limiting the powers and functions of its deities, it naturally admits the Gods of other sects and nations to a share of divinity, and renders all the various deities, as well as rites, ceremonies or traditions compatible with each other."

– Whereas in Theism, "While one sole object of devotion is acknowledged, the worship of other deities is regarded as absurd and impious." Nay he tells us in the same place, "That Theism is opposite to Polytheism both *in its advantages and disadvantages*."[300]

In short, in that Section nothing is alike: in the Section before us every thing is the same. So various in wisdom is antient and modern Infidelity! However a difference between the Jewish and Egyptian Religion, he owns, there was. But it was a difference only in DOGMAS TOO FRIVOLOUS TO DESERVE ATTENTION; being indeed nothing more than this, whether mankind should fall down before a dog, a cat, or a monkey, or whether he should worship the God of the Universe. From this curious specimen of our Author's ideas concerning FAITH and CEREMONIES, we cannot but conclude that he has set up for a writer against Religion, before he had learned his Catechism.

REMARK X.

"MACHIAVEL observes, says our great Philosopher and Divine, that the doctrines of the Christian Religion, (meaning the CATHOLIC, for he knew no other) which recommended only passive courage and suffering, had subdued the spirit of mankind, and fitted them for slavery and subjection. And this observation would certainly be just, were there not

---

[299] Page 77.

[300] Page 58–59.

many other circumstances in human society, which control the genius and character of a Religion."[301]

Machiavel, says he, meant the Catholic Religion. That is, he meant the Roman Catholic, in contradistinction to the Gospel. Machiavel meant no such thing. If he had, the *super-subtile Italian* had wrote like this rambling North-Briton. For it is not the Catholic Religion, so distinguished, but the Gospel itself which gave libertine men the pretence of saying, that *it subdued the spirit of mankind, and fitted them for slavery and subjection.* But here a sudden qualm comes over our Philosopher. He was ashamed of saying this of the Gospel. And well he might. For, tho' he says, *the observation is certainly just,* there never was a ranker calumny. The Gospel recommends no such thing as *passive courage and suffering,* either with regard to the domestic invaders of our civil rights, or to the foreign enemies of our country: And there are but one or two illiterate and fanatic sects, of very small extent, in the whole Christian world, who have so understood and abused the Gospel. The only *passive courage and suffering it recommends* is to particulars, whose consciences civil society hath iniquitously violated. Now, if instead of this *passive courage and suffering* the Gospel had recommended to its private followers to fly to arms and repel the force of the civil magistrate, when he abused his authority, in suppressing truth and the rights of conscience, what tragical exclamations would these very men have raised against the factious spirit of Christianity? Indeed, to our Author's shame be it spoken, the very contrary of all this is the truth. The effects of the Gospel are most salutary to *human Society*: for by encouraging inquiry and by inspiring a spirit of liberty in religious matters, it naturally inclines its followers to carry the same dispositions, into Civil.

REMARK XI.

But this honest man can allow himself, on all occasions, to calumniate the Religion of his country: sometimes openly and grossly; but oftener, as in the following instance, in the oblique way of Insinuation only.

"Were there a Religion (*and we may suspect Mahometanism of this inconsistence*) which sometimes painted the deity in the most sublime colours, as the creator of heaven and earth: sometimes degraded him nearly to a level *with human creatures in his powers and faculties*; while at the same time it ascribed to him *suitable infirmities, passions and partialities of the moral kind*: That Religion, *after it was extinct*, would

---

[301] Page 66–7.

also be cited as an instance of those contradictions, which arise from the gross, vulgar, natural conceptions of mankind, opposed to their continual propensity towards flattery and exaggeration. Nothing indeed would prove more strongly the divine origin of any Religion, than to find (*and happily this is the case with Christianity*) that it is free from a contradiction so incident to human nature."[302]

We see what the man would be at, thro' all his disguises. And, no doubt, he would be much mortified, if we did not; tho' the discovery, we make, is only this, That, of all the slanders against Revelation, this before us is the tritest, the dirtiest and most worn in the drudgery of Freethinking. Not but it may pass with his friends. And they have my free leave to make their best of it. What I quote it for is only to shew the rancour of heart which possesses this unhappy man, and which could induce him to employ an insinuation against the Jewish and Christian Religions; not only of no weight in itself, but of none, I will venture to say, even in his own opinion.

REMARK XII.

"The learned, philosophical Varro (says our no less learned and philosophical Naturalist) discoursing of Religion, pretends not to deliver any thing beyond probabilities and appearances: Such was his good sense and moderation! But the passionate, the zealous Augustin insults the noble Roman on his scepticism and reserve, and professes the most thorough belief and assurance. A Heathen poet, however, contemporary with the Saint, ABSURDLY esteems the religious system of the latter, so false, that even the credulity of children, he says, could not engage them to believe it."[303]

From the fact, as here delivered, we learn, that the Pagans insulted the Christians, and the Christians the Pagans, for the supposed absurdity of each others system. Agreed. And what then? Were their several systems equally absurd? This is what he would insinuate, or his observation is impertinent. Yet does not Mr. David Hume insult the *Religionists*, as absurd; They, him, as ten times more absurd? Will he say, that He and they have equal reason? But what, in the mean time, becomes of *Naturalism*? We must conclude then, that it is possible, one party may be in the right and the other in the wrong. The consequence is, that his approbation of Varro, and his censure of Augustin, is temerarious and unjust. For what hinders but that Augustin's *thorough belief and assurance* might be full as

---

[302] Page 49–50.

[303] Page 80–1.

reasonable when he defended Christianity, as Varro's not venturing *beyond probabilities and appearances*, when he apologized for Paganism? Had our modern Philosopher, who has a much worse cause than Varro's to defend, but imitated Varro's *moderation*, which he commends, instead of Augustin's *thorough assurance*, which he condemns, his reader perhaps would have thought better both of his sense and honesty. – Oh, but for his honesty and impartial indifference between Christianity and Paganism, he has given us such a convincing proof in this very instance, that he ought ever hereafter to go scot-free. We have observed, that he has praised Varro and condemned Augstin: but to shew – Tros Rutulusve fuat[304] – he tells us honestly – *that a Heathen poet, however, contemporary with the Saint,* ABSURDLY *esteems the religious system of the latter* [i.e. Christianity] *so false, that even the credulity of children,* he says *could not engage them to believe it.* Now here, where he has been at the expence of so much fair dealing, he ought to be indulged in rewarding himself for it, which he has done in this modest insinuation, that Christianity was so false and nauseous that even children could not be brought to swallow it.

He may talk what he pleases of the *absurdity* of poets. But while one Philosopher lives, I defy all the poets of antient or modern date to equal him either in absurdity or fiction. The poet, he here abuses, is CLAUDIUS RUTILIUS NUMATIANUS. He tells You, how this poet reviles Christianity: and quotes the Poem, the book, and the page. Would you suspect all this to be a flam, and not one word of truth, from beginning to end? Yet so it is. Rutilius is speaking of a JEW, by name and title; and the Rites of *Judaism*, as they distinguish that Religion from all other, are the subject of his Satire. The whole passage is as follows.

– "Namque loci querulus curam JUDÆUS agebat;
  Humanis animal dissociale *cibis.*
Vexatos frutices, pulsatas imputat algas,
  Damnaque libatæ grandia clamat aquæ.
Reddimus obscænæ convicia debita genti,
  Quæ *genitale caput propudiosa metit*:
Radix stultitiæ, cui frigida *sabbata* cordi;
  Sed cor frigidius religione suâ est.
Septima quæque dies turpi damnata veterno,
  Tanquam lassati mollis imago Dei.
Cetera mendacis deliramenta catastæ,
  Nec pueros omnes credere posse reor."[305]

---

[304] ["Whether he was Trojan or Rutulian."]

[305] Iter. L. I. v. 383. [*A Voyage to Gaul*, Bk. I, v. 383–384. "For a crabbed Jew was in charge of the spot – a creature that quarrels with sound human food. He charges in

The Pagan writers indeed frequently confound the two sects of Judaism and Christianity, with one another. But here, there is not the least room for that poor subterfuge. Rutilius speaks of Judaism by name: and to shew us that he understood his subject, he reviles it for those very rites, which are peculiar to Judaism; namely, the distinction between *clean and unclean meats, circumcision,* and the *Sabbath.* Yet, if You will believe this honest man, Rutilius represents CHRISTIANITY as so false, that even the *credulity of children could not engage them to believe it.* And why should You believe him?[306] He is a Philosopher, a follower of truth, and a virtuous man: One, (as he says of himself) *whose errors should be excused,* ON ACCOUNT OF THE CANDOUR AND SINCERITY WHICH ACCOMPANIES THEM.[307]

REMARK XIII.

"If ever there was a nation or a time (says our Philosopher) in which the public religion lost all authority over mankind, we might expect, that infidelity in *Rome,* during the *Ciceronian* age, would openly have erected it's throne, and that Cicero himself, in every speech and action, would have been its most declared abettor. But, it appears, that, whatever sceptical liberties that great man might use, in his writings or in philosophical conversation; he yet avoided, in the common conduct of life, the imputation of DEISM and PROFANENESS. Even in his own family, and to his wife, *Terentia,* whom he highly trusted, he was willing to appear a devout religionist; and there remains a letter, addrest to her, in which he seriously desires her to offer a sacrifice to *Apollo* and *Æsculapius,* in gratitude for the recovery of his health."[308]

Here he seems to commend Cicero (for his vanity, perverseness, and love of paradox make him always think at large, and write at random) on a

---

our bill for damaging his bushes and hitting the seaweed, and bawls about his enormous loss in water we had sipped. We pay the abuse due to the filthy race that infamously practices circumcision: a root of silliness they are: chill Sabbaths are after their own heart, yet their heart is chillier than their creed. Each seventh day is condemned to ignoble sloth, as 'twere an effeminate picture of a god fatigued. The other wild ravings from their lying bazaar methinks not even a child in his sleep could believe."]

[306] [In the 1788 edition this sentence reads, "And why should You not believe him?"]

[307] Dedicat. p. iii. [In the Dedication to *Four Dissertations,* Hume writes to his cousin, Reverend John Hume, "I still admired your genius, even when I imagined, that you lay under the influence of prejudice; and you sometimes told me, that you excused my errors, on account of the candor and sincerity, which you thought, accompanied them."]

[308] Page 81–2.

topic which exposes his own wicked practice, namely, Cicero's care, *in the common conduct of life*, to set the people an example of reverence for the established Religion. But whether this was said in praise or dispraise of that noble Roman, it matters not, since presently after he contradicts his own account, and assures us that the same Cicero was so far from *avoiding, in the common conduct of life, the imputation of* DEISM *and* PROFANENESS, that *He made no scruple in a public court of Judicature, of teaching the doctrine of a future state, as a* MOST RIDICULOUS FABLE, *to which no body would give any attention.*[309] And this without the least care of reconciling Cicero, to himself; or his own contradictory observations, to his reader.

REMARK XIV.

But he treats whole Bodies of men no better than Particulars.

"We may observe (says he) that, notwithstanding the dogmatical, imperious style of all superstition, the conviction of the Religionists, in all ages, is more affected than real, and scarce ever approaches, in any degree, to that solid belief and persuasion, which governs us in the common affairs of life. Men dare not avow, even to their own hearts, the doubts, which they entertain on such subjects: they make a merit of implicite faith; and disguise to themselves their REAL INFIDELITY, by the strongest asseverations and most positive bigotry. But nature is too hard for all their endeavours, and suffers not the obscure, glimmering light, afforded in those shadowy regions, to equal the strong impressions, made by common sense and by experience. The usual course of men's conduct belies their words, and shews, that the assent in these matters is some unaccountable operation of the mind betwixt disbelief and conviction, but approaching much nearer the former than the latter."[310]

This is superlatively modest. – When the Religionist says that an infidel writer, (like this man) in order to skreen himself from the resentment of the Law, says one thing and thinks another, there is no end of the clamours raised against uncharitable Churchmen. But Mr. David Hume may say all this and more of Religionists, and yet preserve his character of a philosopher and a friend of Truth. But infidelity owed him a shame, and he presently unsays it all; and confesses that Religionists are so far from being tossed about in *doubt* and *unbelief*, that nothing is more constant than the course of even the wisest and most experienced of them, invariably steady to the point of faith. For after having said a great deal to shew that

[309] Page 91.

[310] Page 83.

Socrates and Xenophon did in reality give credit to Augurs and Omens, he concludes thus,

"It is for the same reason, I MAINTAIN, that Newton, Locke, Clarke, &c. being Arians or Socinians, were VERY SINCERE, in the creed they professed: and I ALWAYS OPPOSE THIS ARGUMENT to some Libertines, who will needs have it, that it was impossible but that these great Philosophers must have been HYPOCRITES."[311]

Our modest philosopher had employed the 83d page of this wonderful essay to prove, that notwithstanding *the dogmatical imperious style of all superstition*, yet Religionists are HYPOCRITES; *their conviction in all ages being more* AFFECTED *than* REAL: and a great deal more trash to the same purpose. Yet here in the 91st page he MAINTAINS *against Libertines*, that these Religionists are VERY SINCERE, and no Hypocrites. Nay, in spite, as it were, to his 83d page, he affirms that he ALWAYS *opposes this argument to libertines.*

But are you to think, he talks thus wantonly, for no other end than to shew his contempt of the reader? By no means. For tho' this be, sometimes, motive sufficient for our paradoxical Gentleman to *contradict*, yet we must needs think there was some important occasion which induced him thus *to give the lye to himself.* He had it in his choice (for what hindered him, when unrestrained by the considerations of truth or falshood) to represent the Religionists as either KNAVES or FOOLS. But this did not content his noble passion for mischief. He would have them BOTH. Unluckily this could not be done without a contradiction. To make them *Knaves*, he was to shew they professed one thing and believed another: to make them *Fools*, they were to be represented as *steadily* and *sincerely* believing all things. The contradiction, we see, was unavoidable: but how he came so needlessly to saddle himself with the *lye* – I ALWAYS, says he, *oppose this argument to libertines* – I confess surpasses my comprehension.

Well, having floundered so shamefully, he is for recovering himself; and therefore stops into the gap, between these two extremes, a moderating tenet; and so leaves all Religionists, both antient and modern, in a kind of MIDDLE STATE, between *Knaves* and *Fools*. His conciliating tenet, is this –

"In the meantime it is obvious, that the empire of all religious faith over the understanding is wavering and uncertain, subject to all varieties of humour, and dependent on the present incidents, which strike the imagination. The difference is only in the degrees. An ancient will place a stroke of impiety and one of superstition alternately through a whole

[311] Page 91.

discourse: A modern often thinks in the same way, tho' he may be more guarded in his expressions."[312]

I am so tired with his contradictions that I shall let this passage go, unexamined upon that head, notwithstanding it looks so asquint both to the right and left, and agrees neither with the thorough *Hypocrisy*, nor the *sincere belief* of the two passages, it is brought to reconcile. But, as it stands alone, I may be allowed to ask, Why is the *modern* Christian *more guarded in his expressions*, than the *antient* Pagan? Does not human nature always operate alike in the like circumstances? If therefore, in this *modern superstition*, called *Christianity*, men are more consistent in the profession of their belief, than in that *antient superstition*, called Paganism, does not this shew that the circumstances were not alike? And what other differences in circumstances could there be, if not this, that Christianity having a rational foundation, it's professors stood steady and unmoved; and Paganism only fluctuating in the fancy and unsupported by the understanding, communicated the same inconstancy and variableness to its followers?

Oh, but says our Philosopher, I will not allow that steadiness to be more than pretended, *A modern often thinks in the same way,* [i.e. inconstantly,] *tho' he may be more guarded in his expressions.* How prejudiced! what pretence has he to suppose it an *inconstancy*, only *guarded in the expression*, when the very uniformity of the profession excludes all data whereon to ground his suspicion that the belief is only pretended?

He must take it then for granted (as without doubt he does) that Christianity has no more reasonable foundation than Paganism. No need, will he say, of that, at present. The *fashion*, the fashion, does all. An unsteadiness in Religion is discreditable in these *modern* times: hence the *guarded expression*.

Well, admit it to be so. What, I pray you, made unsteadiness in Religion now discreditable, which was creditable in former times, but this, that Christianity has now the support of, at least, plausible arguments, which Paganism never had?

REMARK XV.

In comparing the two Religions, Paganism and Christianity, our philosopher finds that the former is to be preferred to the latter, both in it's REASONABLENESS and in its BENEVOLENT SPIRIT.

"Upon the whole, the greatest and most observable differences betwixt a *traditional mythological* religion, and a *systematical, scholastic* one, are

---

[312] Page 86–87.

two: The former is often more REASONABLE, as consisting only of a multitude of stories, which however groundless, imply no express absurdity and demonstrative contradiction; and sits also so easy and light on mens minds, that tho' it may be as universally received, it makes no such deep impression on the affections and understanding."[313]

The *reasonableness*, we see, is resolved into this, that You cannot reduce the Professors of Paganism to *an express contradiction*; and that the Profession *sits mighty light and easy on men's minds*. As to the first property of paganism, its incapacity of being reduced to a contradiction, this it has in common with NONSENSE, which is likewise incapable of suffering the same disgrace. And this will account too for its second property, the *sitting so light and easy on the minds of men*. For nothing takes less hold of the mind than NONSENSE, or so little disturbs its tranquility, while we have the discretion to take it for what it is. To this he will tell you, you mistake his aim, if you think it was to credit paganism: the comparison was made only to discredit Christianity; by insinuating that its DOGMAS are *contradictory*, and its SANCTIONS *oppressive*.

As to the superior BENEVOLENCE in the spirit of Paganism, this is made out as follows.

"Lucian observes, that a young man, who reads the history of the Gods in *Homer* or *Hesiod*, and finds their factions, wars, injustice, incest, adultery, and other immoralities so highly celebrated, is much surprized afterwards, when he comes into the world, to observe, that punishments are by Law inflicted on the same actions, which he had been taught to ascribe to superior beings. The contradiction is still perhaps STRONGER betwixt the representations given us by some latter Religions and our natural ideas of generosity, lenity, impartiality, and justice; and in proportion to the multiplied terrors of these religions, the barbarous conceptions of the divinity are multiplied upon us."[314]

You, Sir, who took your idea of the DII MAJORUM GENTIUM[315] from ancient story, seem not to have characterised them amiss where you call them,[316] *"a rabble of Tyrants, Pathics, and Adulterers, Whores,*

---

[313] Page 92–93.

[314] Page 98–99.

[315] [Literally, "Gods of the greater races" (i.e., the gods of the Greeks and Romans).]

[316] [In the 1788 edition the first portion of this sentence reads, "The DII MAJORUM GENTIUM, as we learn from their history, were, 'a rabble...'".]

Vagabonds, Thieves, and Murderers."[317] Yet, gracious Heaven! a Philosopher of North Britain, in the Reign of George the Second, has dared to tell us, with very little disguise, that *the barbarous conceptions of the divinity, multiplied upon us* by Christianity, are still more *contradictory to our natural ideas of generosity, lenity, impartiality, and justice.* But here his *modesty* seemed to labour a little; and he is for casting part of the odium of this diabolic insinuation, from himself upon another.

"But in order, says he, to shew more evidently, that it is possible for *a Religion* to represent the Divinity in a still more immoral, unamiable light than the antient, we shall cite a long passage from an author of TASTE and IMAGINATION, who was surely no enemy of Christianity."[318]

You will suspect him to be just on the point of playing you a trick when you hear him talk of his authority, as an author of *taste and imagination*, when the subject requires that the voucher for it should have a clear judgment and strong understanding. After all there was no occasion for this slight of hand. The trick, I speak of, is to be played, as you will find, not by this *man of taste*, but by our Philosopher himself. His voucher, the Chevalier Ramsey, is perfectly innocent of all our Philosopher brings him to attest.

The words just quoted plainly imply, that in the opinion of this *man of taste*, Revelation, or the Jewish and Christian Religion, as delivered in the Bible, *represents the divinity in a still more immoral and unamiable light than the antient. – It is possible*, says he, *for a* RELIGION – which, I think, implies the Religion itself, and not the superstitious followers, much less the professed enemies of it. Turn now to the *long passage*, which this *man of truth* has quoted in his 100th page, and you will find that this *immoral and unamiable light in which the divinity is represented*, is not the representation of the Religion itself, but of its false friends and open enemies.

"What strange ideas (says the Chevalier Ramsey) would an Indian or a Chinese Philosopher have of our holy Religion, if they judged by the schemes given of it by our MODERN FREE-THINKERS and PHARISAICAL DOCTORS OF ALL SECTS? According to the odious and too vulgar system

---

[317] D.L. iv. B. 4. 5. [William Warburton, *Divine legation of Moses demonstrated* (London, 1761), Vol. II, Bk. 4, Sect. 4, p. 197. Warburton briefly quotes then criticizes the defence of Euhremerism by Samuel Shuckford in the *Sacred and profane history of the world connected* (1728–1737): "*And divine Honours cannot be given with any shew of Decency but to a late Posterity.* It must be owned the Ancients observed much *Decency* when they adopted into the Number of their greater Gods, Ravishers, Adulterers, Pathics; Vagabonds, thieves and Murderers."]

[318] Page 99.

of these INCREDULOUS SCOFFERS and CREDULOUS SCRIBLERS, the God of the Jews is a most cruel, unjust, partial, and fantastic Being. – To accomplish the partial, barbarous decree of predestination and reprobation, God abandoned all nations to darkness, idolatry, superstition, &c."

This turns out ridiculous enough. The Chevalier Ramsey is brought to prove that the Bible *represents the Divinity in a more immoral and unamiable light than Paganism*: and the Chevalier Ramsey turns the tables on him and proves that they are only such as our Philosopher himself and his crew, who so represent the Divinity.

Well, but say you, the Chevalier Ramsey is made by our Philosopher to consider the *representation* as the representation of Revelation, whoever made it. The *man of Truth's* words are these – *To shew more evidently that it is possible for a Religion to represent, &c. we shall cite a long passage from an author, who was surely no enemy to Christianity*. Why were these last words added but to insinuate that the representation, however disadvantagious, was yet owned to be a true one; unwillingly perhaps, as he was a friend of Christianity, but from the mere force of evidence. Whereas turn but your eyes upon the *long passage* and you will find that the representers, the *free-thinkers* and *Pharisaical Doctors*, are heartily censured by the Chevalier for thus *disfiguring* and *dishonouring* Revelation. His concluding words are,

"Thus the *incredulous free-Thinkers*, the *Judaizing Christians*, and the *fatalistic Doctors*, have disfigured and dishonoured the sublime mysteries of our holy faith; thus they have confounded the nature of good and evil; transformed the most monstrous passions into divine attributes, and SURPASSED THE PAGANS IN BLASPHEMY, by ascribing to the eternal nature as perfections, what makes the horridest crimes amongst men."[319]

The sum is this. The *man of truth* calls upon the *man of taste* to prove that the Jewish and Christian religions, as they lye in the bible, *represents the divinity in a more immoral and unamiable light than Paganism*. And the *man of taste* bears evidence that it is not the Bible but the *man of truth* and his crew who give this representation of the Divinity: a representation which SURPASSES indeed the very PAGANS IN BLASPHEMY.

---

[319] [Chevalier Andrew Michael Ramsay, *The philosophical principles of natural and revealed religion* (London, 1751), Part II, p. 406.]

REMARK XVI.

We now come to his account of the origin of that Religion, of which, meaning *Superstition*, he pretends to give a natural History.

"The primary religion of mankind arises chiefly from an anxious fear of future events; and what ideas will naturally be entertained of invisible unknown powers, while men lie under dismal apprehensions of any kind, may easily be conceived. Every image of vengeance, severity, cruelty, and malice must occur and augment the ghastliness and horror, which oppresses the amazed religionist. A panic having once seized the mind, the active fancy still farther multiplies the objects of terror; while that profound darkness, or, what is worse, that glimmering light, with which we are invironed, represents the spectres of divinity under the most dreadful appearances imaginable. And no idea of perverse wickedness can be framed, which those terrified devotees do not readily, without scruple, apply to their deity.

This appears the natural state of religion, when surveyed in one light. But if we consider, on the other hand, that spirit of praise and eulogy, which necessarily has place in all religions, and which is the consequence of these very terrors, we must expect a quite contrary system of theology to prevail. Every virtue, every excellence must be ascribed to the divinity, and no exaggeration be esteemed sufficient to reach those perfections, with which he is endowed. Whatever strains of panegyric can be invented, are immediately embraced, without consulting any arguments or phœnomena. And it is esteemed a sufficient confirmation of them, that they give us more magnificent ideas of the divine object of our worship and adoration.

HERE therefore is a kind of contradiction betwixt the different principles of human nature, which enter into Religion. Our natural terrors present the notion of a devilish and malicious deity: Our propensity to praise leads us to acknowledge an excellent and divine. And the influence of these opposite principles are various, according to the different situation of the human understanding."[320]

Thus has this wretched man misrepresented and calumniated those two simple principles, which under the guidance of natural light, led the people to a deity and kept him always in sight, namely FEAR, and LOVE. A man less maliciously disposed to abuse and slander human nature, would have fairly told us, that FEAR kept the Religionist from evil, as a thing offensive to the deity; and that LOVE inclined him to virtuous practice, as most

[320] Page 94–5.

acceptable to the divine nature. No, says this accuser of his Kind, FEAR presented the Religionist *with the notion of a devilish and malicious deity: and* LOVE *exaggerated the perfections of the deity, without consulting any arguments or phœnomena*: i.e. arguments or phœnomena, which might have convinced him that they were *exaggerations*. Whereas the truth of the case is merely this; whenever simple nature did not work by *fear* and *love*, to avoid evil and to follow good, but instead of that to invent a *fantastic*, or a *diabolic* deity, the impediment was accidental, occasioned by the intervention of some unhappy circumstance foreign to the natural workings of the human mind.

REMARK XVII.

"It is remarked by Xenophon (says our Philosopher) in praise of Socrates, that that philosopher assented not to the VULGAR opinion, which supposed the Gods to know some things, and be ignorant of others: He maintained that they knew every thing, which was done, said, or even thought. But this was a strain of philosophy much above the conception of his countrymen."[321]

This is pleasant. It is but in the foregoing page, he assures us, that not only the *Vulgar* of Greece, but the *Vulgar* of all the world knew that their Gods *were ignorant of nothing*. His words are these. *If we consider that spirit of praise and eulogy*, WHICH NECESSARILY HAS PLACE IN ALL RELIGIONS, *we shall find that every virtue, every excellence must be ascribed to the divinity, and* NO EXAGGERATIONS BE ESTEEMED SUFFICIENT TO REACH THOSE PERFECTIONS, *with which he is endowed*. Now is not OMNISCIENCE a PERFECTION? And was not the spirit of exaggeration, which never thought it said enough, able to reach the idea of *knowing all things*? How happened it then that this exaggerating mob of Religionists wanted a Socrates to tell them, that *the Gods not only knew some things, but all things*? But the man has got his readers, and he uses them as they deserve.

REMARK XVIII.

But now for a discovery indeed. –

"As men further EXALT the idea of their divinity; it is often their NOTION OF HIS POWER AND KNOWLEDGE ONLY, NOT OF HIS GOODNESS, which is

---

[321] Page 96.

improved. On the contrary, in proportion to the supposed extent of his science and authority, their terrors naturally augment."[322]

This is hard. Common sense seems to tell us so much of our common nature, that the *spirit of love*, which is ever *for exalting further and further the idea of* its object, is chiefly delighted in dwelling on the GOODNESS of that object: as *fear* is most conversant in the divine attributes of *power and knowledge.* But this sublime philosopher has discovered that both we and nature are mistaken; and that, *as men further exalt the idea of their divinity, it is often their notion of power and knowledge, not of his goodness,* that is improved. And his kind reader might be disposed perhaps to take his word, but that he sees it contradicts, in express terms, what he had said but two or three pages before: Where he as magisterially assures us, that *a spirit of praise and eulogy makes men ascribe every virtue, every excellence to the Deity, and to* EXAGGERATE THEM ALL: Therefore, I should suppose, GOODNESS, along with the rest.

REMARK XIX.

After all these feats, he will now account how it happens that Religionists are so generally disposed to prefer rites and positive institutions, to morality and natural duties. And the secret is revealed in this manner:

"Perhaps, the following account may be received as a true solution of the difficulty. The duties, which a man performs as a friend or parent, seem merely owing to his benefactor or children, nor can he be wanting to these duties, without breaking thro' all the ties of nature and morality. A strong inclination may prompt him to the performance: A sentiment of order and moral beauty joins its force to these natural ties: And the whole man, if truly virtuous, is drawn to his duty, without any effort or endeavour. Even with regard to the virtues, which are more austere, and more founded on reflection, such as public spirit, filial duty, temperance, or integrity; the moral obligation, in our apprehension, removes all pretence to religious merit; and the virtuous conduct is esteemed no more than what we owe to society and to ourselves. In all this, a superstitious man finds nothing, which he has properly performed for the sake of his deity, or which can peculiarly recommend him to the divine favour and protection. He considers not, that the most genuin method of serving the divinity is by promoting the happiness of his creatures. He still looks out for some more immediate service of the Supreme Being, in order to allay those terrors, with which he is haunted."[323]

[322] Page 97.

[323] Page 106–107.

It is to be lamented that but just before he had proved all this fine reasoning not worth a rush, where he confesses *that there are popular Religions, in which it is expressly declared that nothing but morality can gain the divine favour.*[324] For, if those who prefer rites to moral duties, are yet taught by their Religion that *nothing but morality can gain the divine favour*, it is plain, his solution can have no place, which is that superstitious men give that unjust preference, *because they can find nothing in morality which can peculiarly recommend them to the divine favour.* Had he not therefore done better, as in the former instance of *the genius of Paganism*, to have stolen his solution? He has not boggled at greater matters. And a Philosopher, who deserves no quarter from him, might have saved his credit, and been pillaged with advantage.

"Next to the knowledge of one God, says this excellent man, a clear knowledge of their duty was wanting to mankind. This part of knowledge, tho' cultivated with some care by some of the Heathen philosophers, yet got little footing amongst the people. The priests made it not their business to teach men virtue. If they were diligent in their observations and ceremonies; punctual in their feasts and solemnities, and the tricks of religion, the holy tribe assured them, the Gods were pleased, and they looked no farther. Few went to the schools of the philosophers to be instructed in their duties, and to know what was good and evil in their actions. *The Priests sold the better penny-worths, and therefore had all their custom. Lustrations and processions were much easier than a clean conscience, and a steady course of virtue; and an expiatory sacrifice, that attoned for the want of it, was much more convenient than a steady course of virtue.*"[325]

This is the solution of a philosopher indeed; clear, simple, manly, rational, and striking conviction in every word; unlike the refined and fantastic nonsense of a writer of Paradoxes.

But then don't imagine that our author was not aware of this solution. No, he despised it because it was so reasonable. For he thinks to obviate it by saying, "That it is not satisfactory to allege that the practice of morality is more difficult than that of superstition; *and is therefore rejected.*"[326] *But how does he make out this point? Why, by giving us to understand that the four Lents of the Muscovites, and the austerities of some Roman Catholics, appear more disagreeable than* MEEKNESS AND

---

[324] Page 104.

[325] Locke's works, vol. 2 p. 575. [*The Reasonableness of Christianity as Delivered in the Scriptures*, in *Works* (London, 1833), Vol. VII, pp. 138–139.]

[326] Page 105.

BENEVOLENCE. Let him say, as Mr. Locke does, honestly – than a STEADY COURSE OF VIRTUE. And we shall better judge whether *these austerities* be indeed more difficult than *such* a morality.

REMARK XX.

Well, but he makes ample amends for the slight here shewn of STEADY VIRTUE. For, as a supplement to his account of this mysterious phœnomenon,

"We may add, says he, that even after the commission of crimes, there arise remorses and secret horrors, which give no rest to the mind, but make it have recourse to religious rites and ceremonies, as expiations of its offences. Whatever weakens or disorders the internal frame promotes the interests of superstition: AND NOTHING IS MORE DESTRUCTIVE TO THEM THAN A MANLY STEADY VIRTUE, which either preserves us from disastrous melancholly accidents, or teaches us to bear them."[327]

We may add, says he. That he may safely, whatever he pleases; who has a public to deal with so easily bubbled into the opinion of his being a philosopher. Which makes me the more wonder at the trouble his friends gave him, of refining this *natural history* from the grosser faces[328] of Atheism, before it was presented to the world.[329] But this public, it seems, was become a little squeamish, having been so lately overdosed by the quackery of Bolingbroke.[330]

NOTHING, says our philosopher, IS MORE DESTRUCTIVE TO THE INTEREST OF SUPERSTITION, THAN A MANLY STEADY VIRTUE: Which in plainer English is, "None will be so free from Superstition as the most hardened Rogue." For the fact, from which he deduces this proposition, is this, *That after the commission of crimes, there arise remorses and secret horrors, which make men have recourse to expiatory rites.* These remorses, BY WEAKENING AND DISORDERING THE INTERNAL FRAME, *promote superstition.* Now the

---

[327] Page 109–10.

[328] [The 1788 edition reads "fæces" in place of "faces".]

[329] [Prior to the distribution of *Four dissertations*, Hume altered two passages in the "Natural History" and removed the essays "Of Suicide" and "Of the Immortality of the Soul". A comment similar to Warburton's appears in the *Critical Review* review of the "Natural History": "A deficiency in our author's arrangement of his notions, and a want of method and connection is also visible throughout the whole, occasioned perhaps by some castration of the original." See also the review of Hume's *Essays on suicide* in the *Monthly Review*, included in this volume.]

[330] [In the 1777 and 1788 editions, this paragraph reads "*We may add,* says he, That he may say safely whatever he pleases…".]

contrary state of this internal frame can be no other than such as enables us to bear the retrospect of our rogueries without *remorse and horror*: this he calls *a manly steady Virtue.* Do I wrong him? Let his friends judge. Had he meant, by *manly steady virtue* what common moralists so call, he must have told us, that this *Virtue* produced in the offender, reparation of injuries and amendment of life; things, in reality, *most destructive to the interests of superstition.* Whereas the *manly steady virtue* of our philosopher does no more, by his own confession, than *either preserve us from disastrous melancholly accidents* [i.e. keep us from hanging ourselves] *or teaches us to bear them* [i.e. to recall to memory our past crimes without remorse.] And this, hardened roguery, and nothing but hardened roguery is capable of atchieving. Or, will he, to save himself from this atrocious charge, say, that by a *manly steady virtue* he meant such a *Virtue* as *prevents* the commission of crimes? This had been to the purpose. But let him then shew us how this meaning is to be gathered from his *expression.* To say the least, if, in excess of candour, one must suppose him to have *meant well*, no well-meaning philosopher ever expressed himself so wretchedly.

REMARK XXI.

You have here, Sir, what I promised You; a specimen of his philosophic virtues, his reasoning, his consistency, his knowledge, his truth, his candour and his modesty, as they promiscuously appear in the NATURAL HISTORY OF RELIGION.[331] I have hunted him from track to track. And now what thick cover, do You suppose, has he chosen to skreen himself from the public contempt? He takes shelter in the dark umbrage of SCEPTICISM. These are his concluding words.

"The whole is a riddle, an ænigma, an inexplicable mystery. Doubt, uncertainty, suspence of judgment appear the only result of our most accurate scrutiny, concerning this subject. But such is the frailty of human reason, and such the irresistible contagion of opinion, that even this deliberate doubt could scarce be upheld; did we not enlarge our view, and opposing one species of superstition to another, set them a quarreling; while we ourselves, during their fury and contention, happily make our escape, into THE CALM, THO' OBSCURE, REGIONS OF PHILOSOPHY."

Thus, we see, his last effort is to defend his *dogmatical* nonsense with *scepticism* still more nonsensical. Nor to this, neither, dares he trust

---

[331] [In the 1788 edition this sentence reads "I have given a specimen of...".]

himself: but presently meditates an *escape*, as he calls it, by setting the *Religionists a quarreling*: without which, he frankly owns, that *deliberate doubt could scarce be upheld.* For the sake of this beloved object, DELIB-ERATE DOUBT, there is no mischief he is not ready to commit, even to the unhinging the national Religion, and unloosing all the hold it has on the minds of the people. And all this for the selfish and unnatural lust of *escaping* from right reason and common sense, *into the calm, tho' obscure regions of philosophy.* But here we have earthed him; rolled up in the Scoria of a *dogmatist* and *Sceptic*, run down together. He has been long taken for a Philosopher: and so perhaps he may be found – like Aristotle's statue in the Block.

"Then take him to devellop, if you can,
And hew the block off, and get out the Man."[332]

CONCLUSION.

I have now done with my Philosopher; and, whatever his admirers may think, You, Sir, I persuade myself, will be of opinion that I have treated him but as he deserves. If indeed my purpose had been only to disgrace the *man*, the very recital of his impieties had been sufficient. But finding, that he had somehow usurped to himself the name of *Philosopher*, I thought it not amiss, as occasion offered, to expose his bad logic; and above all to point out to the reader his numerous *inconsistencies and contradictions.* I can readily believe, however, he will be the first to divert himself with this part of my pains. He, who thinks at large, is enslaved to no principles, nor acknowledges any, what should hinder him from writing with as little regard to *truth*, as to Religion? He leaves it, no doubt, to the Religionists to shackle themselves in CONSISTENCY? What is it to him, a free-thinker and a sceptic, whether what he says in one page be of a piece with what he delivers in another?

Well, but this is the feature, of all others, in his philosophical countenance, which I was most ambitious of catching, and presenting to the view of the public. For that public, I would hope, is even yet not so thoroughly abandoned, as to contemplate this profligacy of mind, indifferent to truth and falshood, and which is ready, on all occasions, to neglect common honesty and insult common Sense, without horror. And what so likely way of discrediting such a writer with the people, as to let

---

[332] [Alexander Pope, *The Dunciad*, Bk. IV, 270. The commentary on this passage in Warburton's 1751 edition of Pope's *Works* reads, "A notion of Aristotle, that there was originally in every block of marble, a Statue, which would appear on the removal of superfluous parts".]

them see what a conductor they have taken to themselves in philosophy and religion?

In the mean time how miserable is the condition of depraved humanity! Heaven sends us into life with the seeds and principles, at least, of integrity and honesty. The vulgar of all denominations presently lose these virtues, in the commerce of the WORLD. And the men of science, in the SCHOOLS: The consequence is, A *practice*, void of MORALITY; and a *speculation*, unawed by TRUTH. In this scene of things the good man applies himself to reform the one, and instruct the other: Both, I am afraid, as the Patriarch believed, *against hope*. Yet this does not lessen the merit of his intended services. My concern is only, how they may become effectual. And if there be a way left, it is surely that which you have hitherto taken, "of disgracing every licentious shallow scribler; that dishonours the name of letters, by writing the abused public into an opinion of his being a philosopher."

Hence it is, that CHUBB, MORGAN, COLLINS, MANDEVILLE and BOLINGBROKE are names, which nobody hears, without laughing. It is not for me, perhaps, to predict the fate of Mr. DAVID HUME. But if You, Sir, had taken upon You to read his destiny, the public had, now, seen this Adorer of *Nature*, this *last* hope of his declining family, gathered *to the dull of ancient days*;

"Safe, where no critics, no divines molest,
Where wretched TOLAND, TINDAL, TILLARD rest."

I am, with due respect,
SIR, &c.

FINIS.

18
GÖTTINGISCHE ANZEIGEN

Review of *Four Dissertations*, in *Göttingische Anzeigen von gelehrten Sachen*, April 8, 1758 No. 42, pp. 401–403.
English translation of complete review, translated by Curtis Bowman.

The *Göttingische Anzeigen* was one of the world's longest serial publications, covering over 200 years, from 1739 to 1940. The journal went through several name changes, and was devoted to the review of scholarly books.[333] The journal routinely reviewed Hume's publications and, not unexpectedly, took notice of Hume's *Four Dissertations*. Concerning "The Natural History of Religion", the reviewer senses some hidden intentions behind this piece, but nevertheless states that it contains "exquisitely beautiful truths". The reviewer finds "Of the Passions" less original, but is pleased with the remaining two essays. Below is the first published English translation of the complete review, by Curtis Bowman. Bracketed comments in the notes below are those of the translator.

London.

Last year, in Millar's press, David Hume published four essays (*four dissertations*)[334] on 240 octavo pages. The first essay he calls a *natural history of religion*, under which heading one is not to look for a history of religion drawn from documents and books, but rather a philosophical essay on how natural religion, without revelation, arises, develops, and degenerates. One wanted to discover this otherwise excellent writer's aversion to revealed religion in this history as well; we also do not want to deny that a writer who took the Bible to be God's word would have remembered sometimes that religion may have arisen in a way different from how he recounts its origin; and sometimes it seems that merely the undeniable age of the Bible should have forced one or the other acknowledgment from

---

[333] *Göttingische Zeitungen von gelehrten Sachen* (1739–1752); *Göttingische Anzeigen von gelehrten Sachen, unter der Aufsicht der Königl. Gesellschaft der Wissenschaften* (1753–1801); *Göttingische gelehrte Anzeigen, unter der Aufsicht der Gesellschaft der Wissenschaften* (1802–1940).

[334] [The phrase "four dissertations" is in English in the original review. – CB]

him. But we are not judging hidden intentions; and if one is looking for nothing other than the natural history of religion, then the book contains exquisitely beautiful truths which even the friend of revelation can well use. Naturally, superstition and polytheism come before the religion and worship of a single god, just as a miserable hut comes before a palace. The daily observation that unknown causes make us happy or unhappy first disposes us to a fear of the invisible. These unknown causes are indeed natural, but the common eye does not see this: it assumes invisible beings who dispense happiness and mishap, and appoints them to these matters and those. These are the first gods created by fear: one flatters them, one praises them, and the flattery finally outdoes itself and attributes true infinitude to them. Thus we come to truth by means of error. (It is a wonder that Mr. H. never makes the observation that the most ancient history and the book which is older than any other[335] are contrary to this history[336] and demonstrates the worship of a single infinite God prior to idolatry; religion could thus not have arisen as a natural growth from the soil, but rather must have been given as a revelation at the beginning of the world.) He finds polytheism – who will deny it? – more tolerant than the worship of a single God; but if he records persecution and inquisition in the reckoning of the Christian religion, he seems not merely to forget the history which teaches us that early on Christianity suffered more persecution than it committed, but also to contradict his propositions announced on page 66 which class the papacy with paganism and regard Dominic no differently than Hercules.[337] The abundance of important and unnoticed truths in this first essay nevertheless remains large; and we break off because we cannot compel it into our pages. The second essay treats of the passions. He concerns himself with showing that hope and fear are simply mixtures of joy and sorrow, which he presents as something new, even though it is an old truth. In the case of pride he asserts that one is pleased with the favourable judgment of others only for the reason that it is a confirmation of our own judgment which otherwise appears doubtful to us. Of the other passions he shows how different mixtures alter them; his main intention is to discover what he calls the mechanism of the passions, but we have not found here as much that is unexpected or unusual as we are otherwise accustomed to find in H. The third essay, Of Tragedy, investigates whence arises the pleasure which the representation of the saddest

---

[335] [i.e., the Bible. – CB]

[336] [i.e., contrary to the historical account found in Hume's *Natural History of Religion*. – CB]

[337] [Hume is referring to Saint Dominic (1170–1221), the founder of the Dominican order. The reviewer has in mind the third paragraph of section X of Hume's essay. – CB].

history gives us in so high a degree. He makes use of what others before him have said, but adds yet another new cause: namely, that the beauty and skill of the execution is what actually pleases in tragedy; if, however, we have two passions at the same time, then the weaker, subordinate passion strengthens the superior one. The sadness which the story arouses is, because we know that it is not a true story, even weaker than our enjoyment of the beauty of the work; therefore, it only raises the latter pleasure to a quite incredible magnitude. This material is handled very well. The final essay attempts to formulate a standard of taste.[338]

---

[338] [I thank Heiner Klemme for his comments on this translation. – CB]

19
THOMAS STONA

[Thomas Stona], *Remarks upon The natural history of religion by Mr. Hume. With dialogues on heathen idolatry, and the Christian religion. By S.T.* London: printed for R. and J. Dodsley, 1758, [2], 159, [1] p.
Selections from pages 1–30, 119–127; from 1758 and only edition.

L ittle is known of Thomas Stona (1727/8–1792) other than the fact that he authored *A Letter to the Norfolk Militia, upon the Proceedings of Ancient Nations when Engaged in War. By a Dumpling-Eater...* (London: M. Cooper, 1759). His *Remarks upon the Natural History of Religion* was published anonymously; authorship is attributed to him in John Nichols's *Literary Anecdotes* (London, 1812, Vol. 2, p. 717). The work is divided into three sections: "Remarks on the *Natural History of Religion*" (pp. 1–30), "On Idolatry, a Dialogue" (pp. 30–106), and "Dialogue on the Christian Religion" (pp. (106–159). The first of these sections presents a sustained discussion of Hume's "Natural History of Religion", in which Stona defends the position of original monotheism and attacks Hume's claim that primitive humans were too unsophisticated to deduce monotheism from nature. The second section, "On Idolatry", examines the causes of idolatry; Hume is only briefly discussed. The third section, "A Dialogue on the Christian Religion", defends Christian revelation, and contains a short discussion of Hume's argument against miracles. According to Stona, on Hume's reasoning, we would be forced to deny extraordinary matters of fact such as the existence of Stonehenge, the Pyramids and other wonders, since "we never knew, observed or experienced such a composition of the mechanical powers, as was employed to perform them".

In his brief review of Stona's *Remarks*, William Rose writes in the *Monthly Review* that,

> The Author of these Remarks, &c. appears to be a friend to religion and freedom of enquiry; but he has advanced nothing, in our opinion, that can give the judicious reader any high idea of his discernment or acuteness. His remarks upon Mr. Hume's Natural History of Religion are extremely superficial, and scarce contain any thing that deserves particular notice.

Rose concludes with an unfavourable opinion of the third part of this work:

> In the Dialogue on the *Christian Religion*, there is nothing to be met with but what has been often repeated; nothing urged, but what has been often urged with much greater accuracy and strength of reasoning. [*Monthly Review*, December 1758, Vol. 19, pp. 532–533].

The *Critical Review* devotes a full review article to Stona's *Remarks*. The author opens with an exceptionally sympathetic general assessment of Hume:

> Few writers have been more admired, more opposed, and misrepresented than the ingenious author of the Essays, of which the Natural History of Religion makes one. He has been accused of heterodoxy in religion; of broaching doctrines destructive of Christianity, and the fundamentals of piety and virtue. As a moralist, we have heard him called obscure and paradoxical; as a politician, wild and ideal; though we do not remember to have seen those positions made good by a pen half so masterly as his own. Mr. Hume's sentiments are generally new, ingenious, and deep, the result of a sound judgment, and fine imagination. If sometimes they do not bear the stamp of truth, they have at least the recommendation of novelty, well expressed, and deduced in a manner so obvious and easy, that we are only surprised the reflections did not occur to ourselves; although, upon farther deliberation, we find them drawn from a long and intricate chain of thought. That he is faultless as a politician and moralist, is what we will not assert. His extreme refinement, subtlety, and abstractedness, must undoubtedly lead him often into error; and always fit his maxims rather for the closet than for life and practice. But these are blemishes of a venial nature, if they are blemishes, since they tend to improve the rational faculty, fix the attention, and open the mind to a full display and exertion of its powers. But he himself has given the best defence of this kind of writing prefixed to his Political Essays, to which we refer our readers, as we cannot quote the passage for want of room.

The reviewer continues with a mixed appraisal of Stona's work:

> Mr. Hume is here accused by our author of positions which reflect upon the dignity of the species, as well as the truth of revealed religion. He is attacked with the candor and good breeding of a gentleman, with the erudition of a scholar; but, if we may draw a comparison, with a capacity, a closeness, and precision inferior to his own. There is something easy, polite, but loose and superficial, in the manner of our

author. A few private letters introduce a personal conference among two or three friends, the subject of which turns upon some notions advanced by Mr. Hume. The dialogue, without the depth, or perhaps, the genteel freedom of Plato, Tully, and Berkeley, has at least the merit of being equal to most modern productions in this way. *Inter silvas academiœ quærere verum*, pursuing truth through lawns, woods, and groves, investigating points of abstruse philosophy in common discourse, we fear, is not very suitable to the taste and manners of the age. Most conversations take a turn so very different from the subject of the dialogue before us, that we will not hesitate to affirm it would be condemned by a fine gentleman as forced, unnatural, and favouring of pedantry and the college.

The reviewer concludes with the following recommendation:

We recommend this performance to our readers as a work of learning, taste, and merit; wherein he will find satisfaction without conviction, and an elegant and liberal turn of sentiment, without, perhaps, the strongest powers of the discussive faculty. [*Critical Review*, November 1758, Vol. 6, pp. 411–418]

The following is from the 1758 and only edition of Stona's *Remarks*.

REMARKS
UPON THE
Natural History of Religion.

LETTER to THEOPHILUS

I have lately met with a treatise entitled, *The Natural History of Religion*, in which the author proposes to enquire into the primary religion of mankind upon the principles of reason, unassisted with revelation, and has produced a series of arguments to prove that it was polytheism. I do not pretend to be a judge of the merits of this performance; but must confess, that the air of freedom which enlivens every part of it, delighted me extremely. You know, Theophilus, that I am a friend to liberty in the literary, as well as civil world, since tyrannical authority in either will equally depress the writer, and enslave the subject; to *think* is the prerogative of every rational creature, and freely to declare its sentiments, its happiest privilege. This liberty indeed, you will say, is designed for the investigation of truth, so should be safely preserved from the abuses of the *freethinker* when he endeavours to pervert or corrupt this advantage, as well as from the attacks of the *bigot*, when he wants to destroy it; and, if you read this pamphlet, will think perhaps, that its ingenious author should be ranked under the first class, and that he may be suspected of some such intention, as he has advanced an opinion entirely repugnant to the profession of the Mosaic history. I should be glad then if you would carefully examine it, and tell me whether Mr. Hume has given us a true delineation of human nature in its primitive state, or whether he hath not unjustly depreciated its dignity, by describing our ancient ancestors as altogether *rude, ignorant* and *barbarous*; for as they wore the same frame, possessed the same rational faculty, and were actuated by the same passions with myself, so I am desirous of being acquainted with their civil and religious constitution soon after they were placed upon this beautiful theatre. That affection, which you call benevolence, uninfluenced either by the interest, or connection of relations, friends, or countrymen, uninterrupted with those passions of envy or malice, which are too apt to engage themselves in a party towards our contemporaries, now glows with the purest ardor, and makes me wish to find that advantageous characters are given of the human race, even in the remotest ages of antiquity.

ACASTO.

LETTER to ACASTO.

I Sat down with a full expectation of being highly entertained with the perusal of the pamphlet which you recommended to me in your letter; for the character of its author, and the plan he proposes to pursue, gave me great hopes of finding some new light flung upon the obscure parts of antiquity: but you may judge of the satisfaction it afforded me in this respect by the following abstract.

"It appears to me (says Mr. Hume,) that if we consider the improvement of human society, from rude beginnings to a greater state of perfection, polytheism or idolatry was, and necessarily must have been the first and most ancient religion of mankind. This opinion I shall endeavour to confirm by the following arguments.

'Tis a matter of fact uncontestable, that about 1700 years ago all mankind were idolaters. – Behold then the clear testimony of history. The farther we mount up into antiquity, the more we do find mankind plunged into idolatry. No marks, no symptoms of any more perfect religion. The most ancient records of human race still present us with polytheism, as the popular and established system. As far as writing or history reaches, mankind in ancient times appear universally to have been polytheists. Shall we assert, that in more ancient times, before the

knowledge of letters, or the discovery of any art or science, men entertained the principles of pure theism? That is, while they were ignorant
and barbarous they discovered truth: but fell into error as soon as they
acquired learning and politeness. But in this assertion you not only
contradict all appearance of probability, but also our present experience
concerning the principles and opinions of barbarous nations. The savage
tribes of America, Africa, and Asia, are all idolaters."

The meaning of this argument is, that as far as history reaches, the
popular religion of most countries is found to have been polytheism; and
as mankind were altogether ignorant and barbarous before the knowledge
of letters, or the discovery of any art or science, so unable in such a state
to find out the principles of theism, therefore polytheism must have been
their first and most ancient religion.

But the incapacity of a people unacquainted with the arts and sciences,
to find out the principles of theism, should be demonstrated, before this
argument can have any weight or validity whatever; otherwise mankind
may reasonably be supposed to have made this discovery, long before the
arts and sciences were known. For the works of the creation are the
certain, and have been the perpetual testimony of the existence of a God,
and reason is the medium with which the human creature, from the very
first period of its being, hath been furnished to discover it: it always saw
the sun enlivening every part of the creation, the earth bringing forth
provision for its use, the seasons returning in the utmost regularity and
order; it must always have observed itself to be surrounded by an
innumerable species of creatures, and could not help perceiving its own
inability to form or give life to the meanest insect: and from that reflection
must have been immediately led to conclude, that this beauteous scene of
things must certainly have been created by a being infinitely superior in
wisdom and power to man. But the mind did not want the irradiation of
the arts, to enable it to discover this truth; for neither the utmost perfection
in architecture, sculpture, painting, or statuary, would lead it to such
contemplations as these. In succeeding ages indeed, when mankind were
acquainted with the sciences, they might have acquired more refined proofs
of a deity: as the beautiful symmetry of parts which is conspicuous in the
human frame, is an infallible conviction to the anatomist of the wisdom of
its author; the laws of gravity in the heavenly bodies will afford the
astronomer the most august idea of that being who first put them into
motion. But it will be too peremptory to affirm, that the illiterate *ancient*
might not from pure intellect contemplate this scene of things, with the
same rapture of admiration, with the same emotions of gratitude towards
his Creator, as the cultivated *modern*. Education indeed may polish the
reflections of mankind, but it cannot generate them; and you must neces-

sarily suppose the seeds of knowledge to be planted in the peasant, before they can be expanded into the arts and sciences in the philosopher. So mankind were as able to discover the existence of a God in the remotest ages of antiquity, as at present; and consequently it neither contradicts any appearance of probability to assert, that notwithstanding as far as history reaches, mankind in ancient times appear to have been polytheists; yet in more ancient times, before the knowledge of letters, or the discovery of any art or science, men entertained the principles of theism. That is, while they were ignorant of these accomplishments, they discovered truth, but were afterwards compelled to embrace idolatry, for political purposes (as it will appear in the sequel). Neither doth such an assertion contradict our experience of barbarous nations, who are not all idolaters: the natives of New England believe in a supreme power, that created all things, whom they call Kichtan,[339] and those of Canada believe in the existence of a God.[340]

The Peruvians called the first cause of all things, Pachacamac; by which word they meant the quickener of the universe; or the great soul of the world. This name was so very sacred, and venerable amongst them, that they never mentioned it but upon extreme necessity; and then not without all the signs of devotion imaginable, as bowing the body and head, lifting up the eyes to heaven, and spreading out their hands.[341]

The idolatrous Indians of Asia acknowledge only one infinite God, almighty, and only wise, the creator of heaven and earth, whom they call Permessar, and represent by an oval figure, as the most perfect.[342]

The Africans of Negroland likewise worship Guihimo, i.e. the Lord of heaven.[343]

But to confirm this opinion: Mr. Hume proceeds to tell us, that

"a barbarous necessitous animal (such as man is on the very first origin of society) pressed by such numerous wants and passions, has no leisure to admire the regular face of nature, or make enquiries concerning the cause of objects, to which from his infancy he has been gradually accus-

---

[339] L. 5. c. 30. Harris's coll. of voyages. [John Harris, *Navigantium atque itinerantium bibliotheca: Or a complete collection of voyages and travels* (London, 1705).]

[340] L. 5. c. 18. Ibid.

[341] L. 5. c. 14. Ibid.

[342] L. 2. c. 7. Tavernier's trav. from Harris.

[343] L. 3. c. 1. Harris's coll. of voyages.

tomed. – Imagine not that he will so much as start the question, whence the whole system, or united fabric of the universe arose."[344]

This is a notable observation indeed, and indisputably proves, that as long as man continued to be a *barbarous, necessitous animal*, he was most certainly a *barbarous*, and *necessitous animal*; but it by no means follows from thence, that he was a *polytheist*. A creature starving with hunger would be anxious only of conquering its immediate wants, and not yet curious of enquiring into the order of the universe, or what relation it might have to a superior being; and so, in such a state as this, would be of no religion whatever. Therefore the society must necessarily be supposed to have been amply supplied with the conveniencies of life, and that different stations were allotted to its several members, before curiosity excited any of them, whose employments might engage them the least in their worldly affairs, to enquire from whence they sprung; and man must have been a civilized, contemplative, and reflecting creature, before he could have been a religious one; must be supposed to have argued, and reasoned upon his own nature, to have been sensible of his dependence on a superior power, before he could think of applying to that power for relief.

The question is, whether the human creature, after having exercised its intellectual faculties, and considered the different parts of nature, after having surveyed the stupendous furniture of the heavens, and admired the exquisite order and harmony of this beauteous scene, it would suppose it to be the effect of infinite power, perfect wisdom, and goodness, and so be led to adore its supreme Creator; or whether, (as Mr. H— asserts) it imagined, *each element to be subjected to its invisible power and agent; the province of each god to be separated from that of another; and that its first ideas of religion arose from the incessant hopes and fears which actuate the human mind; so invoked Juno at marriages, Lucina at births.*

In short, the question is, whether the primary religion of a rational creature, was the offspring of its reason, or the monster of its fears. This latter opinion Mr. H— has borrowed from the poet's observation, that *primus in orbe deos fecit timor:*[345] an assertion which deserves rather to be ridiculed, than to be seriously confuted.

To proceed. The author observes,

"it must necessarily be allowed, that, in order to carry men's attention beyond the visible course of things, or lead them into any inference

---

[344] Lord Bolingbroke argues in the same manner. Sect. II. Essay II. Phil. Works. [*Philosophical Works* (London, 1754), Vol. I, Essay II, Sect. 2.]

[345] Statius, Theb. 3. [*Thebiad*, Book. 3, v. 660–62, "Fear first created gods in the world."]

concerning invisible, intelligent power, they must be actuated by some passion, which prompts their thought, and reflection, some motive which urges their first enquiry. But what passion shall we have recourse to, for explaining an effect of such mighty consequence? not speculative curiosity, or the pure love of truth. That motive is too refined for such gross apprehensions, and would lead them into enquiries concerning the frame of nature, a subject too large, and comprehensive for their narrow capacities. No passions therefore can be supposed to work upon such barbarians, but the ordinary affairs of human life: the anxious concern for happiness, the thirst of revenge, the appetite for food, and other necessaries."

Such is Mr. H—'s opinion of our ancient ancestors. He thinks, that they were senseless of every emotion, but *fear, revenge*, and *hunger*; qualities indeed more justly applicable to the beasts of the forest, than to rational creatures. But it may be asked; why was *Speculative curiosity, or the pure love of truth, too refined for their apprehensions?* Doth he imagine that nature did not bestow her talents in so liberal a manner amongst her ancient sons, as amongst us? Doth he suppose that no inquisitive genius, no philosophic mind ever prevailed amongst them, but that reason and reflection are only of modern growth? Why might not a *Bacon, Locke*, or *Newton*, have existed in the remotest ages, since human nature hath always been the same from its first creation? perhaps as the poet observes,[346]

Before great Agamemnon reign'd
Reign'd kings as great as he, and brave,
Whose huge ambition's now contain'd
In the small compass of a grave,
In endless night they sleep unwept, unknown
No *bard* had they to make all time their own.

FRANCIS

But withall, we may demand what right he has to give them the appellation of *ignorant barbarians*, of having *gross apprehensions, narrow capacities?* for a deficiency of records must always deprive an impartial enquirer of that full conviction, by which alone he can be authorized to

---

[346] Vixere fortes ante Agamemnona
Multi: sed omnes illacrymabiles
Urgentur, ignotique longâ
Nocte, carent quia vate sacro.
Hor. l. 4. od. 9. [Horace, *Odes*, Bk. 4, ode 9, v. 25–29.]

pronounce with any decision upon the state and condition of the ancient world. The very invention of letters did not precede the christian æra perhaps above 2000 years, being found out by Thoth in the reign of Tham,[347] and the Greeks wrote nothing in prose before the conquest of Asia by Cyrus the Persian;[348] and consequently as mankind existed many ages before the use of letters, they had no means whatever (if we except hieroglyphicks, which were not to be depended upon, as being capable of various interpretations) of conveying any account of their lives to posterity; so one generation passed away and was but feintly remembered, or entirely forgotten by its succeeding one, and some edifice or column perhaps was the only evidence that mankind then had of the very existence of their ancestors. If a few centuries would thus obliterate the memory of people, and nations, before the use of letters, must not we call it presumption in this author, thus dogmatically to declare that they were altogether *rude*, *ignorant*, and *barbarous* in their manners, and that idolatry was their first religion?

So whether theism or polytheism was the primary religion of mankind, can be determined upon no other authority, than revelation; and if *that* is excluded by this author, then the solution of this question can be only founded on conjecture, and that side of it which is supported by the greatest degree of probability have a right to our assent.

Upon this principle alone must we argue, and let us consider the state of mankind in the remotest ages, upon the testimony of the most ancient monuments, and records, and endeavour from thence to form a reasonable idea of their manners and religion.

The pyramids of Egypt were built before the use of letters,[349] and have still survived the storms, and mouldering hand of time, to convince us, that its builders compounded the mechanical powers in a manner unknown to

---

[347] Soc. Ηκουσα τοινυν περι Ναυκρατιν της Αιγυπτου γενεσθαι των εκει παλαιων τινα θεων, ου και το ορνεον το ιερον ο δη καλουσιν ιβιν αυτω δε ονομα τω δαιμονι ειναι Θευθ. τουτον δε πρωτον αριθμον τε και λογισμον ευρειν και γεωμετριαν και αστρονομιαν, ετι δε πεττειας τε και κυβειασ, και δη και γραμματα.

Platonis Phædrus. [274c–d, "SOCRATES. I heard, then, that at Naucratis, in Egypt, was one of the ancient gods of that country, the one whose sacred bird is called the ibis, and the name of the god himself was Theuth. He it was who invented numbers and arithmetic and geometry and astronomy, also draughts and dice, and, most important of all, letters."]

[348] Newton's Chron. [Isaac Newton, *Chronology of antient kingdoms amended* (London, 1728).]

[349] Pliny speaking of the pyramids says, "Qui de iis scripserunt, sunt Herodotus, Euhemerus, Duris Samius, Aristagoras, Dionysius, Artemidorus, Alexander Polyhistor, Butorides, Antisthenes, Demetrius, Demoteles, Apion, inter omnes eos non constat à quibus factæ sint." Nat. Hist. l. 36. c. 12.

us at present;[350] and their situation likewise proves that they were acquainted with astronomy.[351] Architecture,[352] sculpture,[353] ship building,[354] and embroidery[355] were brought to great perfection in Homer's time. Xenophon speaks of great masters in statuary, and painting:[356] and we find in Plutarch, a remarkable proof of the excellent administration of justice amongst the ancient Egyptians.[357] If we consider withal the descriptions which authors have given us of the magnificent cities of Thebes,[358] Babylon,[359] and Memphis;[360] of the temple of Diana at Ephesus,[361] of the amazing works of the labyrinth,[362] of the lake Mœris,[363] or of the famous statue of Memnon;[364] can we help being astonished at the progress which the ancients had made in the mechanical arts? Is it then reasonable to suppose, with Mr. H—, that these people were *rude* and *ignorant*, and *that speculative curiosity was too refined for their gross apprehensions?* Is it to be imagined that these ancient philosophers, artists, and law-givers, were not curious to enquire from whence they sprung, and what being it is who endued them with that excellent faculty, by which they were enabled to measure time, to calculate the motions of the heavenly bodies, to plan the city and the pyramid; that faculty which taught them how to animate the block into a statue, and to enliven the canvass to a picture? Can we believe that these ingenious people, who by the greatest strength of mind had

[350] All the stones of the pyramid built by Cheops are 30 feet long, well squared, and jointed with the greatest exactness. Herod. [Herodotus, *History*] l. 2. c. 124.

[351] Norden's travels into Ægypt. [Frederick Lewis (Frederik Ludwig) Norden, *Travels in Egypt and Nubia* (London, 1705).]

[352] Homer's Iliad, l. 6. v. 242, &c.

[353] Ibid. l. 18. v. 483, &c.

[354] Ibid. l. 5. v. 62, &c.

[355] Ibid. l. 6. v. 289, &c.

[356] Xenophon's memorab. l. 1. c. 4. [Sect. 3.]

[357] "At Thebes the statues of the magistrates were carried without hands, and that of the chief judge with his eyes looking upon the ground, to signify that they should neither be prevailed upon by bribery, nor influenced by perswasion to act contrary to justice." de Isside & Osiride [Plutarch, *Moralia*, Bk. V, "Iside et Osiride," Ch. 10, Sect. 355.]

[358] Homer's Iliad, l. 9. v. 383.

[359] Herod. [Herodotus, *History*] l. 1. c. 178.

[360] Ibid. l. 2. c. 99.

[361] Pliny's natural history, l. 16. c. 40.

[362] Herod. [Herodotus, *History*] l. 2. c. 148.

[363] Ibid. l. 2. c. 149.

[364] Pliny's natural history, l. 36, c. 7.

invented that amazing art of letters, and the noble science of mathematicks, who had improved their understanding to such a degree of excellence in every respect, were either unable to discover the existence of a God, by the plain evidence of his works, or could refrain from enquiring what power it was, which constituted such beautiful order through the whole creation? Or shall we think with Mr. H—, that they looked upon this scene of things with the same indifference and stupidity, as the irrational brute? No! we cannot, after such indisputable evidence of the ingenuity and wisdom of the remotest ages, believe otherwise, than that they discovered and adored the divine being; for these testimonies are matters of fact, which no prejudice can elude, and as indisputably demonstrate the ability of man, as the works of the creation demonstrate the power and wisdom of God. Permit me then to indulge myself in a conjecture, that my ancient ancestors often turned their eyes to the blue vault of heaven, and chanted to their Creator like Adam in his morning orison, (for they undoubtedly observed, reflected, and admired.)

> These are thy glorious works, parent of good,
> Almighty, thine this universal frame,
> Thus wondrous fair; thyself how wondrous then!
> Unspeakable, who sit'st above the heavens
> To us invisible, or dimly seen
> In these thy lowest works; yet these declare
> Thy goodness beyond thought, and pow'r divine.[365]
>   Mil. par. lost. l. v. 153, &c.

We have likewise great reason to believe that theism was the primary religion of mankind, as the sensible part of them in all ages were of this opinion.

Orpheus,[366] Homer,[367] Thales,[368] Pythagoras,[369] Anaxagoras,[370] Socrates,[371]

---

[365] [John Milton, *Paradise Lost*, Bk. V, v. 153–159.]

[366] εις εστ᾽, αυτογενης, ενος εκγονα παντα τετυκται·
 εν δ᾽ αυτοις αυτος περινισσεται, ουδε τις αυτον
εισοραα θνητων, αυτος δε γε παντας οραται.
      ουτως μεν δη ῟Ορπευς.
Clem. Alex. admon. ad gentes. [Clement of Alexandria, *Exhortation to the Greeks*, Ch. VII, Sect. 64. "'One, self-begotten, lives; all things proceed from one; and in his works he ever moves: no mortal sees him, yet himself sees all.' Thus wrote Orpheus."]

[367] Agamemnon says to Achilles,
ει μαλα καρτερος εσσι, θεος που σοι το γ᾽ εδωκεν.
Iliad l. 1. v. 178 ["Though thou be very valiant, a god, I ween, gave thee this."]

[368] πρεσβυτατον των οντων θεος· αγενητον γαρ. καλλιστον κοσμος· ποιημα γαρ θεου.
Diogen. Laertius in vita Thaletis. [Diogenes Lærtius, *Lives of Eminent Philosophers*,

Plato,[372] and Aristotle[373] believed in the existence of a divine being. The Thebans believed in a self-existent and immortal being, whom they called Kneph,[374] and all the Egyptians in general esteemed God to be the cause of every creature that was generated, and of all the powers in nature, that he is superior to every thing, and that he is an immaterial, immortal, self-

Bk. I, Ch. 1, Thales, Sect. 35. "Of all things that are, the most ancient is God, for he is uncreated. The most beautiful is the universe, for it is God's workmanship."]

[369] Pythagoras censuit animum esse per naturam rerum omnem intentum, & commeantem.
Cic. de nat. deorum. [Cicero, *De Natura Deorum*, Bk. I, Ch. 11, Sect. 28. "As for Pythagoras, who believed that the entire substance of the universe is penetrated and pervaded by a soul....."]

[370] ο δ᾿ Αναξαγορασ φησιν ως ειστηκει κατ᾿ αρχας τα σωματα, νους δε αυτα διακοσμησε θεου, και τας γενεσεις των ογων εποιησεν.
Plutarch. Plac. Philos. l. 1. [Plutarch, *Moralia*, Book. 11, De Placitis Philosophorum, Book. I, Ch. 3. "Anaxagoras avers that bodies did consist from all eternity, but the divine intellect did reduce them into their proper orders, and effected the origination of all beings."]

[371] Xenophon's, memorabilia, l. 1. c. 4.

[372] ο αυτος γαρ ουτος χειροτεχνης ου μονον παντα οιος τε σκευη ποιησαι, αλλα και τα εκ της γης φυομενα απαντα ποιει και ζωα παντα εργαζεται, τα τε αλλα και εαυτον, και προς τουτοις γην και ουρανον και θεους και παντα τα εν ουρανω και τα εν αιδου υπο γης απαντα εργαζεται.
Plato de republica, l. 10 [Plato, *Republic*, Book 10, 596c. "This same handicraftsman is not only able to make all implements, but he produces all plants and animals, including himself, and hereto earth and heaven and the gods and all things in heaven and in Hades under the earth."]

[373] ο τε γαρ θεοσ δοκει των αιτιων πασιν ειναι και αρχη τις.
Aristotle, *Metaphysics*, 983a-8, ["God is thought to be among the causes of all things and to be a first principle."]

[374] τους θηβαιδα κατοικουντασ, ως θνητον θοεν ουδενα νομιζοντας, αλλα ον καλουσιν αυτοι Κνηφ, αγενητον οντα και αθανατον.
Plutarch. de is. & Osir. [Plutarch, *Moralia*, Bk. V, "Iside et Osiride", Ch. 21, Sect. 359. "The inhabitants of the Theban territory only do not contribute because they believe in no mortal god, but only in the god whom they call Kneph, whose existence had no beginning and shall have no end."]

existent being, who governs and sustains every part of the creation.[375] The Ethiopians,[376] the Persians,[377] and Chinese,[378] professed the same belief. Cicero observes, that there is no nation so savage and barbarous, which doth not believe in the being of a God, tho' it may be ignorant of the manner of his existence.[379] Dr. Warburton likewise says,

"It is not only possible that the worship of the first cause of all things was prior to any idol worship, but in the highest degree probable; idol worship having none of the appearances of an original custom, and all the circumstances attending a depraved and corrupted institution."[380]

If we then impartially consider the evidence of probability on either side of this question, we shall certainly be induced to believe that theism was the primary religion of mankind. Nay, if these testimonies which have been produced in favour of this opinion be excluded, let me even then ask you, Acasto, whether it is not more consistent with reason, to suppose that the wise, ingenious, thinking creature which we call man, whom the supreme being hath so eminently distinguished from the rest of the animal creation, by reason and reflection,[381] believed and adored his Creator, in the remotest ages of antiquity, than (according to Mr. Hume's plan) that

---

[375] ο της γενεσεως και φυσεως ολης, και των εν τοις στοιχειοις δυαμεων πασων αιτιος θεος, ατε δη υπερεχων τουτων αυλος και ασωματος και υπερφυης αγενητος τε και αμεριστοσ ολος εξ εαυτου και εν εαυτω αναφανεις, προηγειται παντων τουτων, και εν εαυτω τα ολα περιεχει.

Jamblichus de mysteriis, sect. 7. c. 2. [Iamblichus, *Mysteries of the Egyptians*, Book 7, Ch. 2, Sect. 251. "The God who is the cause of generation, of all nature, and of all the powers in the elements, as transcending these, and as being immaterial, incorporeal, and supernatural, unbegotten and impartible, wholly derived from himself, and concealed in himself, this God precedes all things, and comprehends all things in himself."]

[376] Strabo. l. 17. [Strabo, *Geography*, Book 17, Ch. 2, Sect. 3.]

[377] Hyde de religione vet. Perf. [Thomas Hyde, *Historia religionis veterum Persarum, earumque Magorum; Zoroastris vita, etc.* (Oxford, 1700).]

[378] Tabula chronologicæ monarchiæ Sinicæ ante Christum juxta cyclos, *annorum* 60. ante Christum, 2697. Hoam Ti, hoc est flavus imperator fundator monarchiæ. Templum pacis Xam Ti, id est supremo imperatori seu deo.

Confucius. ["Chronological list of the Chinese monarchs before Christ in accordance with cycles of 60 years, 2697 before Christ. Hoam Ti, namely, the yellow emperor, was founder of the monarchy. The temple of peace Xam Ti, he is the highest of rulers or God."]

[379] De ligibus, l. 1. c. 8. [Cicero, *De Legibus*, Bk. I, Ch. 8, Sect. 24.]

[380] Divine Legation, l. 3. 6th sect. [William Warburton, *The Divine Legation of Moses Demonstrated*, second edition (London, 1738), Vol. I, Bk. III, Sect. 6, page 461.]

[381] Cicero de legibus, l. 1. c. 7. [Sect. 22.]

he worshipped the ridiculous objects of idolatry? So I shall conclude this epistle with the words of Sir Isaac Newton;

> "The believing that the world was framed by one supreme God, and is governed by him, and the loving and worshipping him, and honouring our parents, and loving our neighbours as ourselves, and being merciful even to brute beasts, is the oldest of all religions."[382]

THEOPHILUS.

LETTER to THEOPHILUS

Your arguments in favour of theism have entirely convinced me, that it was the primary religion of mankind; for it is certainly more consistent with our idea of a rational creature to believe, that its religion, or the sense of its duty towards its Creator, at first arose from the conclusions of its reason, rather than from the suggestions of its fears. But as polytheism was undoubtedly the established religion of most of the heathen nations, I should be glad to be informed of the cause which induced mankind thus strangely to degenerate. A farther explanation therefore of your meaning, in idolatry being embraced for political purposes, would much oblige,

ACASTO.

LETTER to ACOSTO.

The satisfaction which my last letter gave you upon the subject of *theism*, has encouraged me to try what success I shall meet with upon *that* of *polytheism*; and if you will spend a few days with me at Pontefract, I will readily communicate my thoughts to you, upon the popular and established religion of the heathen world. I shall not examine the account which Mr. Hume hath given us of it (who says, "that idolatry is derived from the principles of human nature, that a vulgar polytheist deifies every part of the universe, and conceives all the conspicuous productions of nature, to be themselves so many real divinities. The sun, moon and stars, are all gods, according to his system; fountains are inhabited by nymphs, and trees by hamadryads; even monkies, dogs, cats, and other animals, often become sacred in his eyes, and strike him with a religious veneration") but will lay before you the opinion of several authors of antiquity concerning this religion, and I hope that the testimony of an *ancient* will have as much weight with you, as the conjecture of a *modern*. You may perhaps object to the length of my quotations, but I had rather you should accuse me of

---

[382] Newton's Chron. [Isaac Newton, *Chronology of antient kingdoms amended.*]

prolixity in producing my authorities than suspect me of perverting the sense of any author to the support of my plan. The agreeable Philander, whom you have so often heard me mention with respect, has promised to meet you, so I desire that you will not disappoint me of the pleasure of your company.

THEOPHILUS.[383]

...

DIALOGUE
ON THE
CHRISTIAN RELIGION.

PHILANDER, THEOPHILUS, and ACASTO.

...

THEOPH. Your arguments in favour of the christian religion are very strong and satisfactory, and sufficiently convince me of its truth, and divinity; but I should be glad if (agreeable to your promise) you would confute the objections that have been made to the external evidence of its miracles by Mr. Hume

PHILANDER. The whole force of Mr. Hume's arguing against the miracles is founded on the several uses, and observations he makes of *experience*. he says,

"Suppose that the fact which the testimony endeavours to establish, partakes of the extraordinary and the marvellous; in that case, the evidence, resulting from the testimony, receives a diminution greater or less, in proportion as the fact is more or less unusual. The reason, why we place any credit in witnesses and historians, is not from any *connexion* we perceive *a priori* betwixt testimony and reality, but because we are accustomed to find a conformity betwixt them. But when the fact attested is such a one as has seldom fallen under our observation, here is a contest of two opposite experiences; of which the one destroys the other as far as its force goes, and the superior can only operate on the mind by the force which remains. The very same principle of experience, which gives us a certain degree of assurance in the testimony of witnesses,

---

[383] [The text continues with "On Idolatry, a Dialogue" between Theophilus, Philander, and Acasto. This is followed by a "Dialogue on the Christian Religion" with the same three characters.]

gives us also, in this case, another degree of assurance against the fact, which they endeavour to establish; from which contradiction there necessarily arises a counterpoise, and mutual destruction of belief and authority."

Thus doth this gentleman lay it down as a rule, that it must be *experience* alone which can give authority to any human testimony, and consequently that we must refuse our assent to the truth of any thing which is not conformable to our own knowledge and observation, notwithstanding it is attested by the unanimous reports of a number of witnesses of integrity and reputation.

Let us examine the propriety of this rule, by considering some facts which are recorded in history: for instance, the manner in which the mechanical powers were compounded, when Syracuse was defended against the Romans by the engines of Archimedes, and when the Colossus of Rhodes was erected, and when many other magnificent works of the ancients were performed, is not conformable to our knowledge and observation: nay to produce instances of things which are now in being; the art that was made use of to raise those prodigious stones of which the pyramids of Egypt, and Stonehenge upon Salisbury plain, are compounded, is still unknown to us, and contrary to our experience. If then we enquire into the credibility of these facts in Mr. Hume's words, we must say, "That the facts which the testimony endeavours to establish, partake of the extraordinary and the marvellous, so that the evidence resulting from the testimony receives a diminution greater or less, in proportion as the fact is more or less unusual. But the facts attested are such as have seldom fallen under our observation, and consequently here is a contest of two opposite experiences; of which the one destroys the other as far as its force goes, and the superior can only operate on the mind by the force which remains. The very same principle of experience, which gives us a certain degree of assurance in the testimony of the witnesses, gives us also in this case another degree of assurance against the fact which they endeavour to establish; from which contradiction there necessarily arises a counterpoise and mutual destruction of belief and authority; and consequently we are neither to believe that Syracuse was thus defended by Archimedes, or that the Colossus, the pyramids, or Stonehenge, were ever erected, as we never knew, observed or experienced such a composition of the mechanical powers, as was employed to perform them." Thus must we be led by this gentleman's plan of reasoning, to disbelieve not only transactions which are confirmed by the most indisputable evidence, but even matters of fact.

But this is only the introduction, and the mighty difficulty is still to be surmounted: Mr. Hume proceeds to observe, that "in order to increase the probability against the testimony of witnesses, let us suppose that the fact which they affirm, instead of being only marvellous, is really miraculous; and suppose also, that the testimony, considered apart, and in itself, amounts to an entire proof; in that case there is a proof against a proof, of which the strongest must prevail, but still with a diminution of its force, in proportion to that of its antagonist. A miracle is a violation of the laws of nature; and as a firm and inalterable experience has established these laws, the proof against a miracle, from the very nature of the fact, is as entire as any argument from experience can possibly be imagined."

This is undoubtedly a true definition of a miracle, and the proof against this miracle (as he observes) is as entire as any argument from experience can possibly be imagined. But Mr. H. may be pleased to consider, that no proof can be taken against the existence of a miracle from *experience*; for if it was agreeable and common with our experience, it would be no miracle; and its disagreement with it, is no greater proof that there were not such violations of the laws of nature about 1750 years ago, than our having never experienced the terrible eruptions of an earthquake in these kingdoms, is a proof that no such accident happened at Lisbon in 1755. The truth of each fact stands upon the testimony of witnesses, to most people of this nation, and so according to Mr. H. plan, they are neither of them to be believed; for tho' *the testimony of each*

"considered apart amounts to an entire proof, yet here is a proof against a proof. A miracle (or an earthquake) is a violation of the laws of nature; and as a firm and inalterable experience has established these laws, the proof against a miracle (or an earthquake) from the very nature of the fact, is as entire as any argument from experience can possibly be imagined."

Thus then the very nature of miracles being founded in their contradiction to our experience, (however we may be influenced by it in the common affairs of life) yet experience hath certainly no sort of concern, when miraculous events are the objects of our enquiry; and we must necessarily depend upon the testimony of witnesses, for their truth, unless we suppose that the violation of the laws of nature should be frequently made, and this scene of things be changed into confusion and disorder for our conviction.

If the deist then would destroy all credibility that may be given to miracles, he should demonstrate the impossibility of there being effected by any power whatever, either human or divine, or that the testimony which may be at any time given of them, is altogether false. But as I presume he will allow, that the supreme being, who first constituted order, can change it when he pleases, I shall therefore confine myself to the last.

I cannot produce a better answer to the cavils of the deists, against the miracles which were performed to attest to the divine authority of the first propagators of christianity, than is given us in a pamphlet, entitled, *Observations on the conversion and apostleship of St. Paul,* and which I shall beg leave of the author to transcribe.

...